STAR TREK ®

Uchu
宇宙

HAMBURG // LONDON // LOS ANGELES // TOKYO

Star Trek: the manga
Uchu

Lettering and Layout - Michael Paolilli and Lucas Rivera
Associate Editor - Tim Beedle
Cover Art - Felipe Smith
Cover Design - Tina Corrales

Editor - Luis Reyes
Digital Imaging Manager - Chris Buford
Pre-Production Supervisor - Vince Rivera
Art Director - Al-Insan Lashley
Managing Editor - Vy Nguyen
Creative Director - Anne Marie Horne
Editor-in-Chief - Rob Tokar
Publisher - Mike Kiley
President and C.O.O. - John Parker
C.E.O. and Chief Creative Officer - Stu Levy

A  Manga

TOKYOPOP and  are trademarks or registered trademarks of TOKYOPOP Inc.

TOKYOPOP Inc.
5900 Wilshire Blvd. Suite 2000
Los Angeles, CA 90036

E-mail: info@TOKYOPOP.com
Come visit us online at www.TOKYOPOP.com

ISBN: 978-1-4278-0787-8

First TOKYOPOP printing: July 2008
10 9 8 7 6 5 4 3 2 1
Printed in the USA

TABLE OF CONTENTS

Don Hudson

has been an inker on Marvel titles such as *Web of Spider-Man, Silver Surfer* and *Daredevil* and an artist for Sony Animation. Don is also the co-creator of the highly lauded comic rag *Comiculture Magazine* and art director for Mad Science Media. His original credits include illustration for the graphic novel *Gunpowder Girl and The Outlaw Squaw.*

David Gerrold

is the legendary writer of "The Trouble with Tribbles" from the second season of Star Trek: The Original Series. He was also instrumental in shaping the story for the first season of the beloved classic series Land of the Lost, which included authoring four episodes, including the pilot "Cha-Ka." In the time between and since, Gerrold has chalked up a fantastic array of credits for TV and film, as well as penning the novel series The War Against the Chtorr and Star Wolf. And his semi-autobiographical novelette The Martian Child received the Hugo Award in 1995 and was made into a film starring John Cusak in 2007. David is also contributing a story to TOKYOPOP's upcoming Star Trek: The Next Generation manga.

Nathaniel Bowden

is a writer/artist living in Savannah, GA. A graduate of the Savannah College of Art and Design, he stayed in the city to work with his collaborator, Tracy Yardley on the underground indie-comic, *Nate and Steve* as well as TOKYOPOP's *Riding Shotgun.* Currently he is penning the next volume of TOKYOPOP's *Hellgate: London.* Nate spends much of his time working, writing (in a room littered with soda cans) and losing money at the poker table.

Luis Reyes

is a Senior Editor at TOKYOPOP. He is also an arts journalist, playwright, musician, and avid Star Trek fan living in Los Angeles.

EJ Su

...as born in Taiwan and moved to the U.S. at the age of 14. He got his start in comic ...ooks as an artist on Image Comics' *Tech Jacket*. He has been asked to return to *Star ...rek the manga* after his incredible work in Volume 1 on the story "Orphans" and ... Volume 2 on the story "Cura Te Ipsum." EJ is also an artist for IDW Publishing's *...ansformers* series.

Wil Wheaton

...the author of *Just A Geek*, *Dancing Barefoot*, and *The Happiest Days of Our Lives*. ... a previous life, he was an actor best known for work in the film *Stand By Me*, and as ...esley Crusher in *Star Trek: The Next Generation*. Currently, he provides the voices for ...qualad on *Teen Titans* and Cosmic Boy on *Legion of Superheroes*. This is the second ...anga for the self-described comic book geek and life-long Trekkie. His award-winning ...og is at wilwheaton.net.

Heidi Arnhold

...ew up in Orange, VA where she powered the entire town via her bunny plantation. ...rrently she is the artist for Jim Hension's *Legends of the Dark Crystal*. When she's ...t knee-deep in Gelflings, she can often be found on the floor trying to communicate ...ith rabbits. A recent graduate of the Savannah College of Art and Design's prestigious ...quential art program, you can find more of her work at http://chibimaryn.deviantart. ...m.

Nate Watson

...currently working on Scream Queen for Boom! Studios. He had previously worked ... Grim Fairy Tales for Zenescope Entertainment, and the Legend of Isis for Bluewater. ...te is also slated to draw a story for TOKYOPOP's upcoming Ghostbusters manga.

ART OF WAR

STORY BY WIL WHEATON
PENCILS AND INKS BY EJ SU
TONES BY CHOW HON LAM
AND MARA AUM

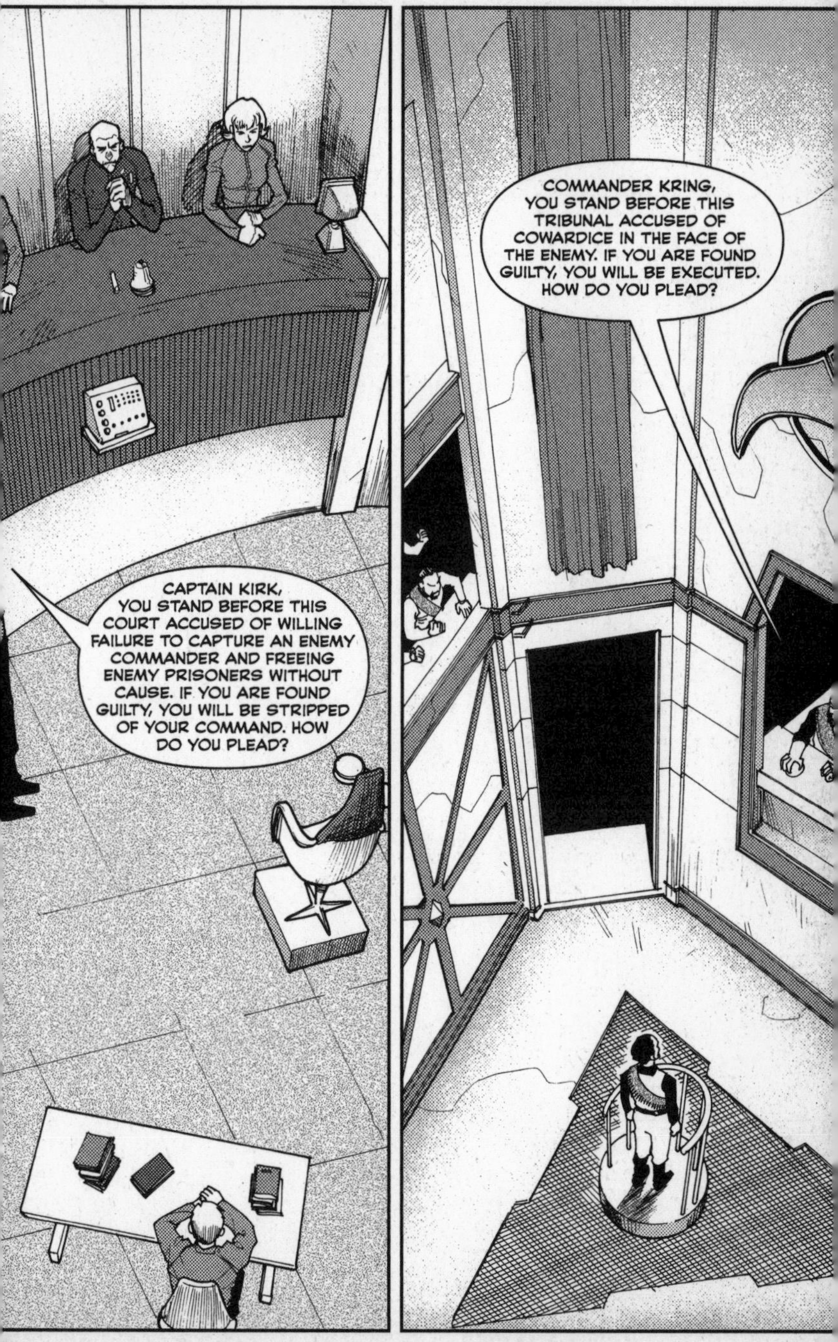
CAPTAIN KIRK, YOU STAND BEFORE THIS COURT ACCUSED OF WILLING FAILURE TO CAPTURE AN ENEMY COMMANDER AND FREEING ENEMY PRISONERS WITHOUT CAUSE. IF YOU ARE FOUND GUILTY, YOU WILL BE STRIPPED OF YOUR COMMAND. HOW DO YOU PLEAD?
COMMANDER KRING, YOU STAND BEFORE THIS TRIBUNAL ACCUSED OF COWARDICE IN THE FACE OF THE ENEMY. IF YOU ARE FOUND GUILTY, YOU WILL BE EXECUTED. HOW DO YOU PLEAD?

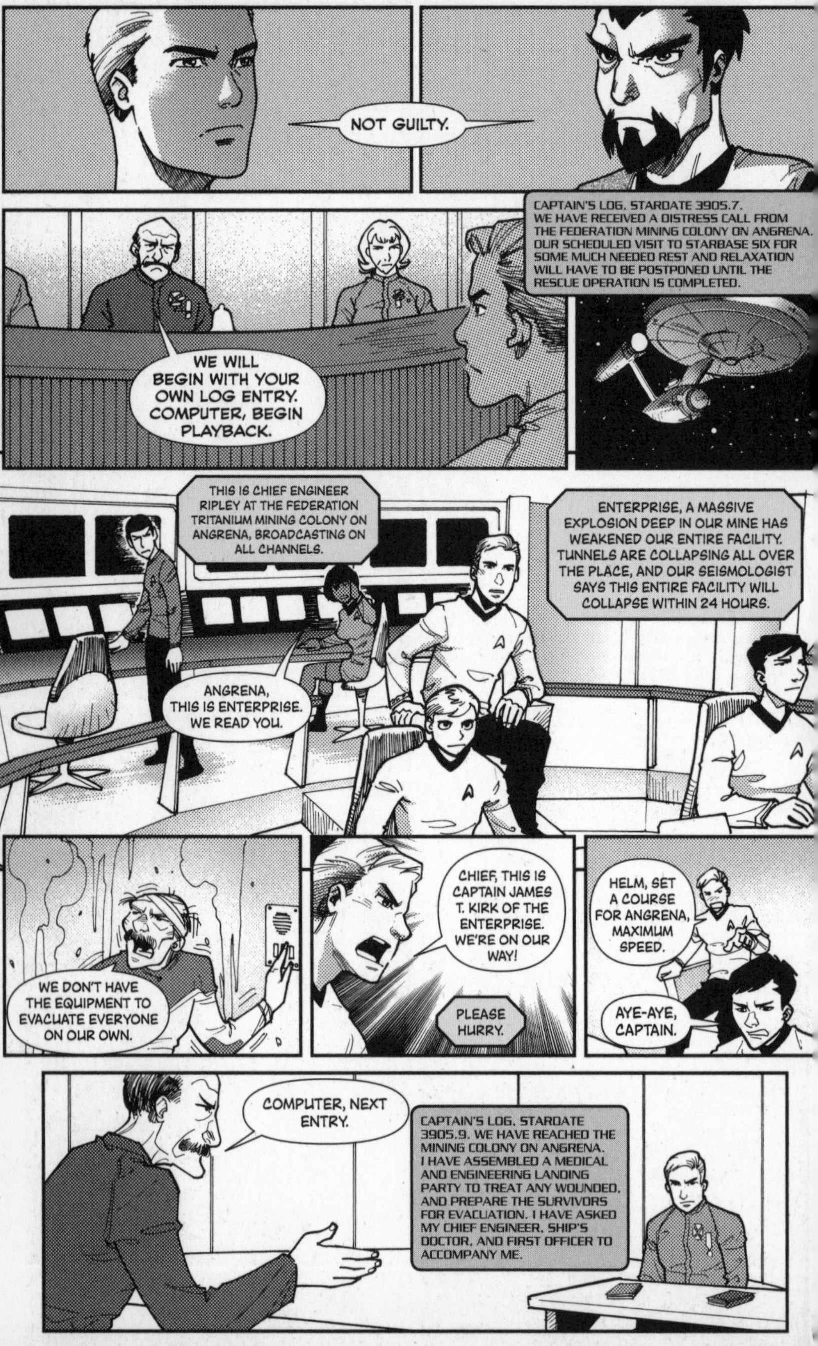
NOT GUILTY.
CAPTAIN'S LOG, STARDATE 3905.7. WE HAVE RECEIVED A DISTRESS CALL FROM THE FEDERATION MINING COLONY ON ANGRENA. OUR SCHEDULED VISIT TO STARBASE SIX FOR SOME MUCH NEEDED REST AND RELAXATION WILL HAVE TO BE POSTPONED UNTIL THE RESCUE OPERATION IS COMPLETED.
WE WILL BEGIN WITH YOUR OWN LOG ENTRY. COMPUTER, BEGIN PLAYBACK.
THIS IS CHIEF ENGINEER RIPLEY AT THE FEDERATION TRITANIUM MINING COLONY ON ANGRENA, BROADCASTING ON ALL CHANNELS.
ENTERPRISE, A MASSIVE EXPLOSION DEEP IN OUR MINE HAS WEAKENED OUR ENTIRE FACILITY. TUNNELS ARE COLLAPSING ALL OVER THE PLACE, AND OUR SEISMOLOGIST SAYS THIS ENTIRE FACILITY WILL COLLAPSE WITHIN 24 HOURS.
ANGRENA, THIS IS ENTERPRISE. WE READ YOU.
WE DON'T HAVE THE EQUIPMENT TO EVACUATE EVERYONE ON OUR OWN.
CHIEF, THIS IS CAPTAIN JAMES T. KIRK OF THE ENTERPRISE. WE'RE ON OUR WAY!
PLEASE HURRY.
HELM, SET A COURSE FOR ANGRENA, MAXIMUM SPEED.
AYE-AYE, CAPTAIN.
COMPUTER, NEXT ENTRY.
CAPTAIN'S LOG, STARDATE 3905.9. WE HAVE REACHED THE MINING COLONY ON ANGRENA. I HAVE ASSEMBLED A MEDICAL AND ENGINEERING LANDING PARTY TO TREAT ANY WOUNDED, AND PREPARE THE SURVIVORS FOR EVACUATION. I HAVE ASKED MY CHIEF ENGINEER, SHIP'S DOCTOR, AND FIRST OFFICER TO ACCOMPANY ME.

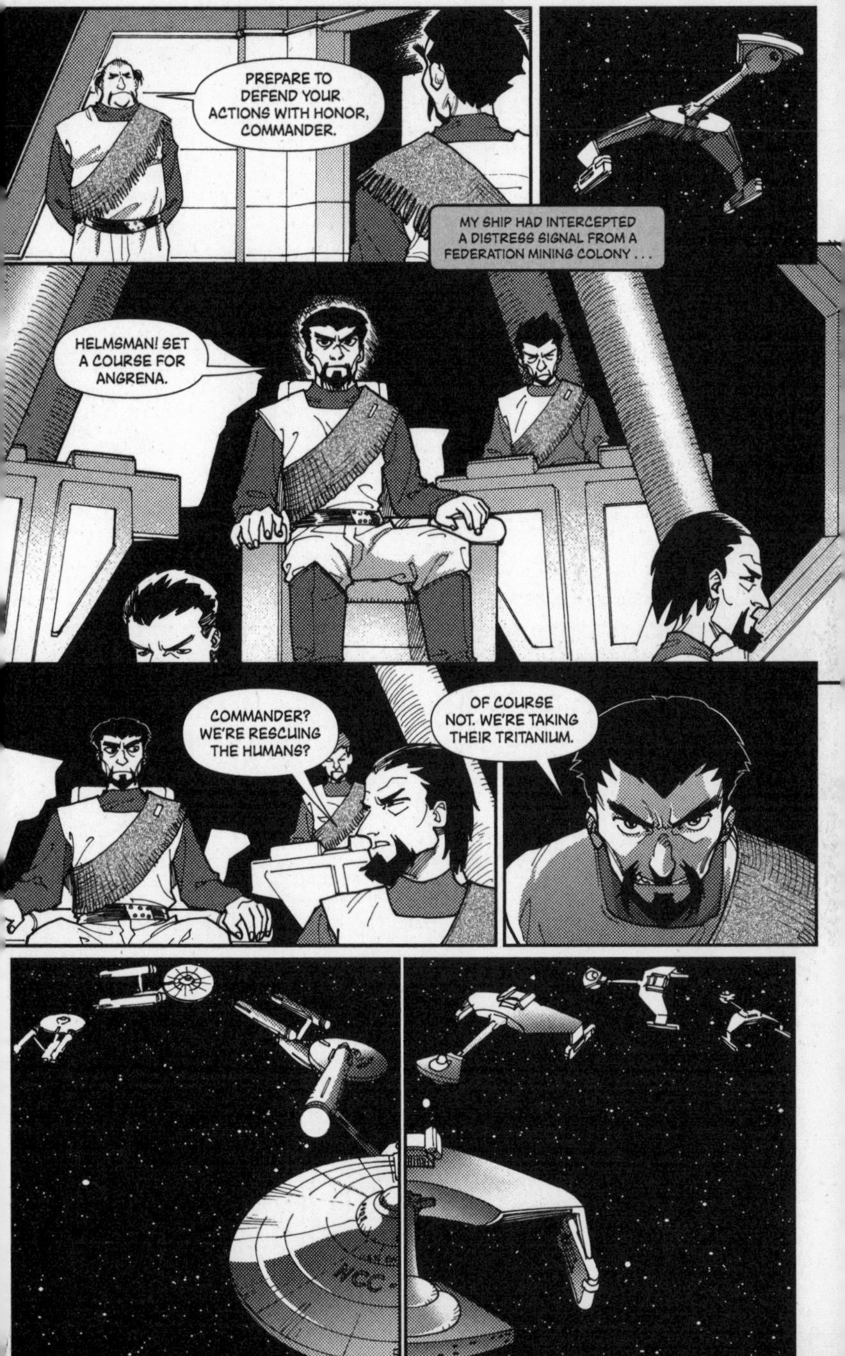
PREPARE TO DEFEND YOUR ACTIONS WITH HONOR, COMMANDER.
MY SHIP HAD INTERCEPTED A DISTRESS SIGNAL FROM A FEDERATION MINING COLONY . . .
HELMSMAN! SET A COURSE FOR ANGRENA.
COMMANDER? WE'RE RESCUING THE HUMANS?
OF COURSE NOT. WE'RE TAKING THEIR TRITANIUM.
NCC

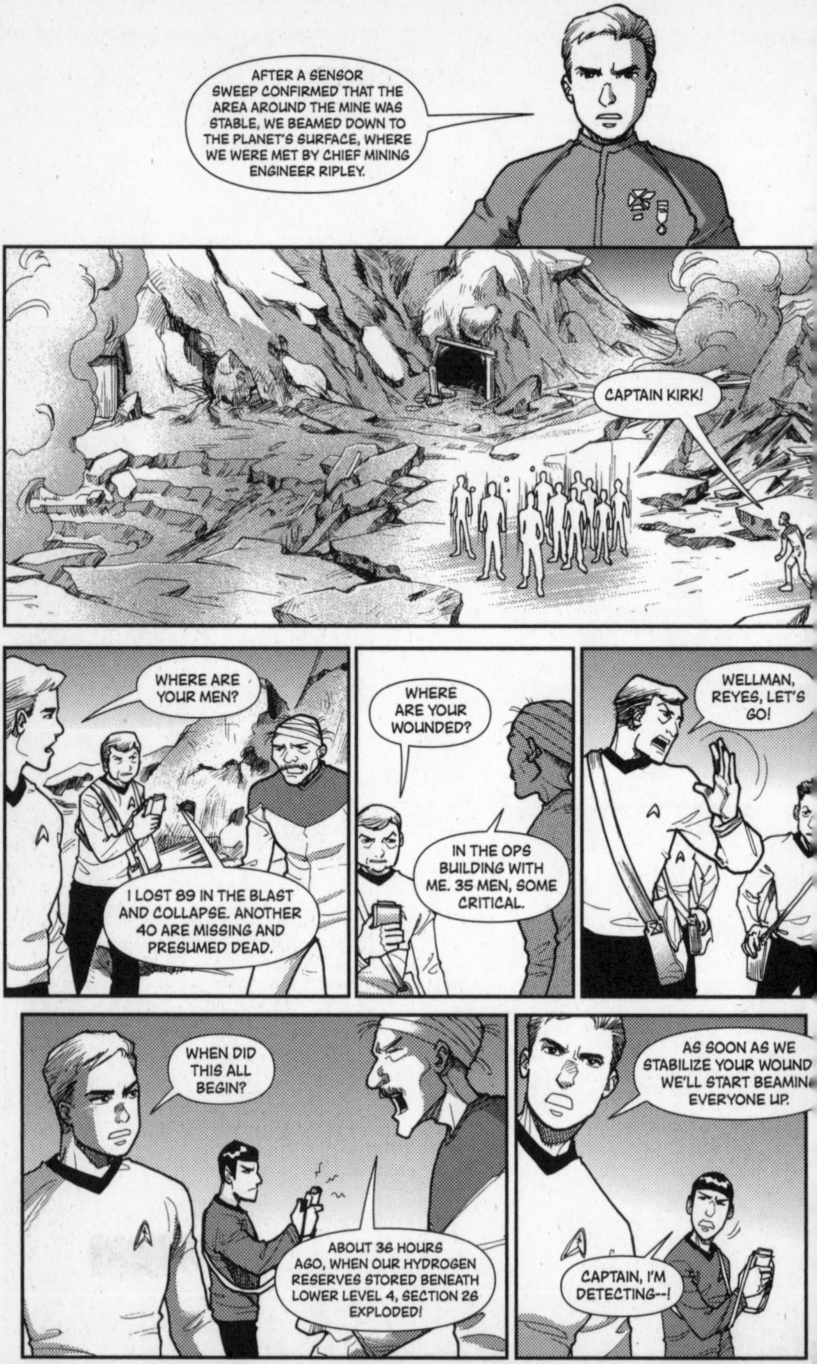
AFTER A SENSOR SWEEP CONFIRMED THAT THE AREA AROUND THE MINE WAS STABLE, WE BEAMED DOWN TO THE PLANET'S SURFACE, WHERE WE WERE MET BY CHIEF MINING ENGINEER RIPLEY.
CAPTAIN KIRK!
WHERE ARE YOUR MEN?
I LOST 89 IN THE BLAST AND COLLAPSE. ANOTHER 40 ARE MISSING AND PRESUMED DEAD.
WHERE ARE YOUR WOUNDED?
IN THE OPS BUILDING WITH ME. 35 MEN, SOME CRITICAL.
WELLMAN, REYES, LET'S GO!
WHEN DID THIS ALL BEGIN?
ABOUT 36 HOURS AGO, WHEN OUR HYDROGEN RESERVES STORED BENEATH LOWER LEVEL 4, SECTION 26 EXPLODED!
AS SOON AS WE STABILIZE YOUR WOUND WE'LL START BEAMIN EVERYONE UP.
CAPTAIN, I'M DETECTING--!

SHZAK

THE FEDERATION STARSHIP ENTERPRISE WAS ALREADY IN ORBIT WHEN WE ARRIVED.

GRUMBLE GRUMBLE KIRK GRUMBLE GRUMBLE SPOCK GRUMBLE PETAQ GRUMBLE

I HID MY SHIP BEHIND A MOON, AND TRANSPORTED DOWN TO THE PLANET'S SURFACE.

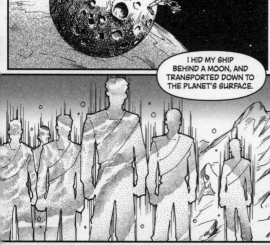

WHAT ARE YOUR ORDERS, COMMANDER?

KILL THEM.

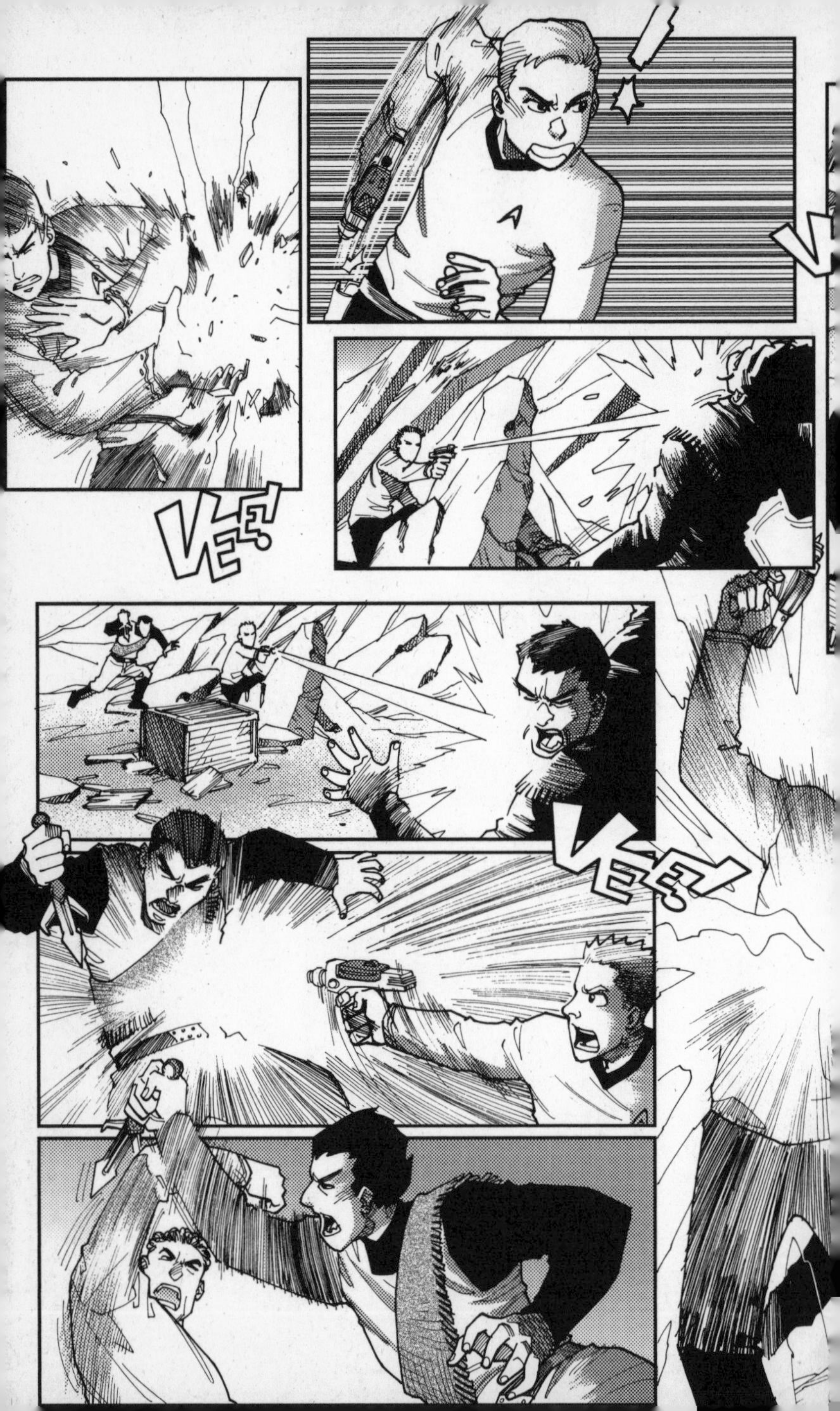
VEE!
VEE!

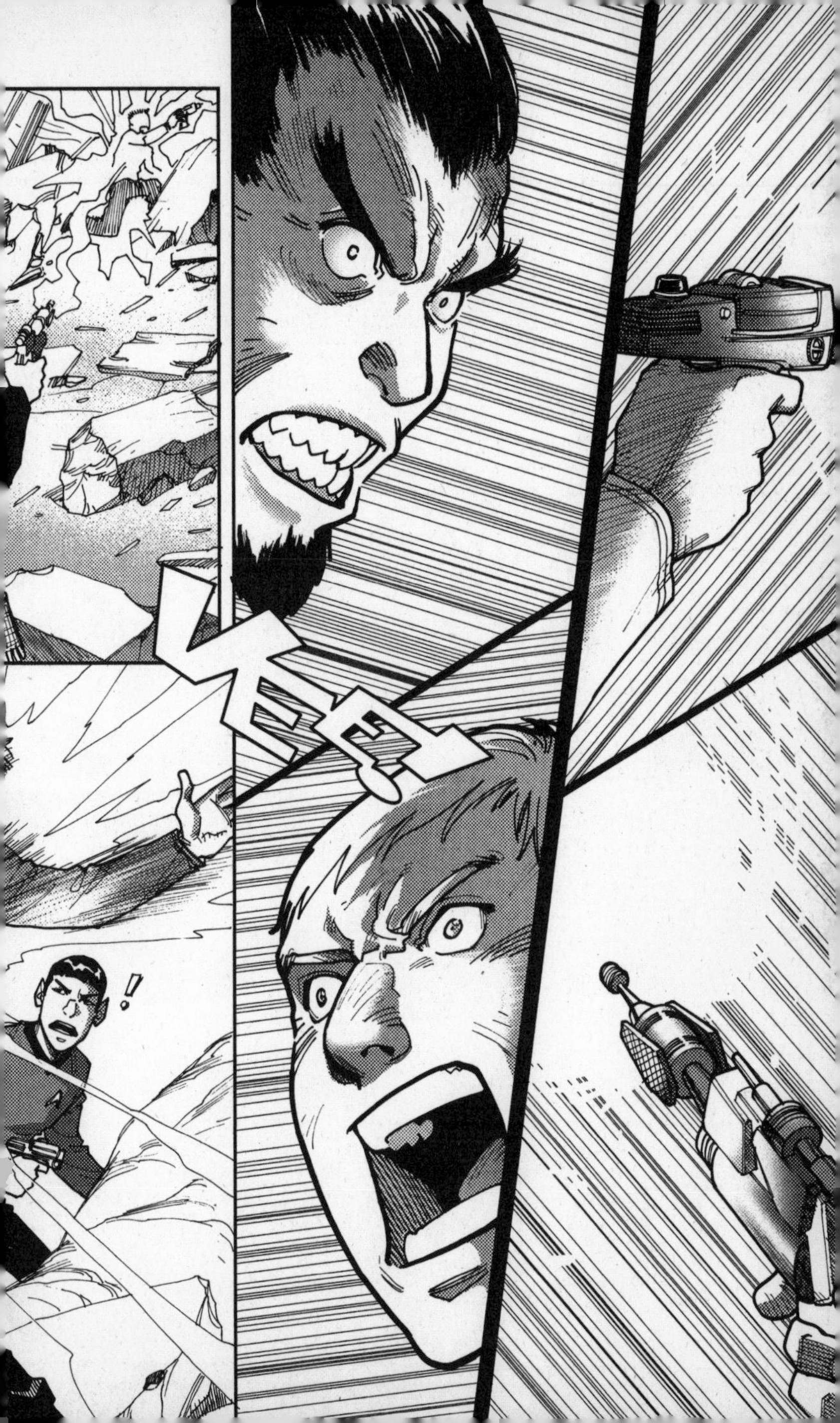
!

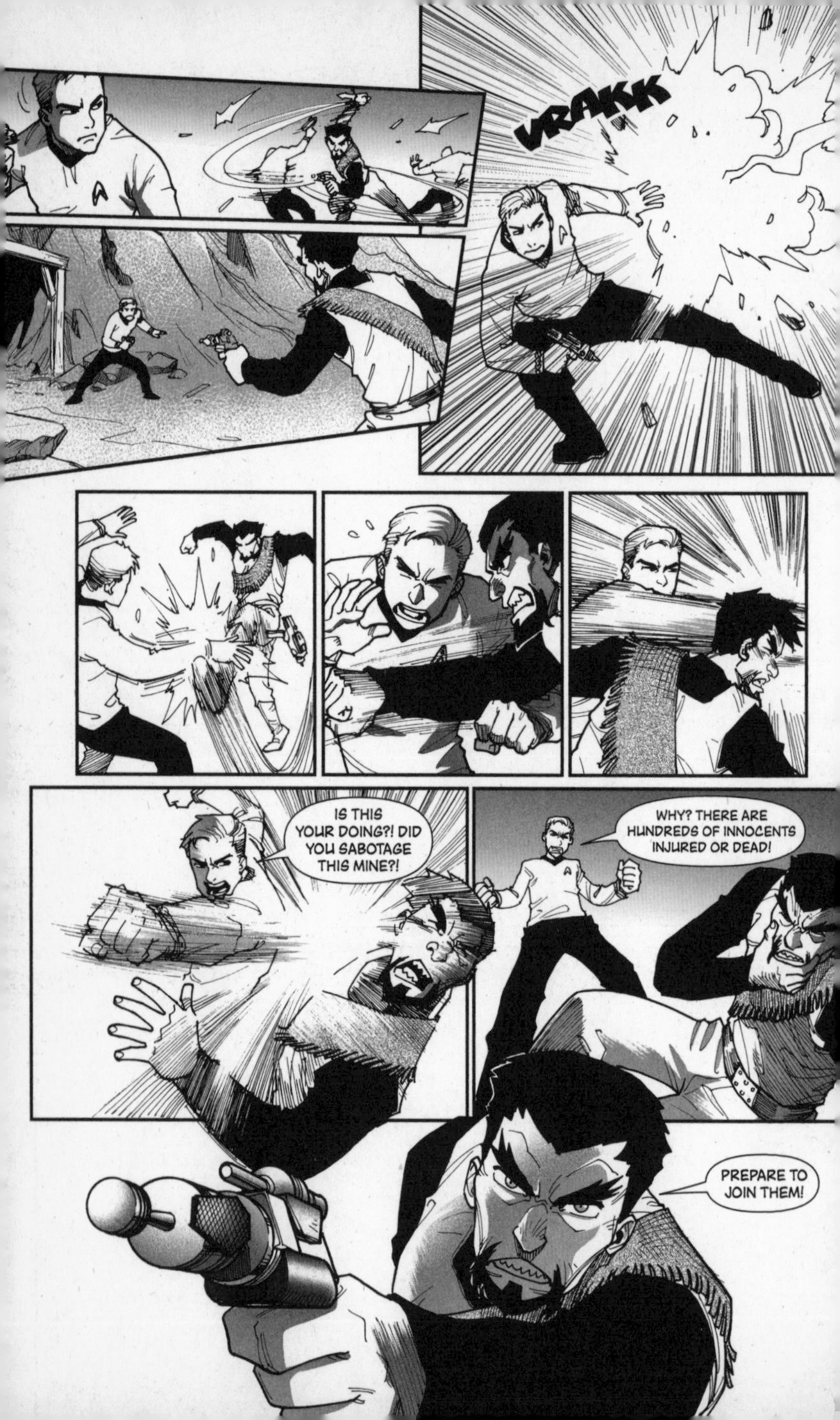
VRAKK
IS THIS YOUR DOING?! DID YOU SABOTAGE THIS MINE?!
WHY? THERE ARE HUNDREDS OF INNOCENTS INJURED OR DEAD!
PREPARE TO JOIN THEM!

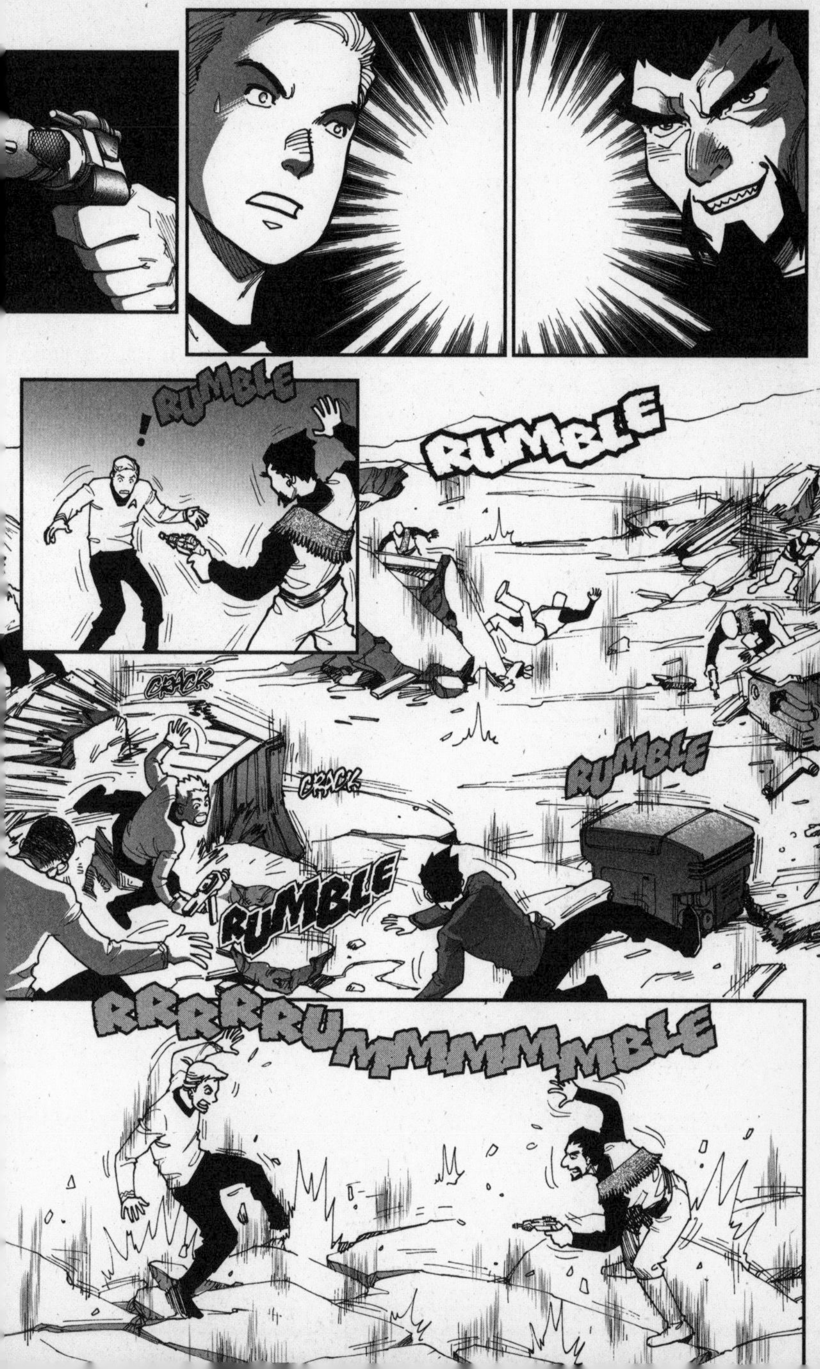
RUMBLE
!
RUMBLE
CRACK
CRACK
RUMBLE
RUMBLE
RRRRRUMMMMMBLE

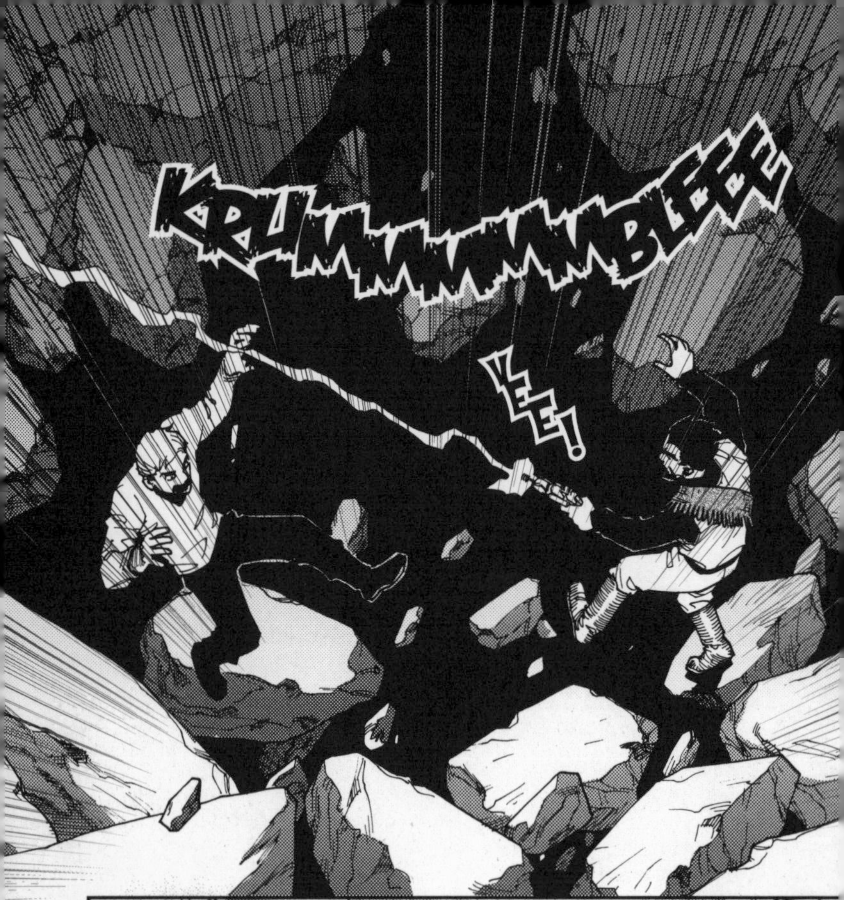
KRUMMMMMBLEEE
YEE!
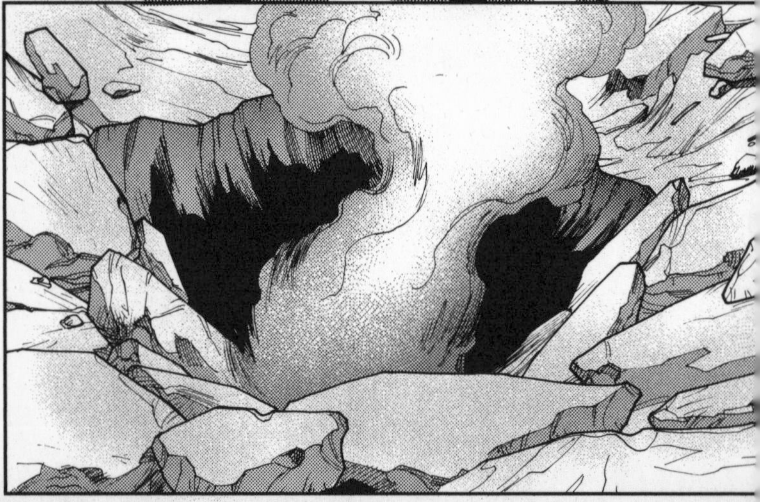

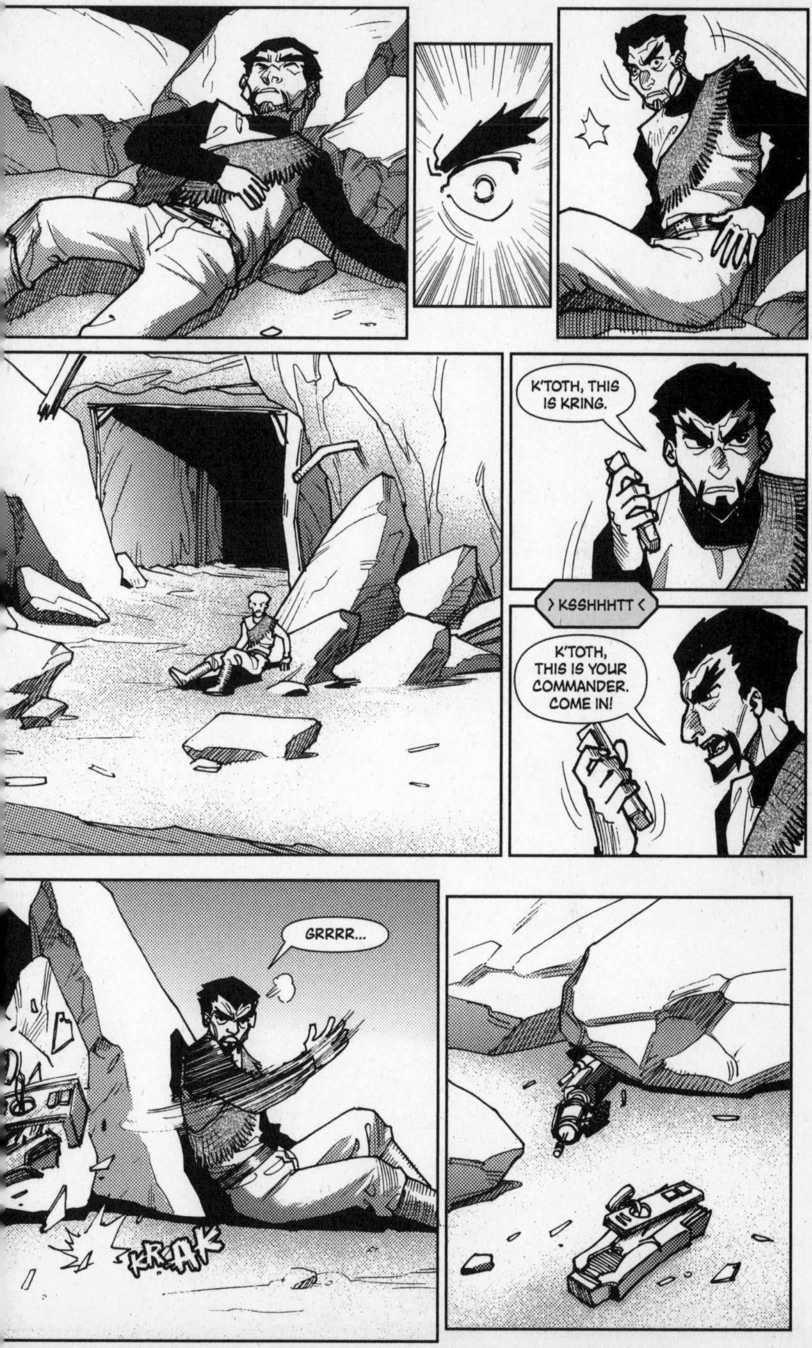
K'TOTH, THIS IS KRING.
KSSHHHTT
K'TOTH, THIS IS YOUR COMMANDER. COME IN!
GRRRR...
KRAK

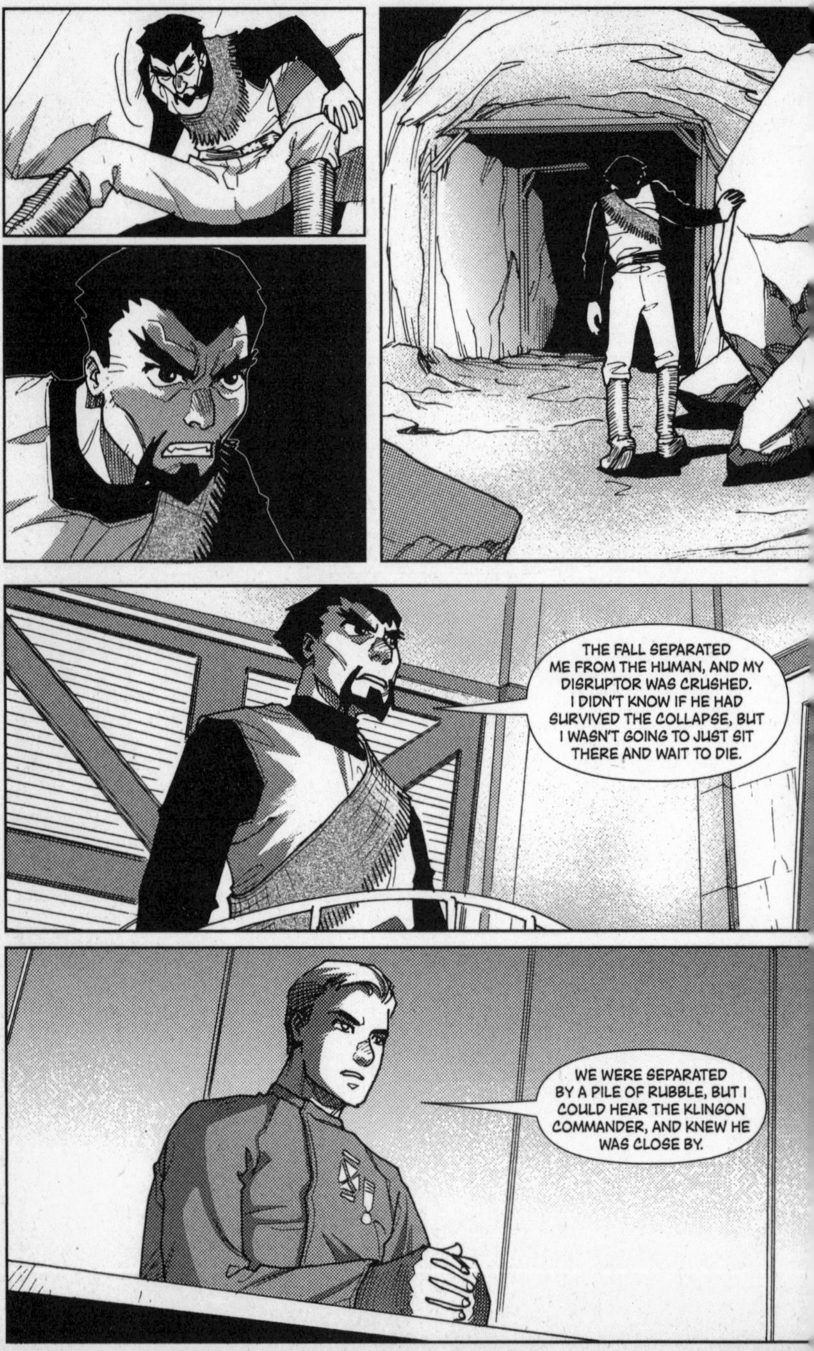
THE FALL SEPARATED ME FROM THE HUMAN, AND MY DISRUPTOR WAS CRUSHED. I DIDN'T KNOW IF HE HAD SURVIVED THE COLLAPSE, BUT I WASN'T GOING TO JUST SIT THERE AND WAIT TO DIE.
WE WERE SEPARATED BY A PILE OF RUBBLE, BUT I COULD HEAR THE KLINGON COMMANDER, AND KNEW HE WAS CLOSE BY.

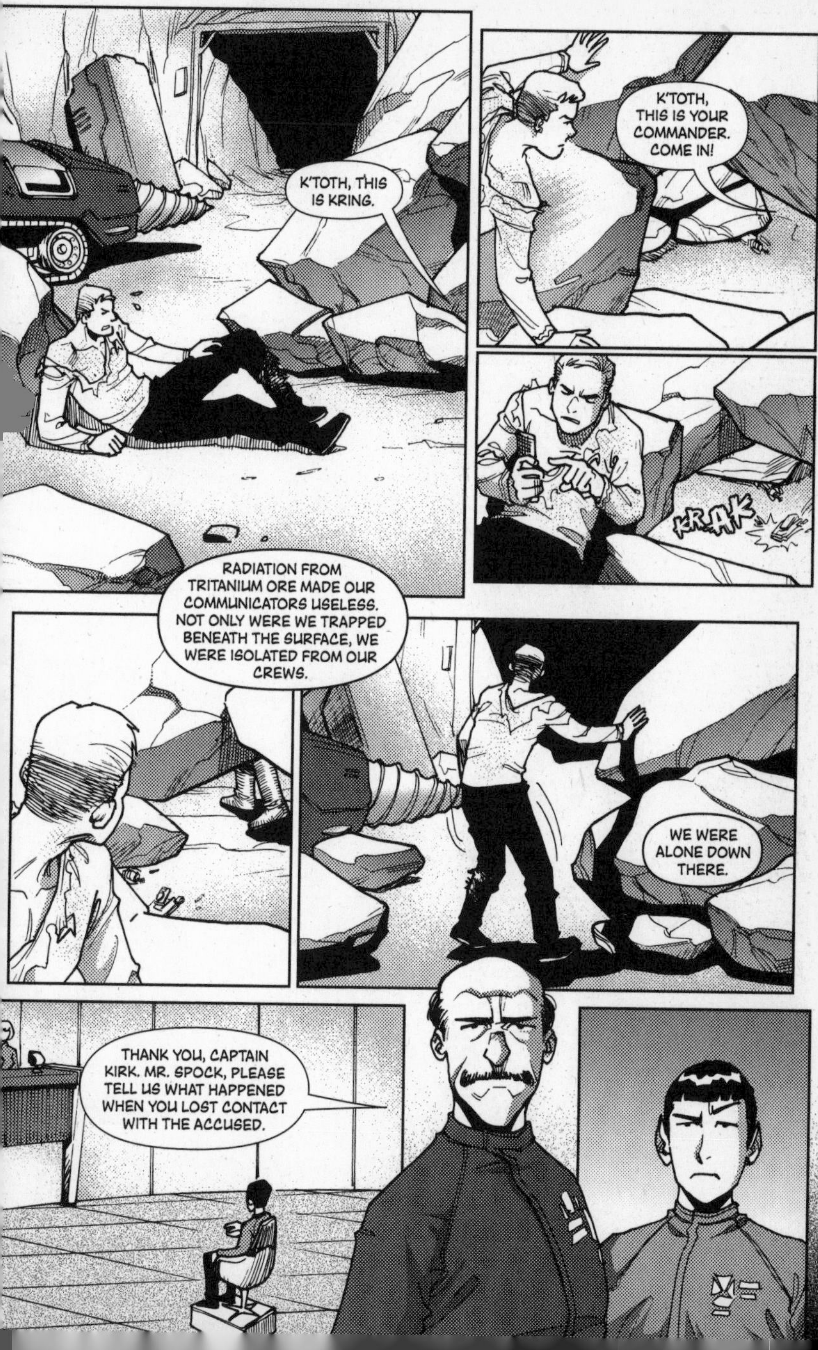
K'TOTH, THIS IS KRING.
K'TOTH, THIS IS YOUR COMMANDER. COME IN!
KRAK
RADIATION FROM TRITANIUM ORE MADE OUR COMMUNICATORS USELESS. NOT ONLY WERE WE TRAPPED BENEATH THE SURFACE, WE WERE ISOLATED FROM OUR CREWS.
WE WERE ALONE DOWN THERE.
THANK YOU, CAPTAIN KIRK. MR. SPOCK, PLEASE TELL US WHAT HAPPENED WHEN YOU LOST CONTACT WITH THE ACCUSED.

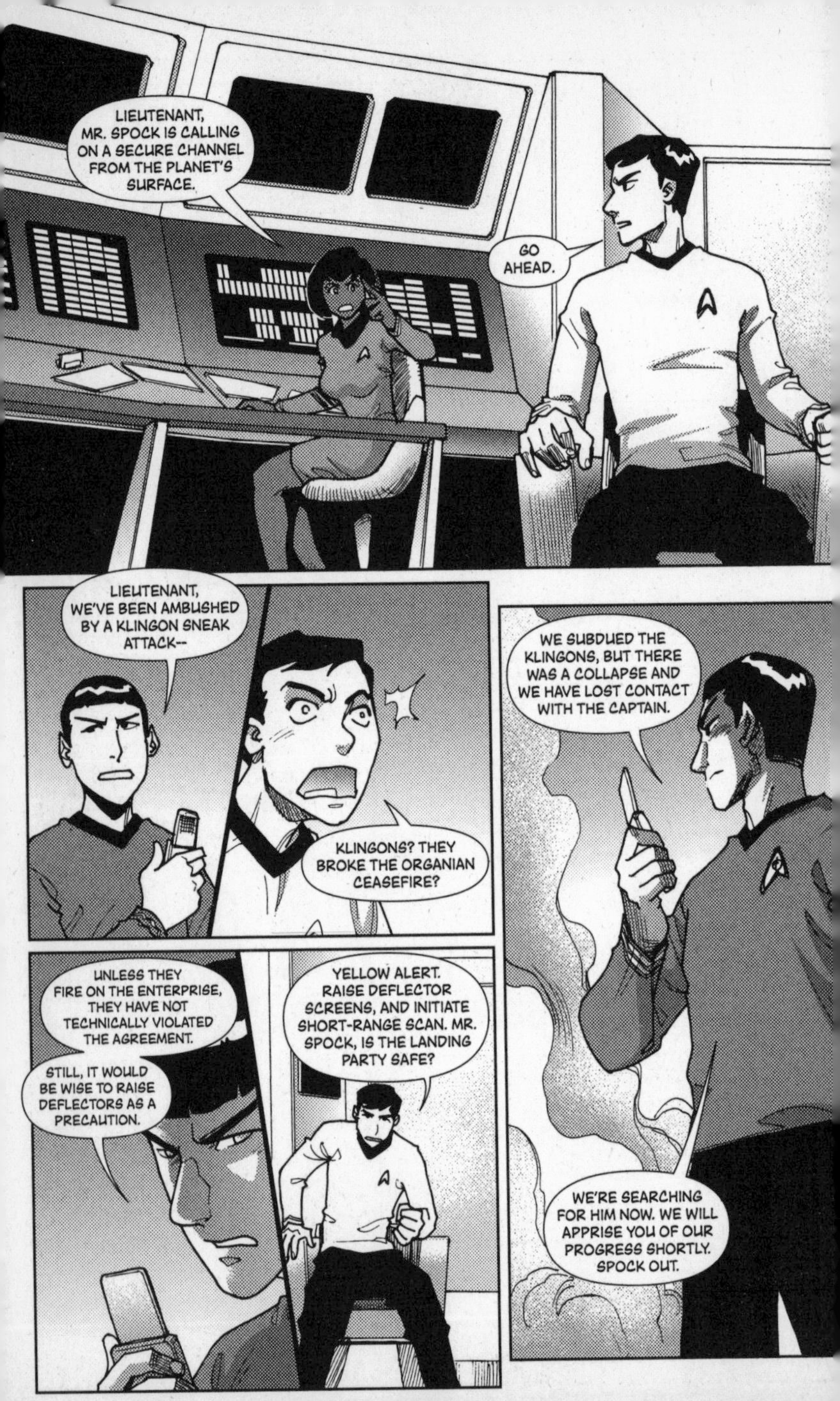
LIEUTENANT, MR. SPOCK IS CALLING ON A SECURE CHANNEL FROM THE PLANET'S SURFACE.
GO AHEAD.
LIEUTENANT, WE'VE BEEN AMBUSHED BY A KLINGON SNEAK ATTACK--
KLINGONS? THEY BROKE THE ORGANIAN CEASEFIRE?
UNLESS THEY FIRE ON THE ENTERPRISE, THEY HAVE NOT TECHNICALLY VIOLATED THE AGREEMENT.
STILL, IT WOULD BE WISE TO RAISE DEFLECTORS AS A PRECAUTION.
YELLOW ALERT. RAISE DEFLECTOR SCREENS, AND INITIATE SHORT-RANGE SCAN. MR. SPOCK, IS THE LANDING PARTY SAFE?
WE SUBDUED THE KLINGONS, BUT THERE WAS A COLLAPSE AND WE HAVE LOST CONTACT WITH THE CAPTAIN.
WE'RE SEARCHING FOR HIM NOW. WE WILL APPRISE YOU OF OUR PROGRESS SHORTLY. SPOCK OUT.

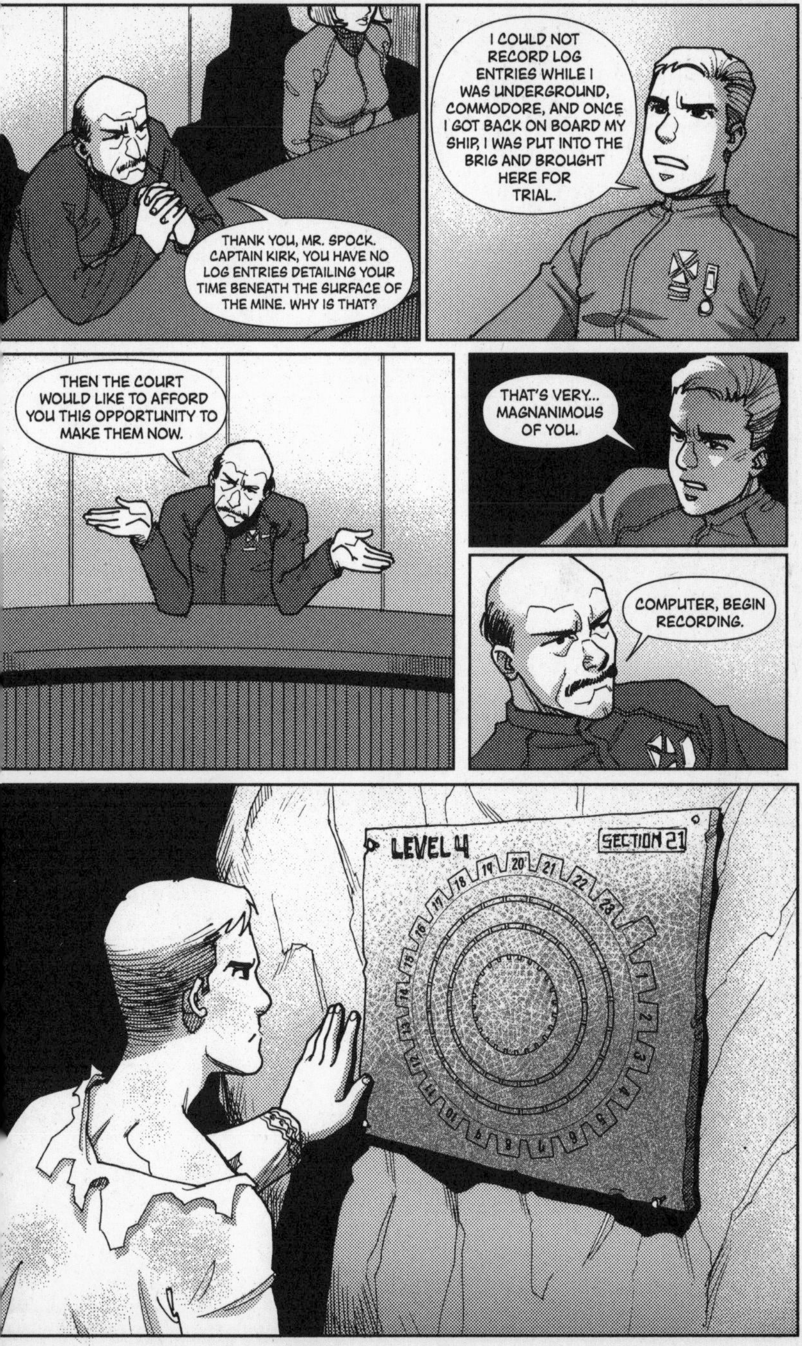
THANK YOU, MR. SPOCK. CAPTAIN KIRK, YOU HAVE NO LOG ENTRIES DETAILING YOUR TIME BENEATH THE SURFACE OF THE MINE. WHY IS THAT?
I COULD NOT RECORD LOG ENTRIES WHILE I WAS UNDERGROUND, COMMODORE, AND ONCE I GOT BACK ON BOARD MY SHIP, I WAS PUT INTO THE BRIG AND BROUGHT HERE FOR TRIAL.
THEN THE COURT WOULD LIKE TO AFFORD YOU THIS OPPORTUNITY TO MAKE THEM NOW.
THAT'S VERY... MAGNANIMOUS OF YOU.
COMPUTER, BEGIN RECORDING.
LEVEL 4
SECTION 21

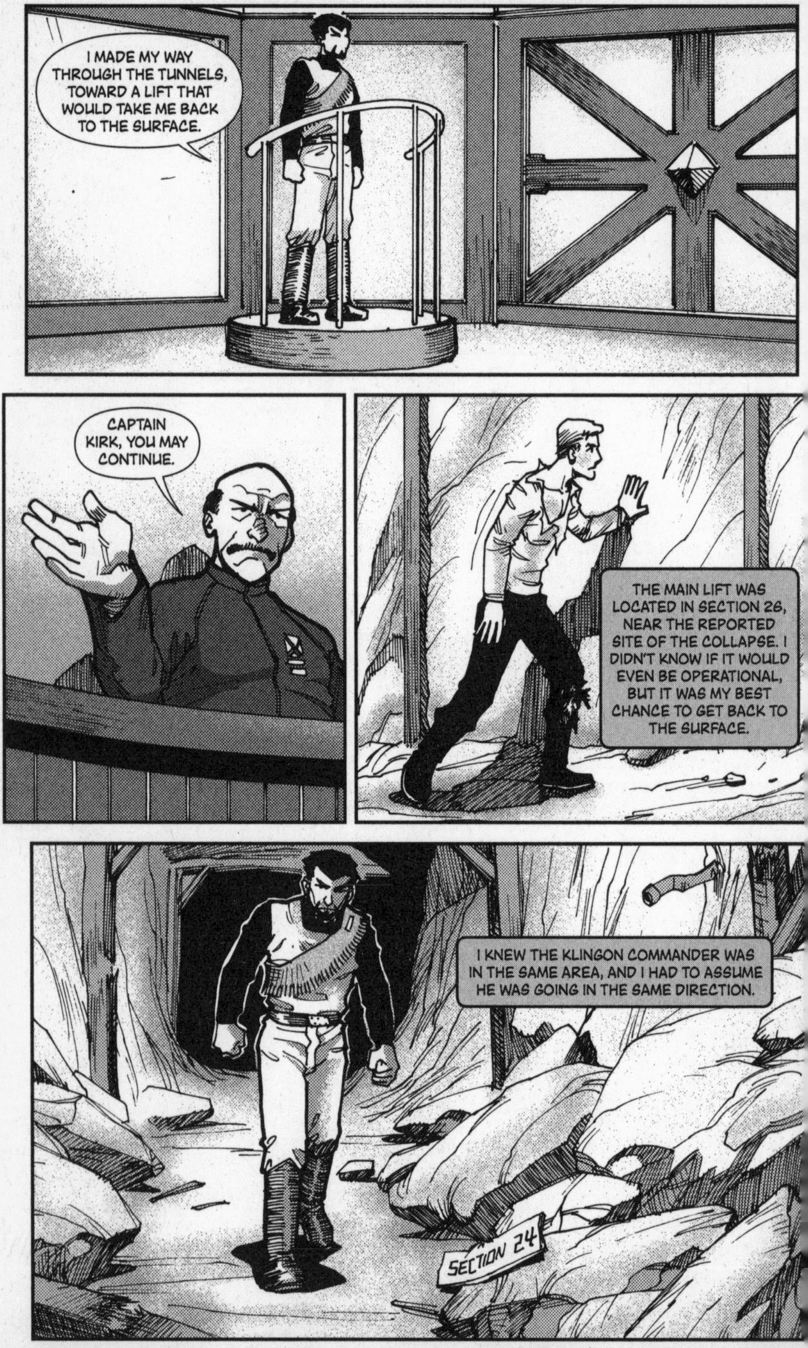
I MADE MY WAY THROUGH THE TUNNELS, TOWARD A LIFT THAT WOULD TAKE ME BACK TO THE SURFACE.
CAPTAIN KIRK, YOU MAY CONTINUE.
THE MAIN LIFT WAS LOCATED IN SECTION 26, NEAR THE REPORTED SITE OF THE COLLAPSE. I DIDN'T KNOW IF IT WOULD EVEN BE OPERATIONAL, BUT IT WAS MY BEST CHANCE TO GET BACK TO THE SURFACE.
I KNEW THE KLINGON COMMANDER WAS IN THE SAME AREA, AND I HAD TO ASSUME HE WAS GOING IN THE SAME DIRECTION.
SECTION 24

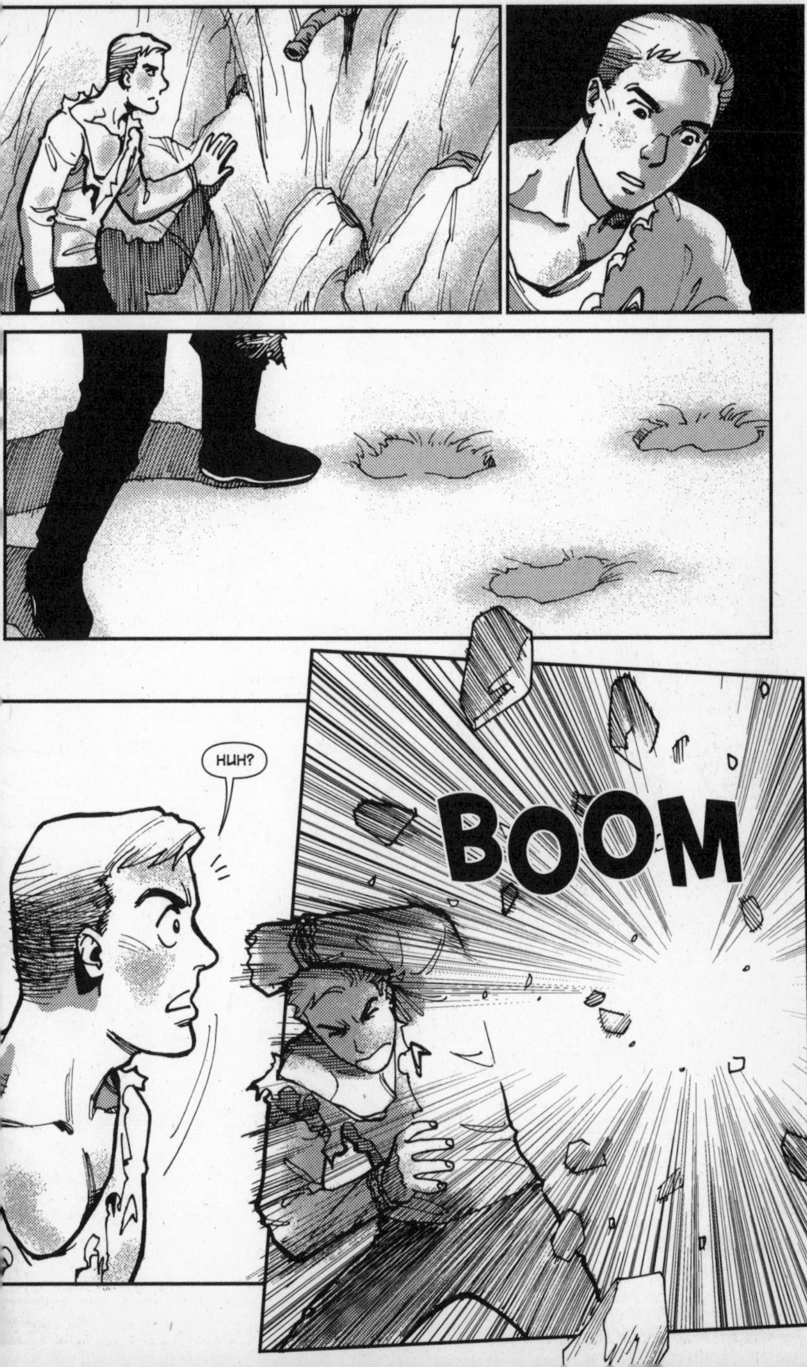
HUH?
BOOM

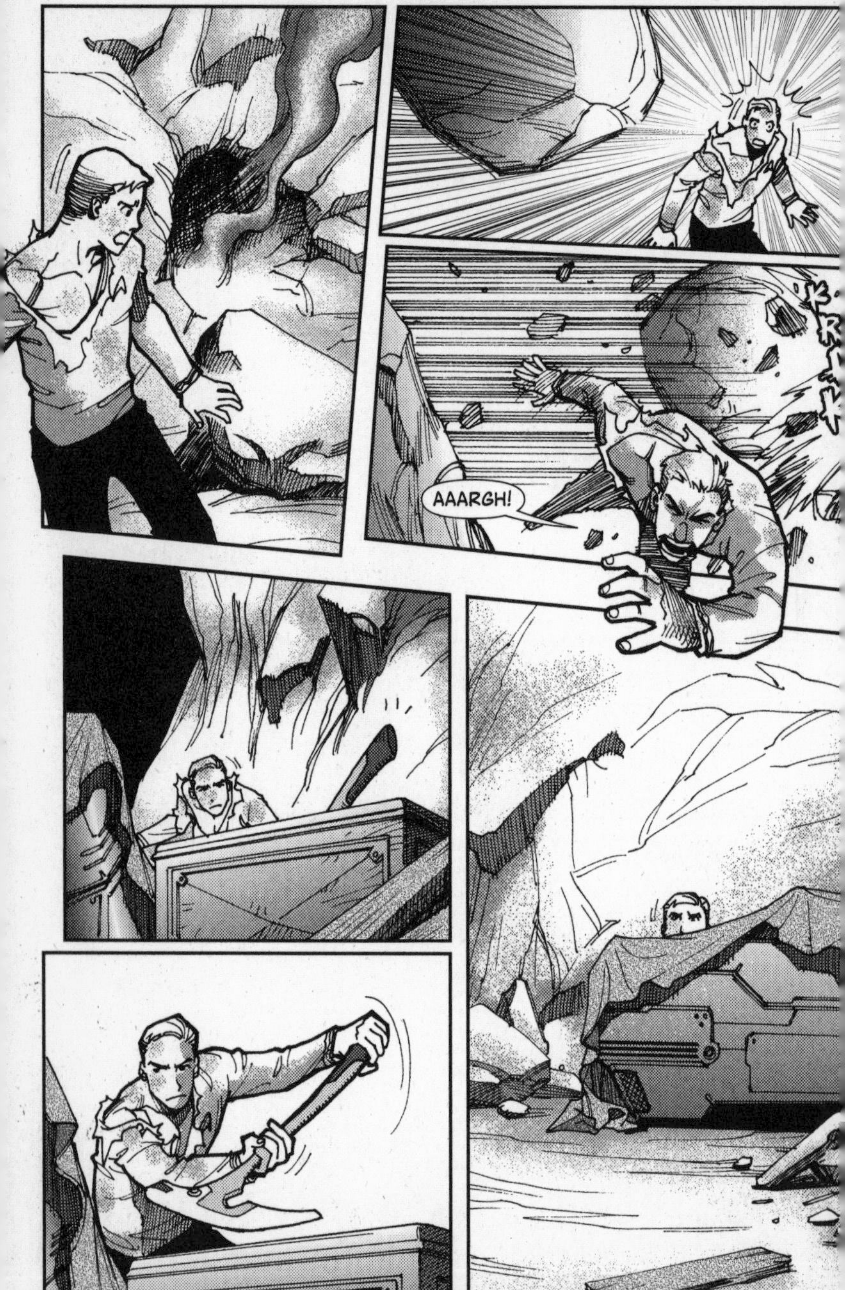
AAARGH!

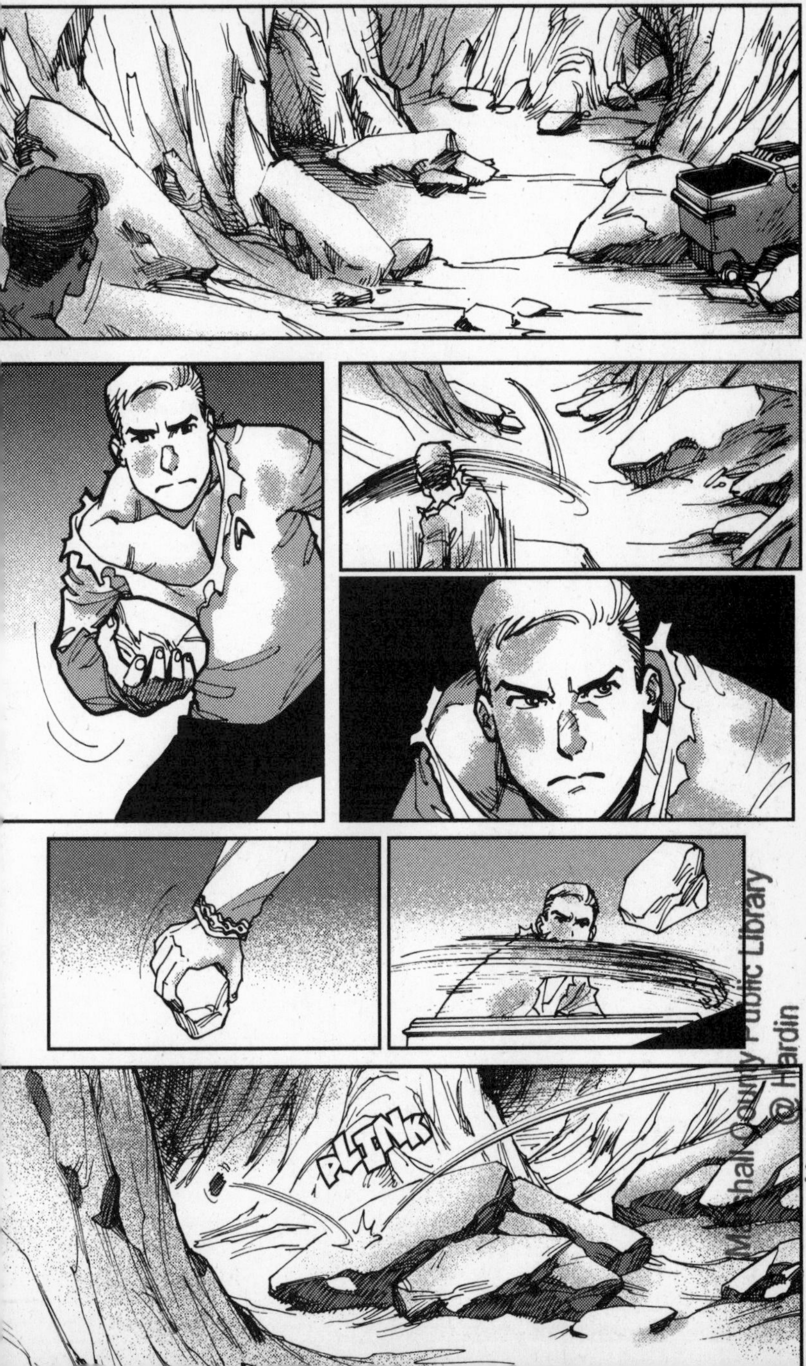
PLINK

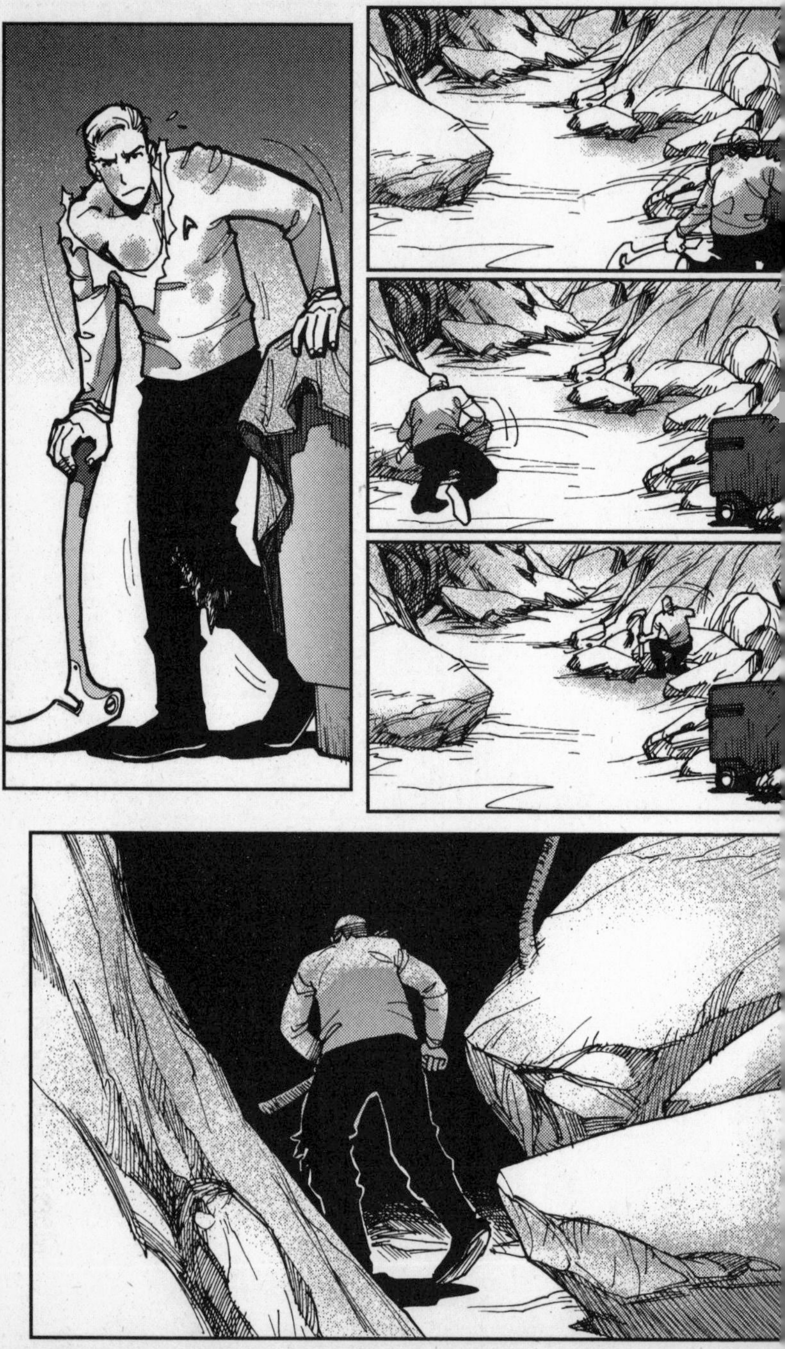

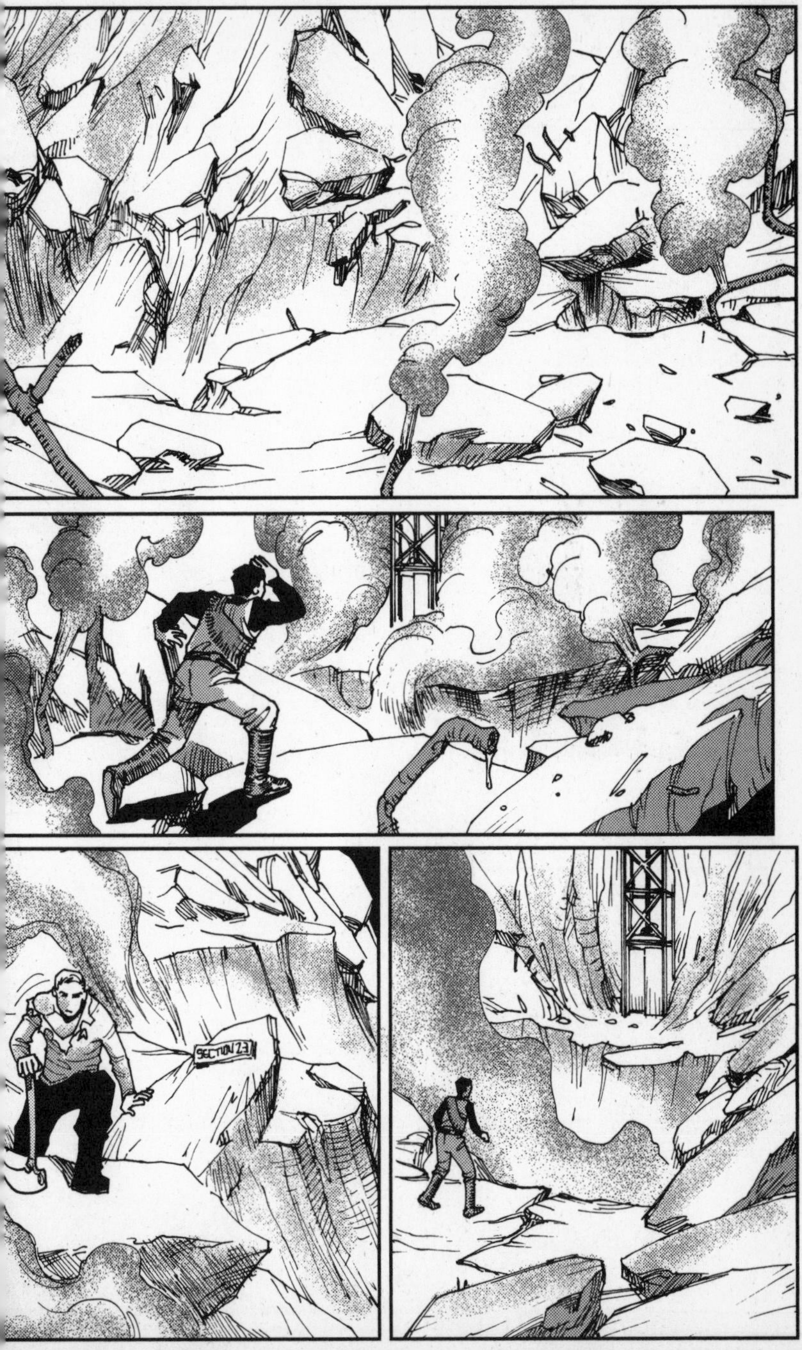
SECTION 23

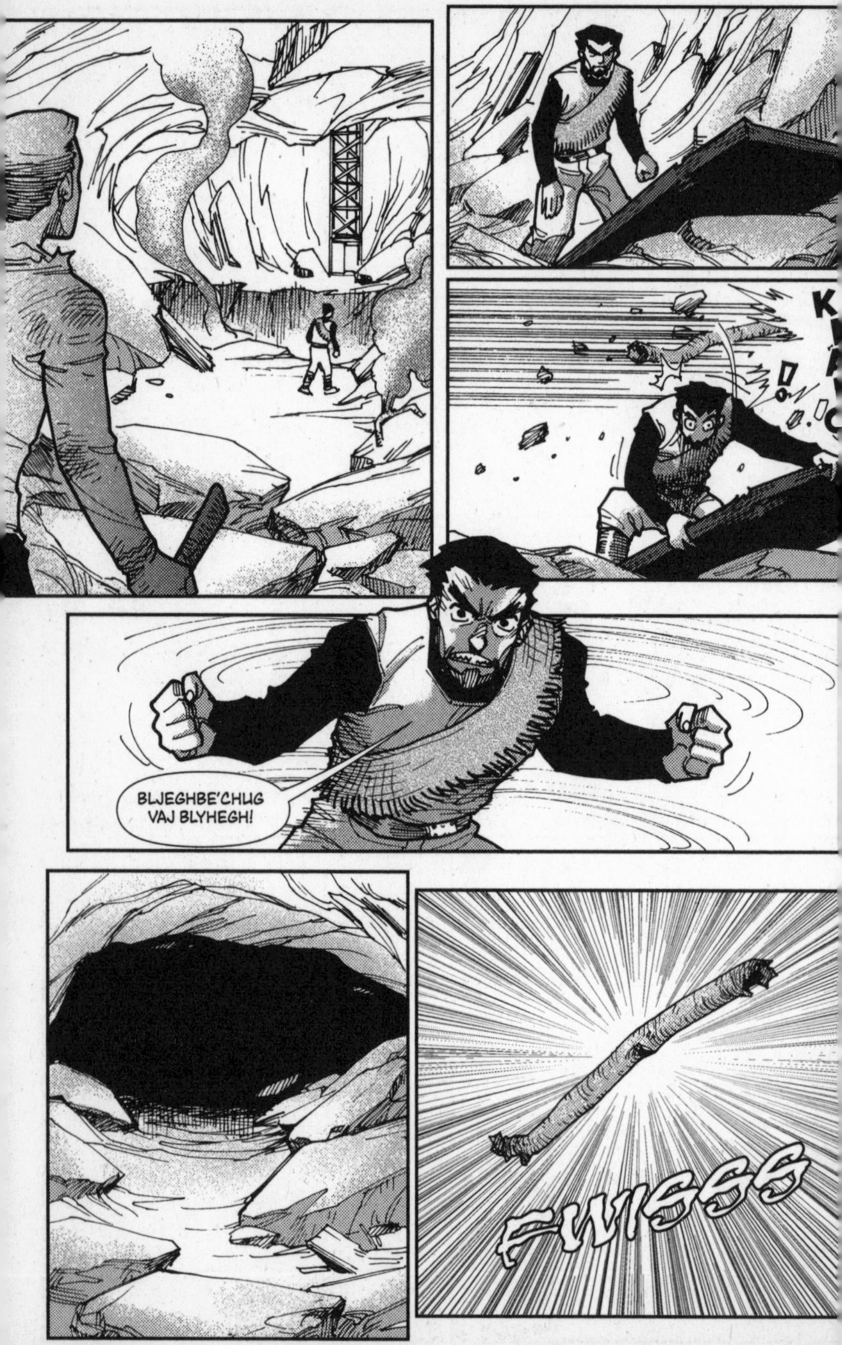
BLJEGHBE'CHUG VAJ BLYHEGH!
FWISSS

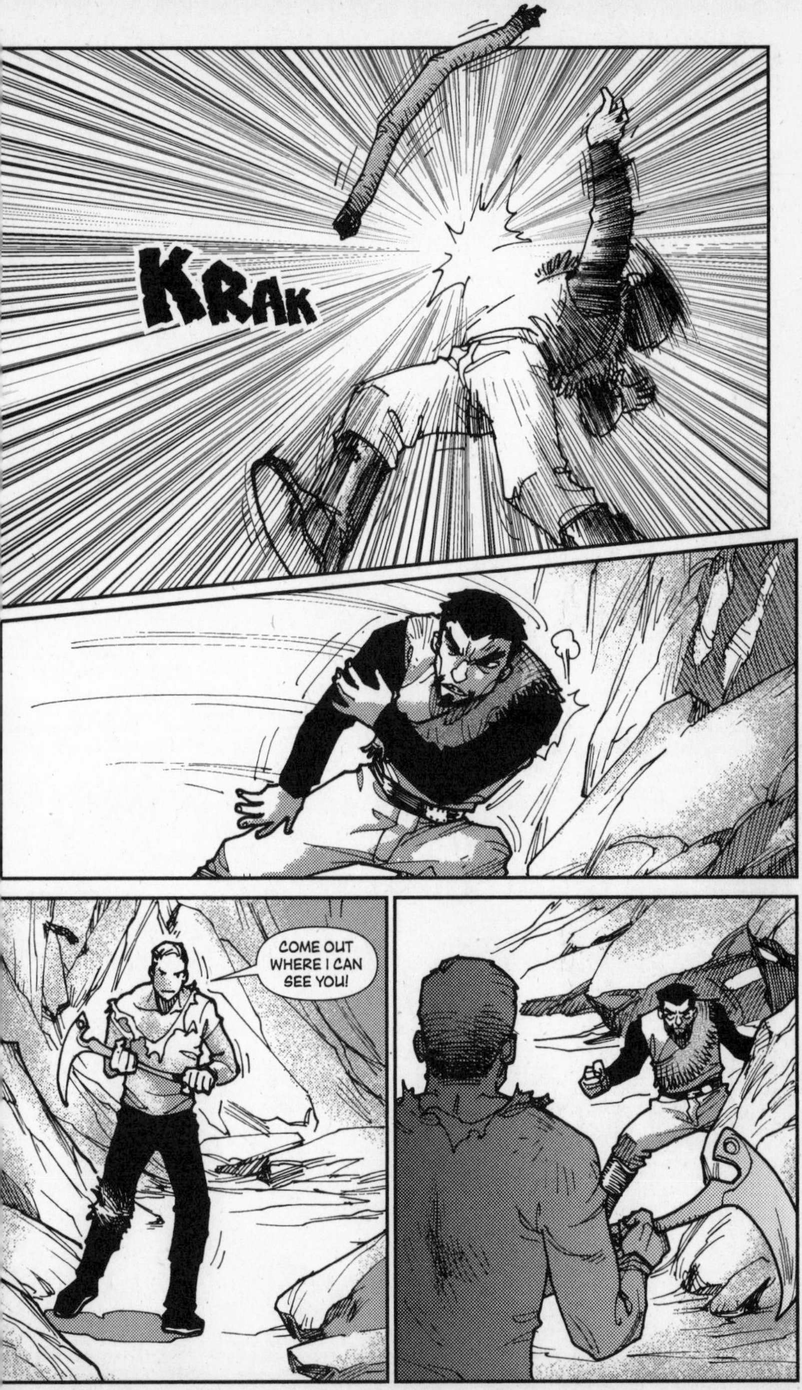
KRAK
COME OUT WHERE I CAN SEE YOU!

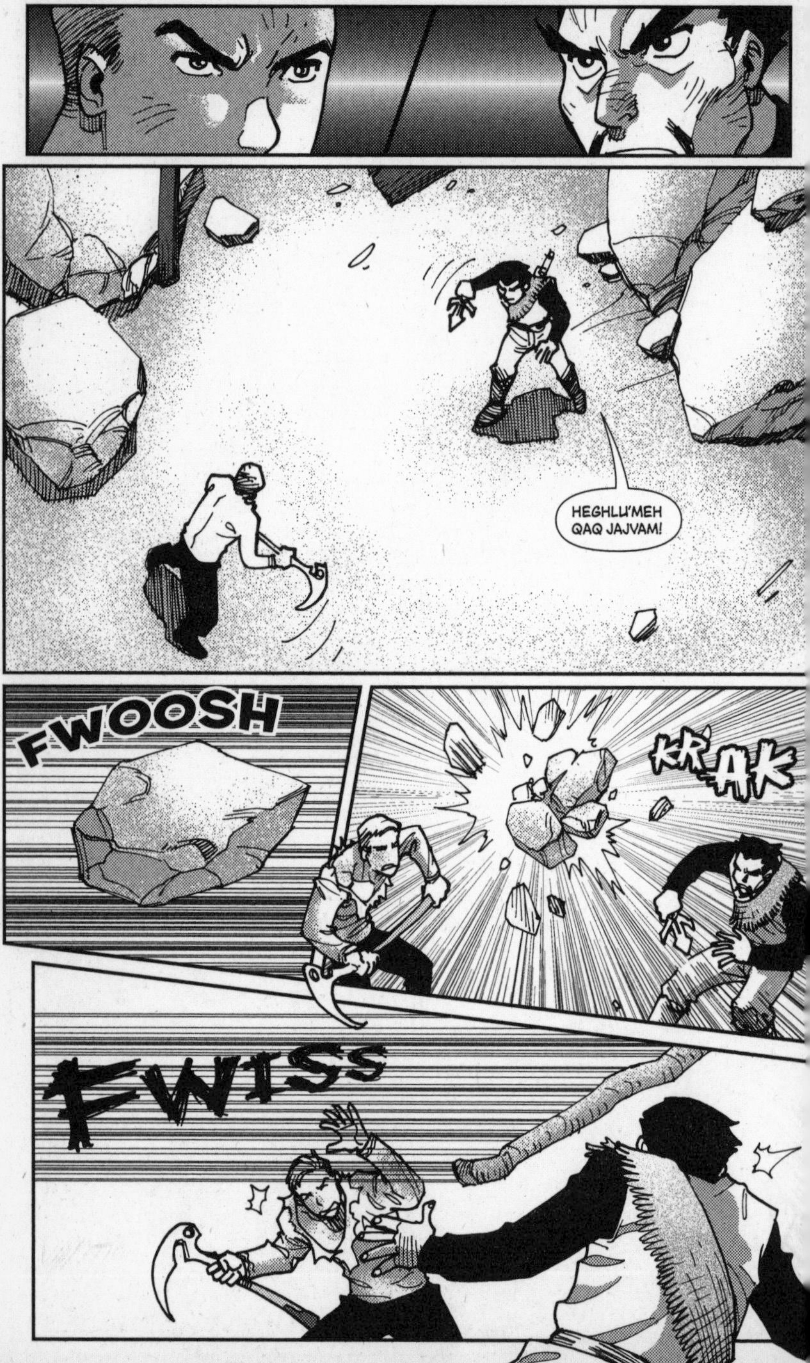
HEGHLU'MEH
QAQ JAJVAM!
FWOOSH
KRAK
FWISS

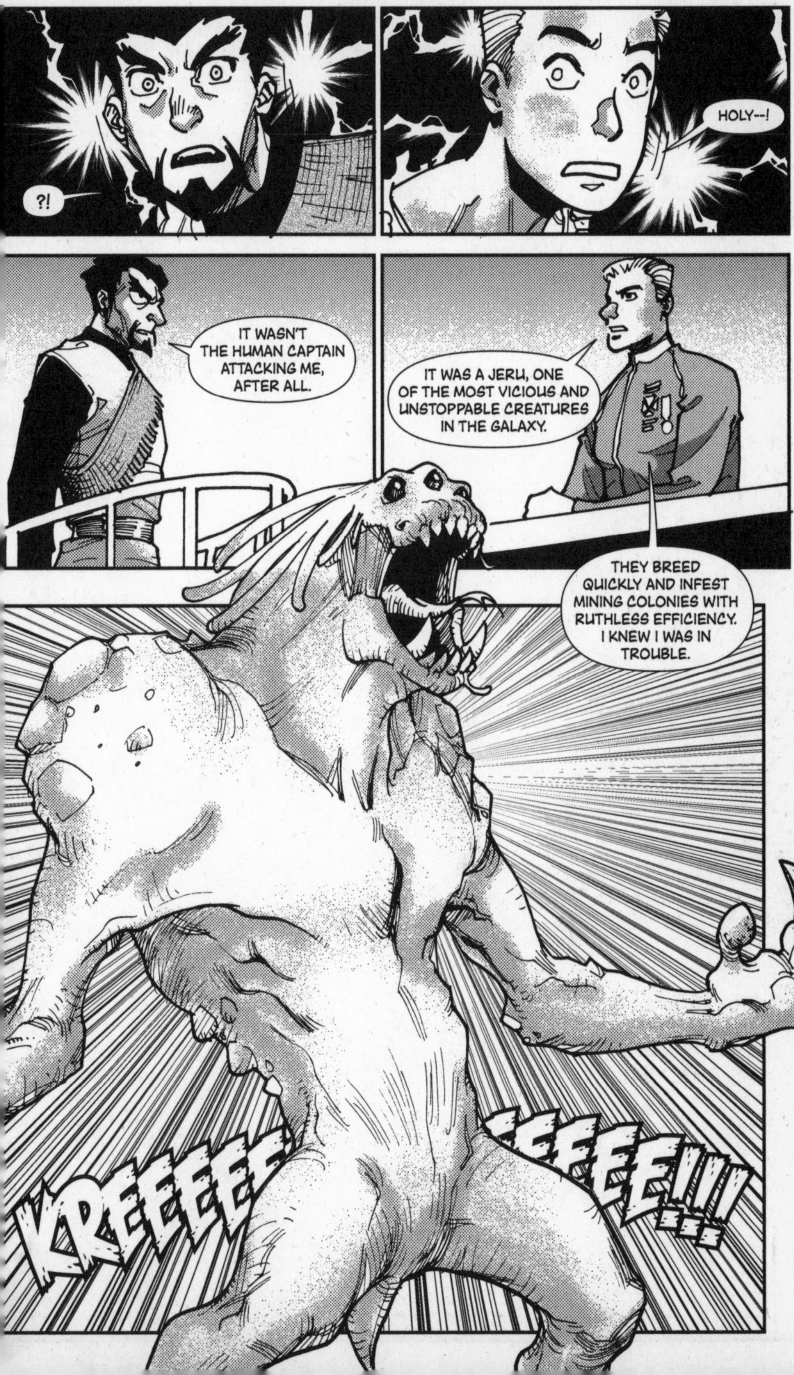
?!
HOLY--!
IT WASN'T THE HUMAN CAPTAIN ATTACKING ME, AFTER ALL.
IT WAS A JERU, ONE OF THE MOST VICIOUS AND UNSTOPPABLE CREATURES IN THE GALAXY.
THEY BREED QUICKLY AND INFEST MINING COLONIES WITH RUTHLESS EFFICIENCY. I KNEW I WAS IN TROUBLE.
KREEEEE--EEEEE!!!

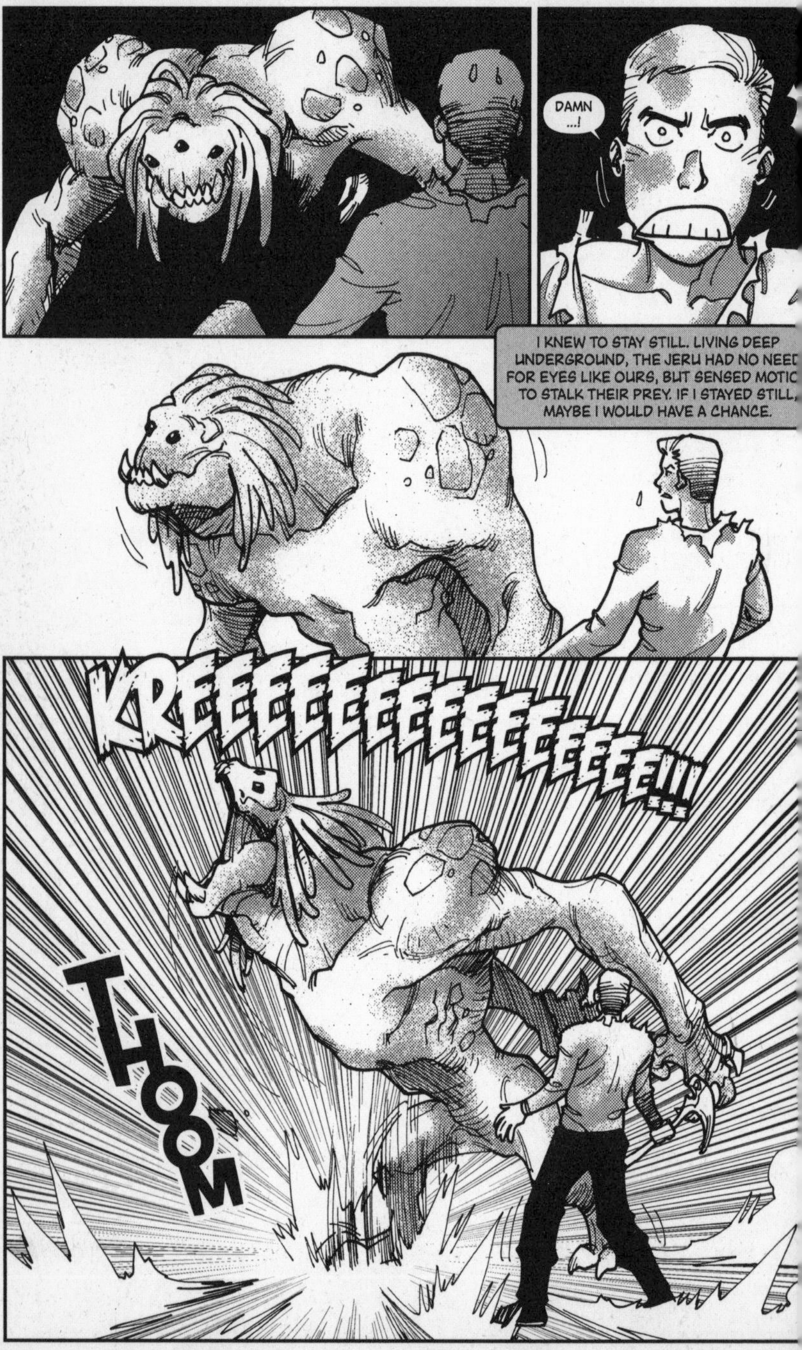
DAMN ...!
I KNEW TO STAY STILL. LIVING DEEP UNDERGROUND, THE JERU HAD NO NEED FOR EYES LIKE OURS, BUT SENSED MOTIC TO STALK THEIR PREY. IF I STAYED STILL, MAYBE I WOULD HAVE A CHANCE.
KREEEEEEEEEEEEEEEEE!!!
THOOM

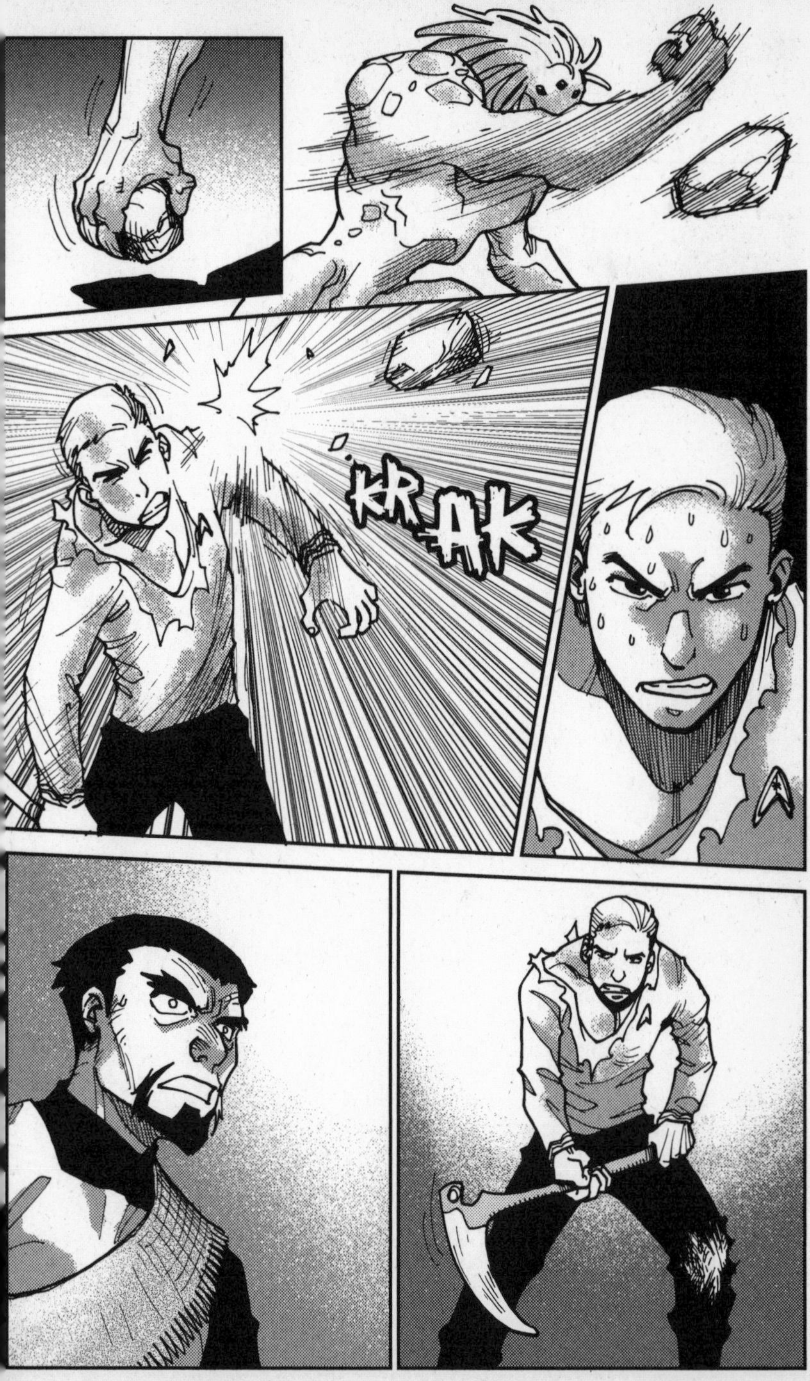
KRAK

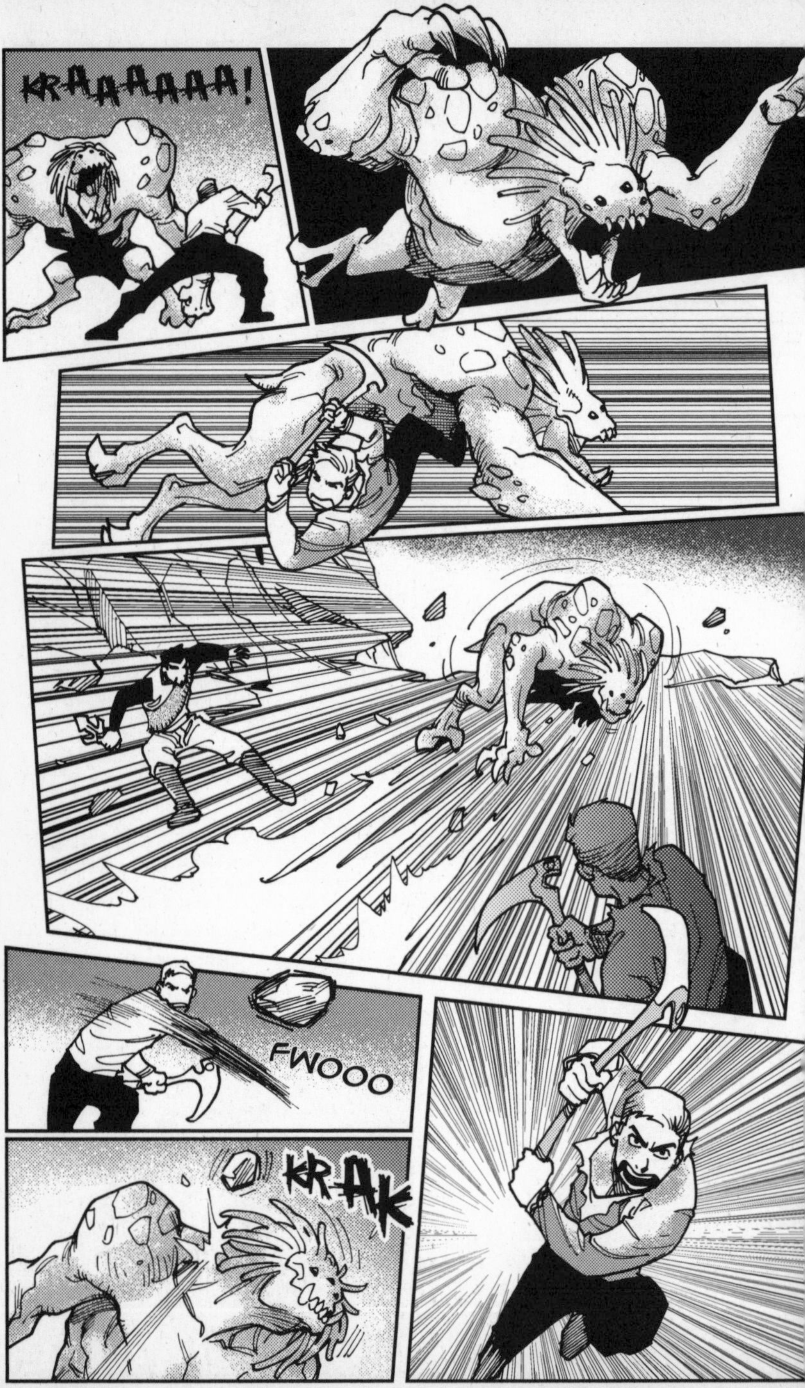
KRAAAAAAA!
FWOOO
KRAK

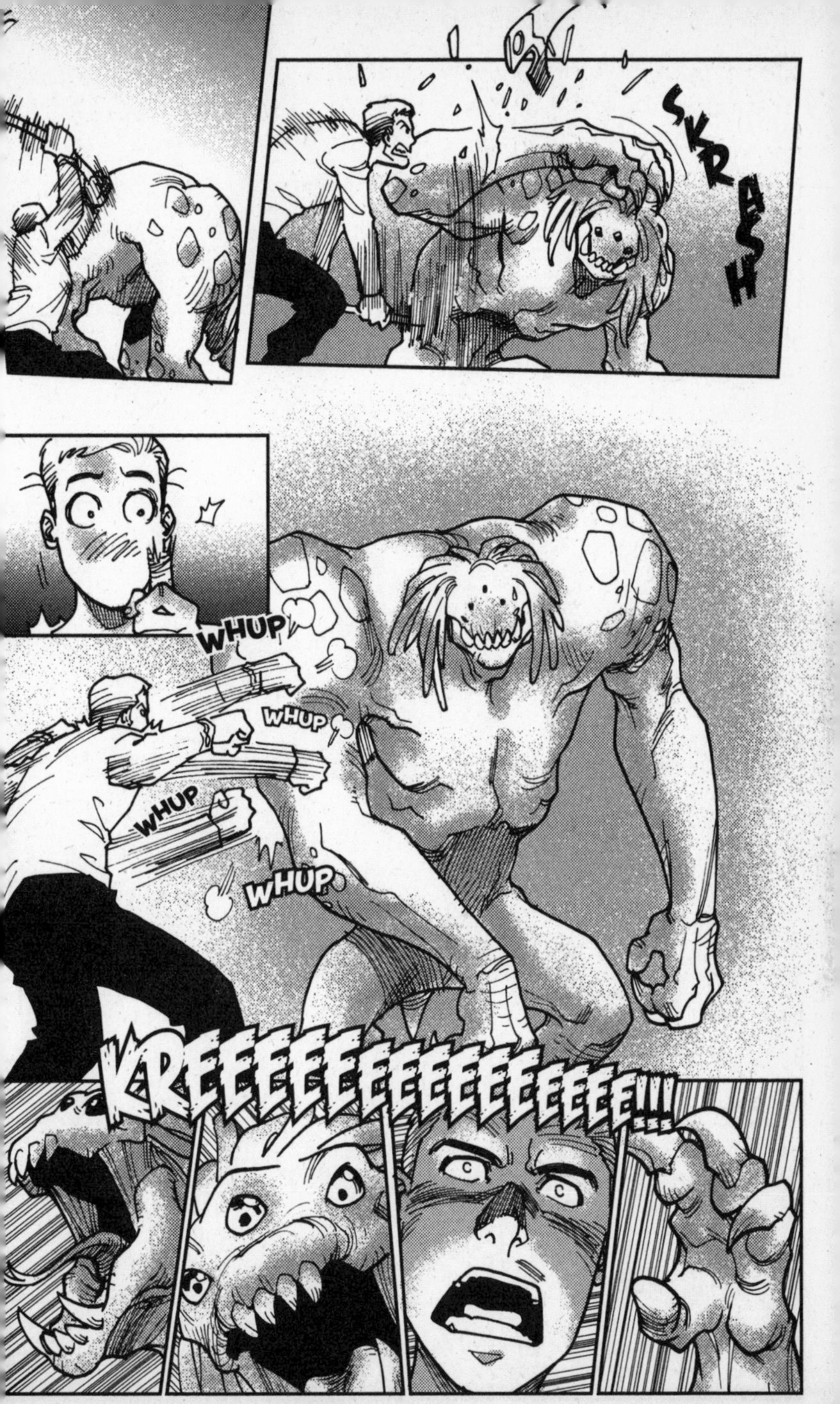
SKRASH
WHUP
WHUP
WHUP
WHUP
KREEEEEEEEEEEEEEEEE!!!

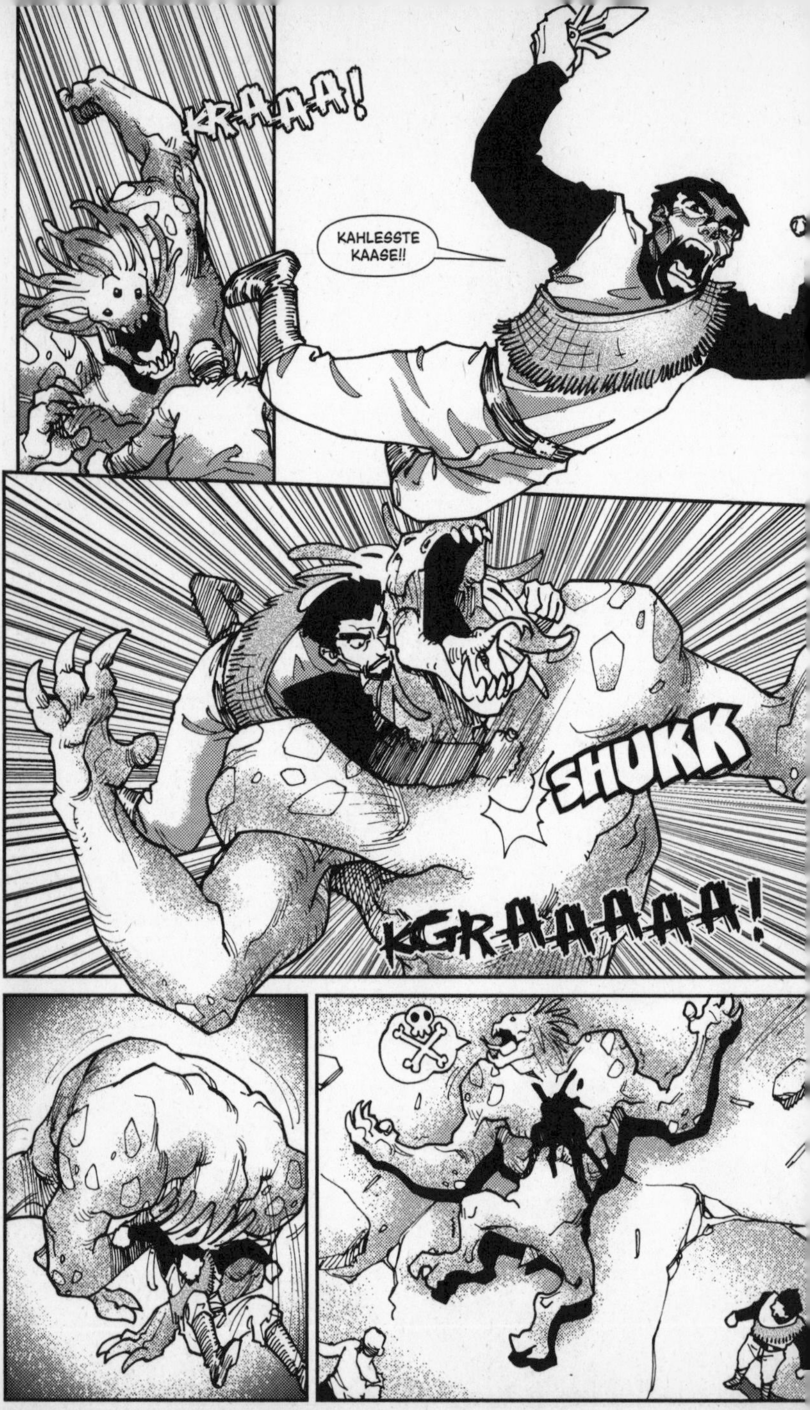
KRAAAA!
KAHLESSTE KAASE!!
SHUKK
KGRAAAAAA!

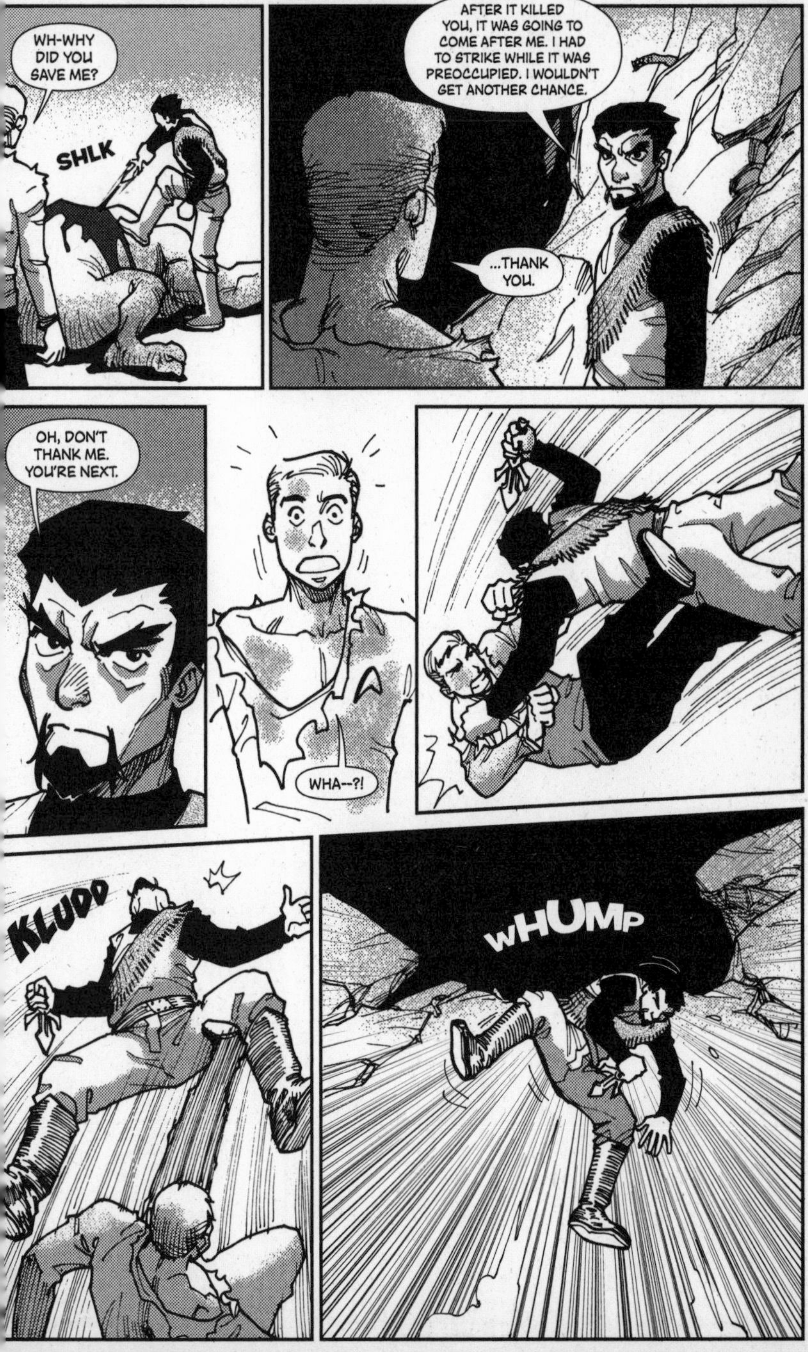
WH-WHY DID YOU SAVE ME?
SHLK
AFTER IT KILLED YOU, IT WAS GOING TO COME AFTER ME. I HAD TO STRIKE WHILE IT WAS PREOCCUPIED. I WOULDN'T GET ANOTHER CHANCE.
...THANK YOU.
OH, DON'T THANK ME. YOU'RE NEXT.
WHA--?!
KLUDD
wHUMp

RUMBLE

KRUUMMM!

KR-AK

KR-AK

KR-AK

WHAP

KL-AK

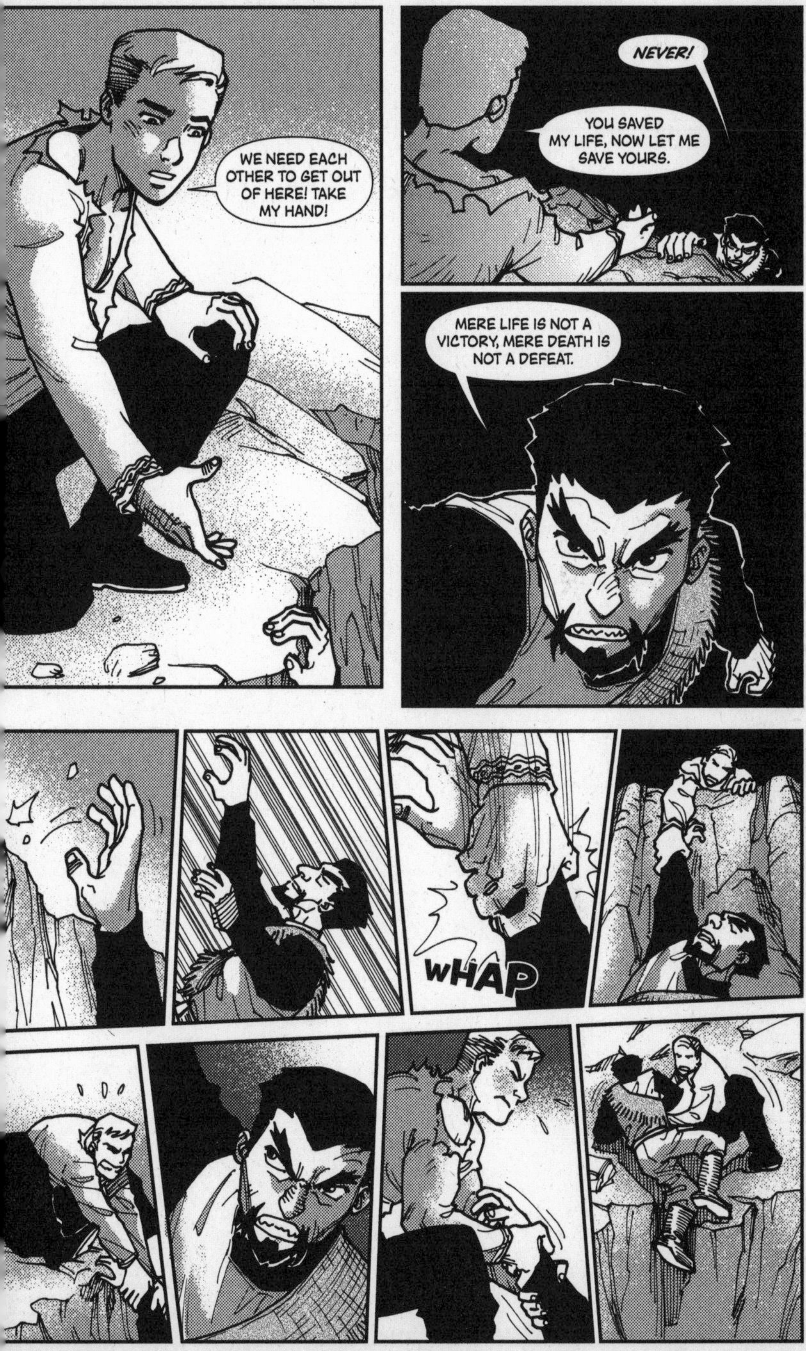
WE NEED EACH OTHER TO GET OUT OF HERE! TAKE MY HAND!
YOU SAVED MY LIFE, NOW LET ME SAVE YOURS.
NEVER!
MERE LIFE IS NOT A VICTORY, MERE DEATH IS NOT A DEFEAT.
WHAP

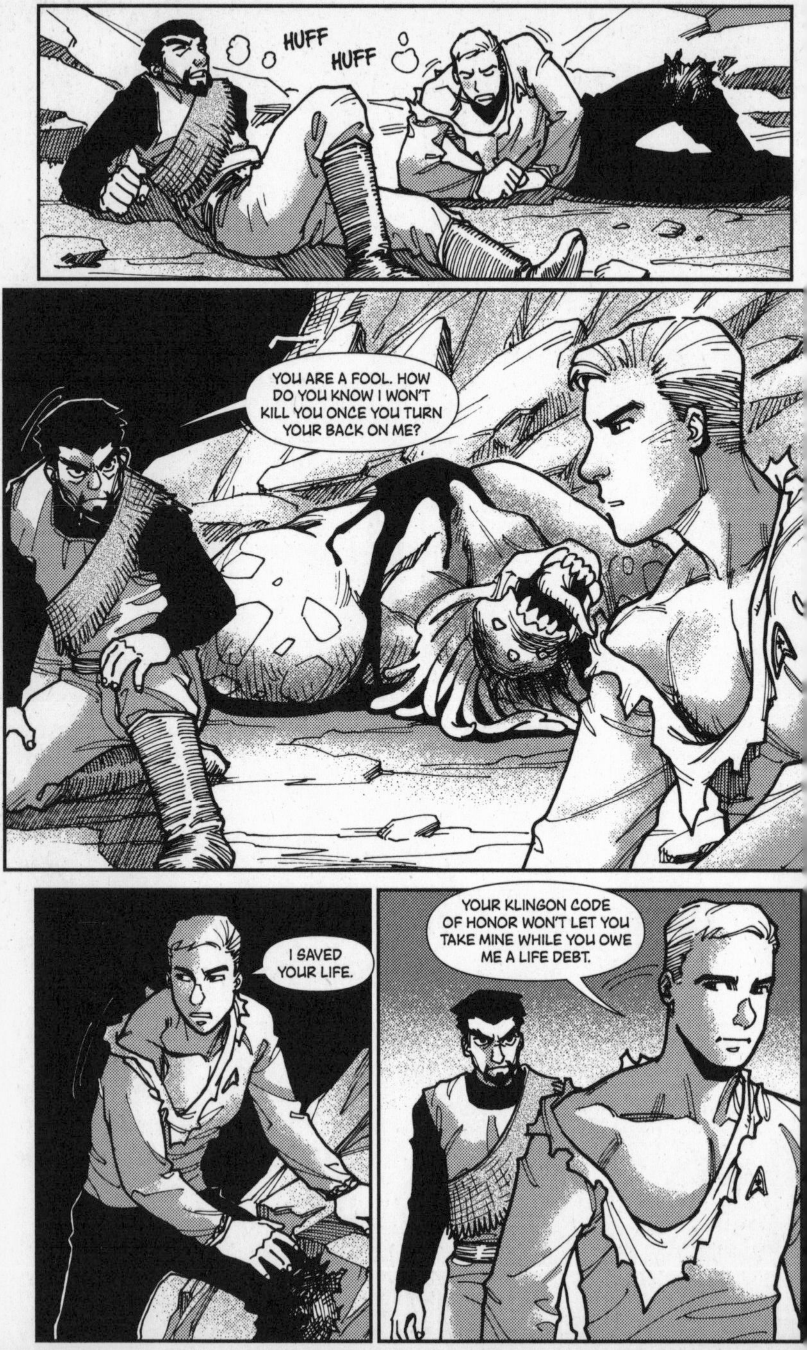

HUFF
HUFF
YOU ARE A FOOL. HOW DO YOU KNOW I WON'T KILL YOU ONCE YOU TURN YOUR BACK ON ME?
I SAVED YOUR LIFE.
YOUR KLINGON CODE OF HONOR WON'T LET YOU TAKE MINE WHILE YOU OWE ME A LIFE DEBT.

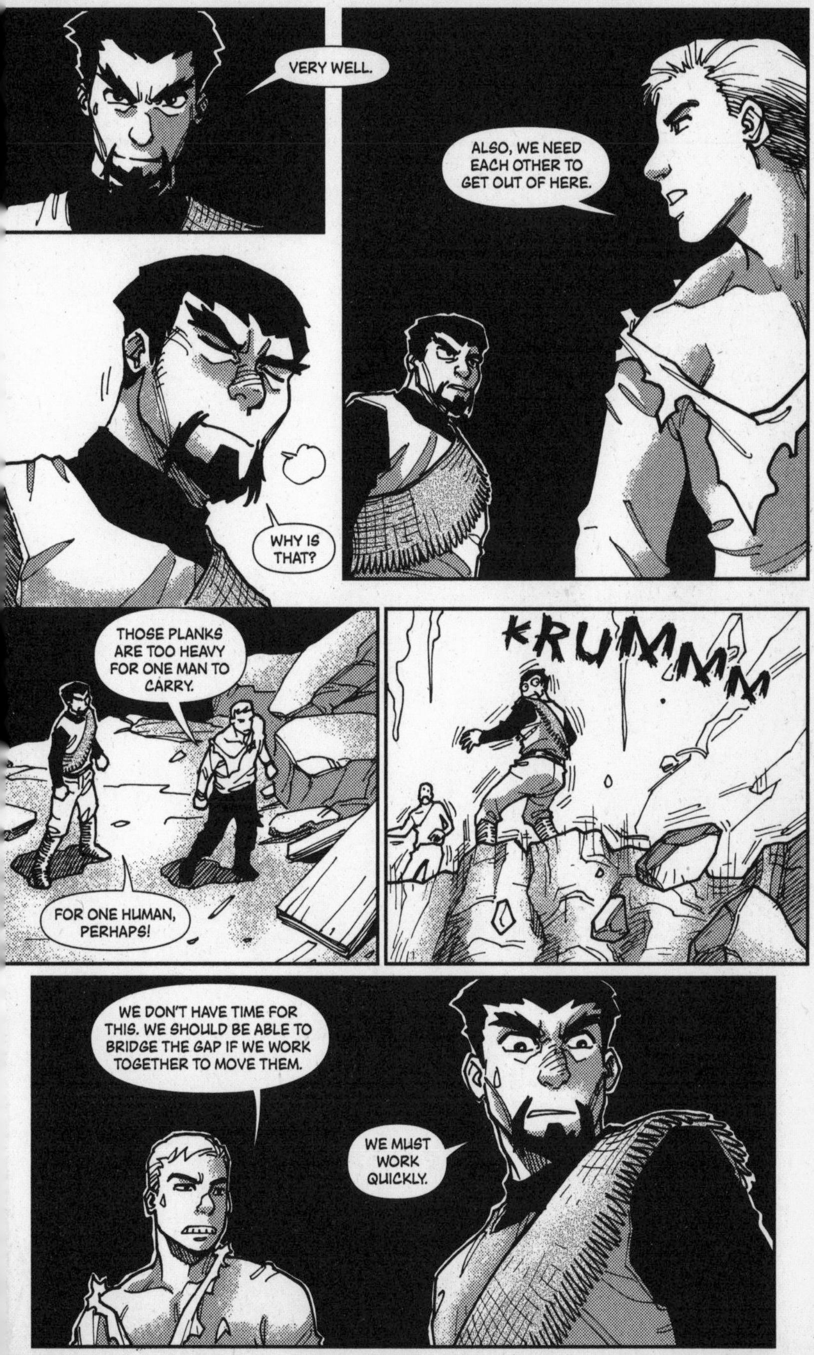
VERY WELL.
ALSO, WE NEED EACH OTHER TO GET OUT OF HERE.
WHY IS THAT?
THOSE PLANKS ARE TOO HEAVY FOR ONE MAN TO CARRY.
FOR ONE HUMAN, PERHAPS!
KRUMMM
WE DON'T HAVE TIME FOR THIS. WE SHOULD BE ABLE TO BRIDGE THE GAP IF WE WORK TOGETHER TO MOVE THEM.
WE MUST WORK QUICKLY.

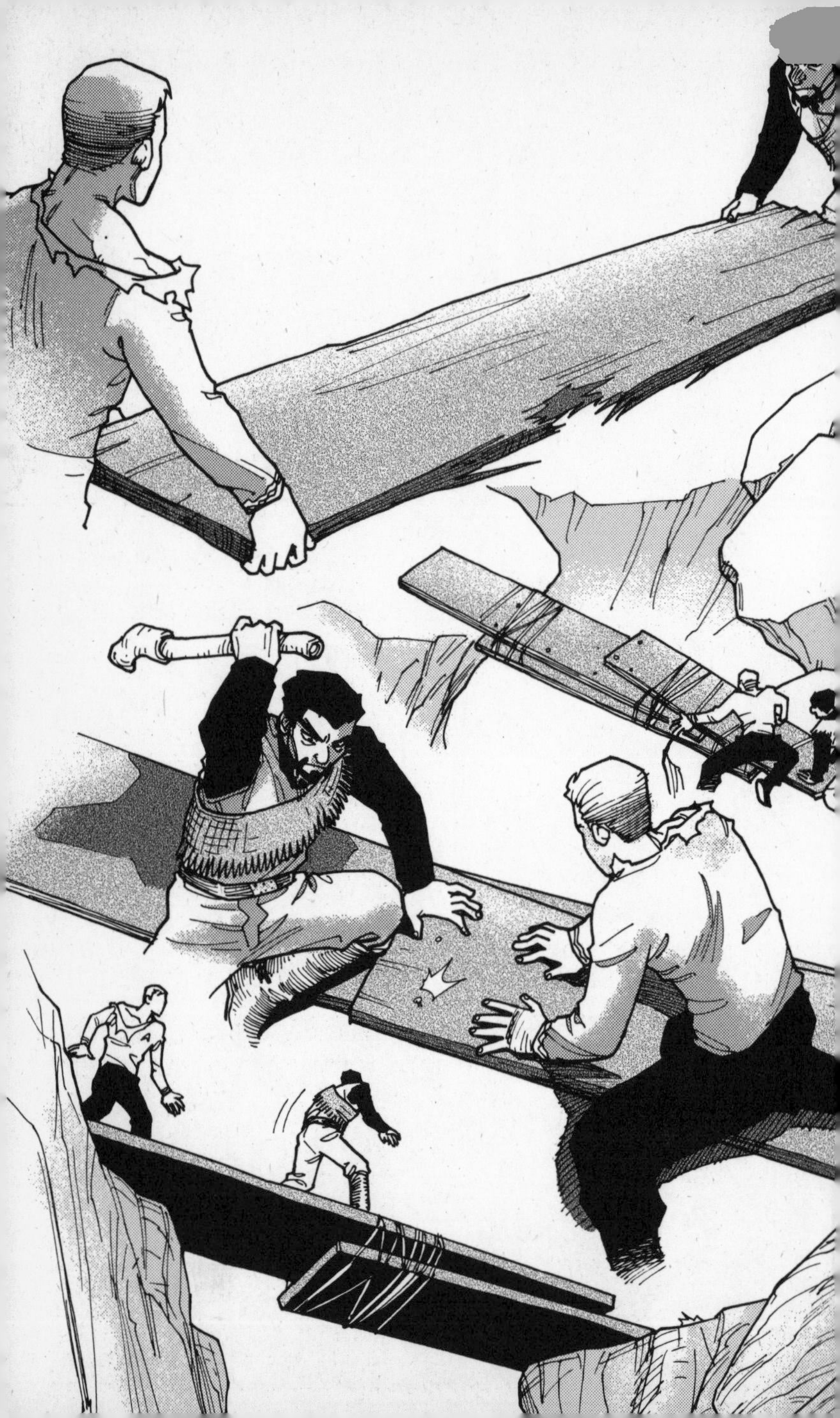

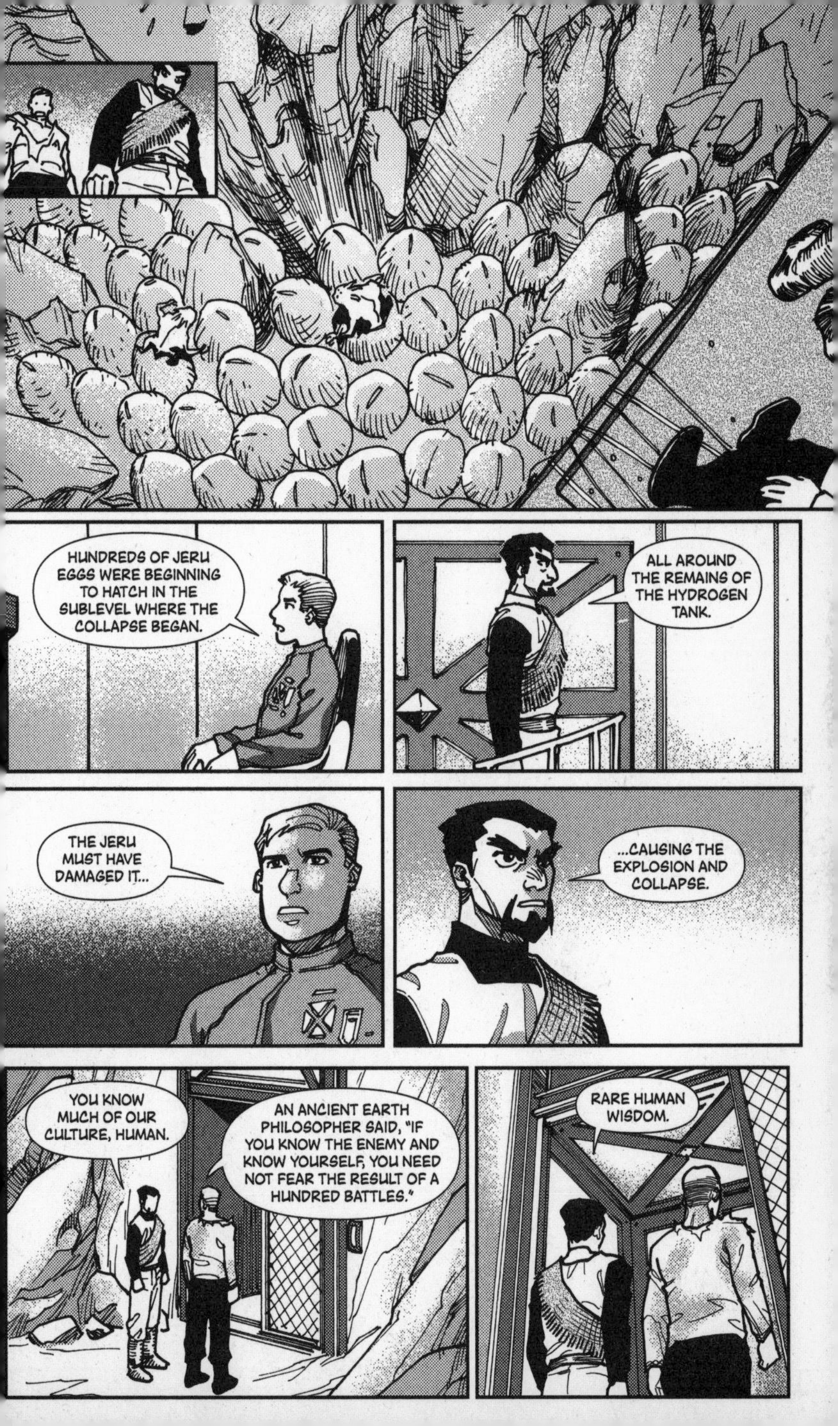
HUNDREDS OF JERU EGGS WERE BEGINNING TO HATCH IN THE SUBLEVEL WHERE THE COLLAPSE BEGAN.
ALL AROUND THE REMAINS OF THE HYDROGEN TANK.
THE JERU MUST HAVE DAMAGED IT...
...CAUSING THE EXPLOSION AND COLLAPSE.
YOU KNOW MUCH OF OUR CULTURE, HUMAN.
AN ANCIENT EARTH PHILOSOPHER SAID, "IF YOU KNOW THE ENEMY AND KNOW YOURSELF, YOU NEED NOT FEAR THE RESULT OF A HUNDRED BATTLES."
RARE HUMAN WISDOM.

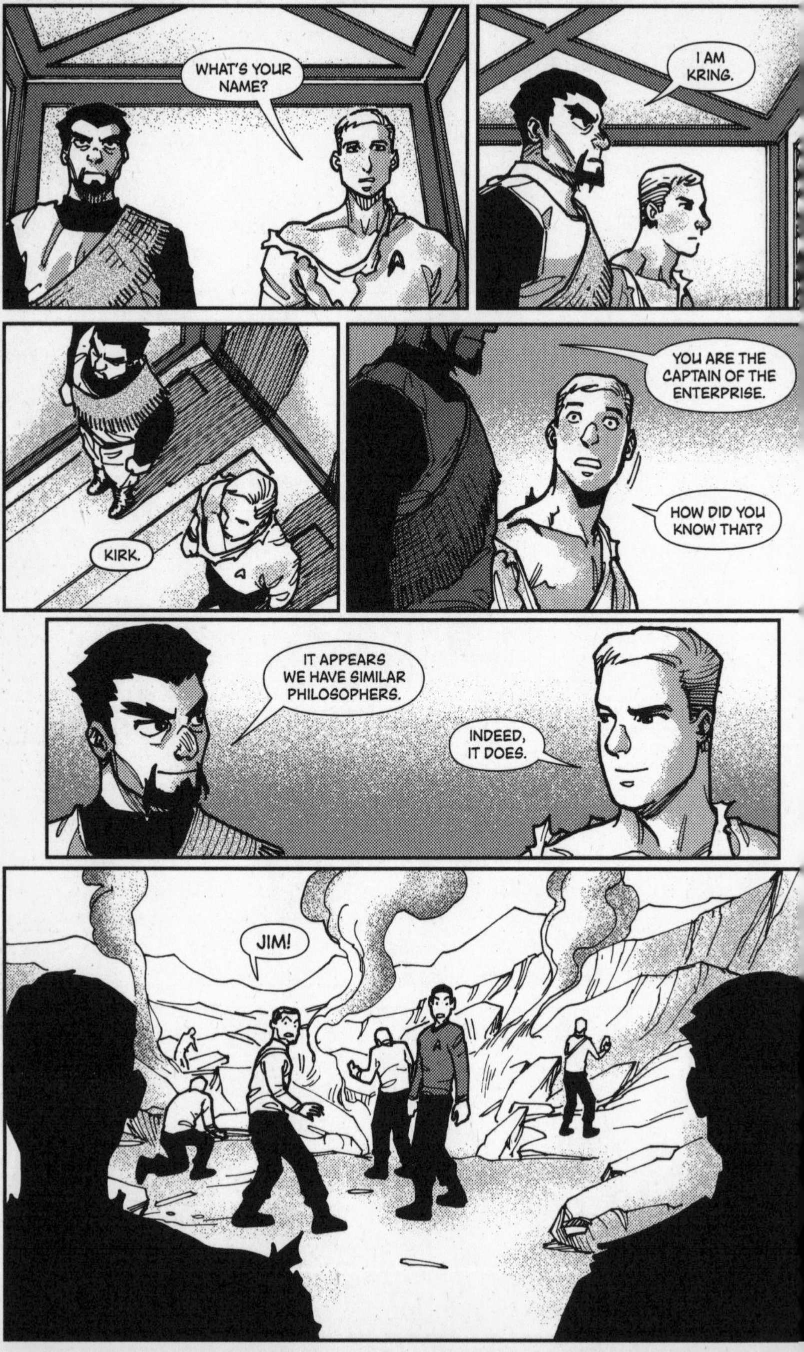
WHAT'S YOUR NAME?
I AM KRING.
KIRK.
YOU ARE THE CAPTAIN OF THE ENTERPRISE.
HOW DID YOU KNOW THAT?
IT APPEARS WE HAVE SIMILAR PHILOSOPHERS.
INDEED, IT DOES.
JIM!

HOLSTER YOUR WEAPONS.

SIR?

YOU HEARD ME! HOLSTER YOUR WEAPONS!

SPOCK, THERE'S A JERU COLONY BENEATH THE MINE AND THE EGGS ARE HATCHING. IF WE DON'T GET OFF THIS PLANET SOON, THE COLLAPSE WILL BE THE LEAST OF OUR WORRIES. BONES, HOW ARE THE MINERS?

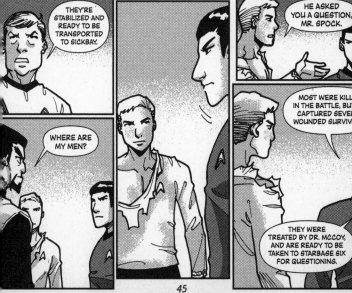

THEY'RE STABILIZED AND READY TO BE TRANSPORTED TO SICKBAY.

WHERE ARE MY MEN?

HE ASKED YOU A QUESTION, MR. SPOCK.

MOST WERE KILLED IN THE BATTLE, BUT WE CAPTURED SEVERAL WOUNDED SURVIVORS.

THEY WERE TREATED BY DR. MCCOY, AND ARE READY TO BE TAKEN TO STARBASE SIX FOR QUESTIONING.

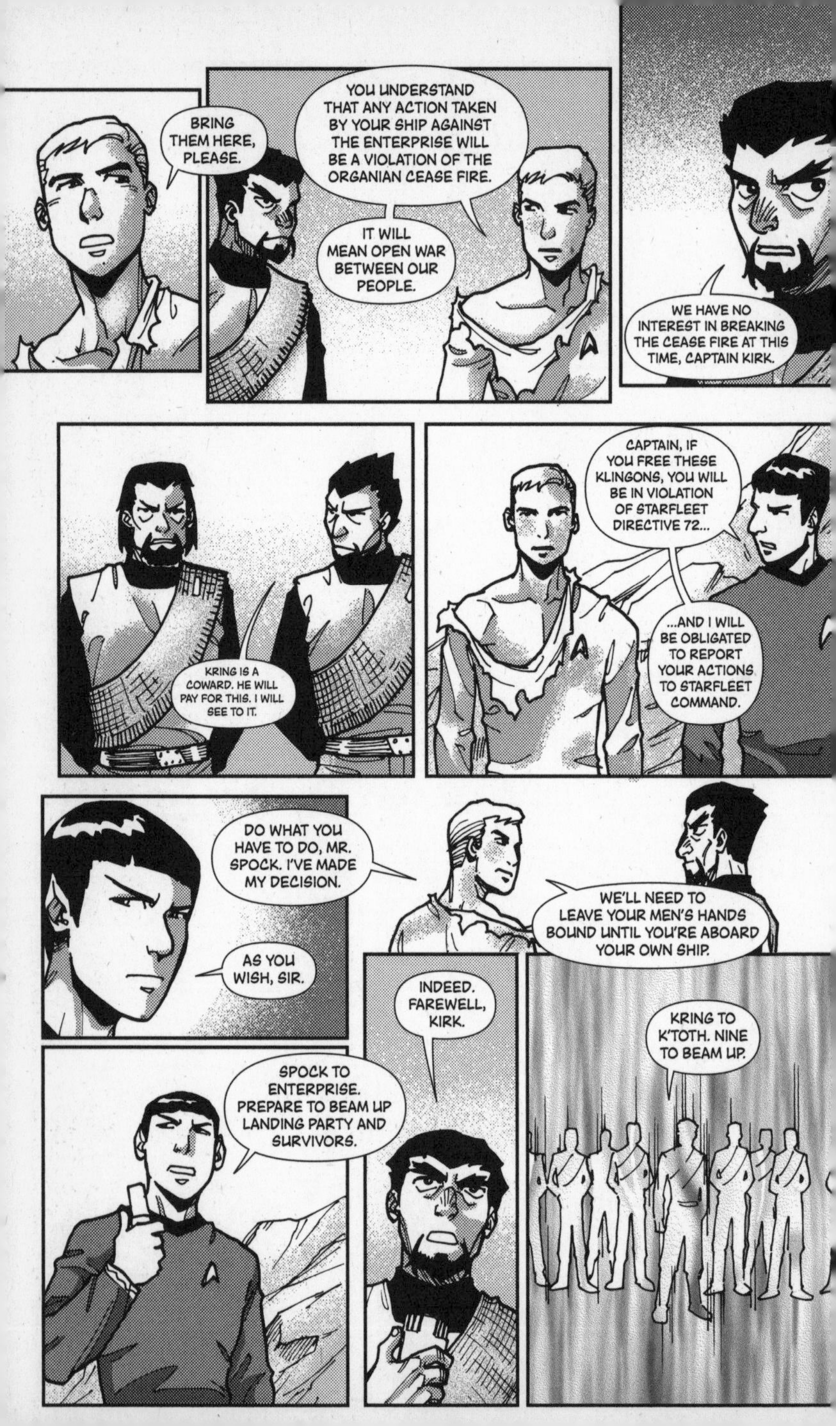
BRING THEM HERE, PLEASE.
YOU UNDERSTAND THAT ANY ACTION TAKEN BY YOUR SHIP AGAINST THE ENTERPRISE WILL BE A VIOLATION OF THE ORGANIAN CEASE FIRE.
IT WILL MEAN OPEN WAR BETWEEN OUR PEOPLE.
WE HAVE NO INTEREST IN BREAKING THE CEASE FIRE AT THIS TIME, CAPTAIN KIRK.
KRING IS A COWARD. HE WILL PAY FOR THIS. I WILL SEE TO IT.
CAPTAIN, IF YOU FREE THESE KLINGONS, YOU WILL BE IN VIOLATION OF STARFLEET DIRECTIVE 72...
...AND I WILL BE OBLIGATED TO REPORT YOUR ACTIONS TO STARFLEET COMMAND.
DO WHAT YOU HAVE TO DO, MR. SPOCK. I'VE MADE MY DECISION.
AS YOU WISH, SIR.
WE'LL NEED TO LEAVE YOUR MEN'S HANDS BOUND UNTIL YOU'RE ABOARD YOUR OWN SHIP.
SPOCK TO ENTERPRISE. PREPARE TO BEAM UP LANDING PARTY AND SURVIVORS.
INDEED. FAREWELL, KIRK.
KRING TO K'TOTH. NINE TO BEAM UP.

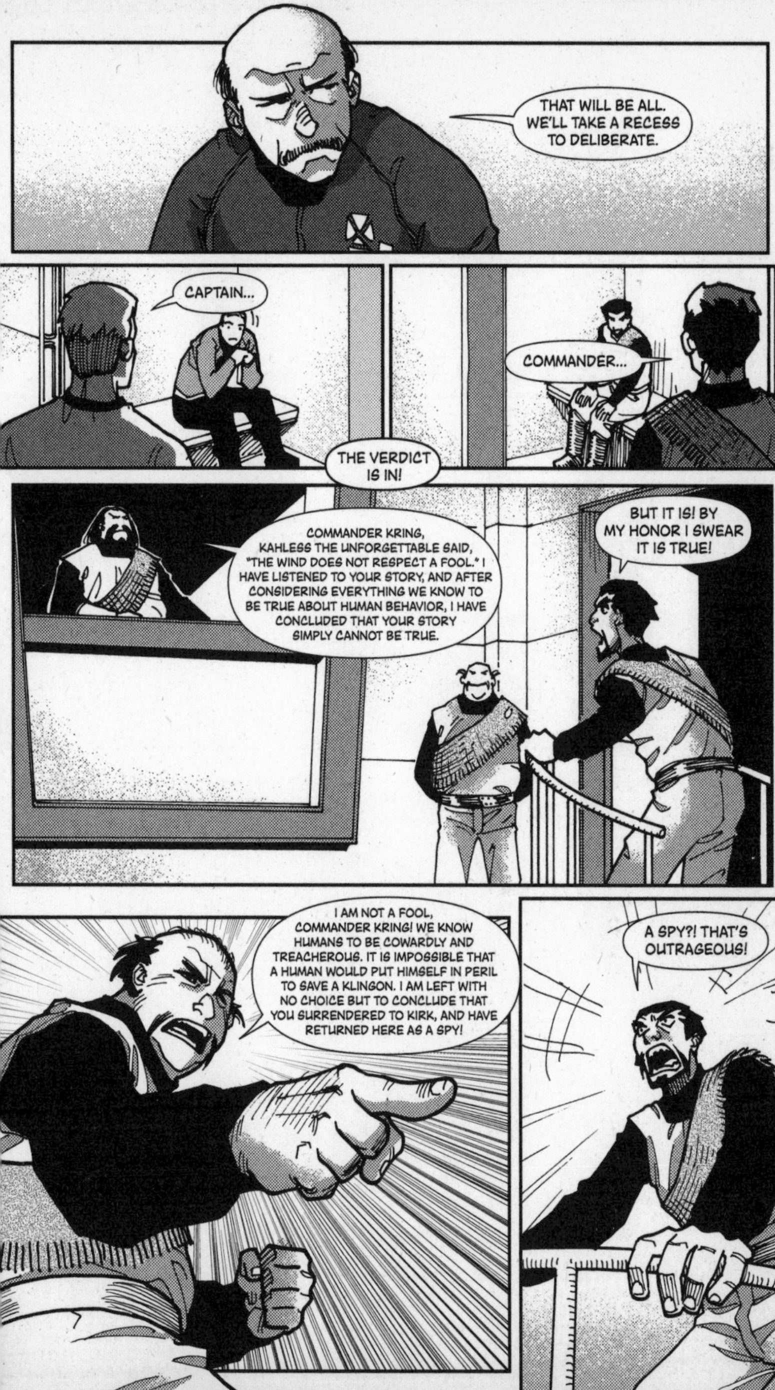
THAT WILL BE ALL. WE'LL TAKE A RECESS TO DELIBERATE.
CAPTAIN...
COMMANDER...
THE VERDICT IS IN!
COMMANDER KRING, KAHLESS THE UNFORGETTABLE SAID, "THE WIND DOES NOT RESPECT A FOOL." I HAVE LISTENED TO YOUR STORY, AND AFTER CONSIDERING EVERYTHING WE KNOW TO BE TRUE ABOUT HUMAN BEHAVIOR, I HAVE CONCLUDED THAT YOUR STORY SIMPLY CANNOT BE TRUE.
BUT IT IS! BY MY HONOR I SWEAR IT IS TRUE!
I AM NOT A FOOL, COMMANDER KRING! WE KNOW HUMANS TO BE COWARDLY AND TREACHEROUS. IT IS IMPOSSIBLE THAT A HUMAN WOULD PUT HIMSELF IN PERIL TO SAVE A KLINGON. I AM LEFT WITH NO CHOICE BUT TO CONCLUDE THAT YOU SURRENDERED TO KIRK, AND HAVE RETURNED HERE AS A SPY!
A SPY?! THAT'S OUTRAGEOUS!

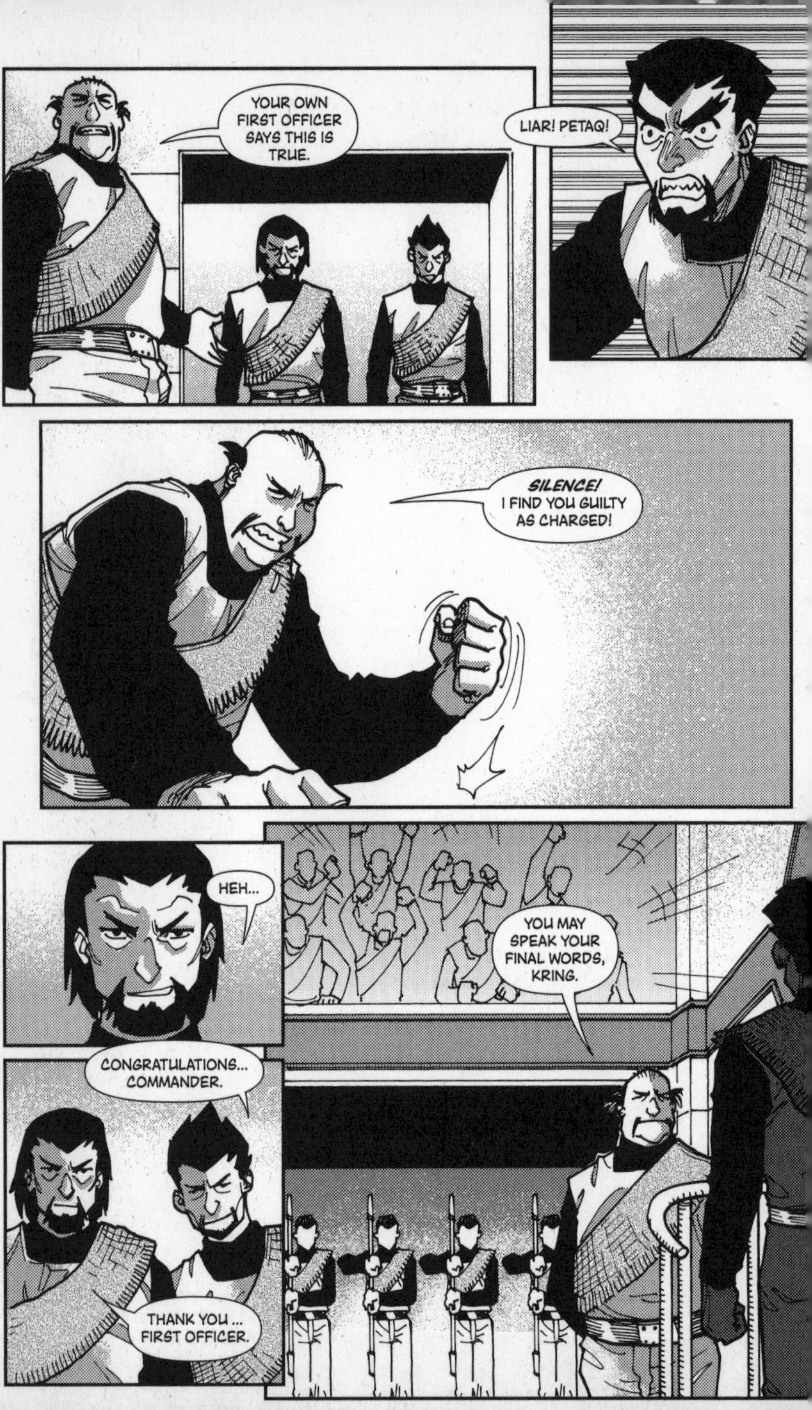
YOUR OWN FIRST OFFICER SAYS THIS IS TRUE.
LIAR! PETAQ!
SILENCE! I FIND YOU GUILTY AS CHARGED!
HEH...
CONGRATULATIONS... COMMANDER.
THANK YOU ... FIRST OFFICER.
YOU MAY SPEAK YOUR FINAL WORDS, KRING.

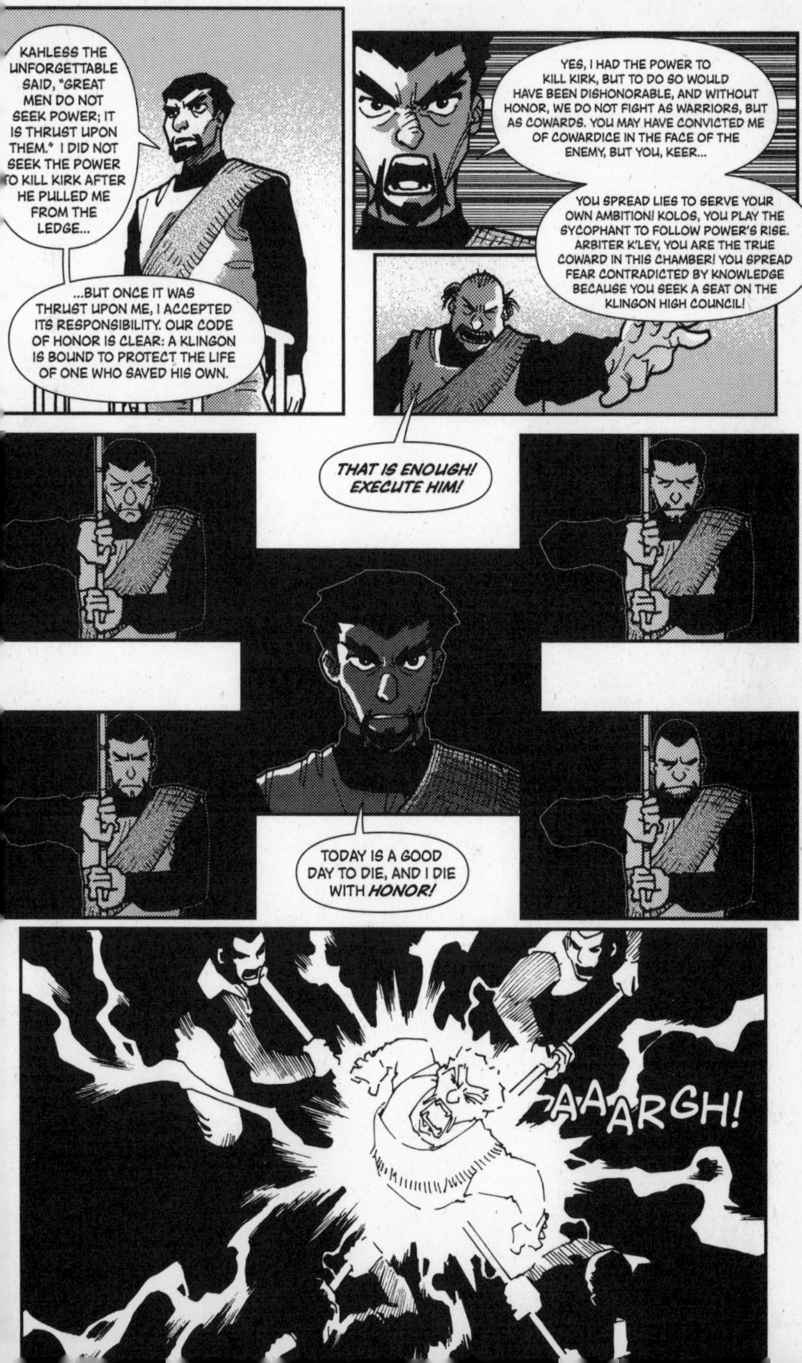
KAHLESS THE UNFORGETTABLE SAID, "GREAT MEN DO NOT SEEK POWER; IT IS THRUST UPON THEM." I DID NOT SEEK THE POWER TO KILL KIRK AFTER HE PULLED ME FROM THE LEDGE...
...BUT ONCE IT WAS THRUST UPON ME, I ACCEPTED ITS RESPONSIBILITY. OUR CODE OF HONOR IS CLEAR: A KLINGON IS BOUND TO PROTECT THE LIFE OF ONE WHO SAVED HIS OWN.
YES, I HAD THE POWER TO KILL KIRK, BUT TO DO SO WOULD HAVE BEEN DISHONORABLE, AND WITHOUT HONOR, WE DO NOT FIGHT AS WARRIORS, BUT AS COWARDS. YOU MAY HAVE CONVICTED ME OF COWARDICE IN THE FACE OF THE ENEMY, BUT YOU, KEER...
YOU SPREAD LIES TO SERVE YOUR OWN AMBITION! KOLOS, YOU PLAY THE SYCOPHANT TO FOLLOW POWER'S RISE. ARBITER K'LEY, YOU ARE THE TRUE COWARD IN THIS CHAMBER! YOU SPREAD FEAR CONTRADICTED BY KNOWLEDGE BECAUSE YOU SEEK A SEAT ON THE KLINGON HIGH COUNCIL!
THAT IS ENOUGH! EXECUTE HIM!
TODAY IS A GOOD DAY TO DIE, AND I DIE WITH ***HONOR!***
AAAARGH!

CAPTAIN KIRK, MANY IN THIS COURTROOM-- INCLUDING MEMBERS OF YOUR OWN CREW -- BELIEVE IT WAS WRONG FOR YOU TO FREE COMMANDER KRING AND HIS CREW.

INDEED, WILLINGLY RELEASING AN ENEMY DURING WARTIME WITHOUT AUTHORIZATION FROM STARFLEET COMMAND IS EXPRESSLY PROHIBITED BY GENERAL ORDER 72.

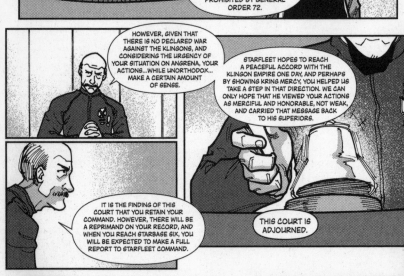

HOWEVER, GIVEN THAT THERE IS NO DECLARED WAR AGAINST THE KLINGONS, AND CONSIDERING THE URGENCY OF YOUR SITUATION ON ANGRENA, YOUR ACTIONS...WHILE UNORTHODOX... MAKE A CERTAIN AMOUNT OF SENSE.

STARFLEET HOPES TO REACH A PEACEFUL ACCORD WITH THE KLINGON EMPIRE ONE DAY, AND PERHAPS BY SHOWING KRING MERCY, YOU HELPED US TAKE A STEP IN THAT DIRECTION. WE CAN ONLY HOPE THAT HE VIEWED YOUR ACTIONS AS MERCIFUL AND HONORABLE, NOT WEAK, AND CARRIED THAT MESSAGE BACK TO HIS SUPERIORS.

IT IS THE FINDING OF THIS COURT THAT YOU RETAIN YOUR COMMAND. HOWEVER, THERE WILL BE A REPRIMAND ON YOUR RECORD, AND WHEN YOU REACH STARBASE SIX, YOU WILL BE EXPECTED TO MAKE A FULL REPORT TO STARFLEET COMMAND.

THIS COURT IS ADJOURNED.

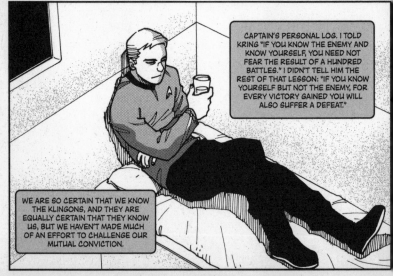

CAPTAIN'S PERSONAL LOG. I TOLD KRING "IF YOU KNOW THE ENEMY AND KNOW YOURSELF, YOU NEED NOT FEAR THE RESULT OF A HUNDRED BATTLES." I DIDN'T TELL HIM THE REST OF THAT LESSON: "IF YOU KNOW YOURSELF BUT NOT THE ENEMY, FOR EVERY VICTORY GAINED YOU WILL ALSO SUFFER A DEFEAT."

WE ARE SO CERTAIN THAT WE KNOW THE KLINGONS, AND THEY ARE EQUALLY CERTAIN THAT THEY KNOW US, BUT WE HAVEN'T MADE MUCH OF AN EFFORT TO CHALLENGE OUR MUTUAL CONVICTION.

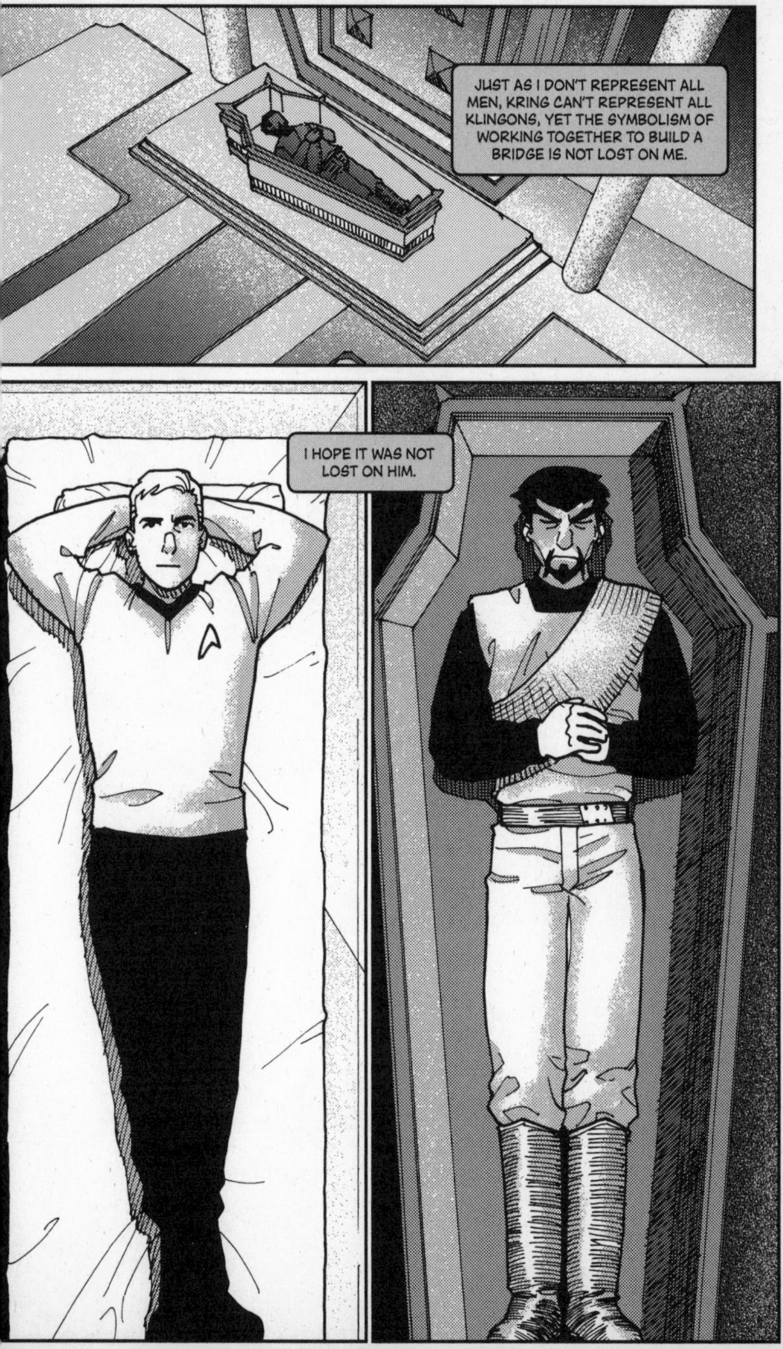
JUST AS I DON'T REPRESENT ALL MEN, KRING CAN'T REPRESENT ALL KLINGONS, YET THE SYMBOLISM OF WORKING TOGETHER TO BUILD A BRIDGE IS NOT LOST ON ME.
I HOPE IT WAS NOT LOST ON HIM.

THE END

BANDI

STORY BY DAVID GERROLD
PENCILS AND INKS BY DON HUDSON
TONES BY STEVE BUCCELLATO

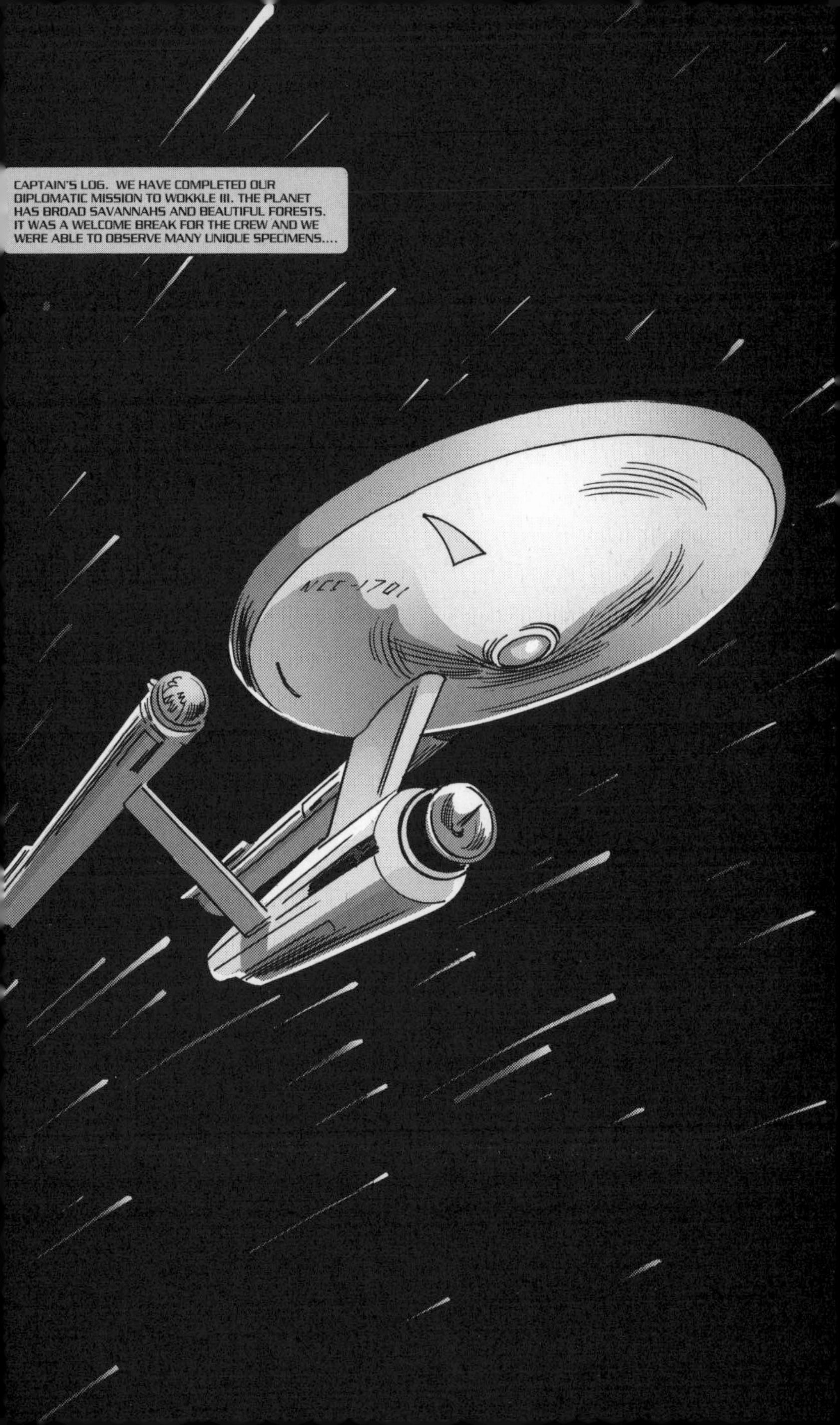
CAPTAIN'S LOG. WE HAVE COMPLETED OUR DIPLOMATIC MISSION TO WOKKLE III. THE PLANET HAS BROAD SAVANNAHS AND BEAUTIFUL FORESTS. IT WAS A WELCOME BREAK FOR THE CREW AND WE WERE ABLE TO OBSERVE MANY UNIQUE SPECIMENS....
NCC-1701

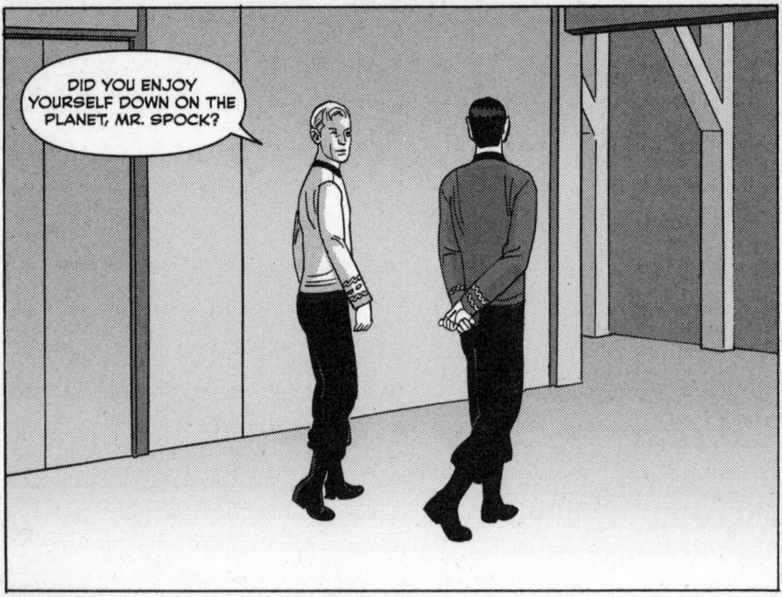
DID YOU ENJOY YOURSELF DOWN ON THE PLANET, MR. SPOCK?

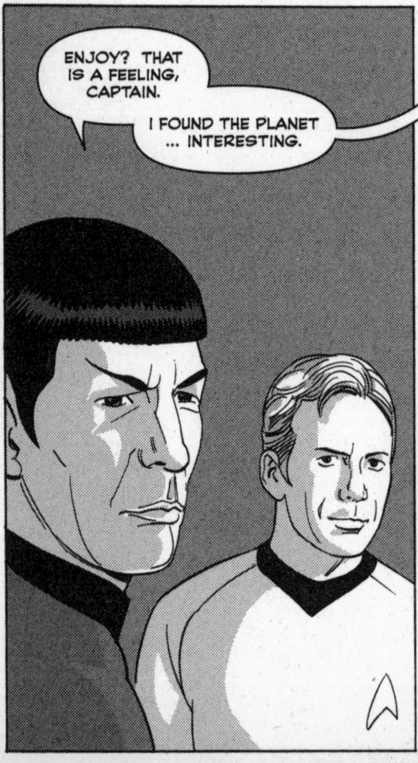
ENJOY? THAT IS A FEELING, CAPTAIN.
I FOUND THE PLANET ... INTERESTING.

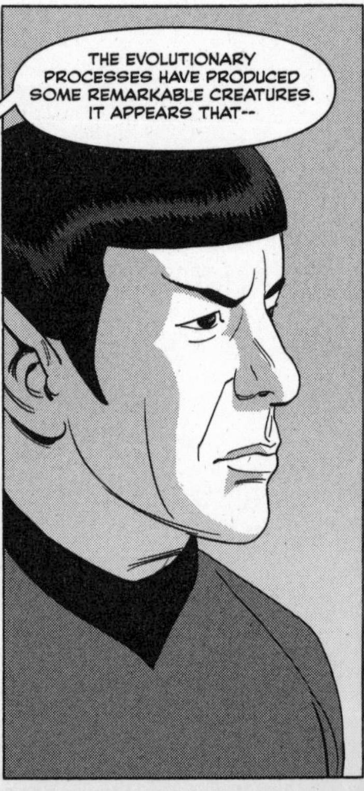
THE EVOLUTIONARY PROCESSES HAVE PRODUCED SOME REMARKABLE CREATURES. IT APPEARS THAT--

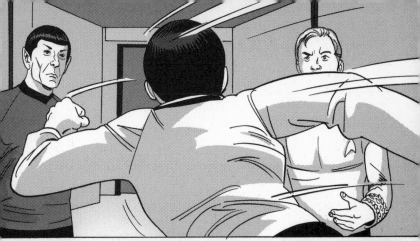

DID YOU SEE IT?

WHICH WAY DID IT GO?

WHAT CAME THIS WAY?

YOU DIDN'T SEE IT?

SEE WHAT?

UH--

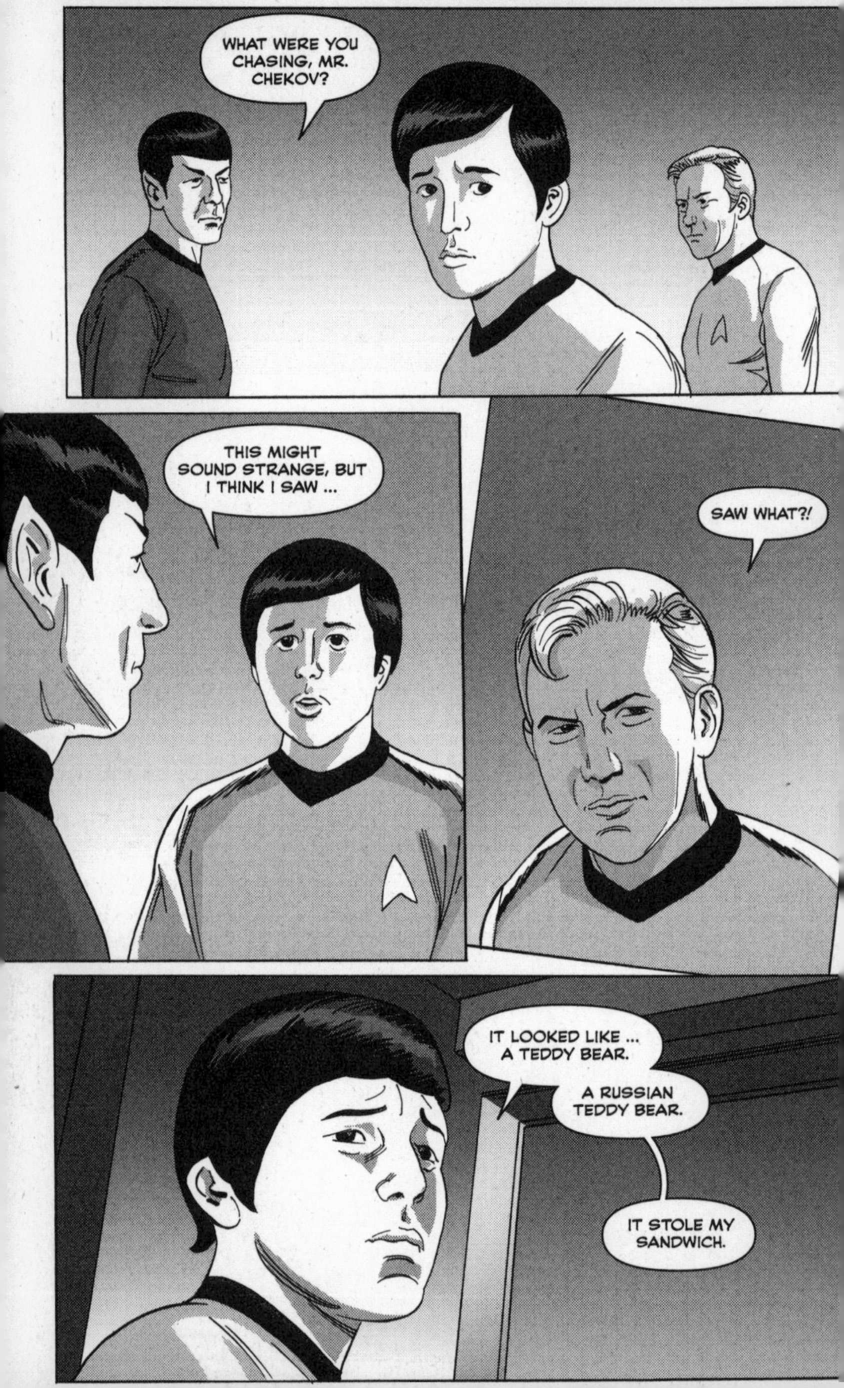
WHAT WERE YOU CHASING, MR. CHEKOV?
THIS MIGHT SOUND STRANGE, BUT I THINK I SAW ...
SAW WHAT?!
IT LOOKED LIKE ... A TEDDY BEAR.
A RUSSIAN TEDDY BEAR.
IT STOLE MY SANDWICH.

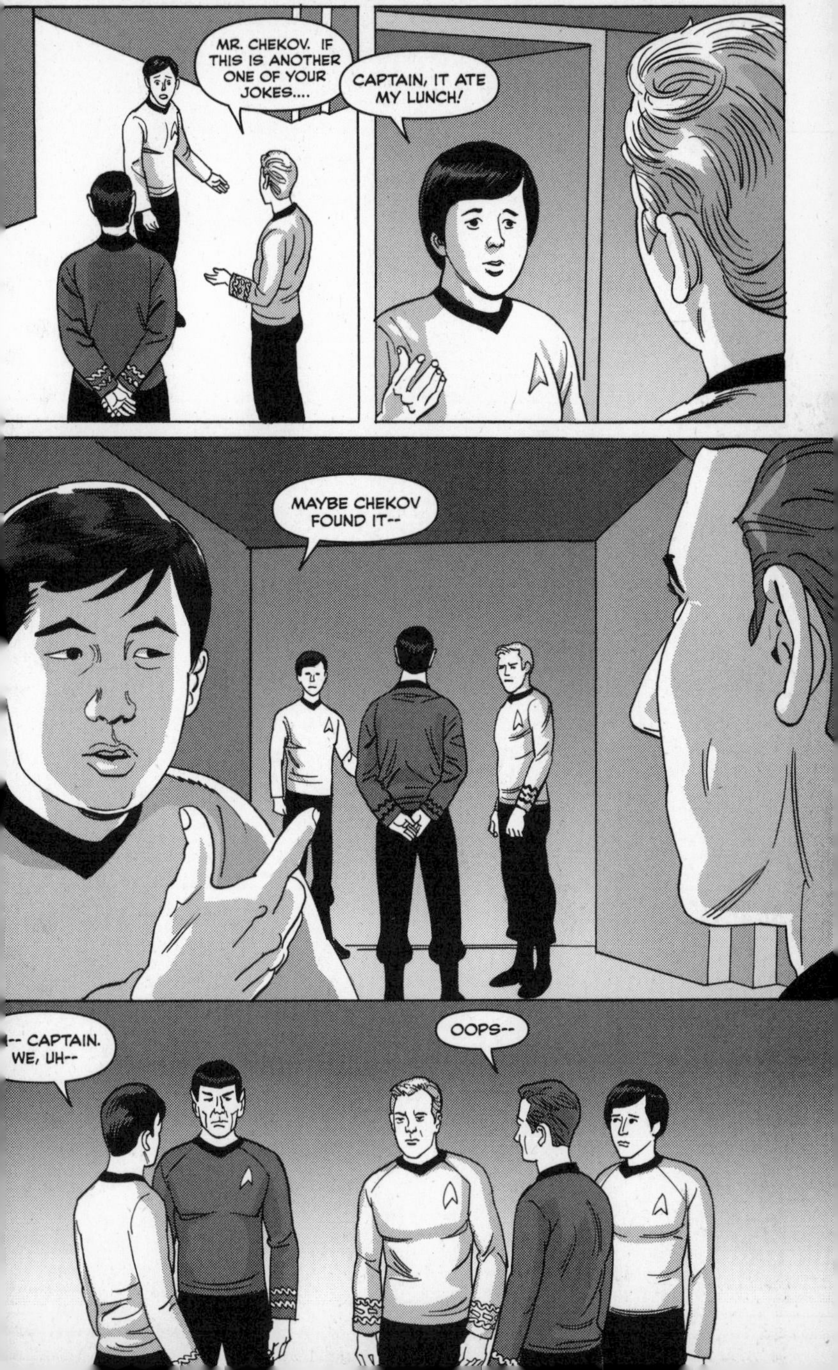
MR. CHEKOV. IF THIS IS ANOTHER ONE OF YOUR JOKES....
CAPTAIN, IT ATE MY LUNCH!
MAYBE CHEKOV FOUND IT--
-- CAPTAIN. WE, UH--
OOPS--

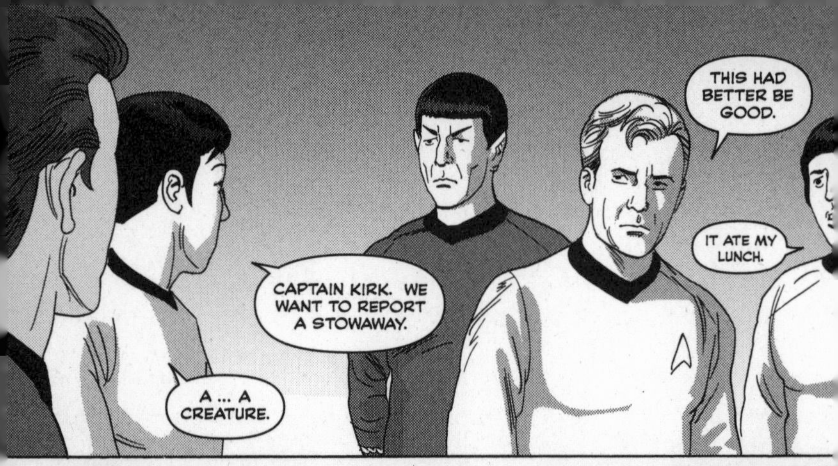
THIS HAD BETTER BE GOOD.
CAPTAIN KIRK. WE WANT TO REPORT A STOWAWAY.
A ... A CREATURE.
IT ATE MY LUNCH.

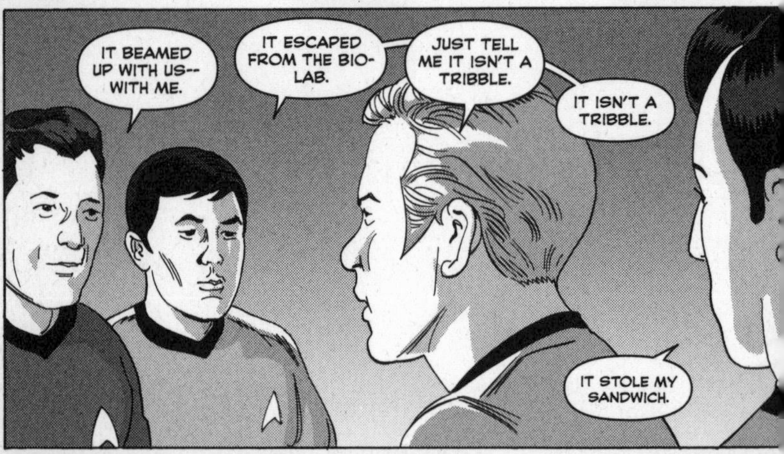
IT BEAMED UP WITH US-- WITH ME.
IT ESCAPED FROM THE BIO-LAB.
JUST TELL ME IT ISN'T A TRIBBLE.
IT ISN'T A TRIBBLE.
IT STOLE MY SANDWICH.

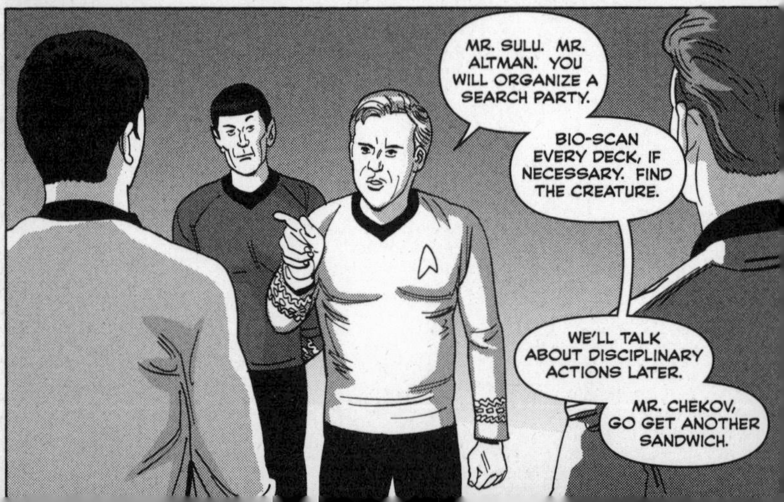
MR. SULU. MR. ALTMAN. YOU WILL ORGANIZE A SEARCH PARTY.
BIO-SCAN EVERY DECK, IF NECESSARY. FIND THE CREATURE.
WE'LL TALK ABOUT DISCIPLINARY ACTIONS LATER.
MR. CHEKOV, GO GET ANOTHER SANDWICH.

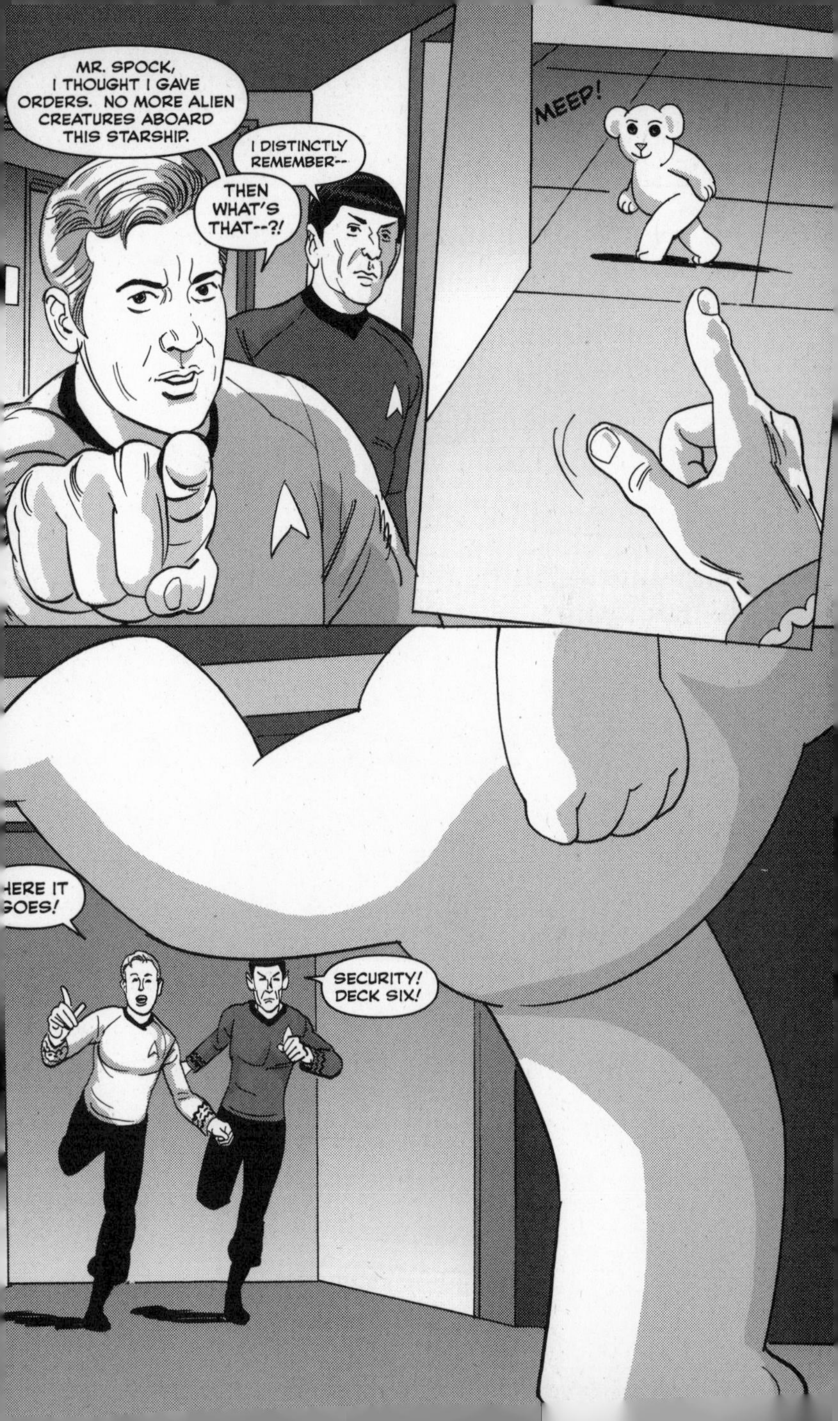
MR. SPOCK, I THOUGHT I GAVE ORDERS. NO MORE ALIEN CREATURES ABOARD THIS STARSHIP.
I DISTINCTLY REMEMBER--
THEN WHAT'S THAT--?!
MEEP!
HERE IT GOES!
SECURITY! DECK SIX!

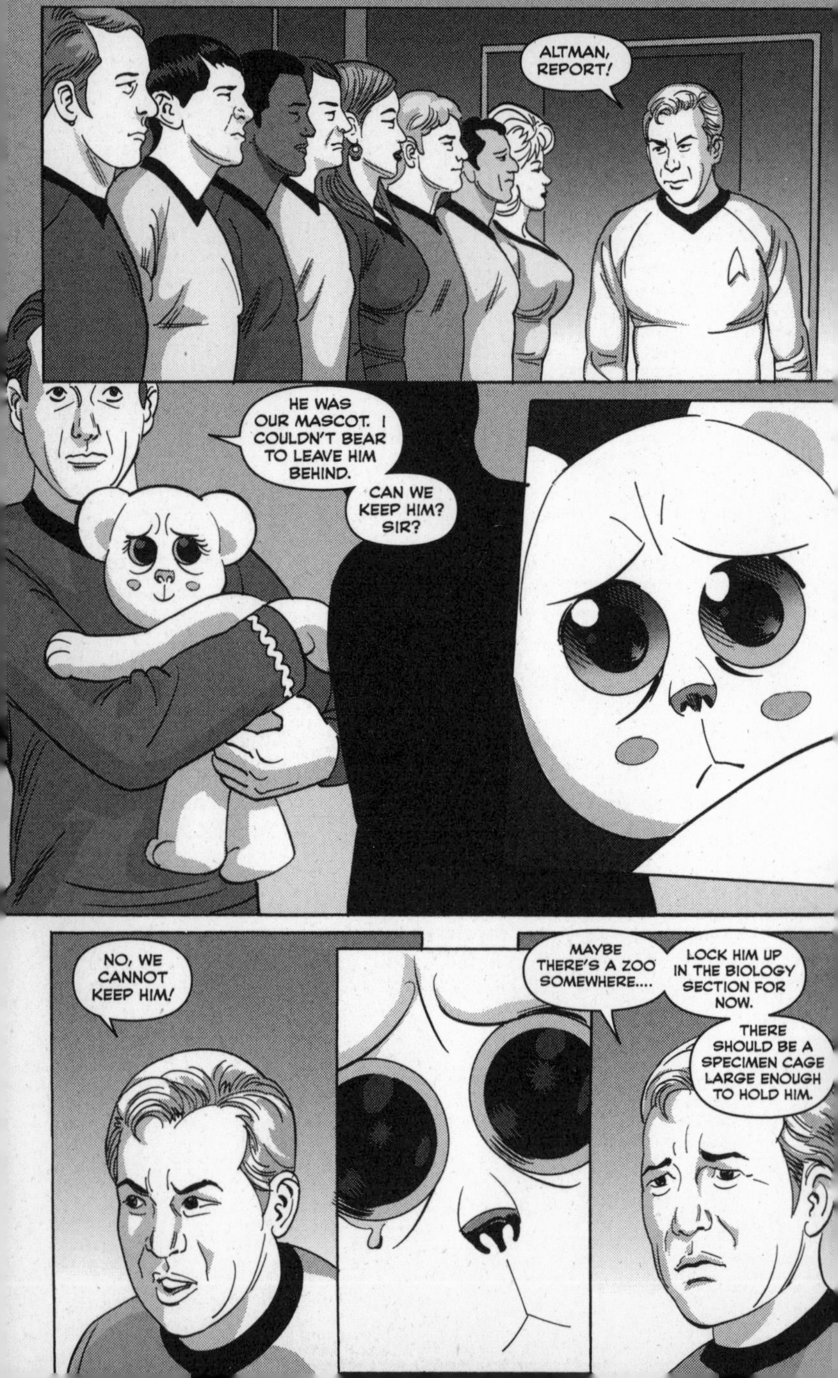
ALTMAN, REPORT!
HE WAS OUR MASCOT. I COULDN'T BEAR TO LEAVE HIM BEHIND.
CAN WE KEEP HIM? SIR?
NO, WE CANNOT KEEP HIM!
MAYBE THERE'S A ZOO SOMEWHERE....
LOCK HIM UP IN THE BIOLOGY SECTION FOR NOW.
THERE SHOULD BE A SPECIMEN CAGE LARGE ENOUGH TO HOLD HIM.

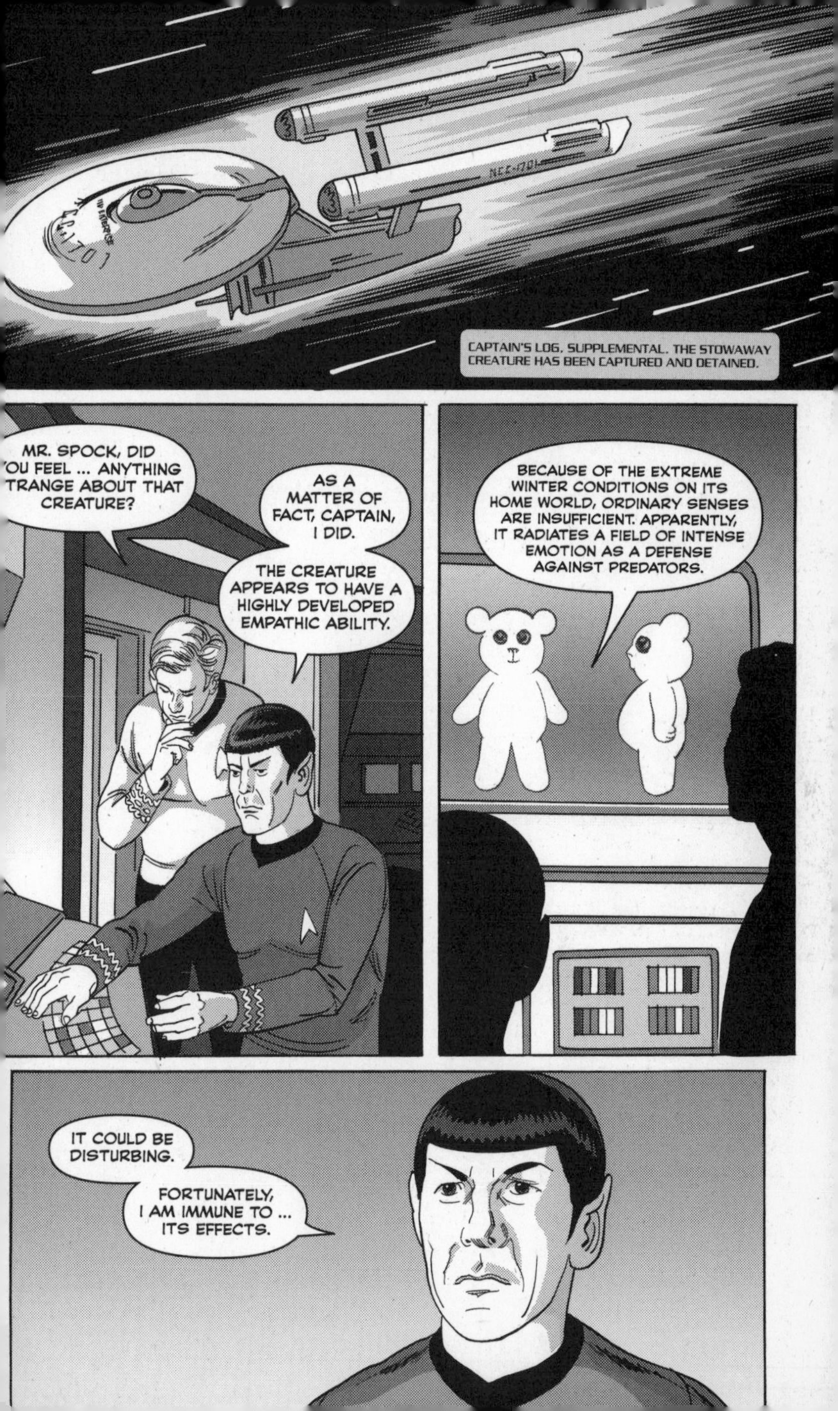
CAPTAIN'S LOG, SUPPLEMENTAL. THE STOWAWAY CREATURE HAS BEEN CAPTURED AND DETAINED.
MR. SPOCK, DID OU FEEL ... ANYTHING TRANGE ABOUT THAT CREATURE?
AS A MATTER OF FACT, CAPTAIN, I DID.
THE CREATURE APPEARS TO HAVE A HIGHLY DEVELOPED EMPATHIC ABILITY.
BECAUSE OF THE EXTREME WINTER CONDITIONS ON ITS HOME WORLD, ORDINARY SENSES ARE INSUFFICIENT. APPARENTLY, IT RADIATES A FIELD OF INTENSE EMOTION AS A DEFENSE AGAINST PREDATORS.
IT COULD BE DISTURBING.
FORTUNATELY, I AM IMMUNE TO ... ITS EFFECTS.

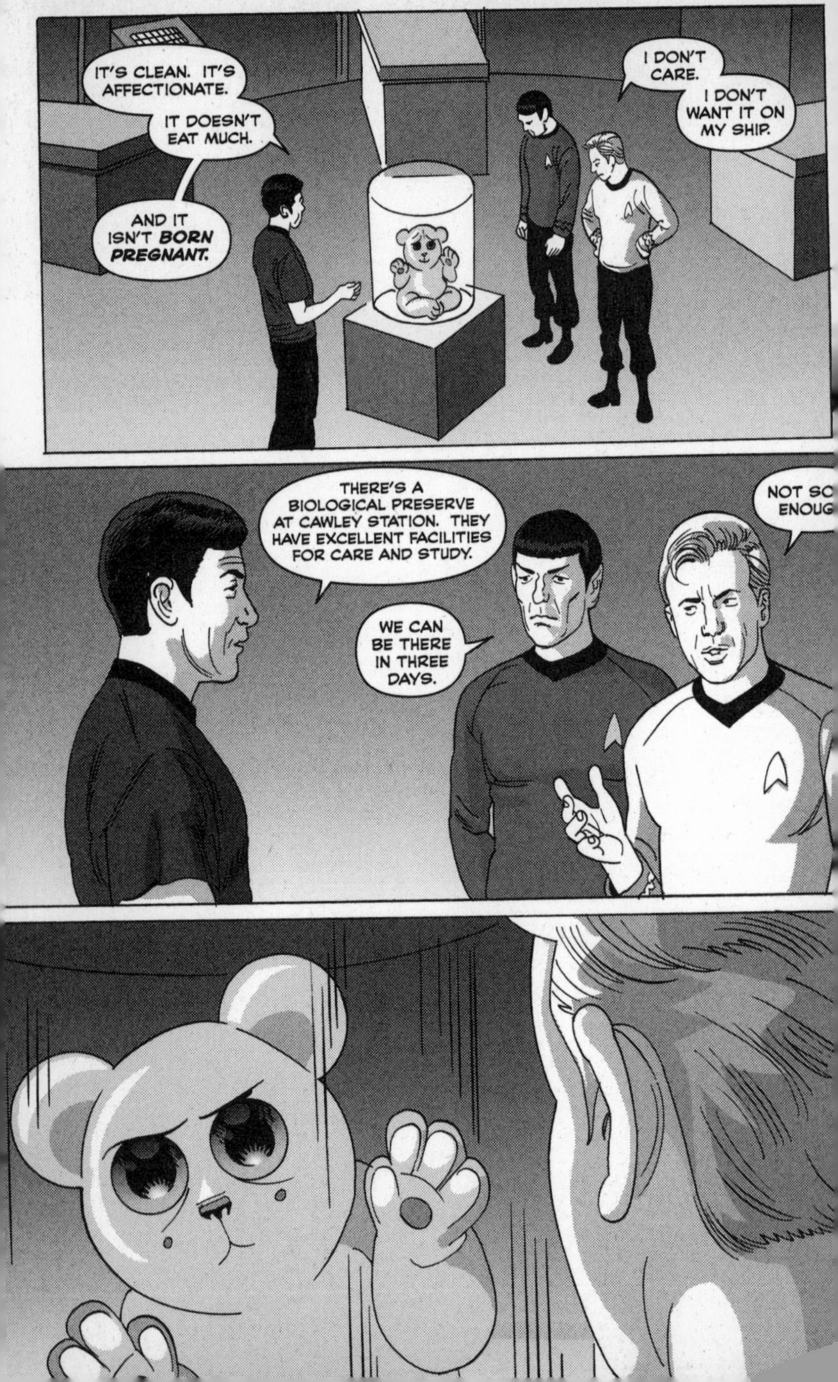

IT'S CLEAN. IT'S AFFECTIONATE.
IT DOESN'T EAT MUCH.
AND IT ISN'T **BORN PREGNANT.**
I DON'T CARE.
I DON'T WANT IT ON MY SHIP.
THERE'S A BIOLOGICAL PRESERVE AT CAWLEY STATION. THEY HAVE EXCELLENT FACILITIES FOR CARE AND STUDY.
WE CAN BE THERE IN THREE DAYS.

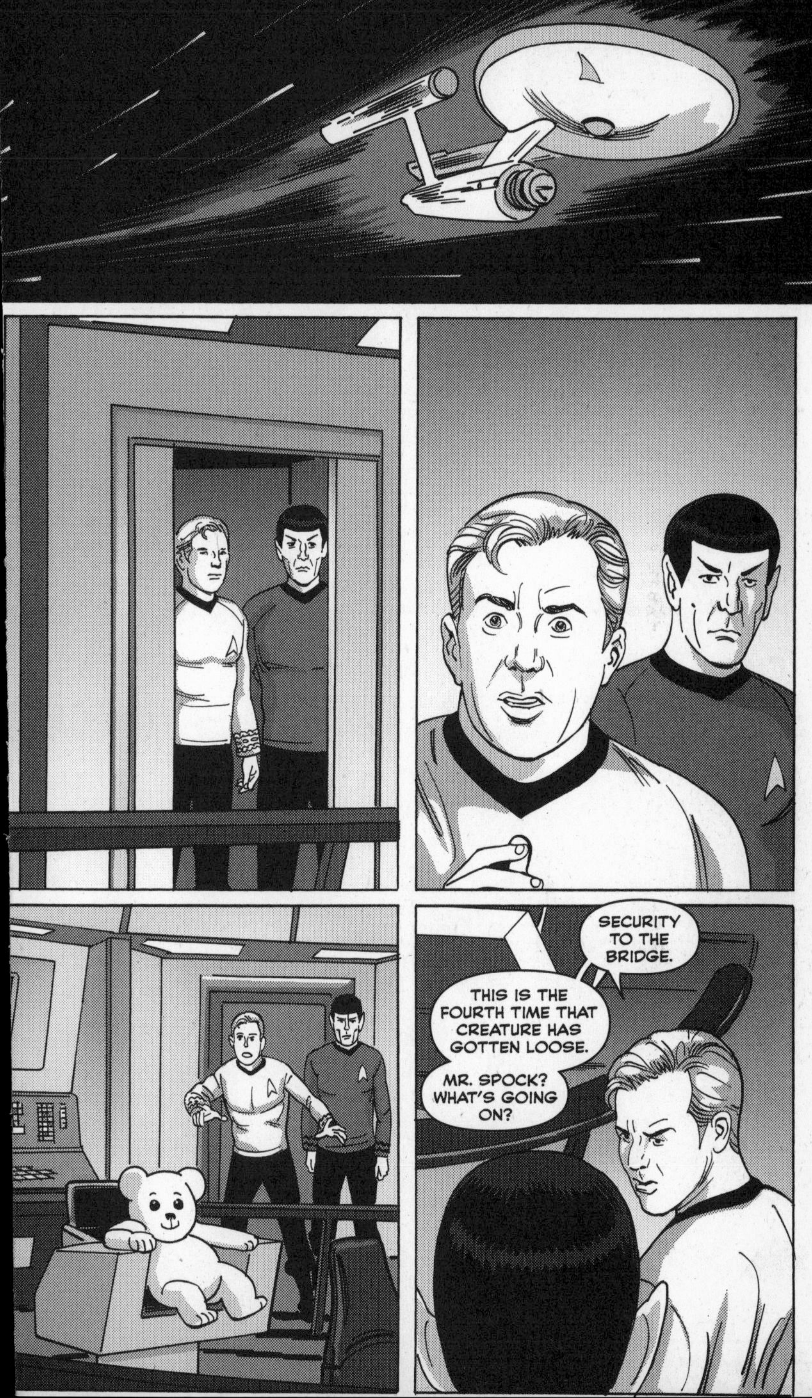
SECURITY TO THE BRIDGE.
THIS IS THE FOURTH TIME THAT CREATURE HAS GOTTEN LOOSE.
MR. SPOCK? WHAT'S GOING ON?

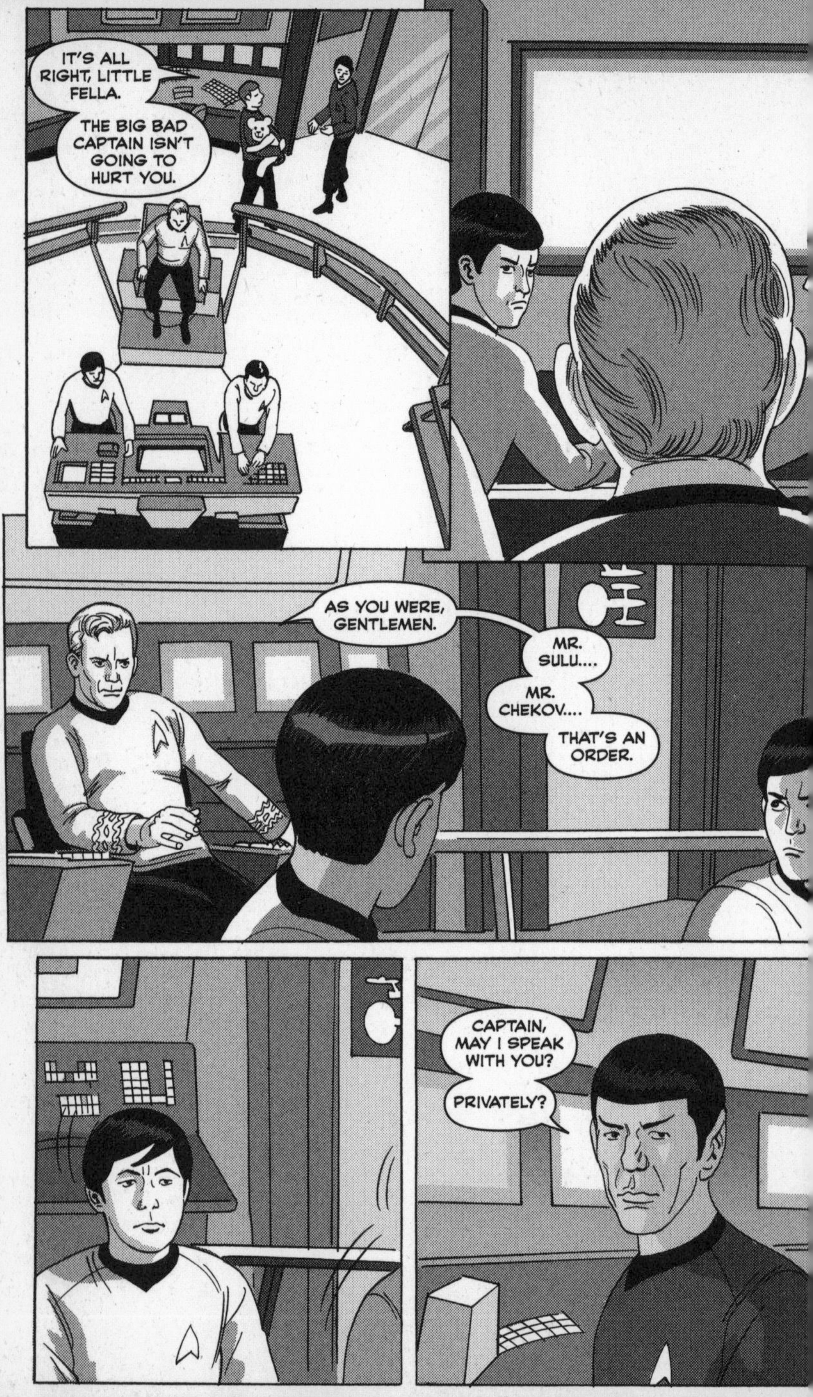
IT'S ALL RIGHT, LITTLE FELLA.
THE BIG BAD CAPTAIN ISN'T GOING TO HURT YOU.
AS YOU WERE, GENTLEMEN.
MR. SULU....
MR. CHEKOV....
THAT'S AN ORDER.
CAPTAIN, MAY I SPEAK WITH YOU?
PRIVATELY?

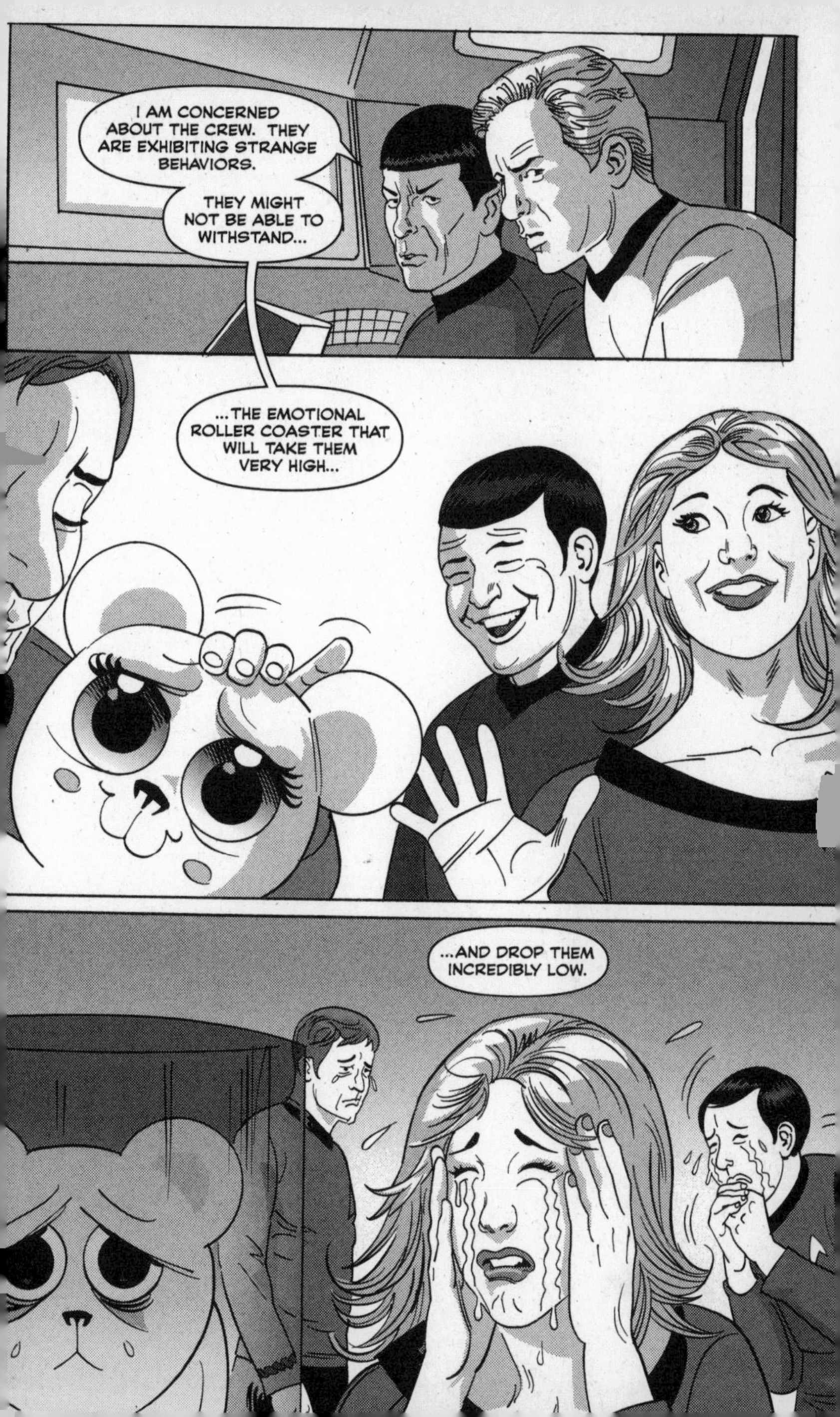
I AM CONCERNED ABOUT THE CREW. THEY ARE EXHIBITING STRANGE BEHAVIORS.
THEY MIGHT NOT BE ABLE TO WITHSTAND...
...THE EMOTIONAL ROLLER COASTER THAT WILL TAKE THEM VERY HIGH...
...AND DROP THEM INCREDIBLY LOW.

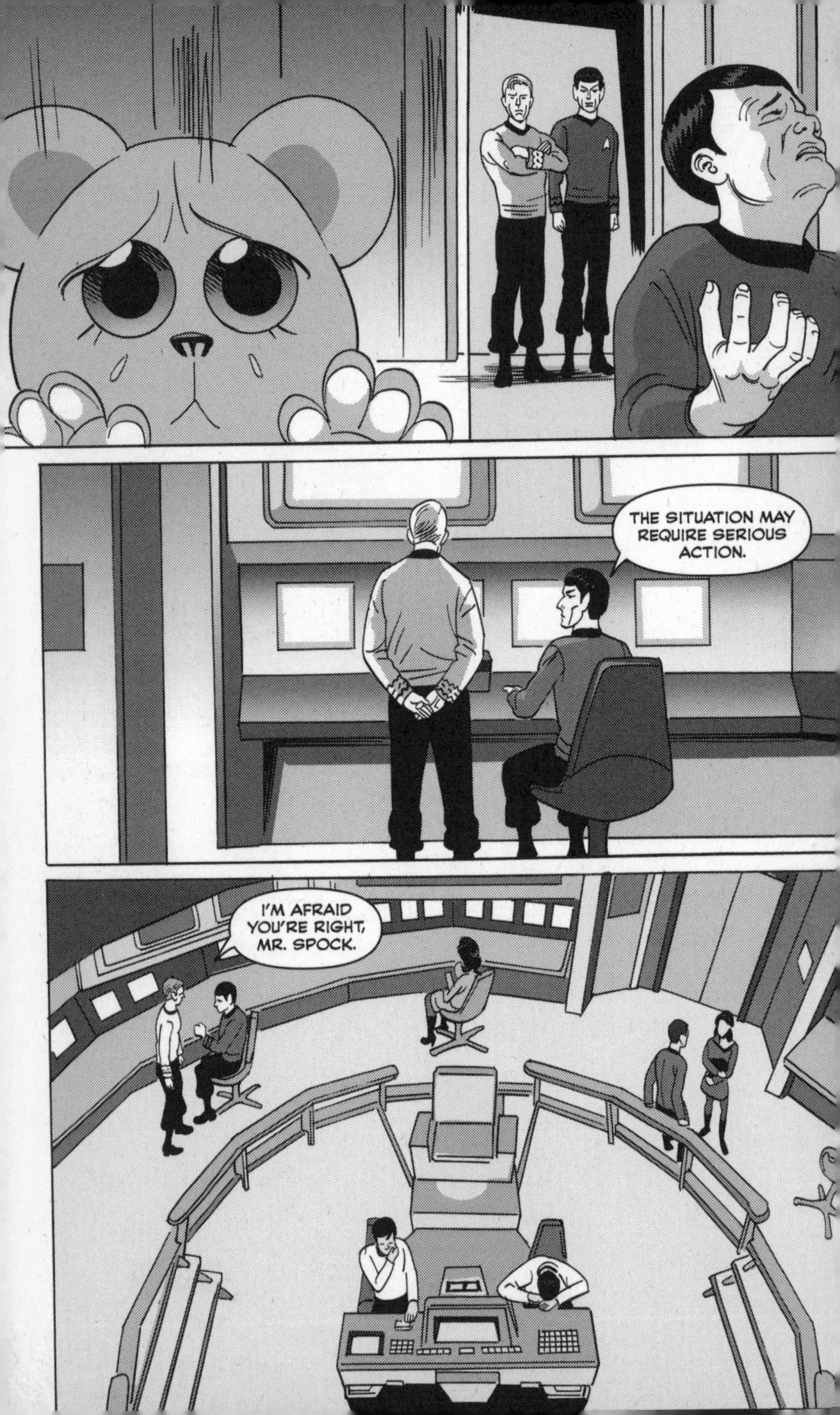
THE SITUATION MAY REQUIRE SERIOUS ACTION.
I'M AFRAID YOU'RE RIGHT, MR. SPOCK.

CAN YOU SEDATE IT?

IT'S AN ALIEN BIOLOGY, JIM.

I'M NOT SURE HOW IT WILL REACT.

I DON'T WANT TO KILL IT.

IS THERE SOMETHING WE CAN DO TO SHIELD ITS EMOTIONAL PROJECTIONS?

I CAN'T THINK OF ANYTHING.

SPOCK...?

CAPTAIN, IF THERE WERE A WAY TO SHIELD AGAINST EMOTIONS, VULCANS WOULD HAVE APPLIED IT TO HUMANS A LONG TIME AGO.

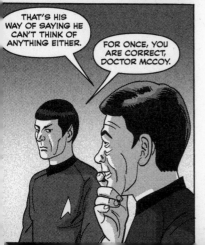

THAT'S HIS WAY OF SAYING HE CAN'T THINK OF ANYTHING EITHER.

FOR ONCE, YOU ARE CORRECT, DOCTOR MCCOY.

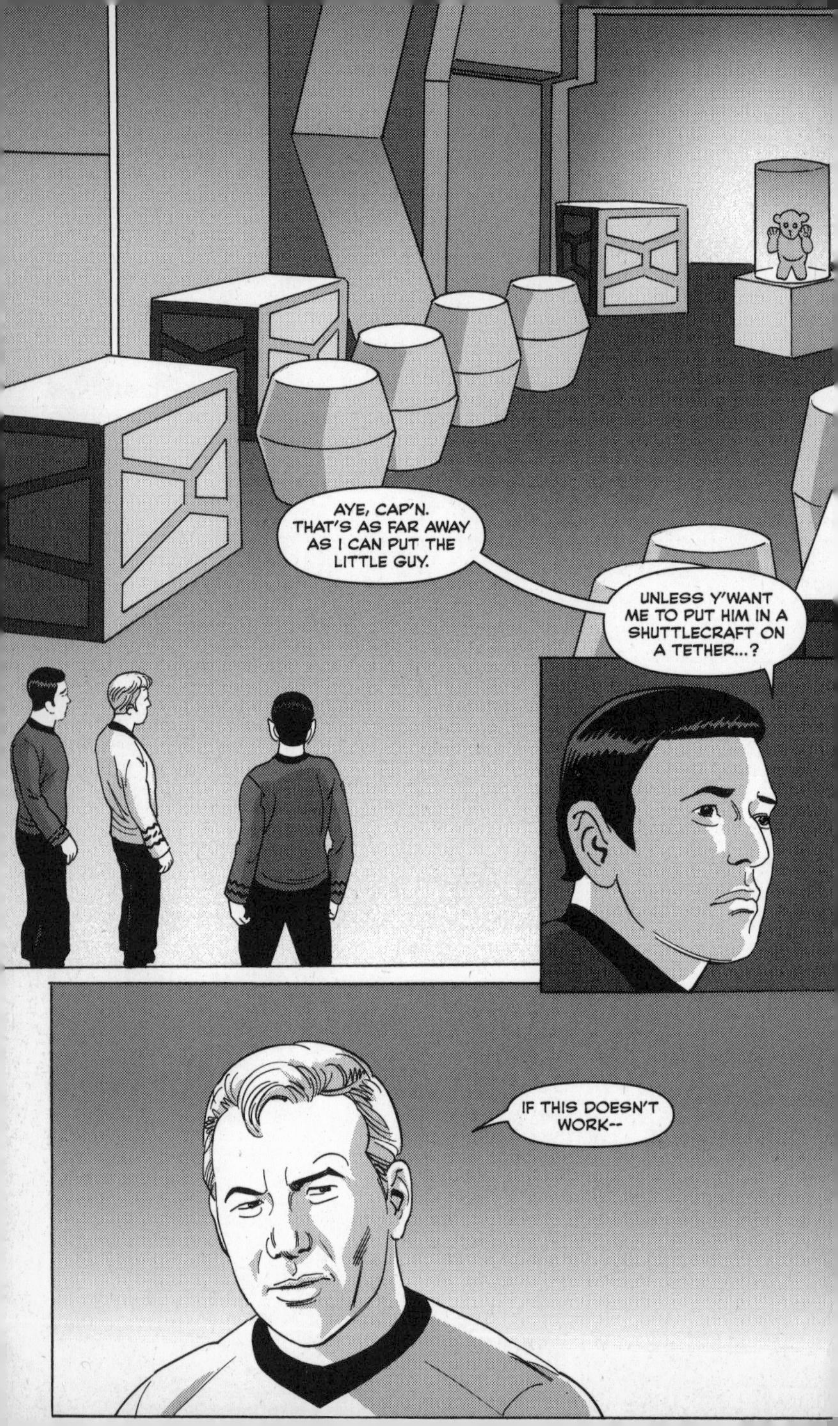
AYE, CAP'N. THAT'S AS FAR AWAY AS I CAN PUT THE LITTLE GUY.
UNLESS Y'WANT ME TO PUT HIM IN A SHUTTLECRAFT ON A TETHER...?
IF THIS DOESN'T WORK--

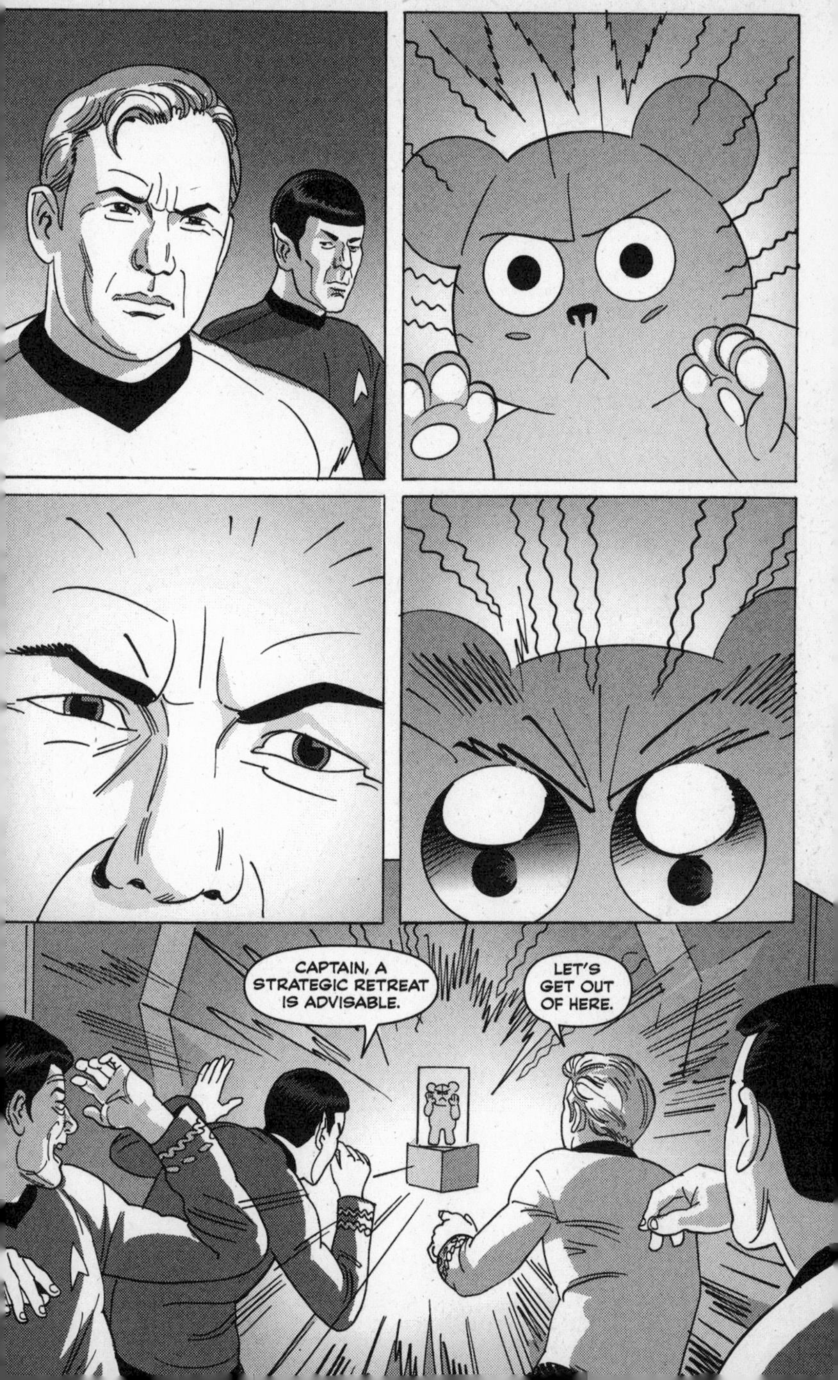
CAPTAIN, A STRATEGIC RETREAT IS ADVISABLE.
LET'S GET OUT OF HERE.

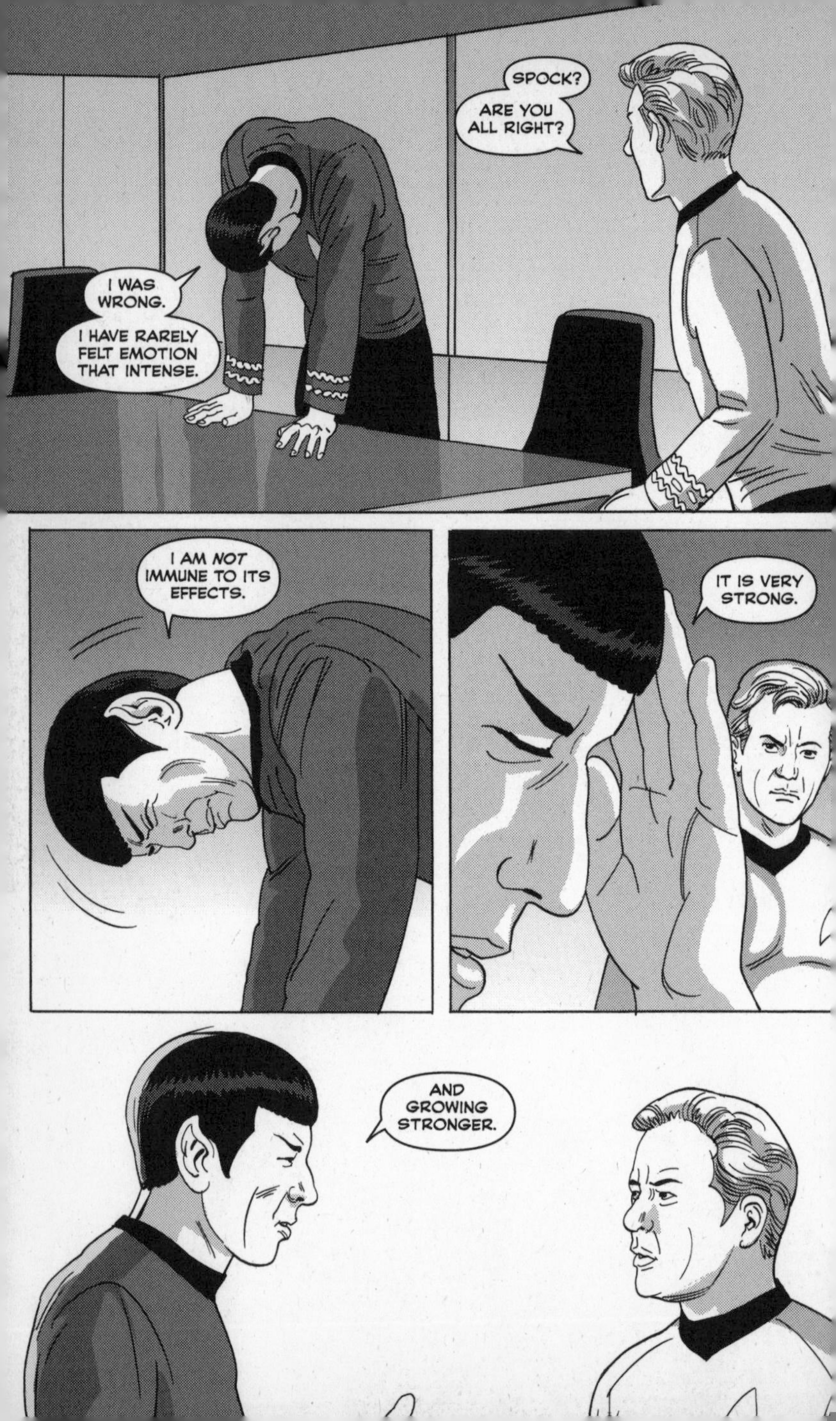
SPOCK?
ARE YOU ALL RIGHT?
I WAS WRONG.
I HAVE RARELY FELT EMOTION THAT INTENSE.
I AM *NOT* IMMUNE TO ITS EFFECTS.
IT IS VERY STRONG.
AND GROWING STRONGER.

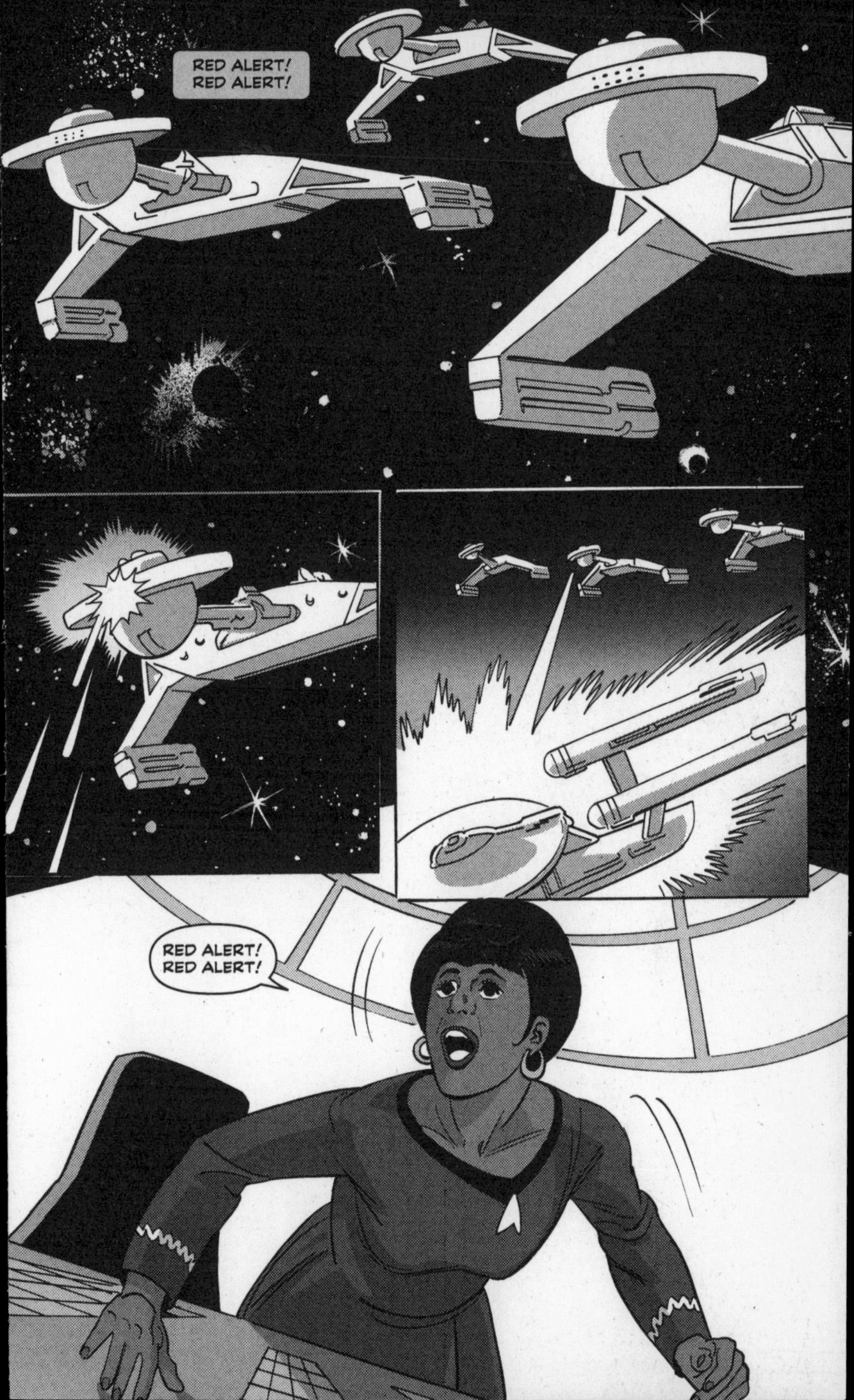
RED ALERT!
RED ALERT!
RED ALERT!
RED ALERT!

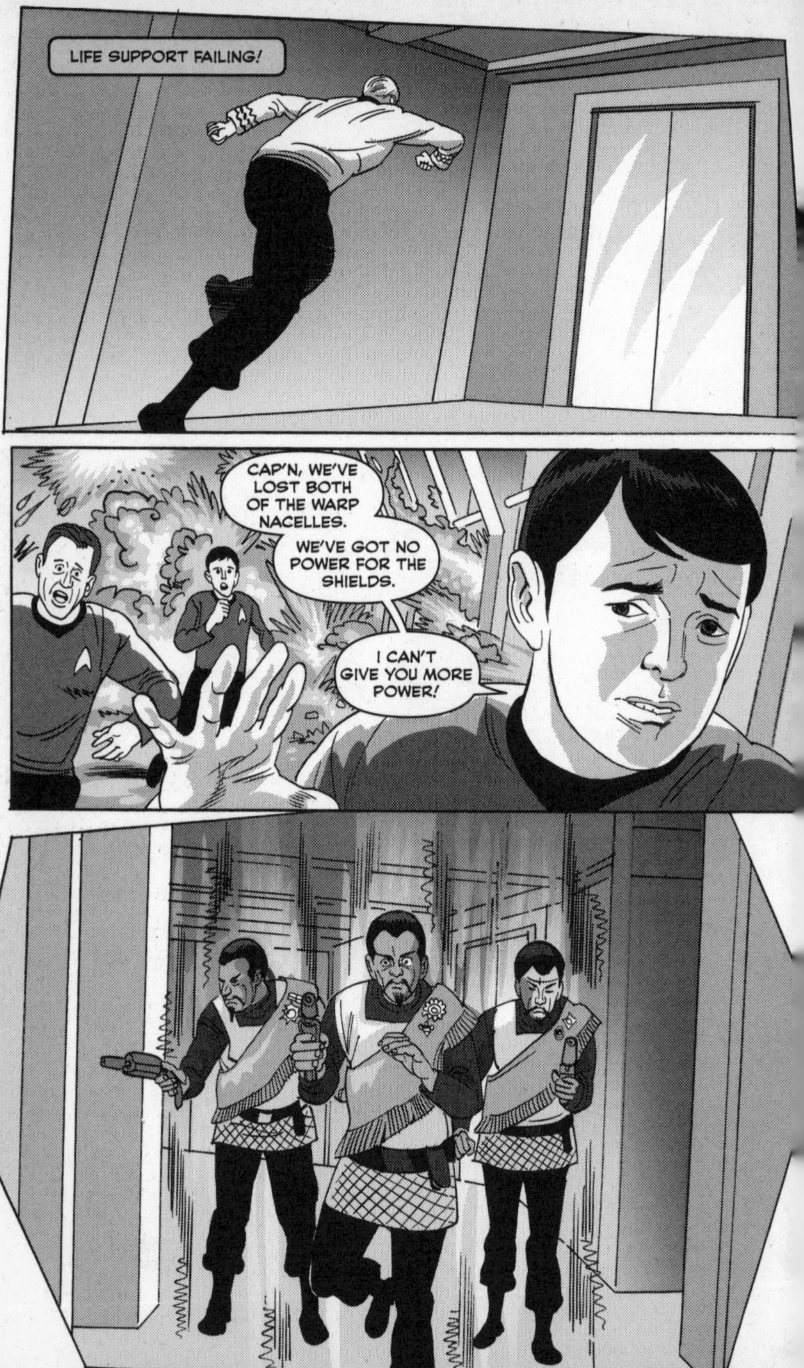
LIFE SUPPORT FAILING!
CAP'N, WE'VE LOST BOTH OF THE WARP NACELLES.
WE'VE GOT NO POWER FOR THE SHIELDS.
I CAN'T GIVE YOU MORE POWER!

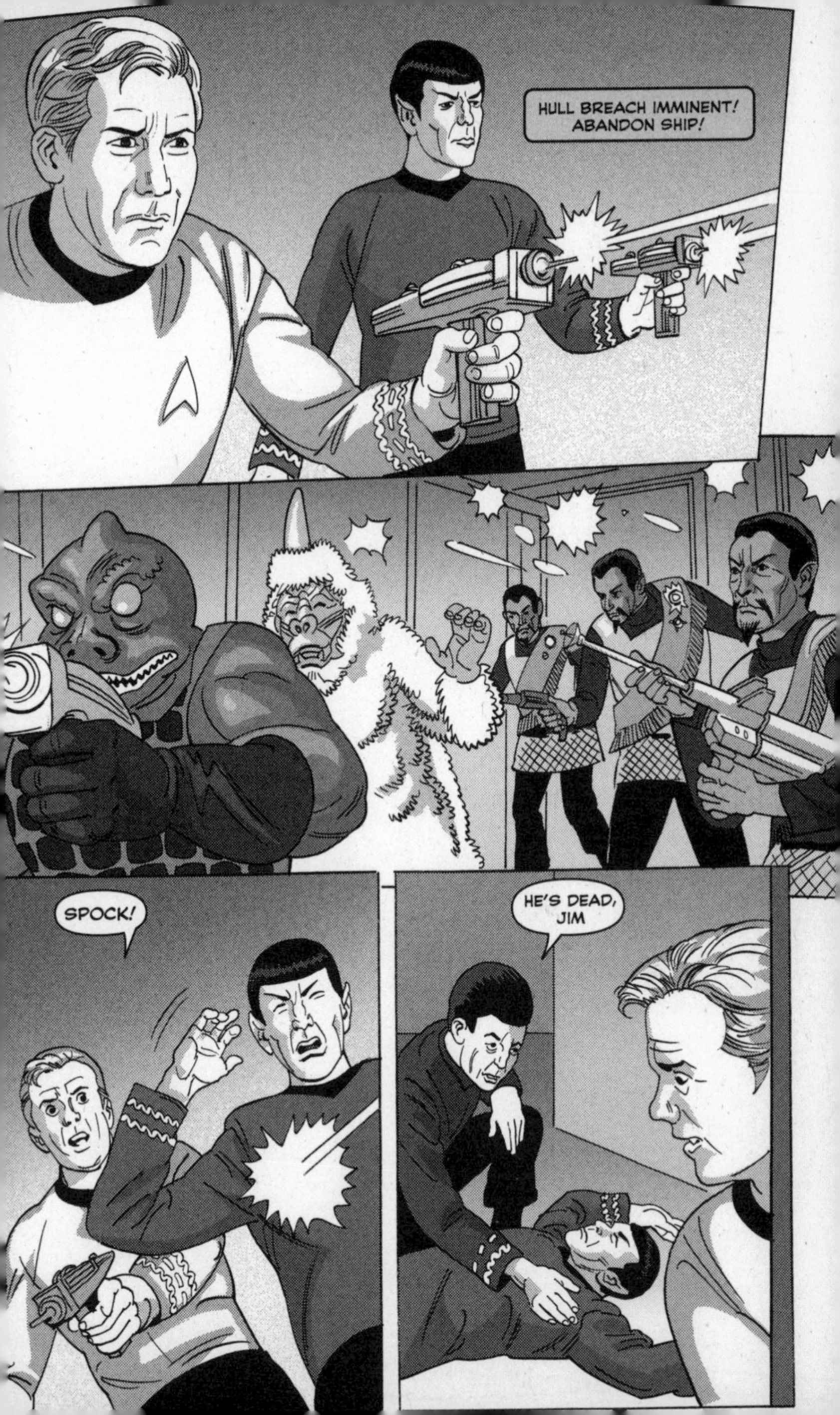
HULL BREACH IMMINENT! ABANDON SHIP!
SPOCK!
HE'S DEAD, JIM

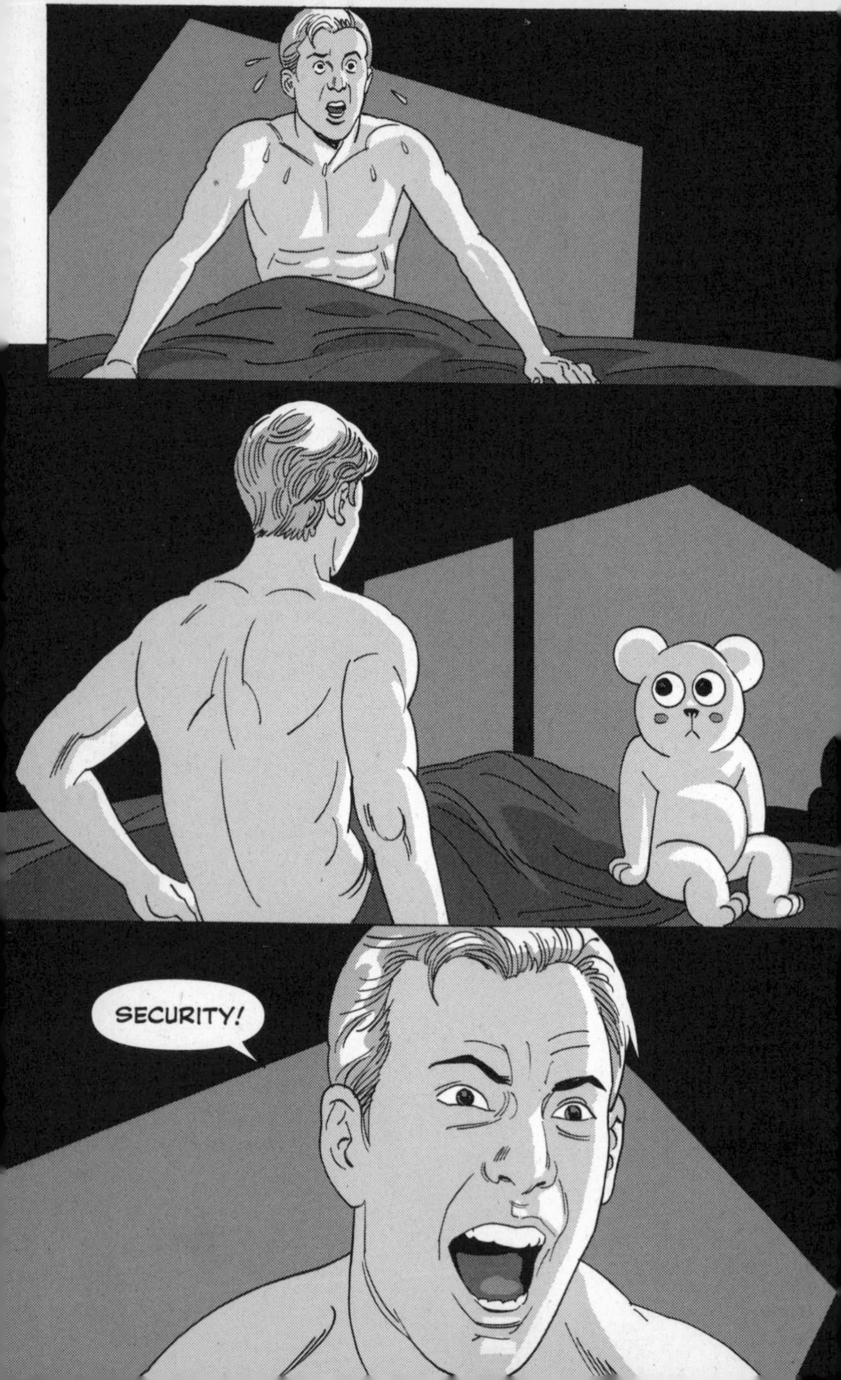
SECURITY!

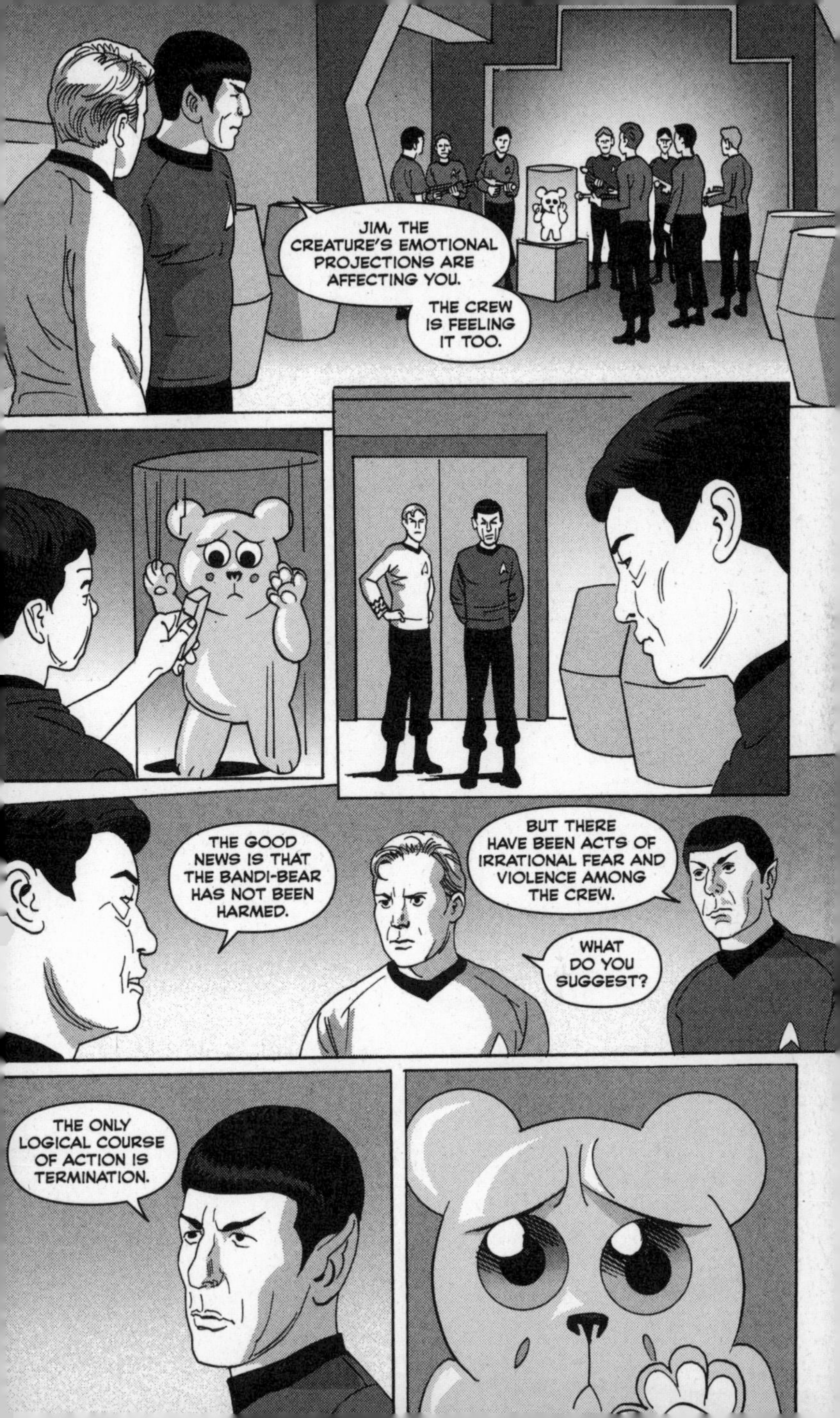
JIM, THE CREATURE'S EMOTIONAL PROJECTIONS ARE AFFECTING YOU.
THE CREW IS FEELING IT TOO.
THE GOOD NEWS IS THAT THE BANDI-BEAR HAS NOT BEEN HARMED.
BUT THERE HAVE BEEN ACTS OF IRRATIONAL FEAR AND VIOLENCE AMONG THE CREW.
WHAT DO YOU SUGGEST?
THE ONLY LOGICAL COURSE OF ACTION IS TERMINATION.

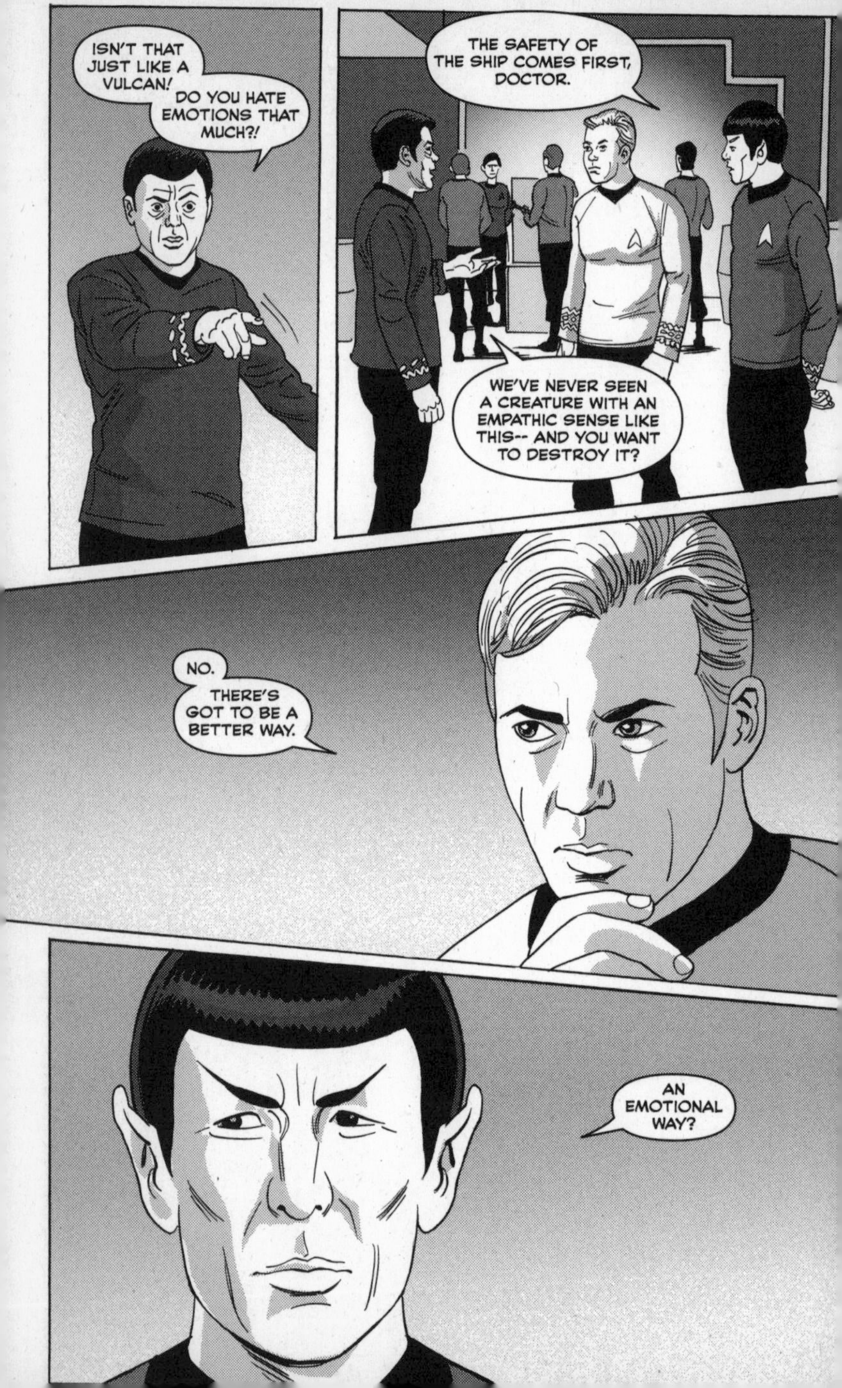
ISN'T THAT JUST LIKE A VULCAN!
DO YOU HATE EMOTIONS THAT MUCH?!
THE SAFETY OF THE SHIP COMES FIRST, DOCTOR.
WE'VE NEVER SEEN A CREATURE WITH AN EMPATHIC SENSE LIKE THIS-- AND YOU WANT TO DESTROY IT?
NO.
THERE'S GOT TO BE A BETTER WAY.
AN EMOTIONAL WAY?

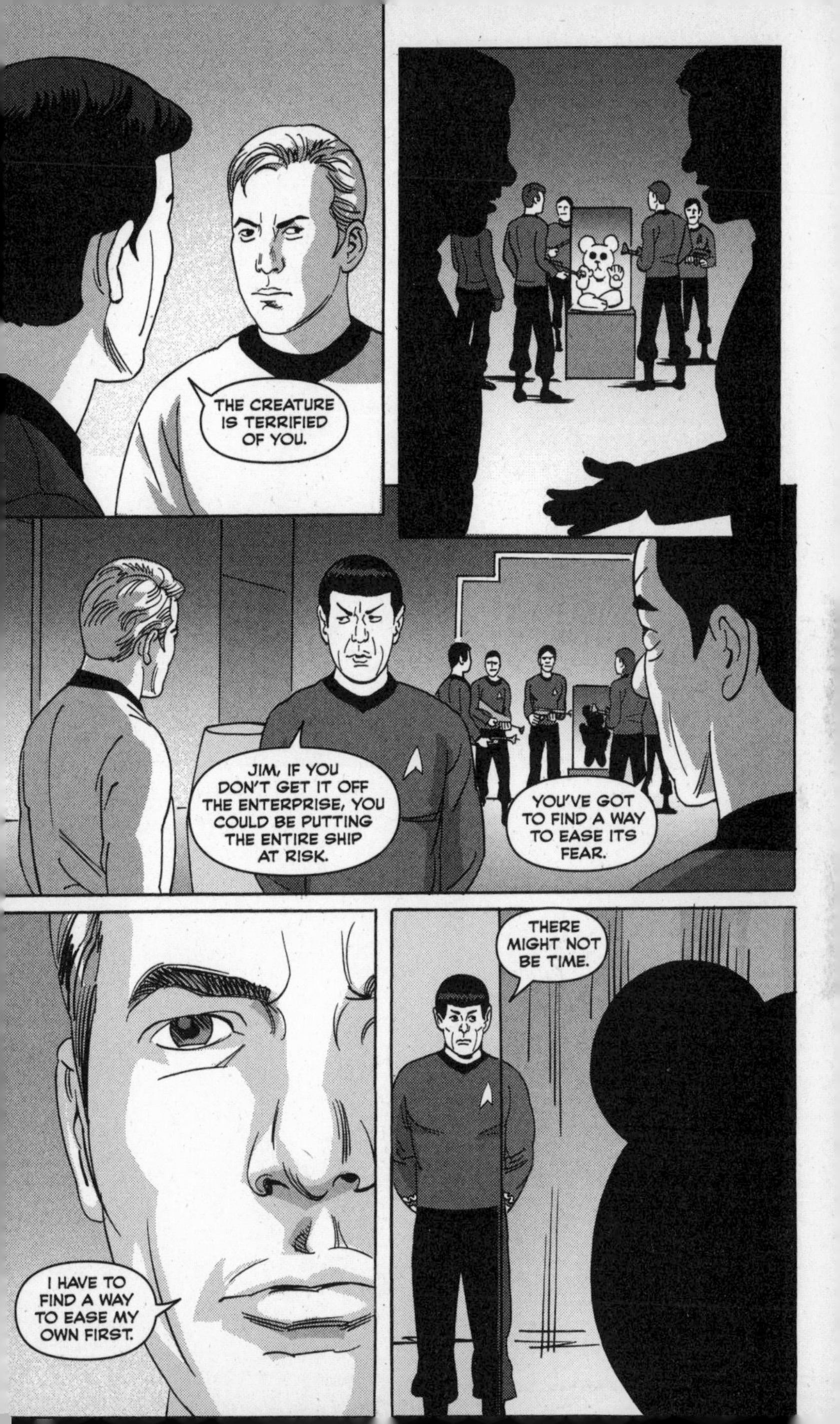
THE CREATURE IS TERRIFIED OF YOU.
JIM, IF YOU DON'T GET IT OFF THE ENTERPRISE, YOU COULD BE PUTTING THE ENTIRE SHIP AT RISK.
YOU'VE GOT TO FIND A WAY TO EASE ITS FEAR.
I HAVE TO FIND A WAY TO EASE MY OWN FIRST.
THERE MIGHT NOT BE TIME.

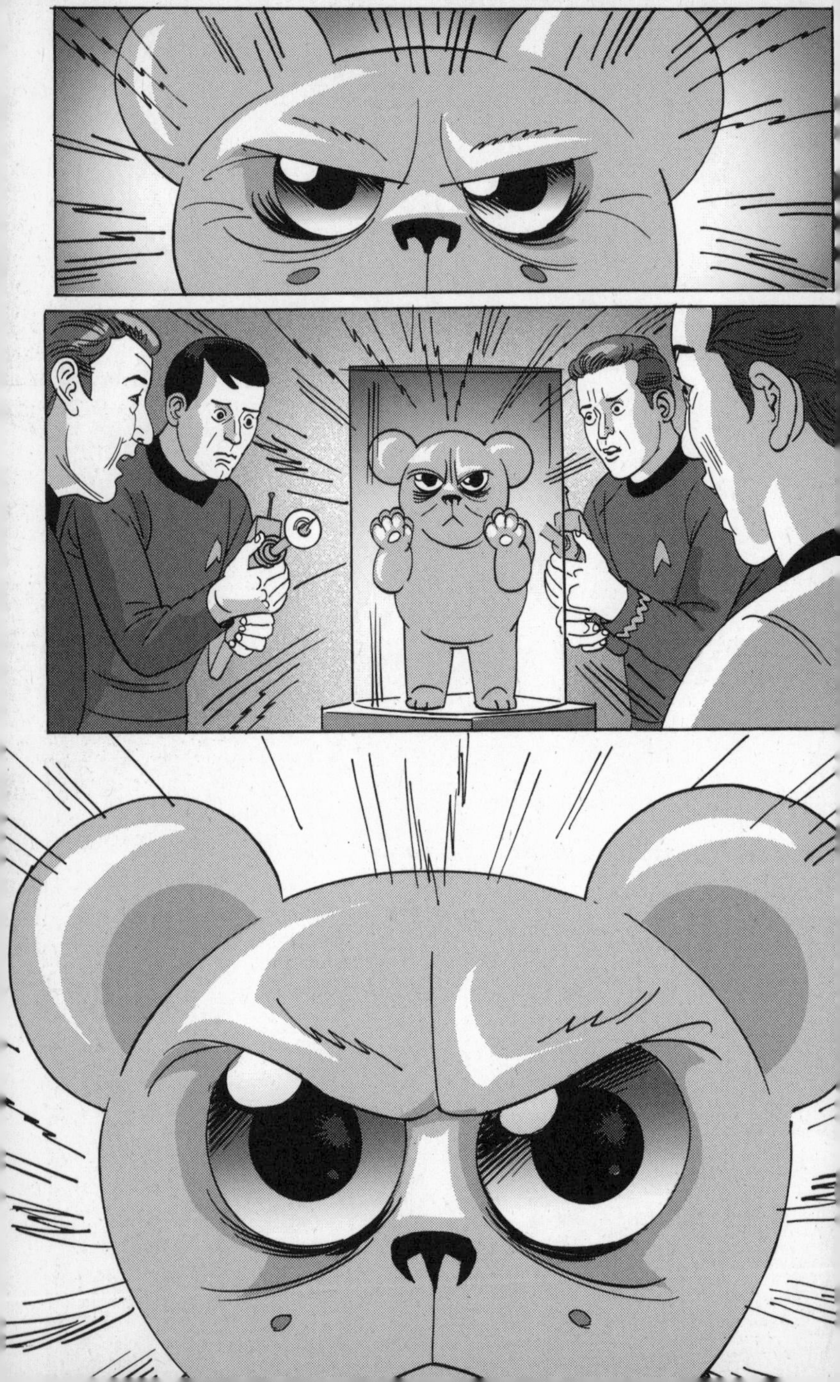

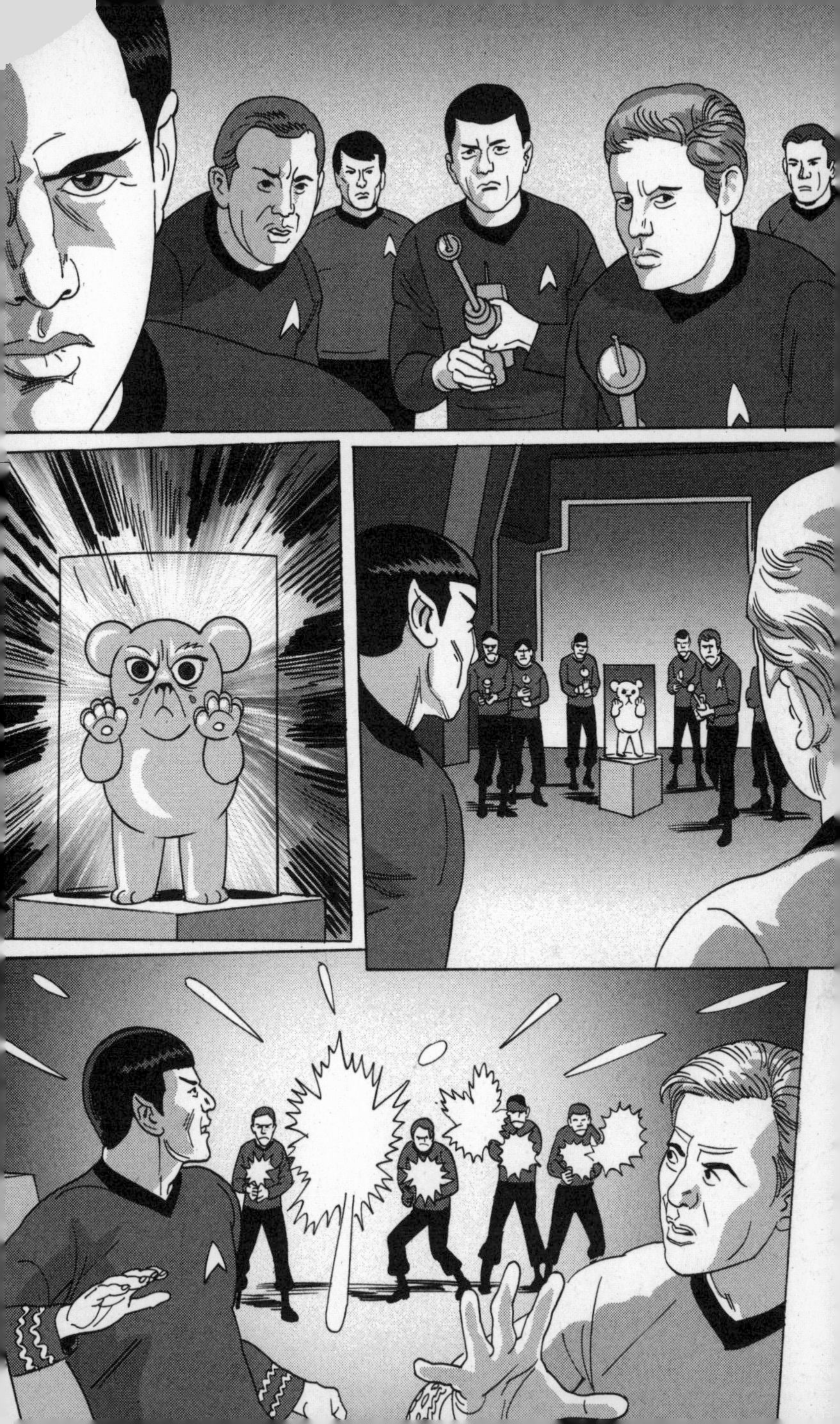

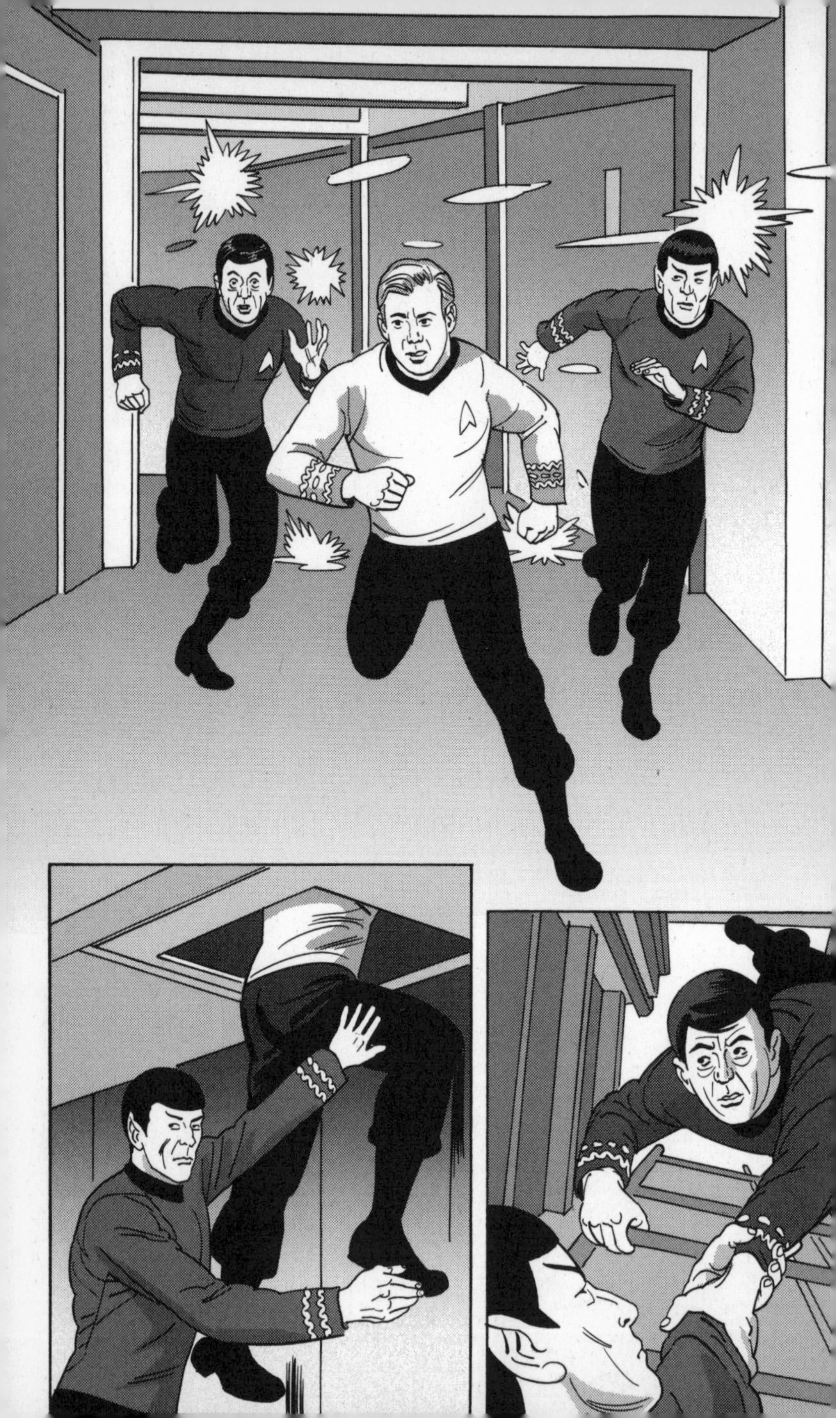

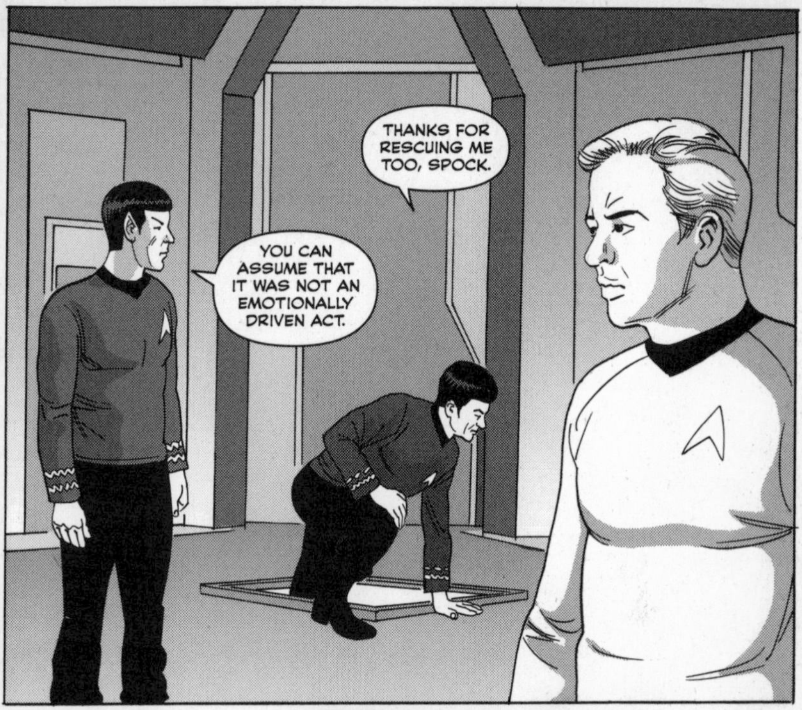
THANKS FOR RESCUING ME TOO, SPOCK.
YOU CAN ASSUME THAT IT WAS NOT AN EMOTIONALLY DRIVEN ACT.

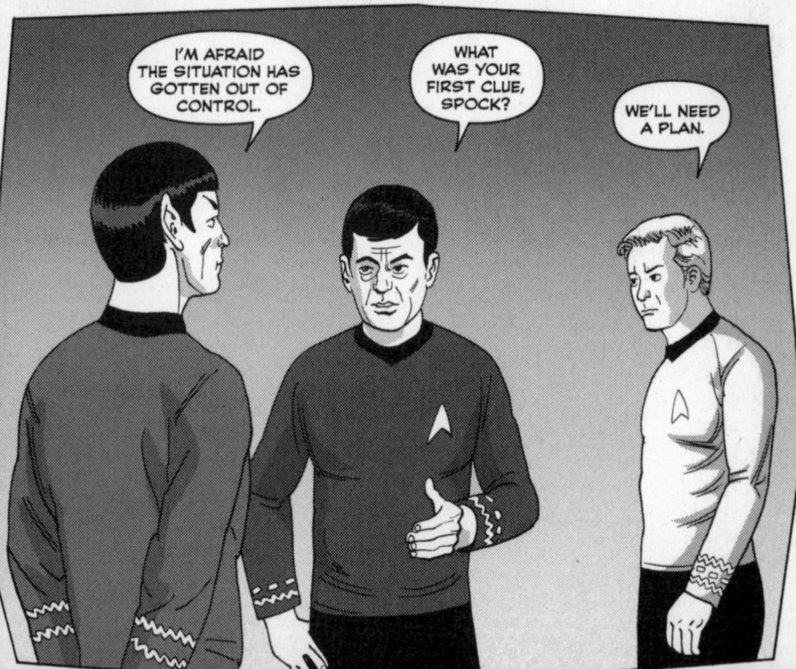
I'M AFRAID THE SITUATION HAS GOTTEN OUT OF CONTROL.
WHAT WAS YOUR FIRST CLUE, SPOCK?
WE'LL NEED A PLAN.

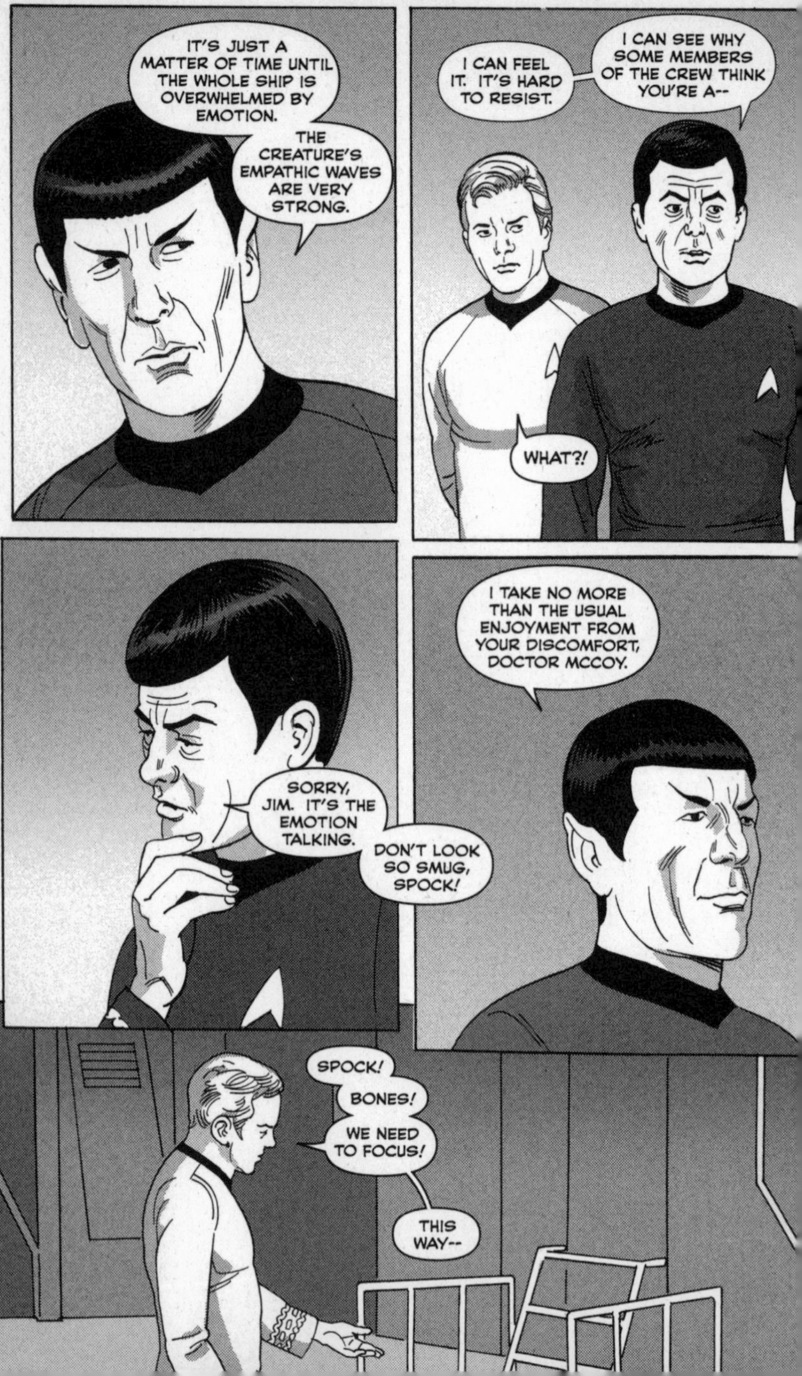
IT'S JUST A MATTER OF TIME UNTIL THE WHOLE SHIP IS OVERWHELMED BY EMOTION.
THE CREATURE'S EMPATHIC WAVES ARE VERY STRONG.
I CAN FEEL IT. IT'S HARD TO RESIST.
I CAN SEE WHY SOME MEMBERS OF THE CREW THINK YOU'RE A--
WHAT?!
SORRY, JIM. IT'S THE EMOTION TALKING.
DON'T LOOK SO SMUG, SPOCK!
I TAKE NO MORE THAN THE USUAL ENJOYMENT FROM YOUR DISCOMFORT, DOCTOR MCCOY.
SPOCK!
BONES!
WE NEED TO FOCUS!
THIS WAY--

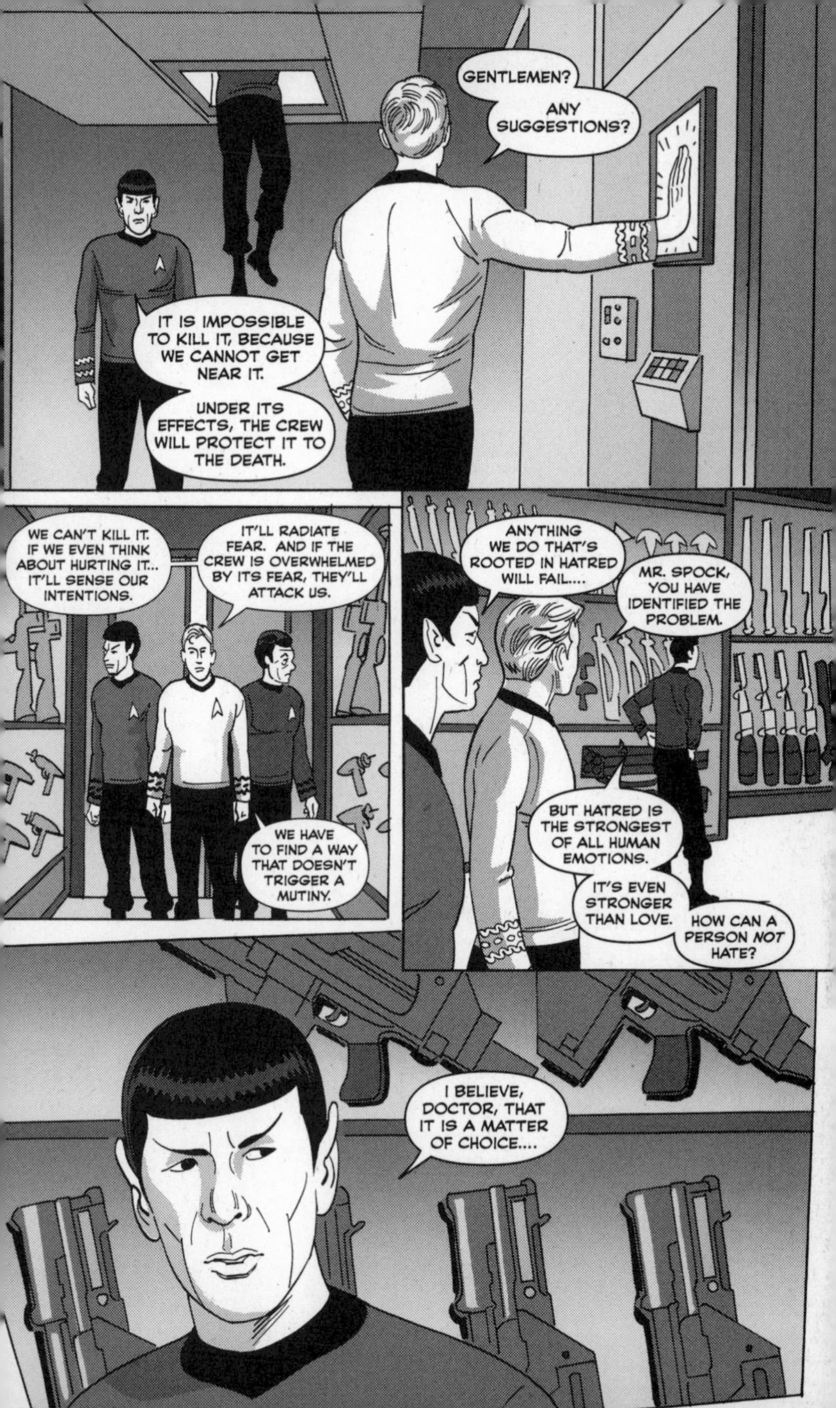
GENTLEMEN?
ANY SUGGESTIONS?
IT IS IMPOSSIBLE TO KILL IT, BECAUSE WE CANNOT GET NEAR IT.
UNDER ITS EFFECTS, THE CREW WILL PROTECT IT TO THE DEATH.
WE CAN'T KILL IT. IF WE EVEN THINK ABOUT HURTING IT... IT'LL SENSE OUR INTENTIONS.
IT'LL RADIATE FEAR. AND IF THE CREW IS OVERWHELMED BY ITS FEAR, THEY'LL ATTACK US.
WE HAVE TO FIND A WAY THAT DOESN'T TRIGGER A MUTINY.
ANYTHING WE DO THAT'S ROOTED IN HATRED WILL FAIL....
MR. SPOCK, YOU HAVE IDENTIFIED THE PROBLEM.
BUT HATRED IS THE STRONGEST OF ALL HUMAN EMOTIONS.
IT'S EVEN STRONGER THAN LOVE.
HOW CAN A PERSON *NOT* HATE?
I BELIEVE, DOCTOR, THAT IT IS A MATTER OF CHOICE....

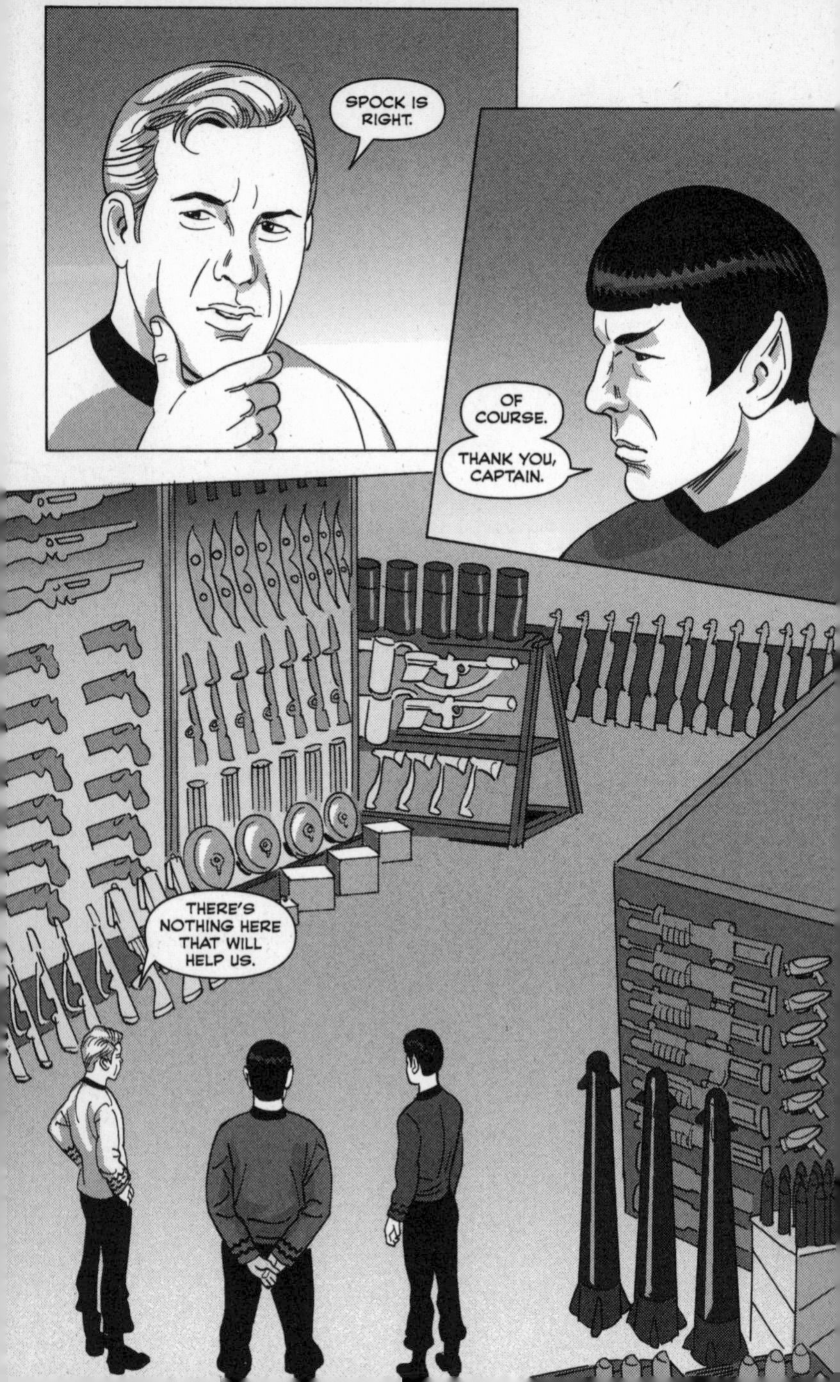
SPOCK IS RIGHT.
OF COURSE.
THANK YOU, CAPTAIN.
THERE'S NOTHING HERE THAT WILL HELP US.

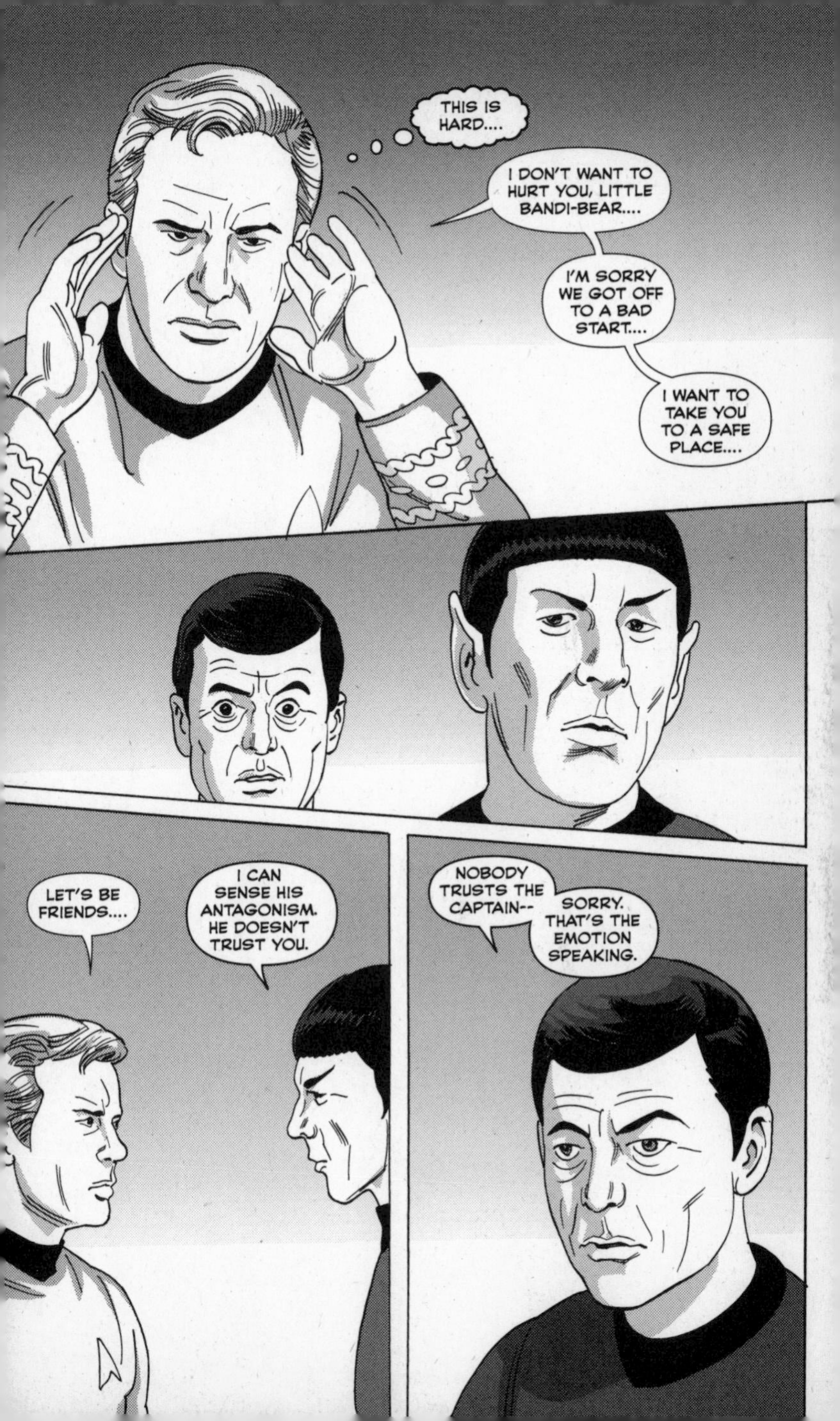
THIS IS HARD....
I DON'T WANT TO HURT YOU, LITTLE BANDI-BEAR....
I'M SORRY WE GOT OFF TO A BAD START....
I WANT TO TAKE YOU TO A SAFE PLACE....
LET'S BE FRIENDS....
I CAN SENSE HIS ANTAGONISM. HE DOESN'T TRUST YOU.
NOBODY TRUSTS THE CAPTAIN--
SORRY. THAT'S THE EMOTION SPEAKING.

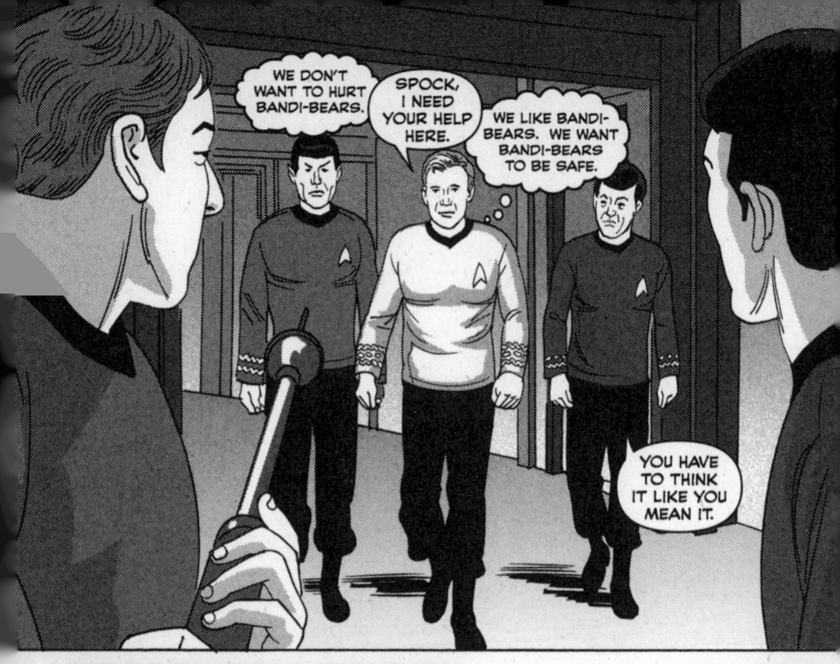
WE DON'T WANT TO HURT BANDI-BEARS.
SPOCK, I NEED YOUR HELP HERE.
WE LIKE BANDI-BEARS. WE WANT BANDI-BEARS TO BE SAFE.
YOU HAVE TO THINK IT LIKE YOU MEAN IT.

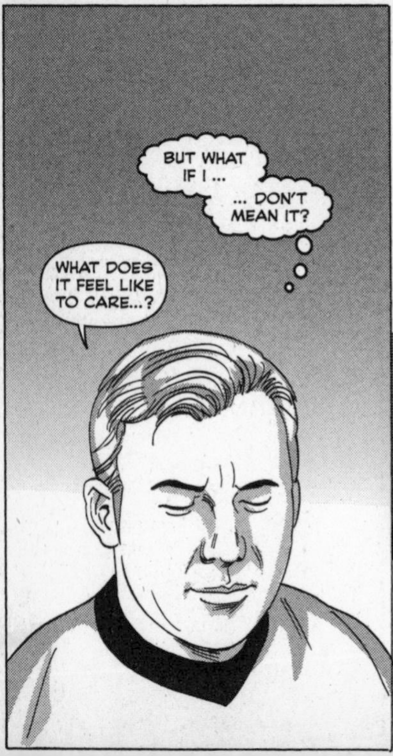
BUT WHAT IF I ...
... DON'T MEAN IT?
WHAT DOES IT FEEL LIKE TO CARE...?

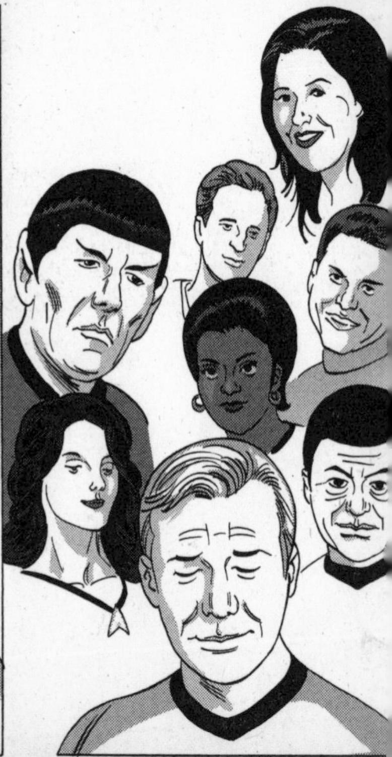

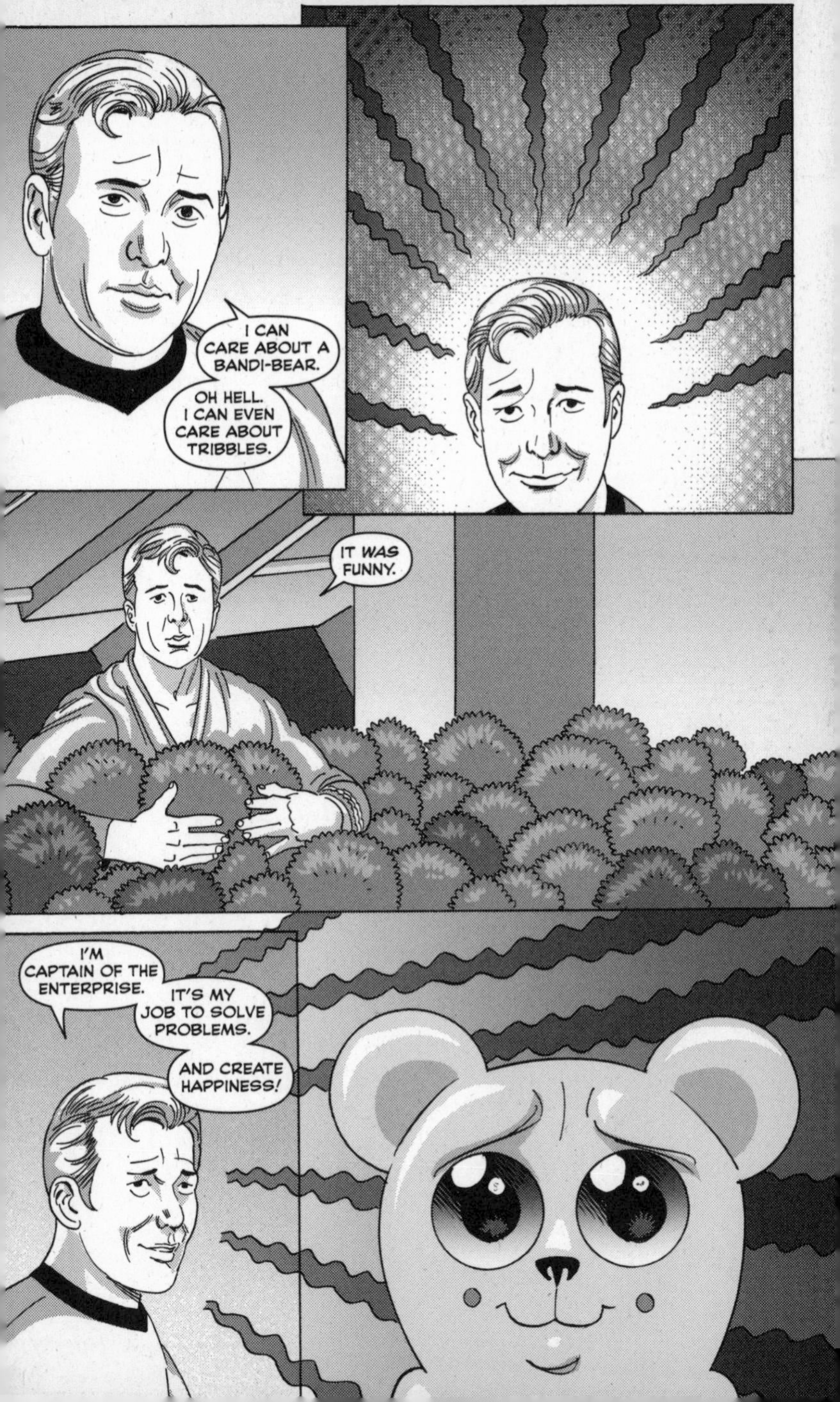

I CAN CARE ABOUT A BANDI-BEAR.
OH HELL. I CAN EVEN CARE ABOUT TRIBBLES.
IT *WAS* FUNNY.
I'M CAPTAIN OF THE ENTERPRISE.
IT'S MY JOB TO SOLVE PROBLEMS.
AND CREATE HAPPINESS!

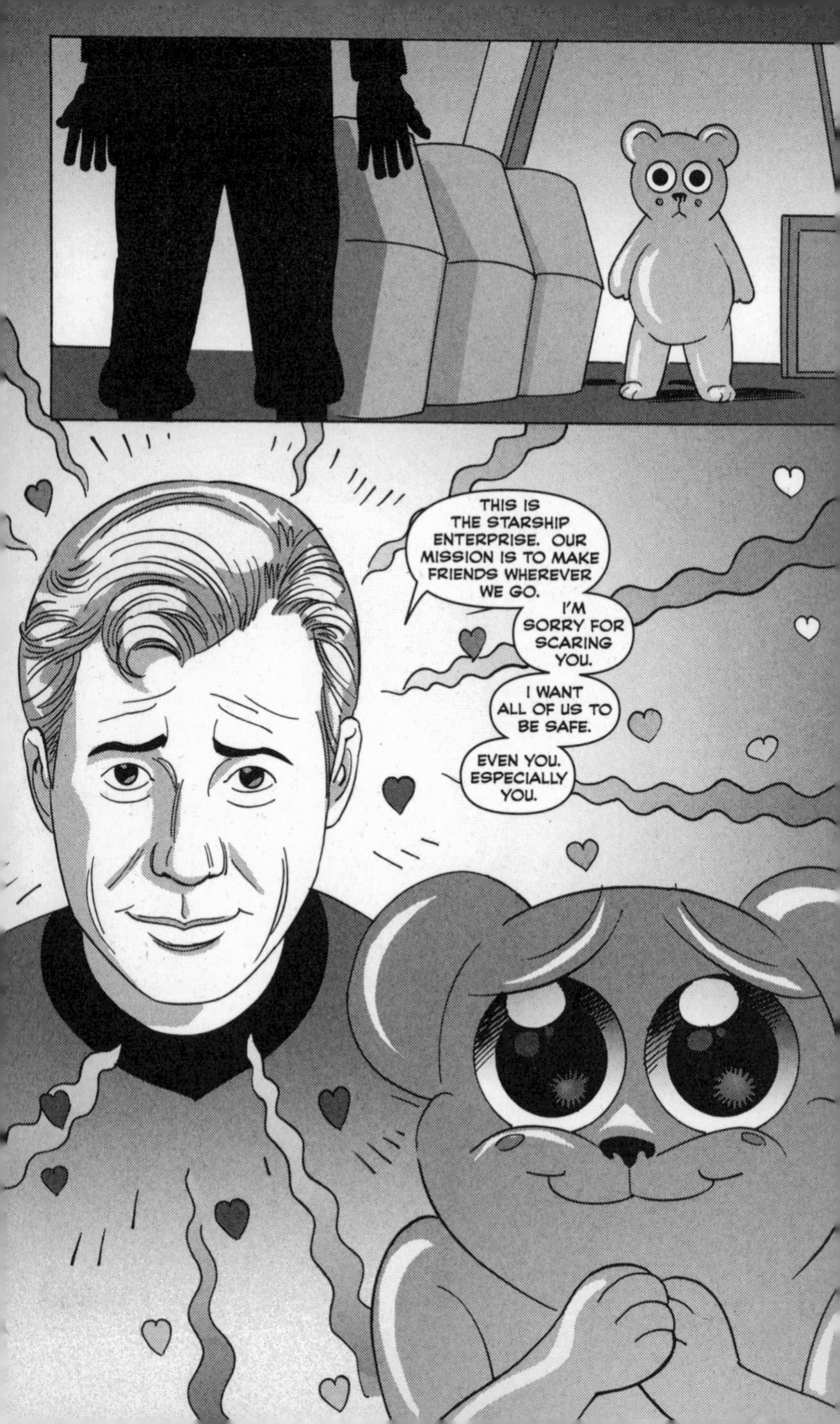

THIS IS THE STARSHIP ENTERPRISE. OUR MISSION IS TO MAKE FRIENDS WHEREVER WE GO.
I'M SORRY FOR SCARING YOU.
I WANT ALL OF US TO BE SAFE.
EVEN YOU. ESPECIALLY YOU.

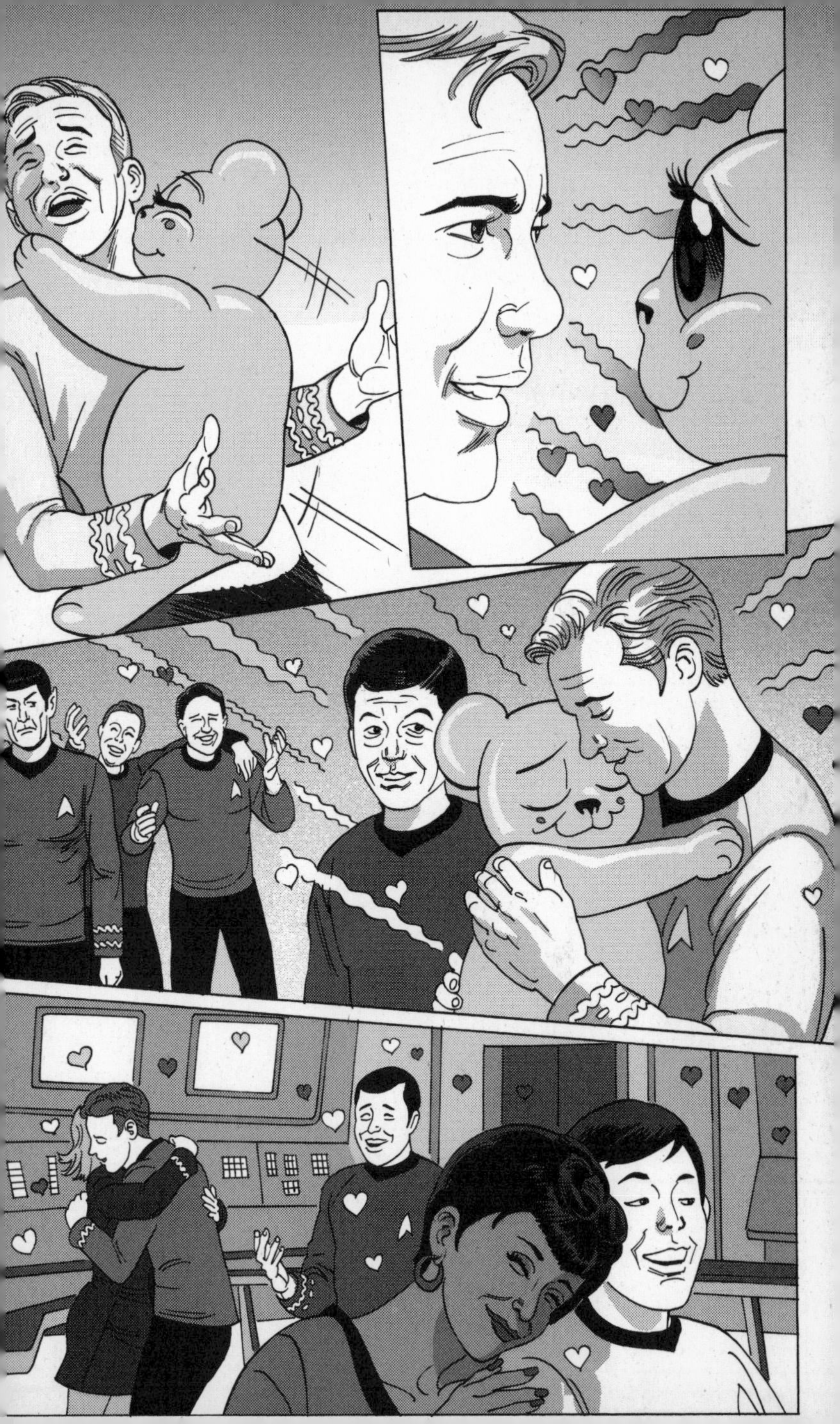

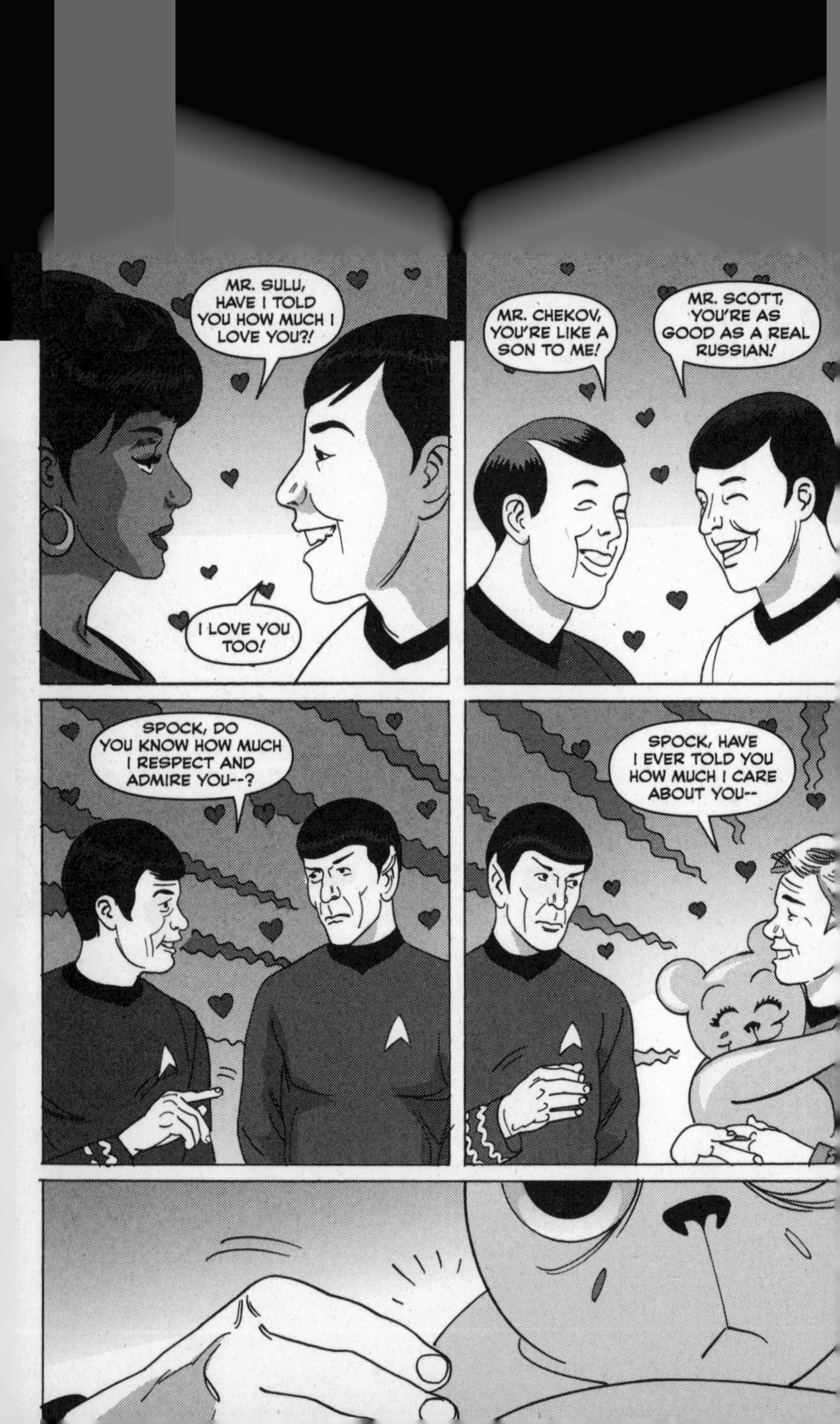
MR. SULU, HAVE I TOLD YOU HOW MUCH I LOVE YOU?!
I LOVE YOU TOO!
MR. CHEKOV, YOU'RE LIKE A SON TO ME!
MR. SCOTT, YOU'RE AS GOOD AS A REAL RUSSIAN!
SPOCK, DO YOU KNOW HOW MUCH I RESPECT AND ADMIRE YOU--?
SPOCK, HAVE I EVER TOLD YOU HOW MUCH I CARE ABOUT YOU--

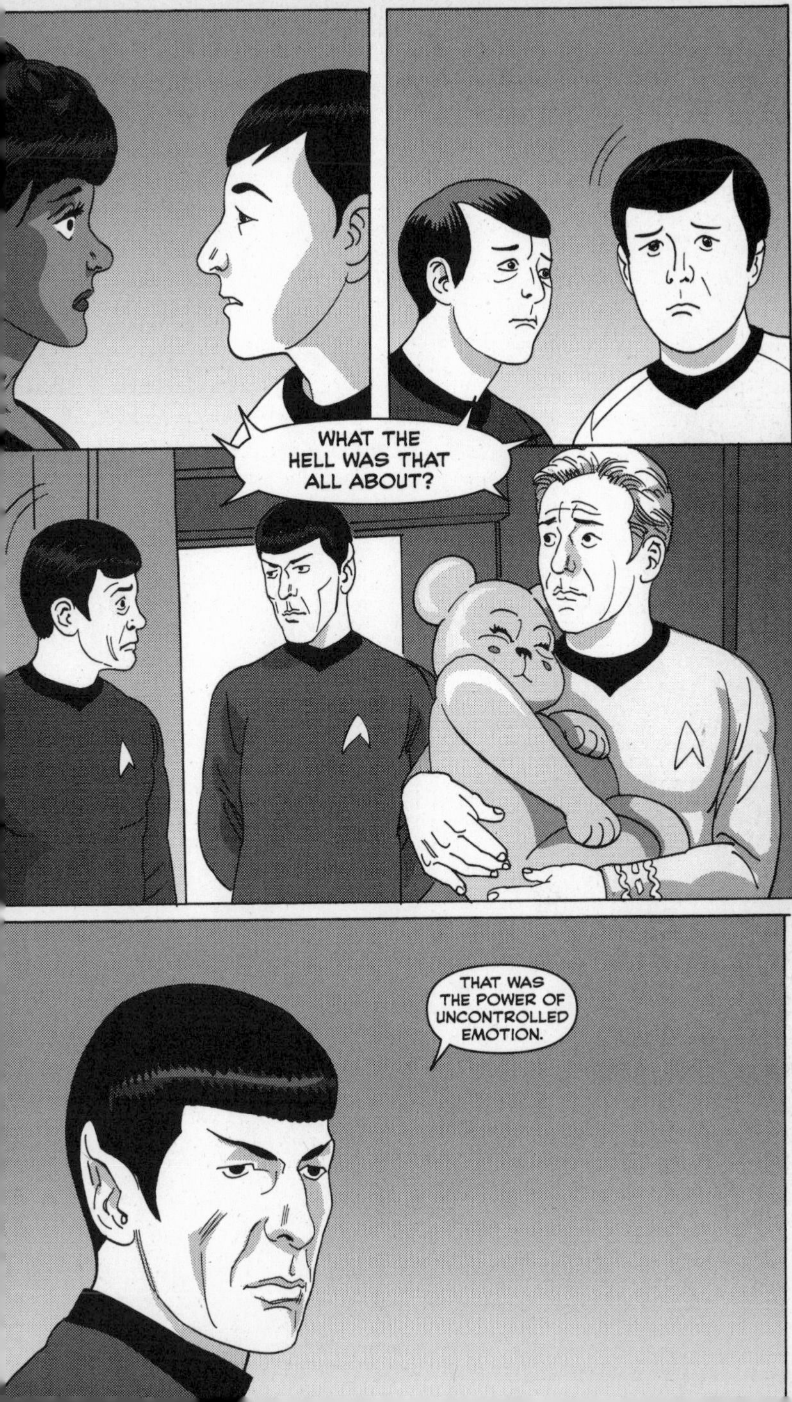
WHAT THE HELL WAS THAT ALL ABOUT?
THAT WAS THE POWER OF UNCONTROLLED EMOTION.

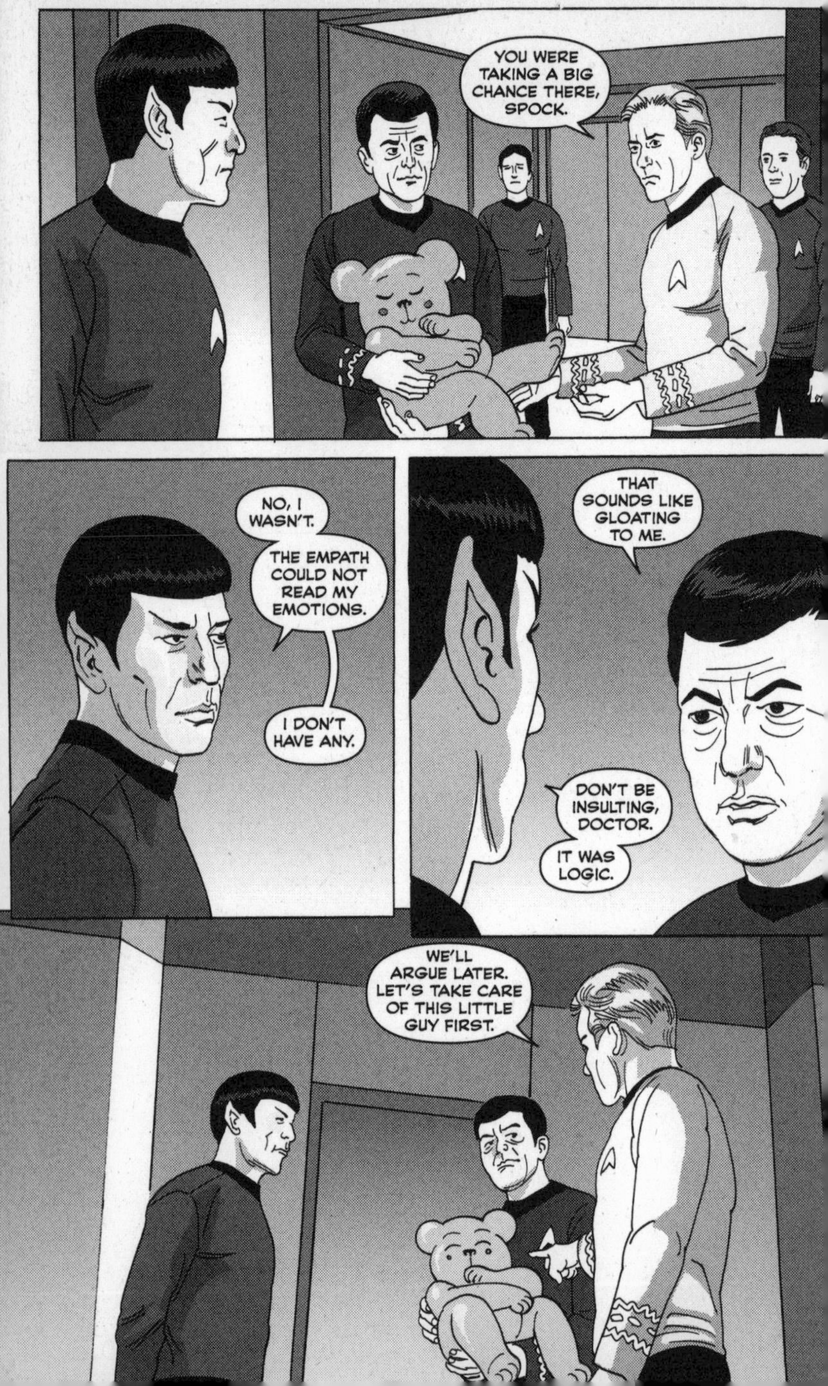
YOU WERE TAKING A BIG CHANCE THERE, SPOCK.
NO, I WASN'T.
THE EMPATH COULD NOT READ MY EMOTIONS.
I DON'T HAVE ANY.
THAT SOUNDS LIKE GLOATING TO ME.
DON'T BE INSULTING, DOCTOR.
IT WAS LOGIC.
WE'LL ARGUE LATER. LET'S TAKE CARE OF THIS LITTLE GUY FIRST.

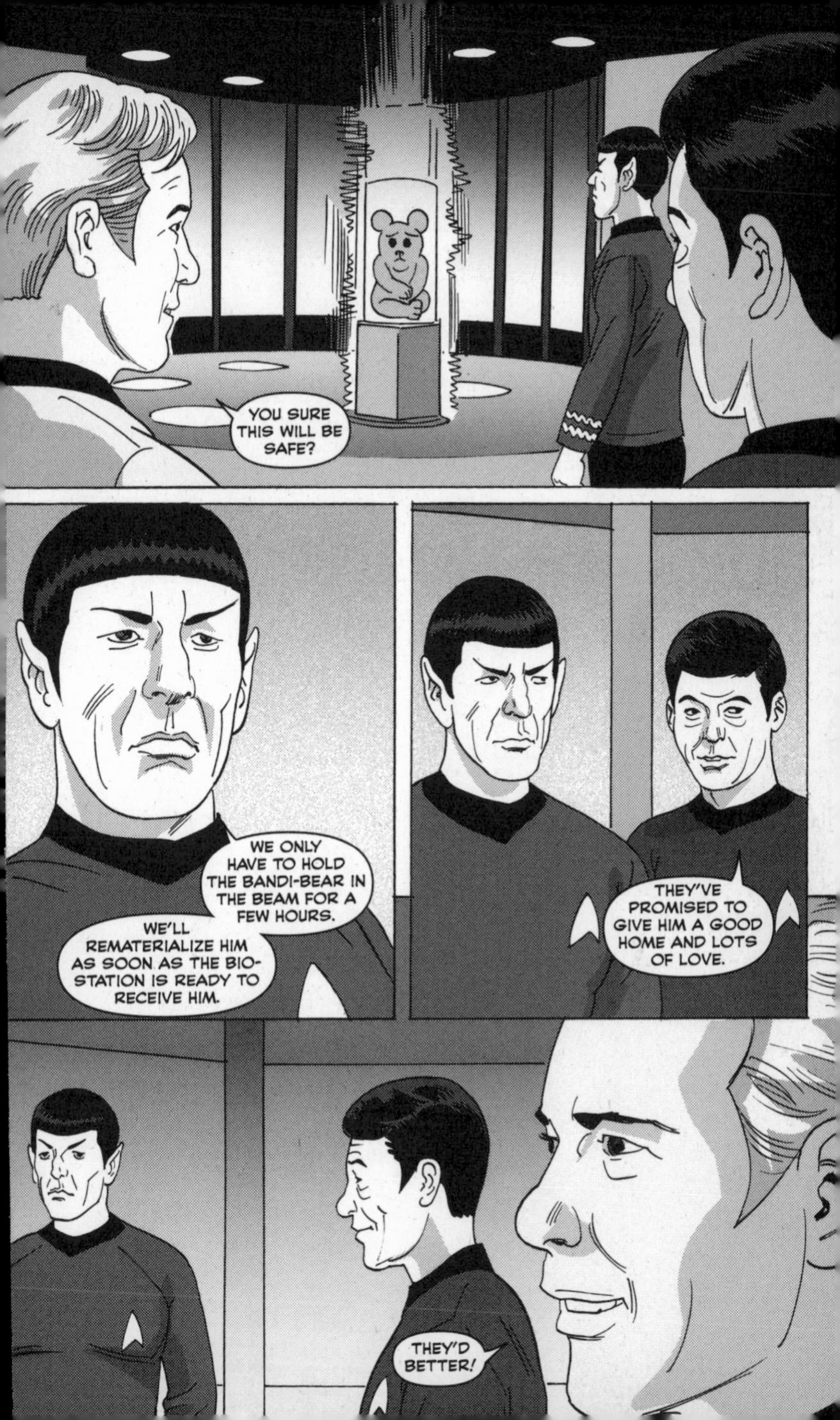
YOU SURE THIS WILL BE SAFE?
WE ONLY HAVE TO HOLD THE BANDI-BEAR IN THE BEAM FOR A FEW HOURS.
WE'LL REMATERIALIZE HIM AS SOON AS THE BIO-STATION IS READY TO RECEIVE HIM.
THEY'VE PROMISED TO GIVE HIM A GOOD HOME AND LOTS OF LOVE.
THEY'D BETTER!

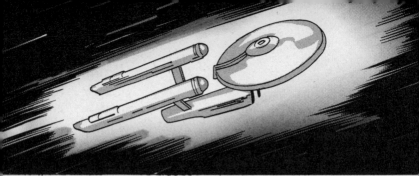

SO, TELL US SPOCK, WHAT DID IT FEEL LIKE TO BE THE TARGET OF SO MUCH LOVE?

IT WAS ... EMBARRASSING.

I DIDN'T SAY ANYTHING, DID I?

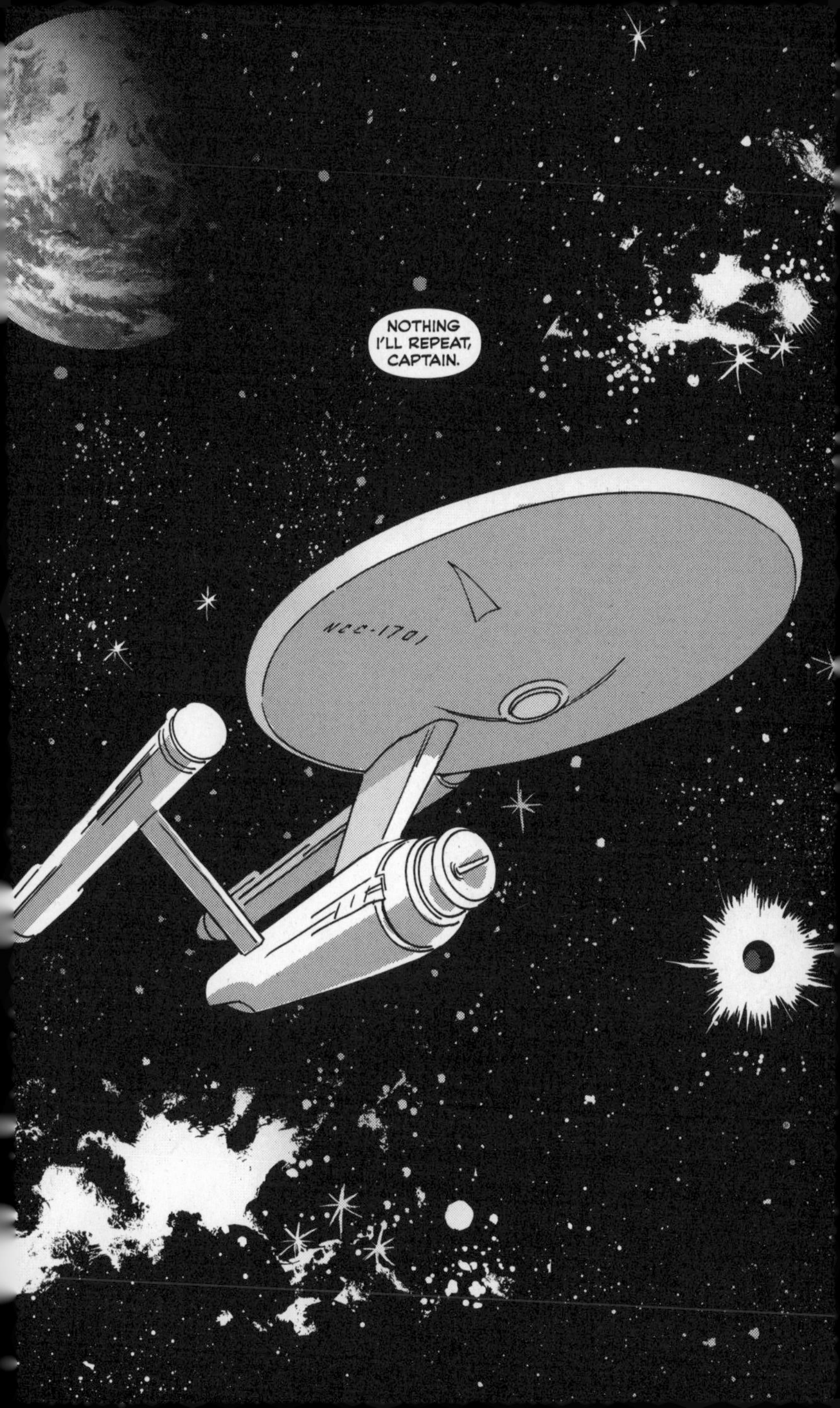
NOTHING I'LL REPEAT, CAPTAIN.

THE HUMANITARIAN

STORY BY LUIS A. REYES
PENCILS AND INKS BY NATE WATSON
TONES BY CHOW HON LAM

CAPTAIN'S LOG, STARDATE 3347.6. FIRST OFFICER SPOCK IN COMMAND.

AS CAPTAIN KIRK IS RECUPERATING ON STARBASE 47, THE ENTERPRISE HAS BEEN ORDERED TO THE PLANET RUDIMON FOR A REMARKABLE MISSION OF PEACE.

THOUGH ONCE ON THE PATH TO MEMBERSHIP IN THE UNITED FEDERATION OF PLANETS, RUDIMON'S INTERNAL POLITICAL UNREST DROVE THEM TO SEVER ALL GALACTIC TIES. NOW, SEVENTY YEARS LATER, THE FEDERATION HAS BEEN ASKED TO RETURN AND HELP A FLEDGLING PEACE PROSPER.

OUR MISSION IS TO AID THE PEOPLE OF THIS WORLD BY INITIATING A PROGRAM TO REBUILD INFRASTRUCTURES WEATHERED AND TORN BY DECADES OF WAR AND NEGLECT. IT IS A UNIQUE PRIVILEGE.

IF I WERE HUMAN, I WOULD MOST LIKELY BE BORDERING ON EXCITEMENT...

...IF I WERE HUMAN.

97

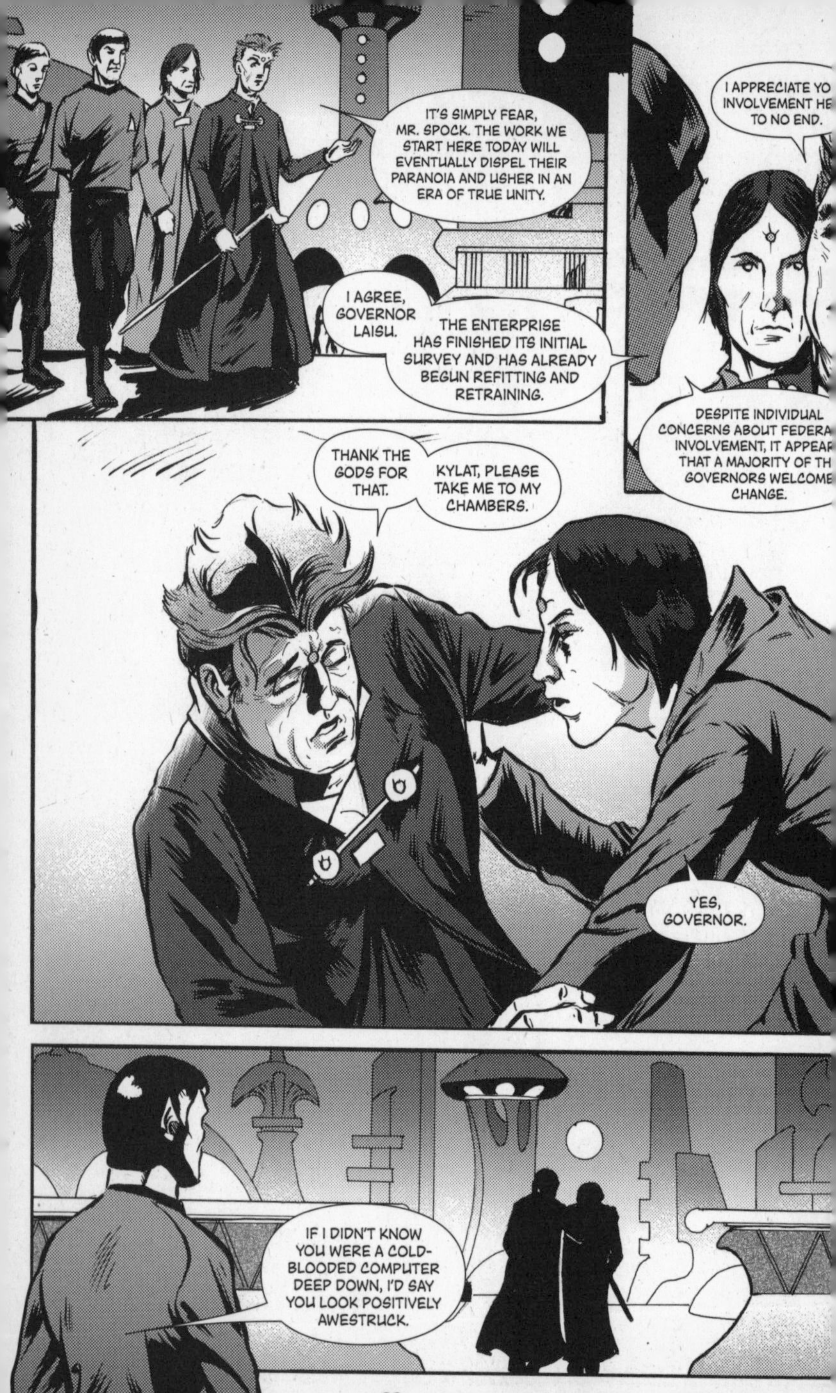
IT'S SIMPLY FEAR, MR. SPOCK. THE WORK WE START HERE TODAY WILL EVENTUALLY DISPEL THEIR PARANOIA AND USHER IN AN ERA OF TRUE UNITY.
I AGREE, GOVERNOR LAISU.
THE ENTERPRISE HAS FINISHED ITS INITIAL SURVEY AND HAS ALREADY BEGUN REFITTING AND RETRAINING.
I APPRECIATE YO INVOLVEMENT HE TO NO END.
DESPITE INDIVIDUAL CONCERNS ABOUT FEDERA INVOLVEMENT, IT APPEAR THAT A MAJORITY OF TH GOVERNORS WELCOME CHANGE.
THANK THE GODS FOR THAT.
KYLAT, PLEASE TAKE ME TO MY CHAMBERS.
YES, GOVERNOR.
IF I DIDN'T KNOW YOU WERE A COLD-BLOODED COMPUTER DEEP DOWN, I'D SAY YOU LOOK POSITIVELY AWESTRUCK.

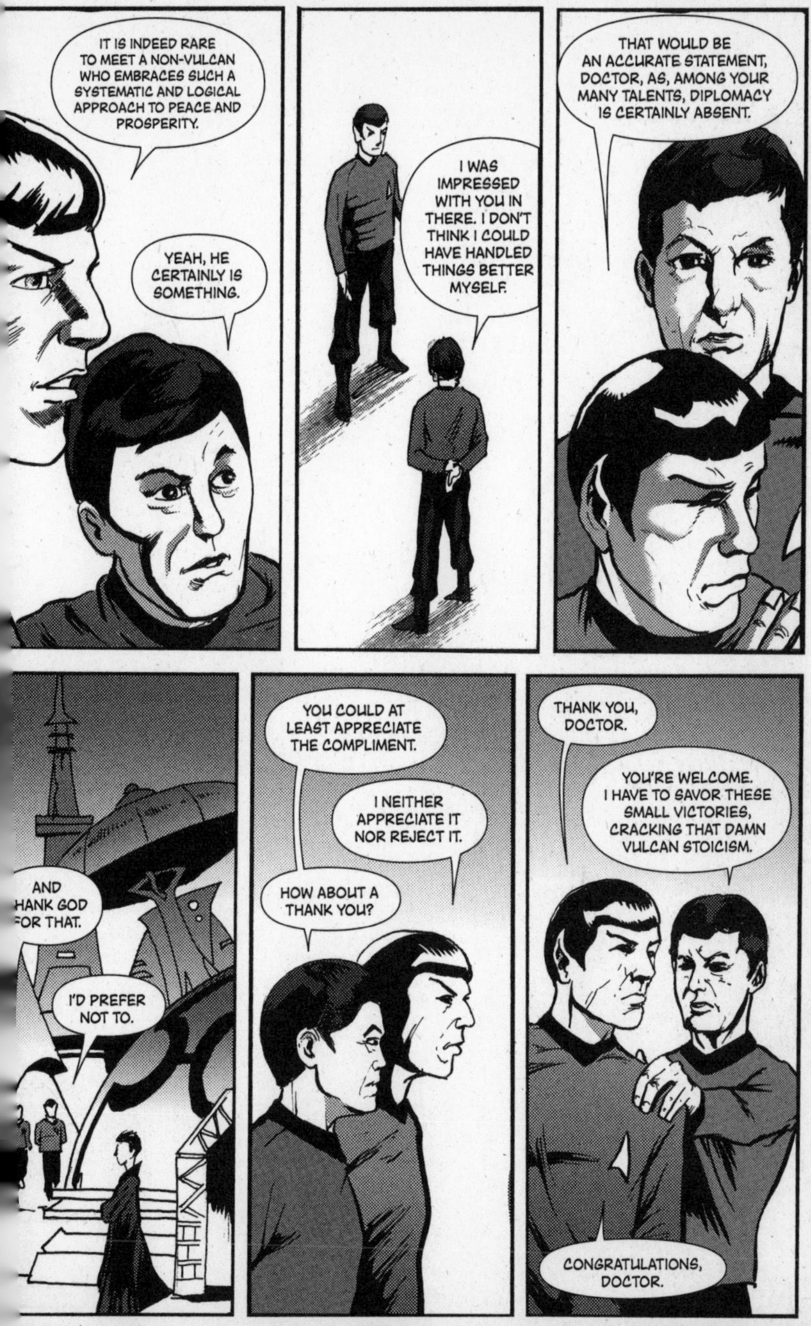
IT IS INDEED RARE TO MEET A NON-VULCAN WHO EMBRACES SUCH A SYSTEMATIC AND LOGICAL APPROACH TO PEACE AND PROSPERITY.
YEAH, HE CERTAINLY IS SOMETHING.
I WAS IMPRESSED WITH YOU IN THERE. I DON'T THINK I COULD HAVE HANDLED THINGS BETTER MYSELF.
THAT WOULD BE AN ACCURATE STATEMENT, DOCTOR, AS, AMONG YOUR MANY TALENTS, DIPLOMACY IS CERTAINLY ABSENT.
AND HANK GOD FOR THAT.
I'D PREFER NOT TO.
YOU COULD AT LEAST APPRECIATE THE COMPLIMENT.
I NEITHER APPRECIATE IT NOR REJECT IT.
HOW ABOUT A THANK YOU?
THANK YOU, DOCTOR.
YOU'RE WELCOME. I HAVE TO SAVOR THESE SMALL VICTORIES, CRACKING THAT DAMN VULCAN STOICISM.
CONGRATULATIONS, DOCTOR.

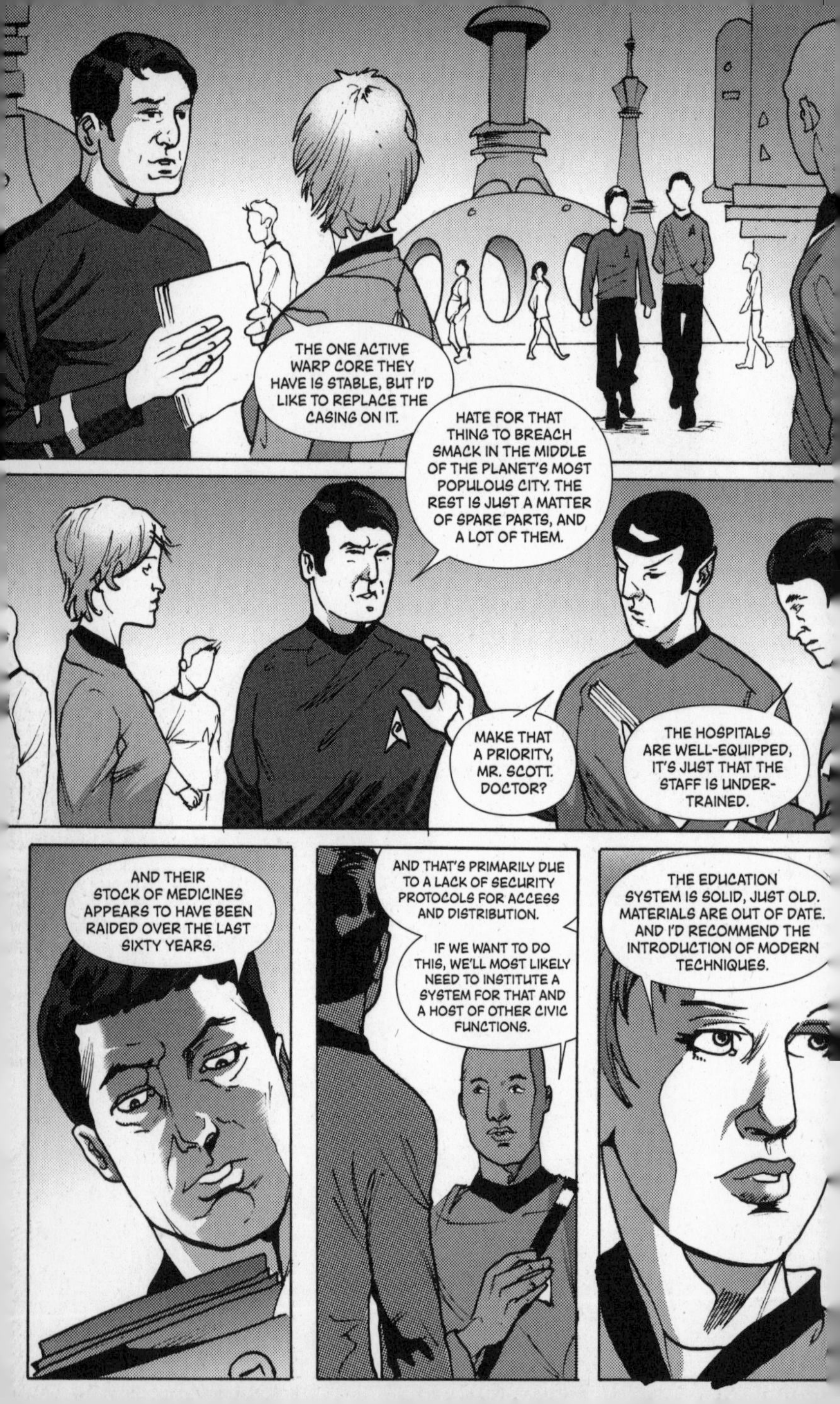
THE ONE ACTIVE WARP CORE THEY HAVE IS STABLE, BUT I'D LIKE TO REPLACE THE CASING ON IT.
HATE FOR THAT THING TO BREACH SMACK IN THE MIDDLE OF THE PLANET'S MOST POPULOUS CITY. THE REST IS JUST A MATTER OF SPARE PARTS, AND A LOT OF THEM.
MAKE THAT A PRIORITY, MR. SCOTT. DOCTOR?
THE HOSPITALS ARE WELL-EQUIPPED, IT'S JUST THAT THE STAFF IS UNDER-TRAINED.
AND THEIR STOCK OF MEDICINES APPEARS TO HAVE BEEN RAIDED OVER THE LAST SIXTY YEARS.
AND THAT'S PRIMARILY DUE TO A LACK OF SECURITY PROTOCOLS FOR ACCESS AND DISTRIBUTION.
IF WE WANT TO DO THIS, WE'LL MOST LIKELY NEED TO INSTITUTE A SYSTEM FOR THAT AND A HOST OF OTHER CIVIC FUNCTIONS.
THE EDUCATION SYSTEM IS SOLID, JUST OLD. MATERIALS ARE OUT OF DATE. AND I'D RECOMMEND THE INTRODUCTION OF MODERN TECHNIQUES.

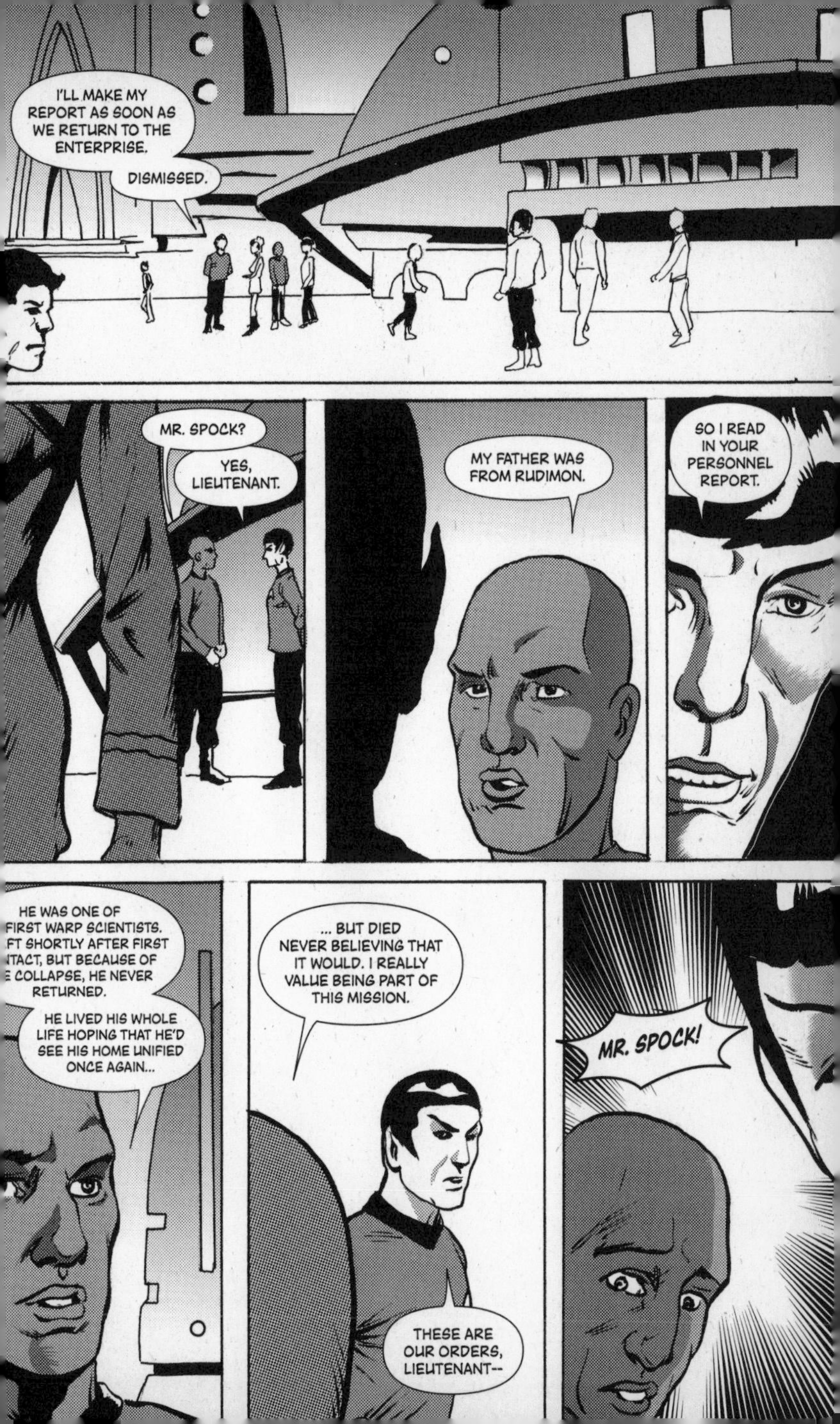

I'LL MAKE MY REPORT AS SOON AS WE RETURN TO THE ENTERPRISE.
DISMISSED.
MR. SPOCK?
YES, LIEUTENANT.
MY FATHER WAS FROM RUDIMON.
SO I READ IN YOUR PERSONNEL REPORT.
HE WAS ONE OF FIRST WARP SCIENTISTS. FT SHORTLY AFTER FIRST ITACT, BUT BECAUSE OF E COLLAPSE, HE NEVER RETURNED.
HE LIVED HIS WHOLE LIFE HOPING THAT HE'D SEE HIS HOME UNIFIED ONCE AGAIN...
... BUT DIED NEVER BELIEVING THAT IT WOULD. I REALLY VALUE BEING PART OF THIS MISSION.
THESE ARE OUR ORDERS, LIEUTENANT--
MR. SPOCK!

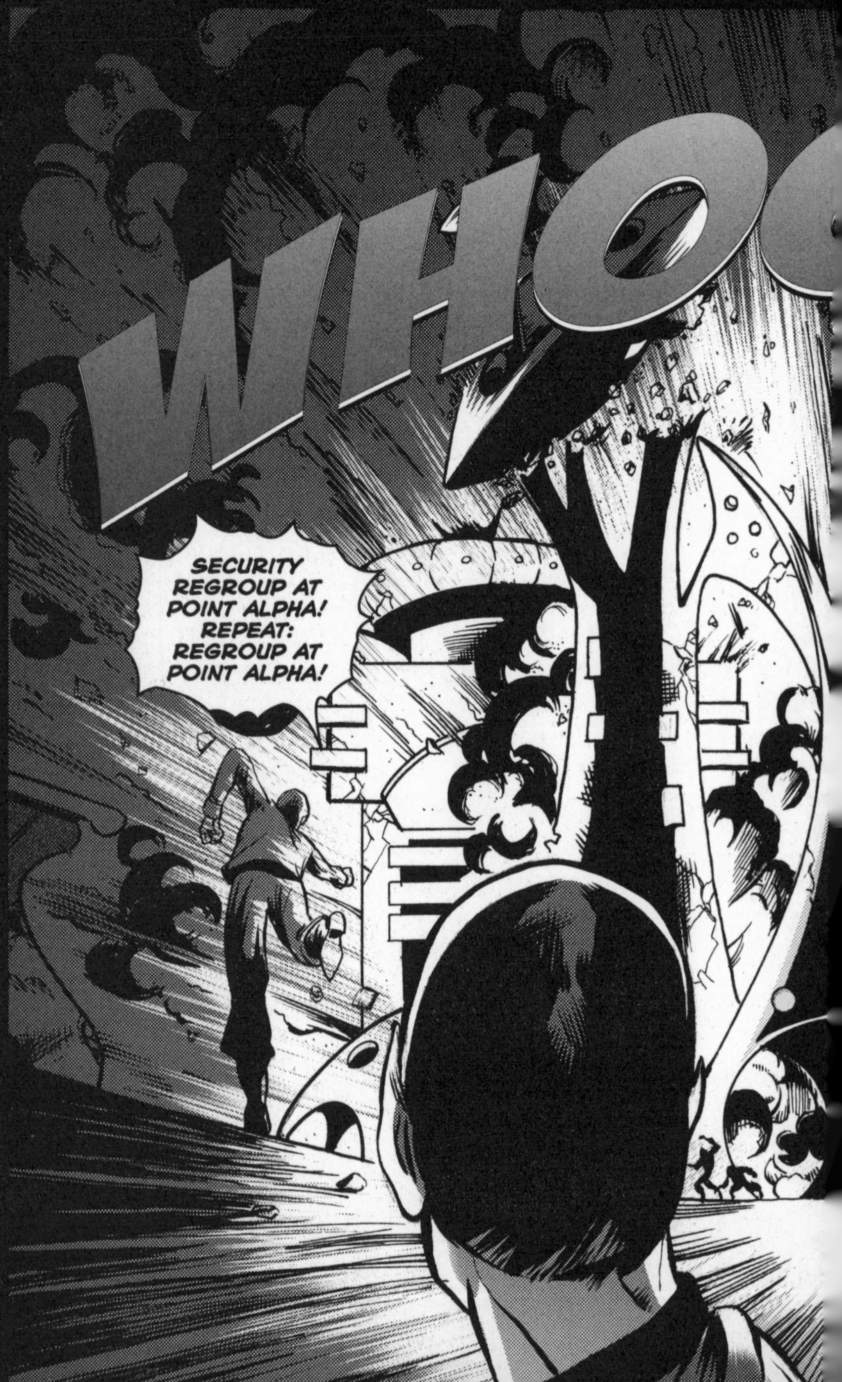
WHOO
SECURITY REGROUP AT POINT ALPHA! REPEAT: REGROUP AT POINT ALPHA!

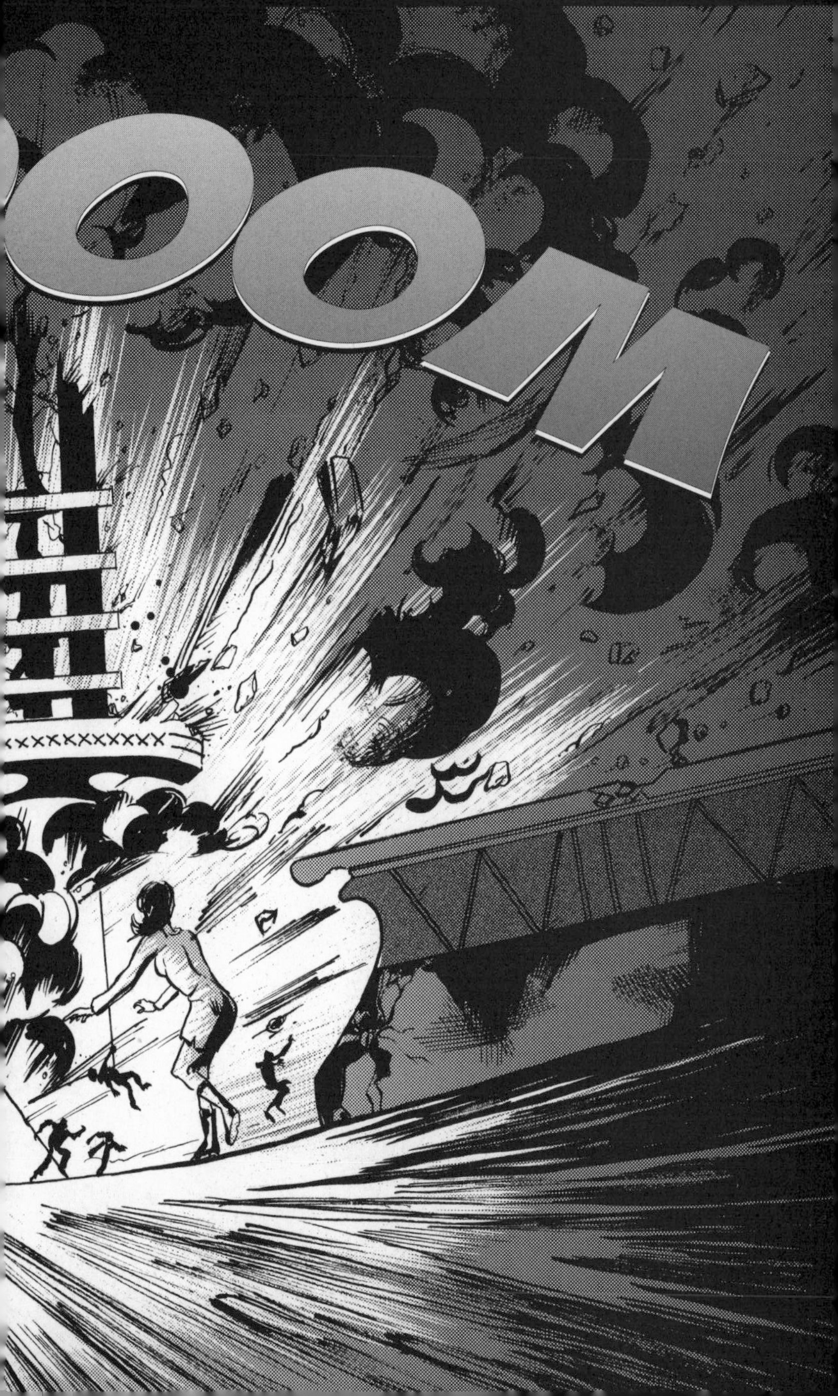
OOM

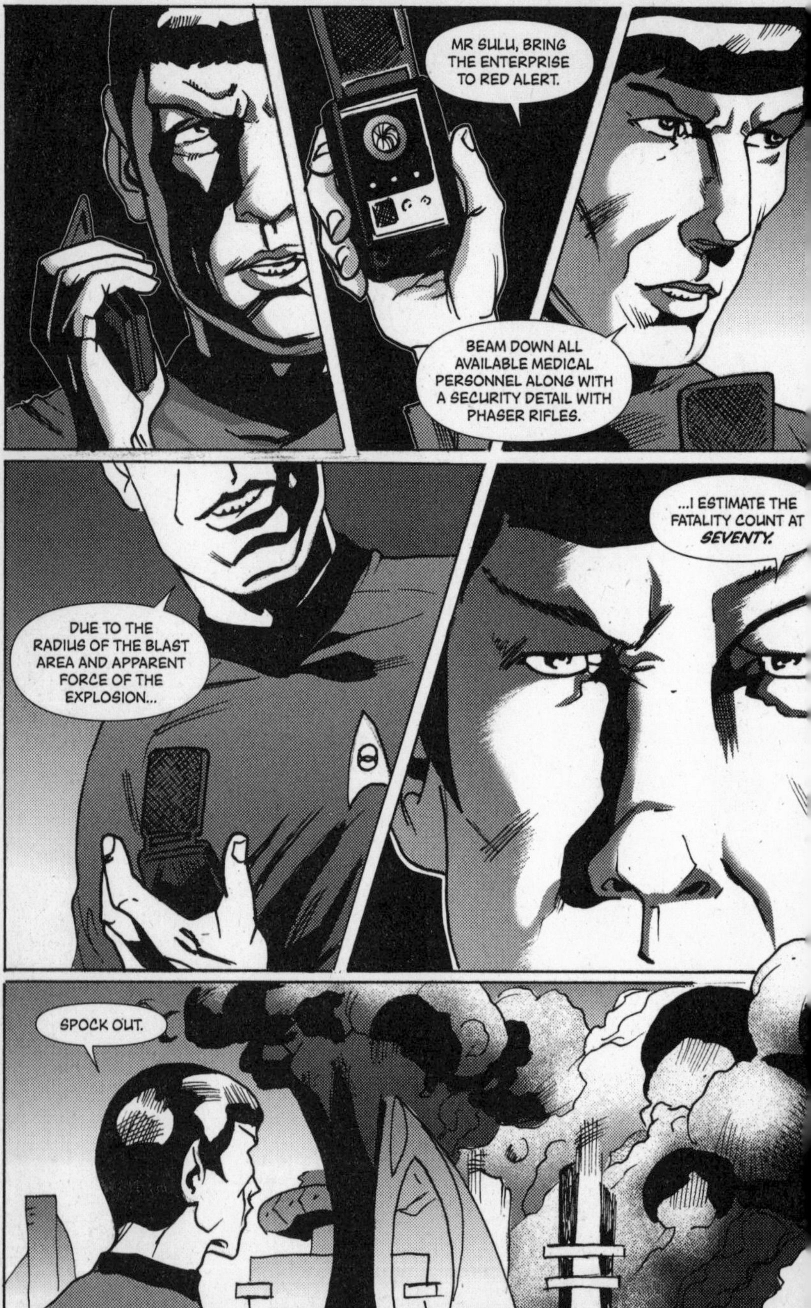
MR SULU, BRING THE ENTERPRISE TO RED ALERT.
BEAM DOWN ALL AVAILABLE MEDICAL PERSONNEL ALONG WITH A SECURITY DETAIL WITH PHASER RIFLES.
DUE TO THE RADIUS OF THE BLAST AREA AND APPARENT FORCE OF THE EXPLOSION...
...I ESTIMATE THE FATALITY COUNT AT *SEVENTY.*
SPOCK OUT.

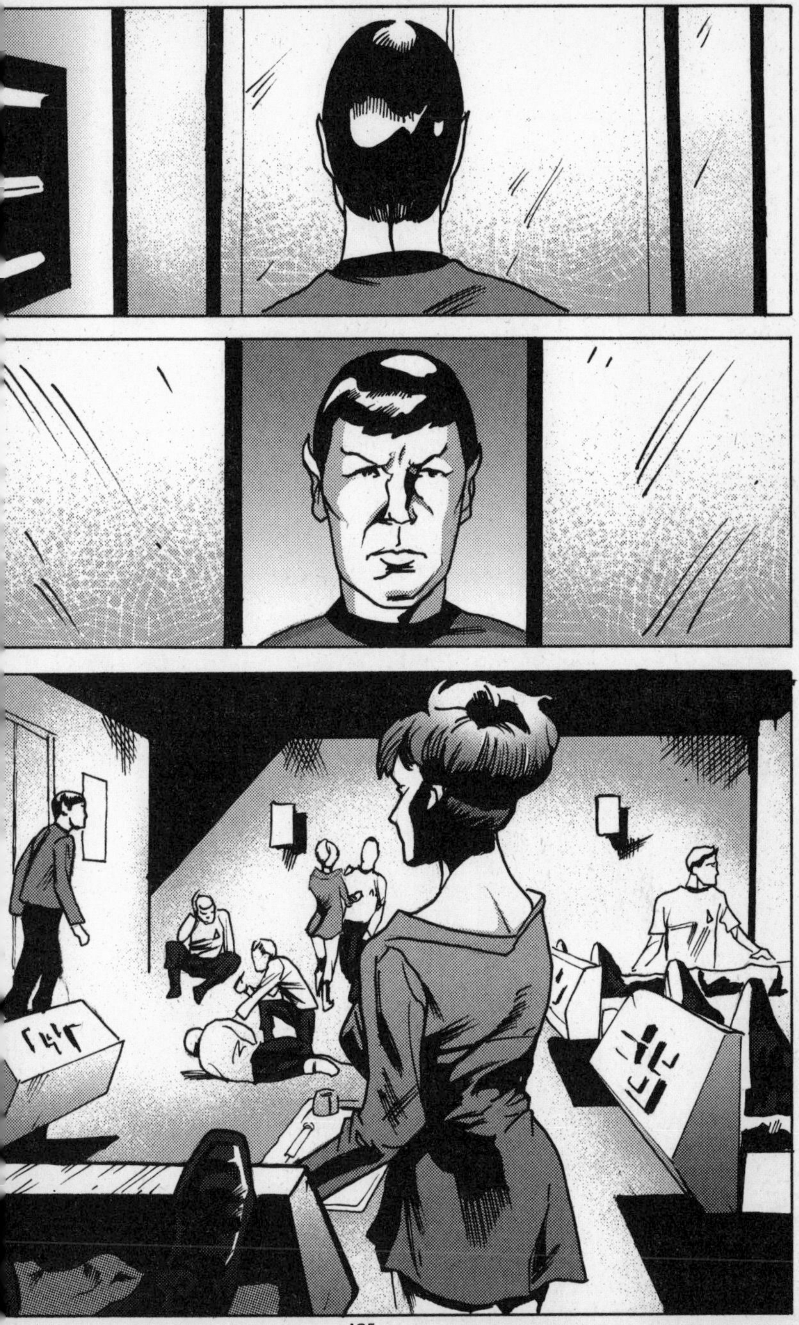

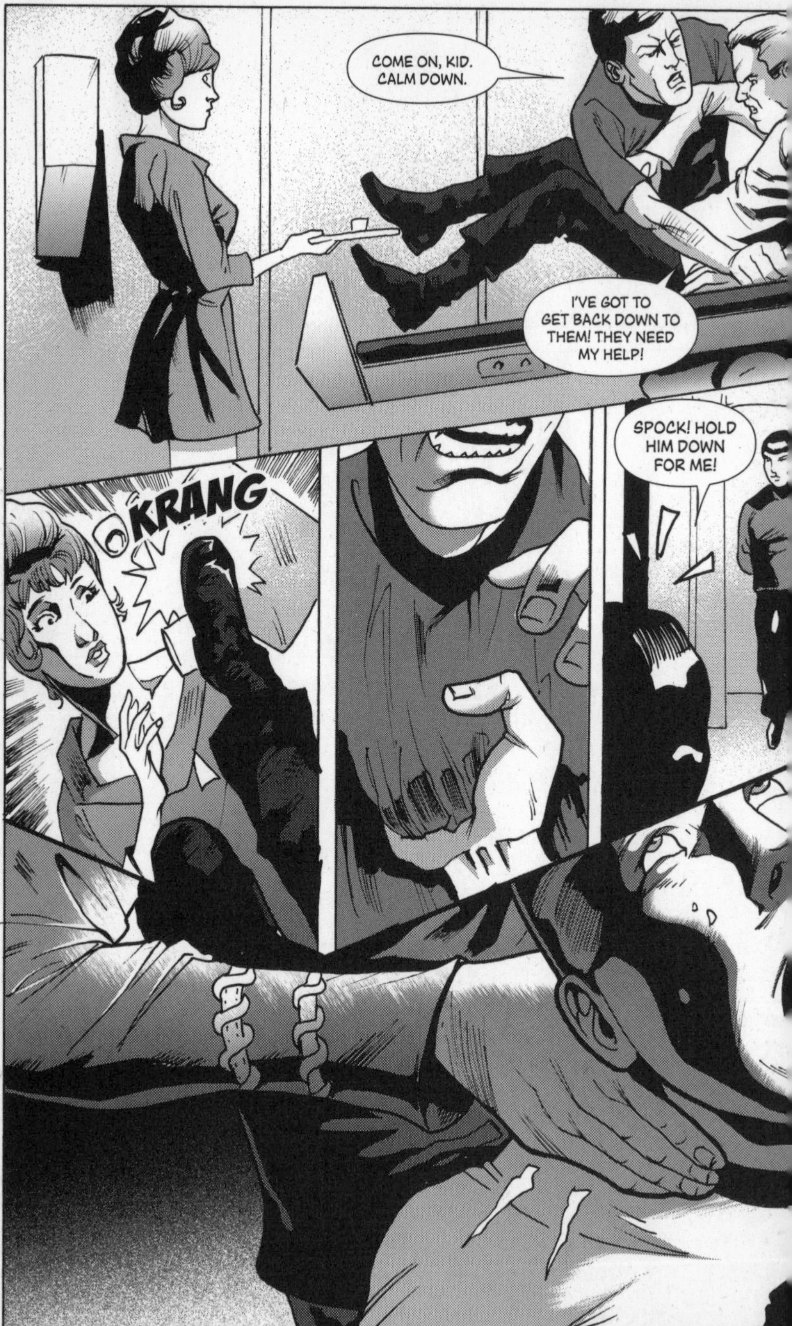
COME ON, KID. CALM DOWN.
I'VE GOT TO GET BACK DOWN TO THEM! THEY NEED MY HELP!
KRANG
SPOCK! HOLD HIM DOWN FOR ME!

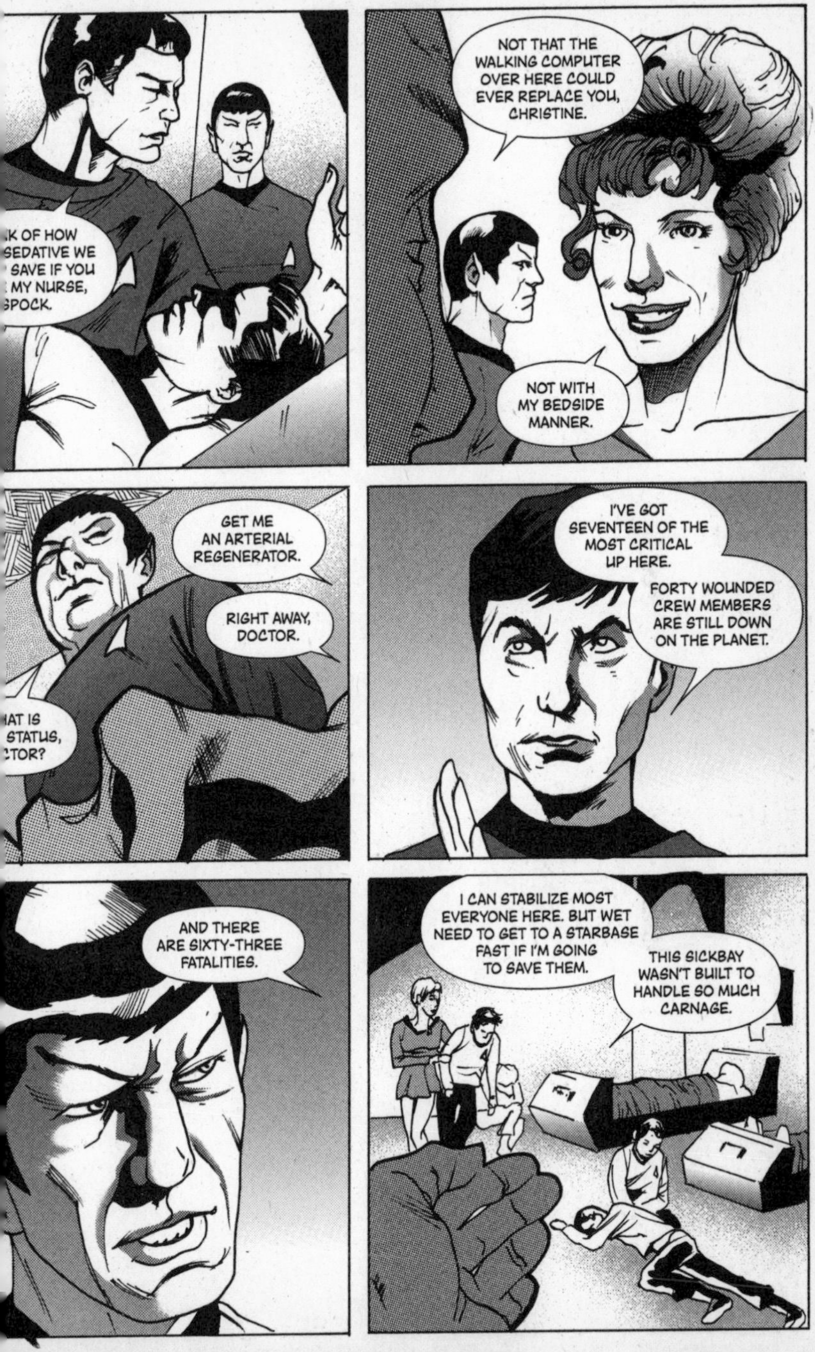
K OF HOW
SEDATIVE WE
SAVE IF YOU
MY NURSE,
SPOCK.
NOT THAT THE WALKING COMPUTER OVER HERE COULD EVER REPLACE YOU, CHRISTINE.
NOT WITH MY BEDSIDE MANNER.
GET ME AN ARTERIAL REGENERATOR.
RIGHT AWAY, DOCTOR.
HAT IS
STATUS,
CTOR?
I'VE GOT SEVENTEEN OF THE MOST CRITICAL UP HERE.
FORTY WOUNDED CREW MEMBERS ARE STILL DOWN ON THE PLANET.
AND THERE ARE SIXTY-THREE FATALITIES.
I CAN STABILIZE MOST EVERYONE HERE. BUT WET NEED TO GET TO A STARBASE FAST IF I'M GOING TO SAVE THEM.
THIS SICKBAY WASN'T BUILT TO HANDLE SO MUCH CARNAGE.

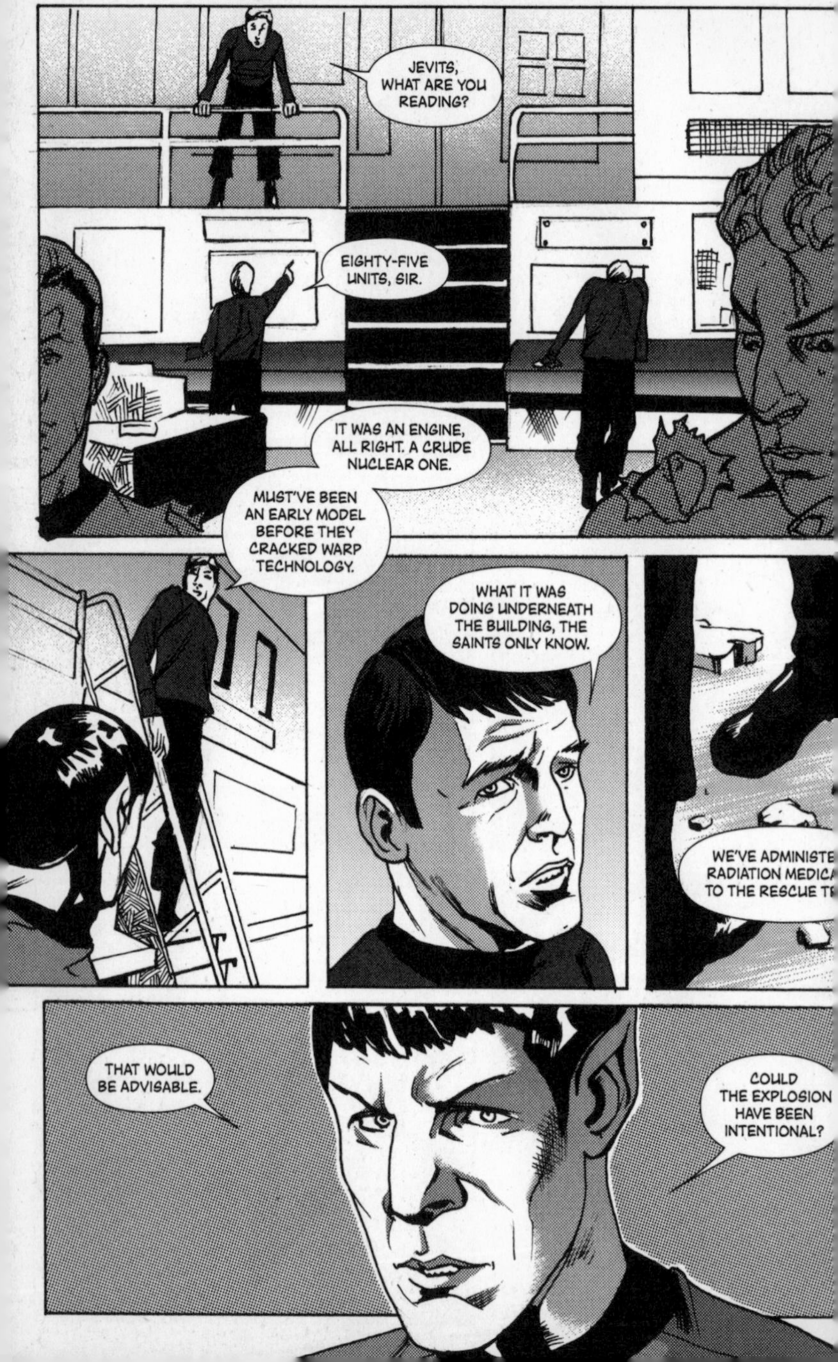
JEVITS, WHAT ARE YOU READING?
EIGHTY-FIVE UNITS, SIR.
IT WAS AN ENGINE, ALL RIGHT. A CRUDE NUCLEAR ONE.
MUST'VE BEEN AN EARLY MODEL BEFORE THEY CRACKED WARP TECHNOLOGY.
WHAT IT WAS DOING UNDERNEATH THE BUILDING, THE SAINTS ONLY KNOW.
WE'VE ADMINISTE
RADIATION MEDICA
TO THE RESCUE T
THAT WOULD BE ADVISABLE.
COULD THE EXPLOSION HAVE BEEN INTENTIONAL?

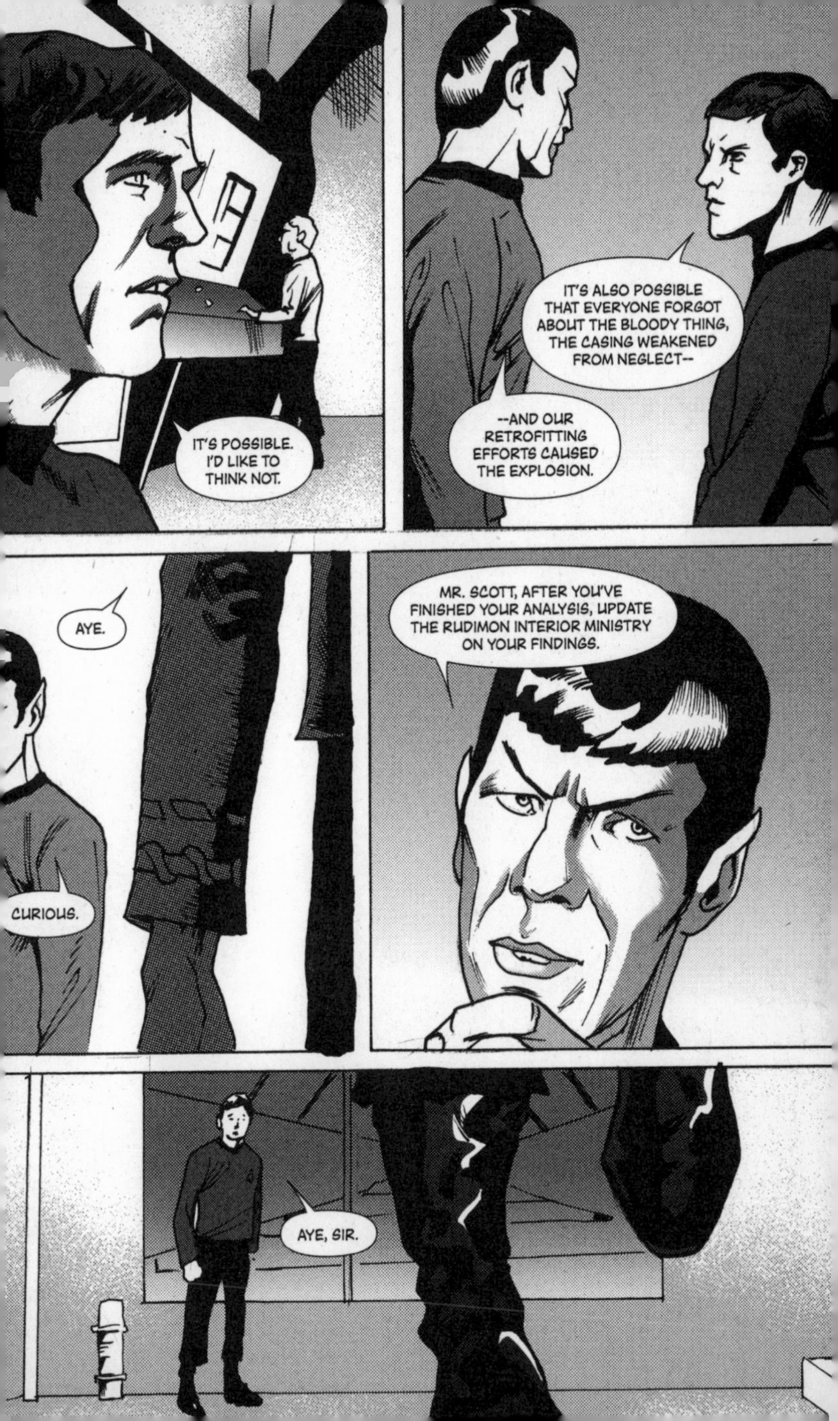
IT'S POSSIBLE. I'D LIKE TO THINK NOT.
IT'S ALSO POSSIBLE THAT EVERYONE FORGOT ABOUT THE BLOODY THING, THE CASING WEAKENED FROM NEGLECT--
--AND OUR RETROFITTING EFFORTS CAUSED THE EXPLOSION.
AYE.
CURIOUS.
MR. SCOTT, AFTER YOU'VE FINISHED YOUR ANALYSIS, UPDATE THE RUDIMON INTERIOR MINISTRY ON YOUR FINDINGS.
AYE, SIR.

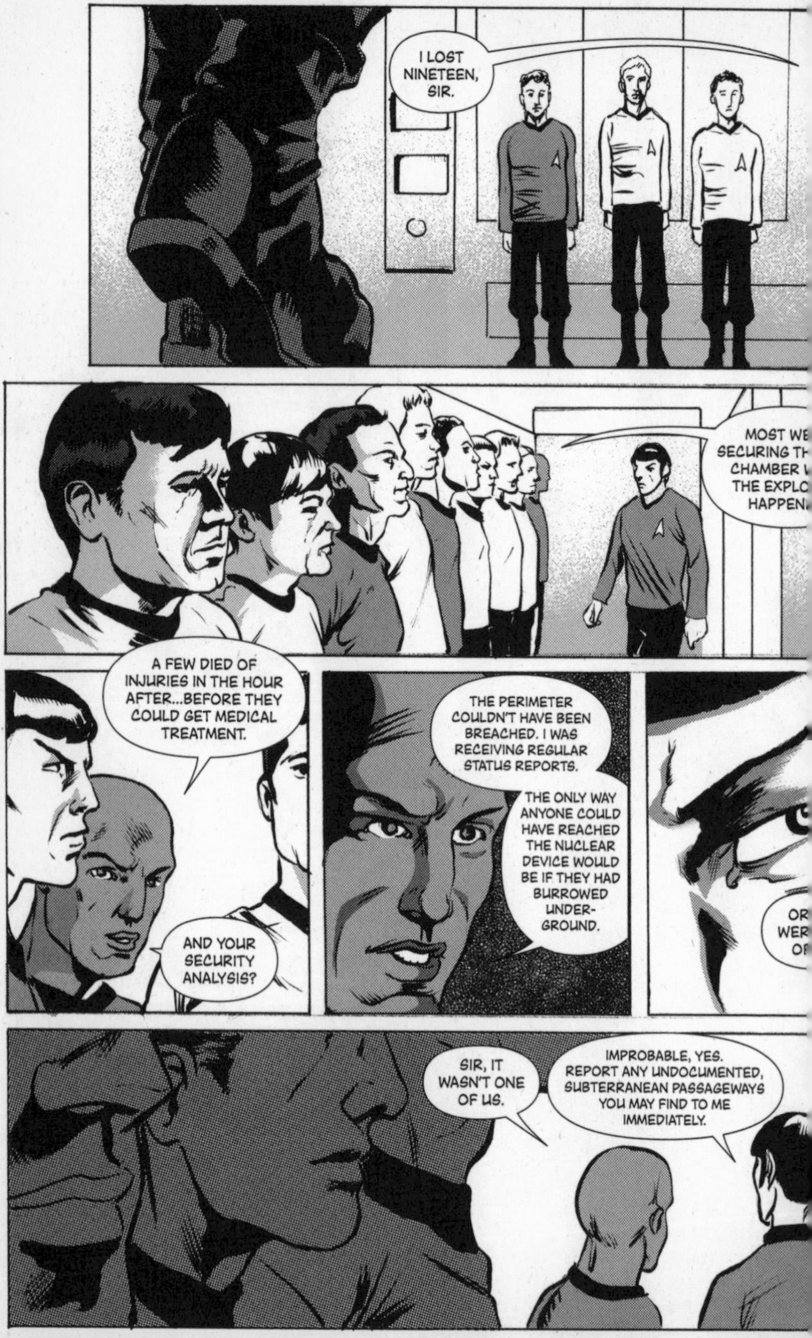
I LOST NINETEEN, SIR.
MOST WE
SECURING TH
CHAMBER W
THE EXPLO
HAPPEN
A FEW DIED OF INJURIES IN THE HOUR AFTER...BEFORE THEY COULD GET MEDICAL TREATMENT.
AND YOUR SECURITY ANALYSIS?
THE PERIMETER COULDN'T HAVE BEEN BREACHED. I WAS RECEIVING REGULAR STATUS REPORTS.
THE ONLY WAY ANYONE COULD HAVE REACHED THE NUCLEAR DEVICE WOULD BE IF THEY HAD BURROWED UNDER-GROUND.
OR
WER
OF
SIR, IT WASN'T ONE OF US.
IMPROBABLE, YES. REPORT ANY UNDOCUMENTED, SUBTERRANEAN PASSAGEWAYS YOU MAY FIND TO ME IMMEDIATELY.

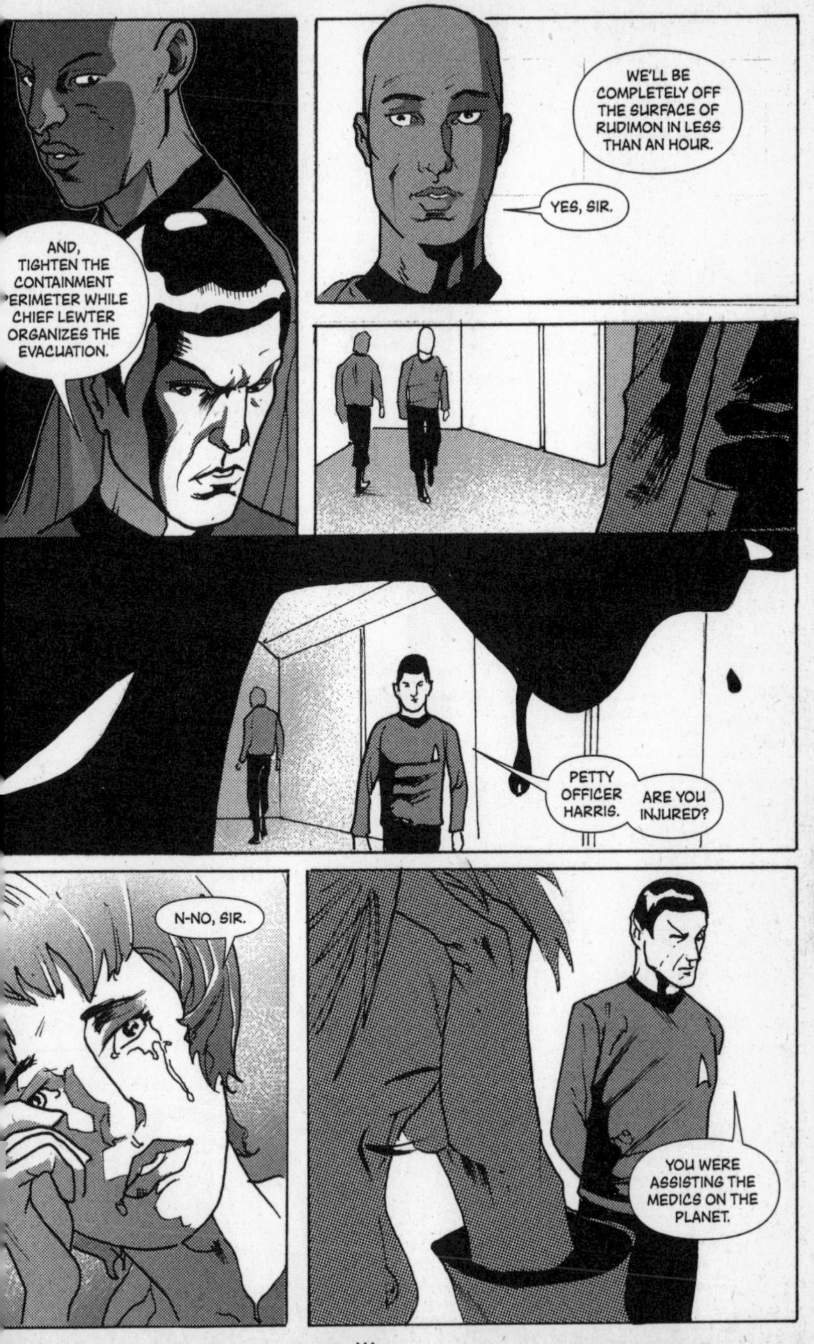

AND, TIGHTEN THE CONTAINMENT PERIMETER WHILE CHIEF LEWTER ORGANIZES THE EVACUATION.
WE'LL BE COMPLETELY OFF THE SURFACE OF RUDIMON IN LESS THAN AN HOUR.
YES, SIR.
PETTY OFFICER HARRIS.
ARE YOU INJURED?
N-NO, SIR.
YOU WERE ASSISTING THE MEDICS ON THE PLANET.

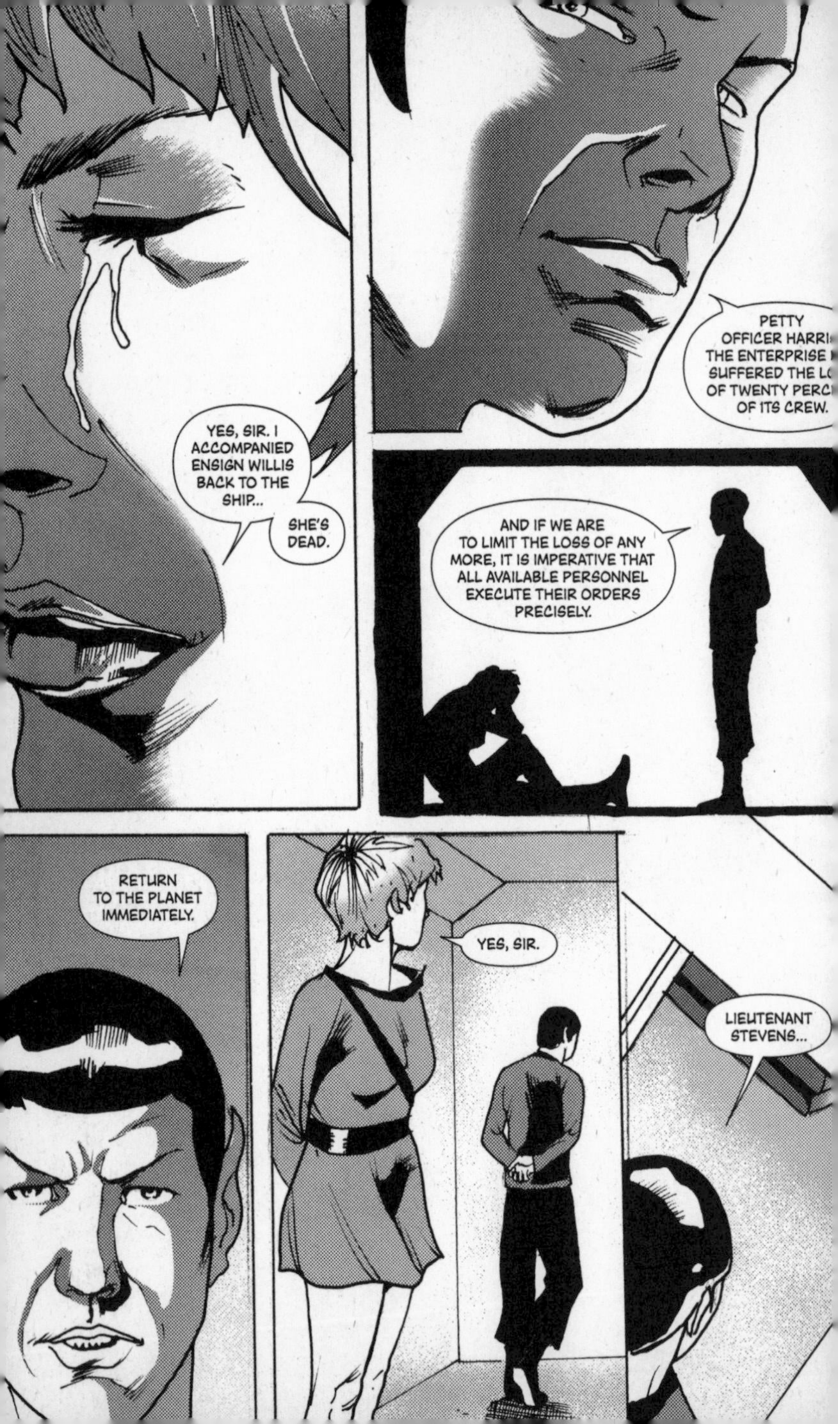

YES, SIR. I ACCOMPANIED ENSIGN WILLIS BACK TO THE SHIP...
SHE'S DEAD.
PETTY OFFICER HARRI THE ENTERPRISE SUFFERED THE LO OF TWENTY PERC OF ITS CREW.
AND IF WE ARE TO LIMIT THE LOSS OF ANY MORE, IT IS IMPERATIVE THAT ALL AVAILABLE PERSONNEL EXECUTE THEIR ORDERS PRECISELY.
RETURN TO THE PLANET IMMEDIATELY.
YES, SIR.
LIEUTENANT STEVENS...

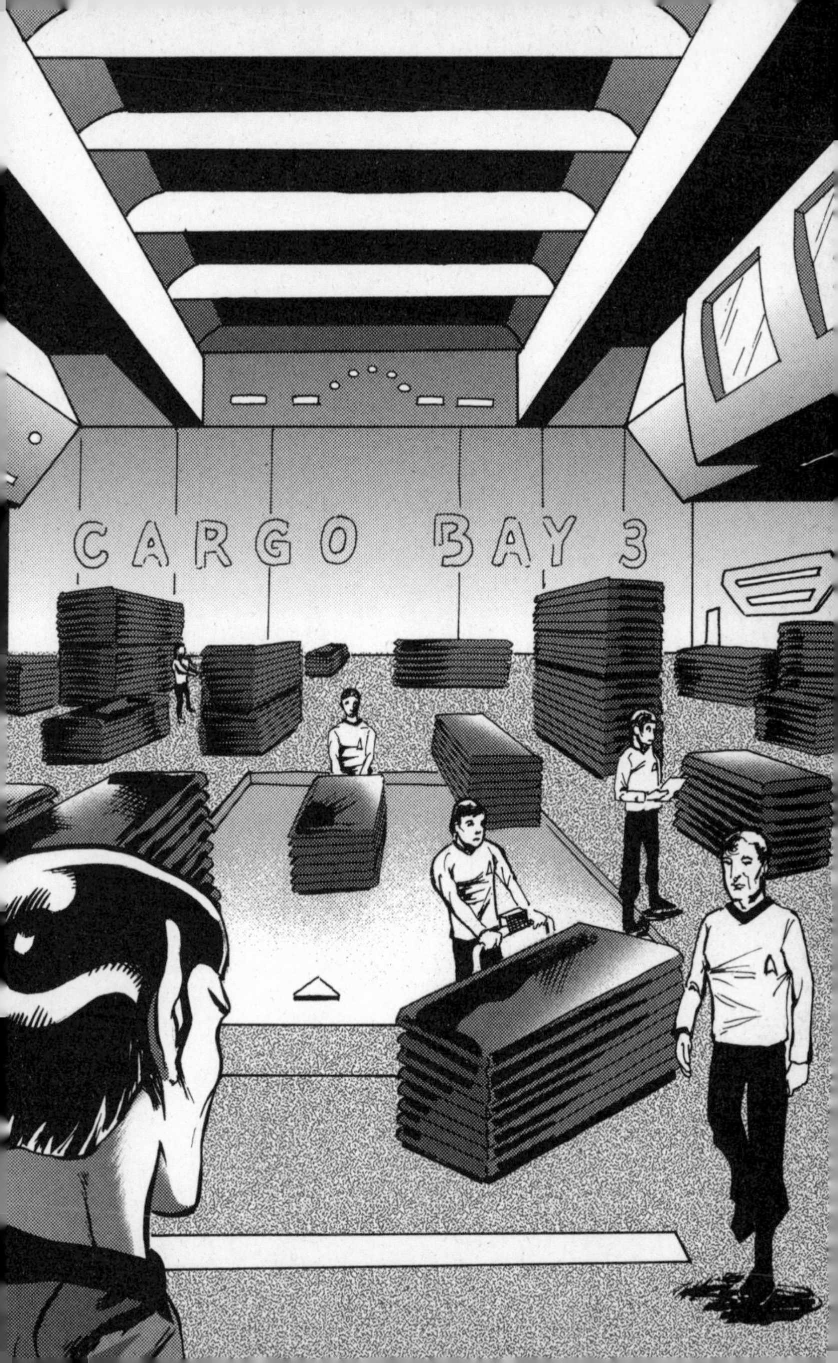
CARGO BAY 3

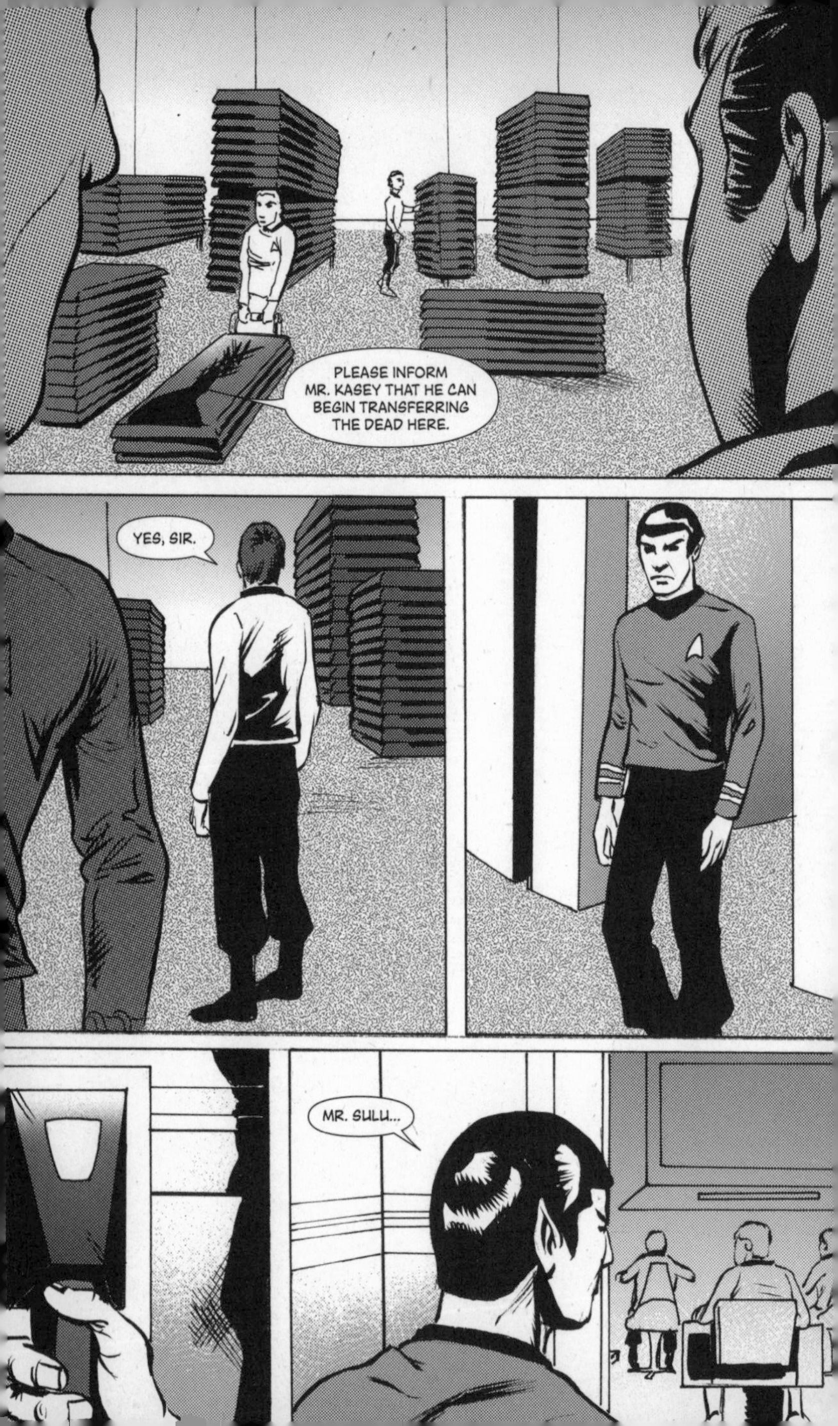
PLEASE INFORM MR. KASEY THAT HE CAN BEGIN TRANSFERRING THE DEAD HERE.
YES, SIR.
MR. SULU...

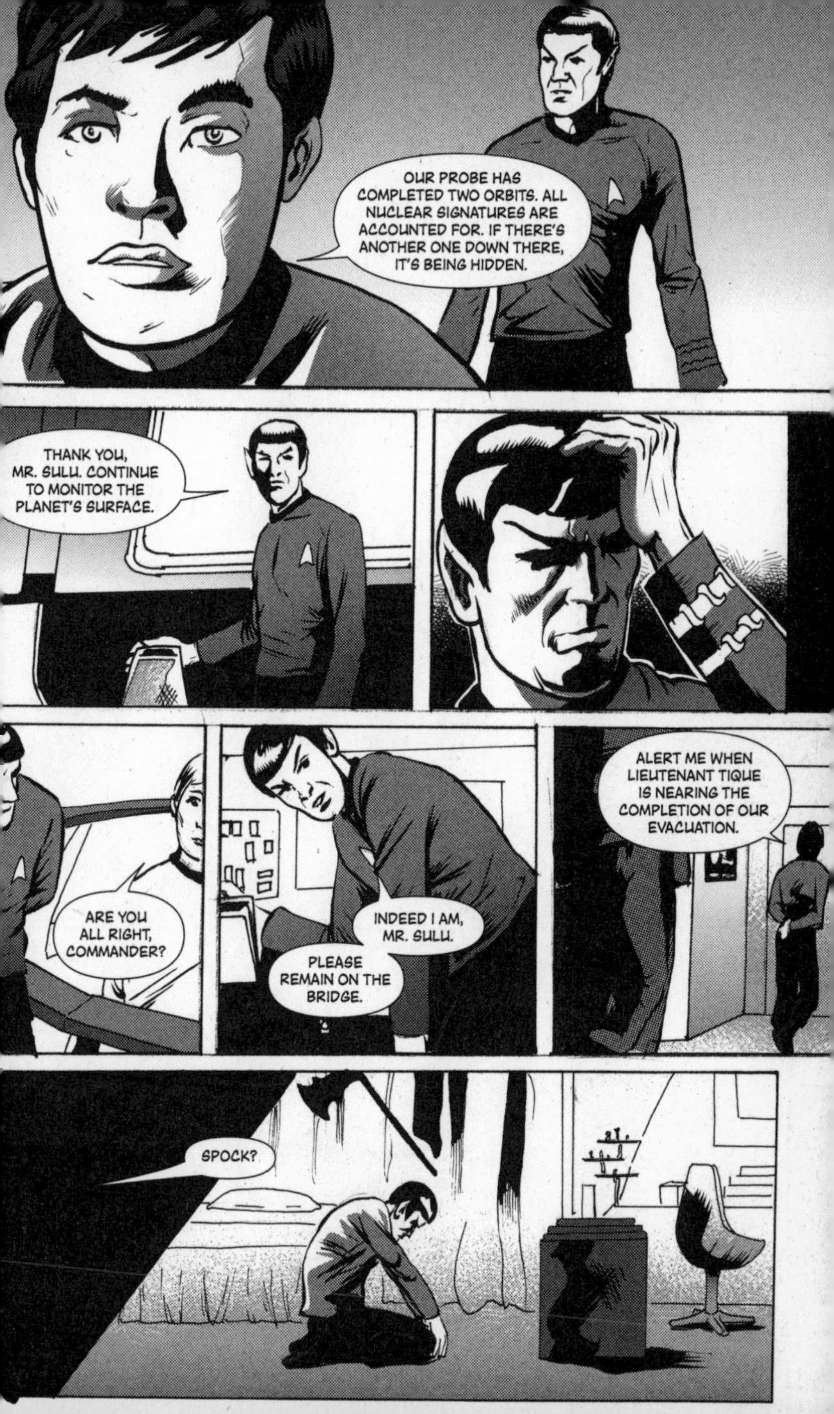
OUR PROBE HAS COMPLETED TWO ORBITS. ALL NUCLEAR SIGNATURES ARE ACCOUNTED FOR. IF THERE'S ANOTHER ONE DOWN THERE, IT'S BEING HIDDEN.
THANK YOU, MR. SULU. CONTINUE TO MONITOR THE PLANET'S SURFACE.
ARE YOU ALL RIGHT, COMMANDER?
INDEED I AM, MR. SULU.
PLEASE REMAIN ON THE BRIDGE.
ALERT ME WHEN LIEUTENANT TIQUE IS NEARING THE COMPLETION OF OUR EVACUATION.
SPOCK?

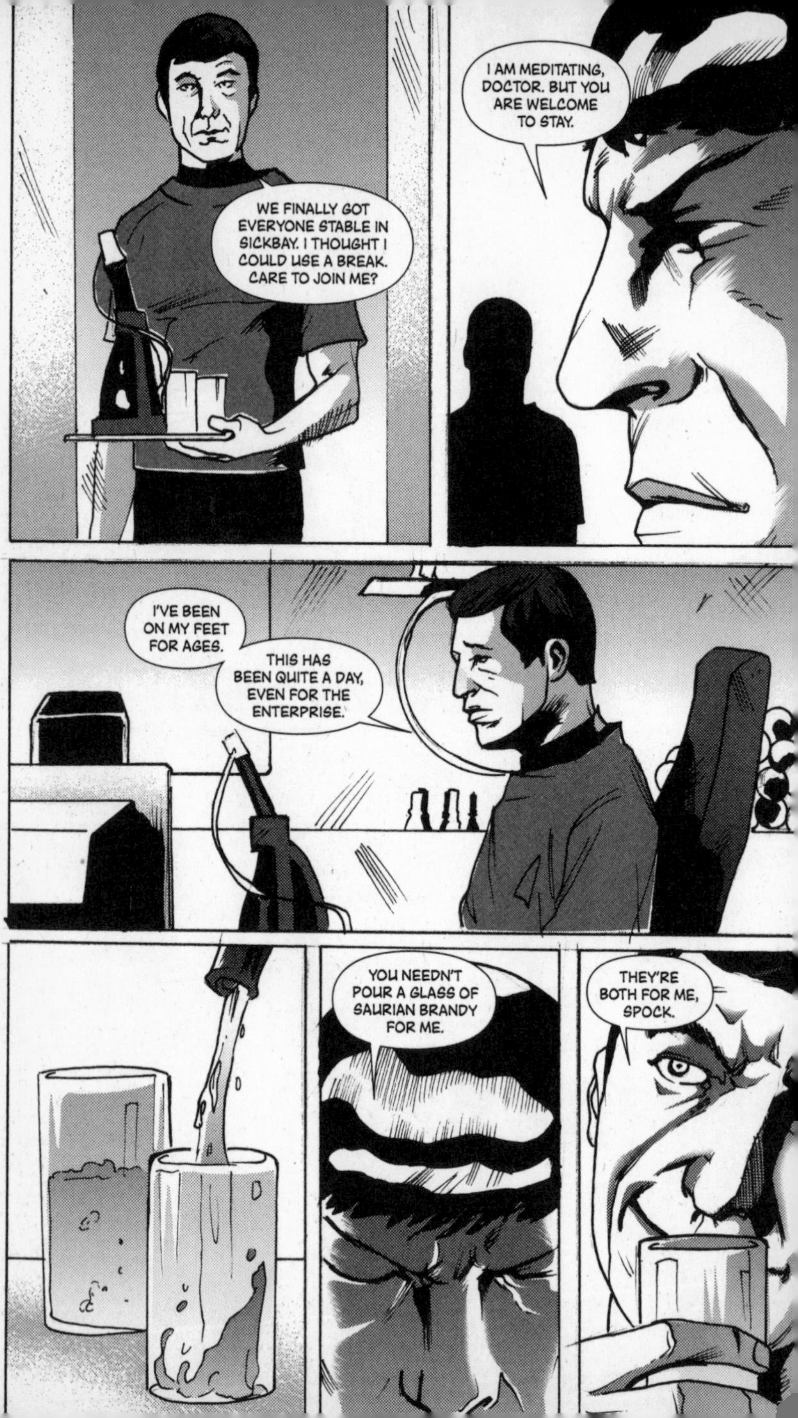
WE FINALLY GOT EVERYONE STABLE IN SICKBAY. I THOUGHT I COULD USE A BREAK. CARE TO JOIN ME?
I AM MEDITATING, DOCTOR. BUT YOU ARE WELCOME TO STAY.
I'VE BEEN ON MY FEET FOR AGES.
THIS HAS BEEN QUITE A DAY, EVEN FOR THE ENTERPRISE.
YOU NEEDN'T POUR A GLASS OF SAURIAN BRANDY FOR ME.
THEY'RE BOTH FOR ME, SPOCK.

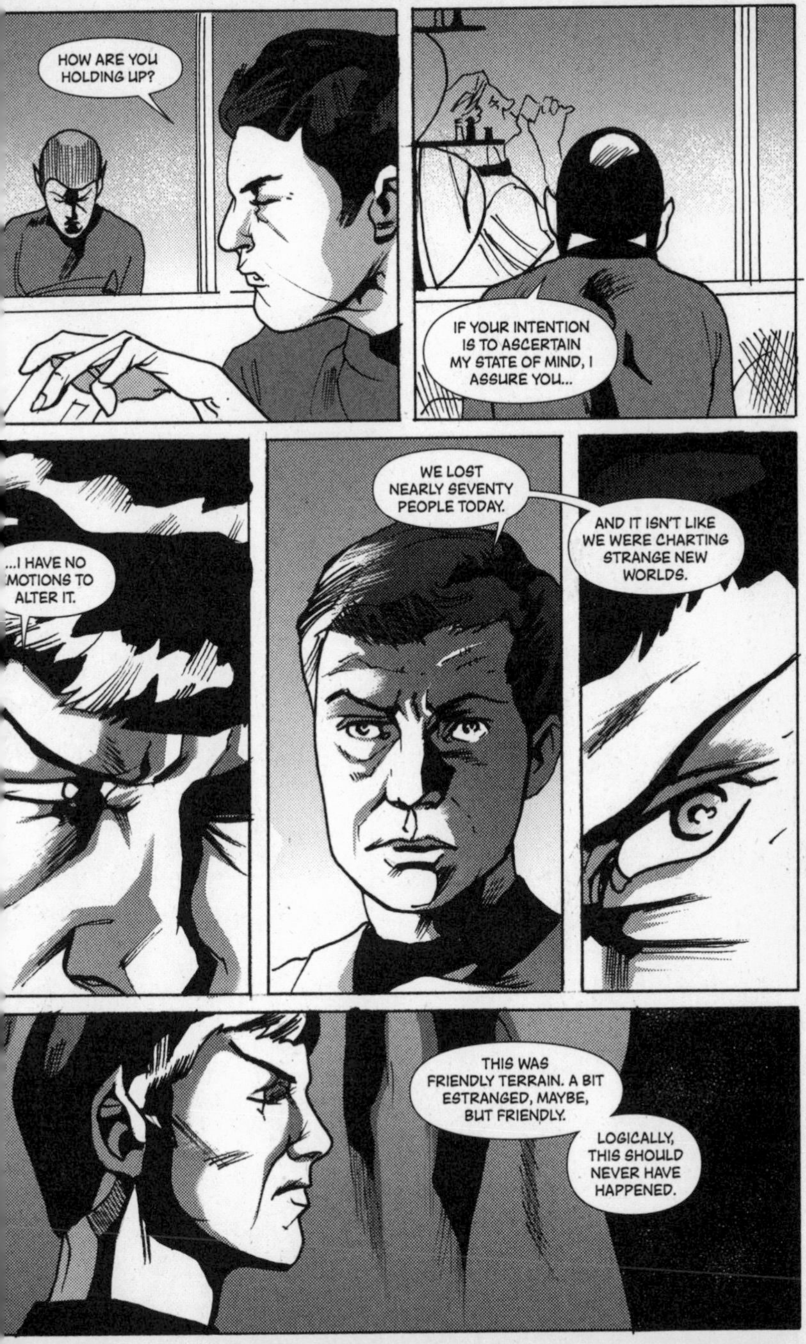
HOW ARE YOU HOLDING UP?
IF YOUR INTENTION IS TO ASCERTAIN MY STATE OF MIND, I ASSURE YOU...
...I HAVE NO EMOTIONS TO ALTER IT.
WE LOST NEARLY SEVENTY PEOPLE TODAY.
AND IT ISN'T LIKE WE WERE CHARTING STRANGE NEW WORLDS.
THIS WAS FRIENDLY TERRAIN. A BIT ESTRANGED, MAYBE, BUT FRIENDLY.
LOGICALLY, THIS SHOULD NEVER HAVE HAPPENED.

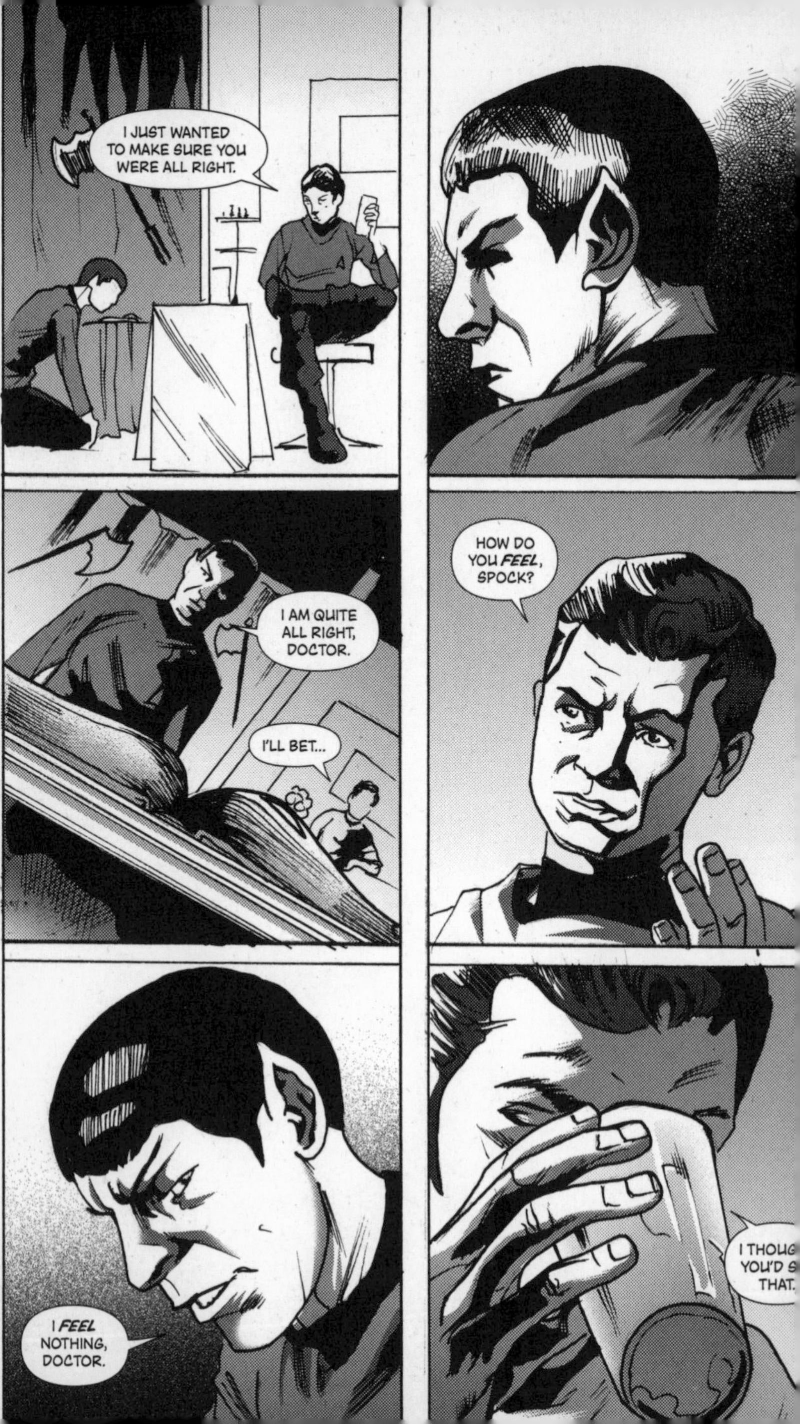
I JUST WANTED TO MAKE SURE YOU WERE ALL RIGHT.
I AM QUITE ALL RIGHT, DOCTOR.
I'LL BET...
HOW DO YOU *FEEL*, SPOCK?
I *FEEL* NOTHING, DOCTOR.
I THOUG YOU'D S THAT.

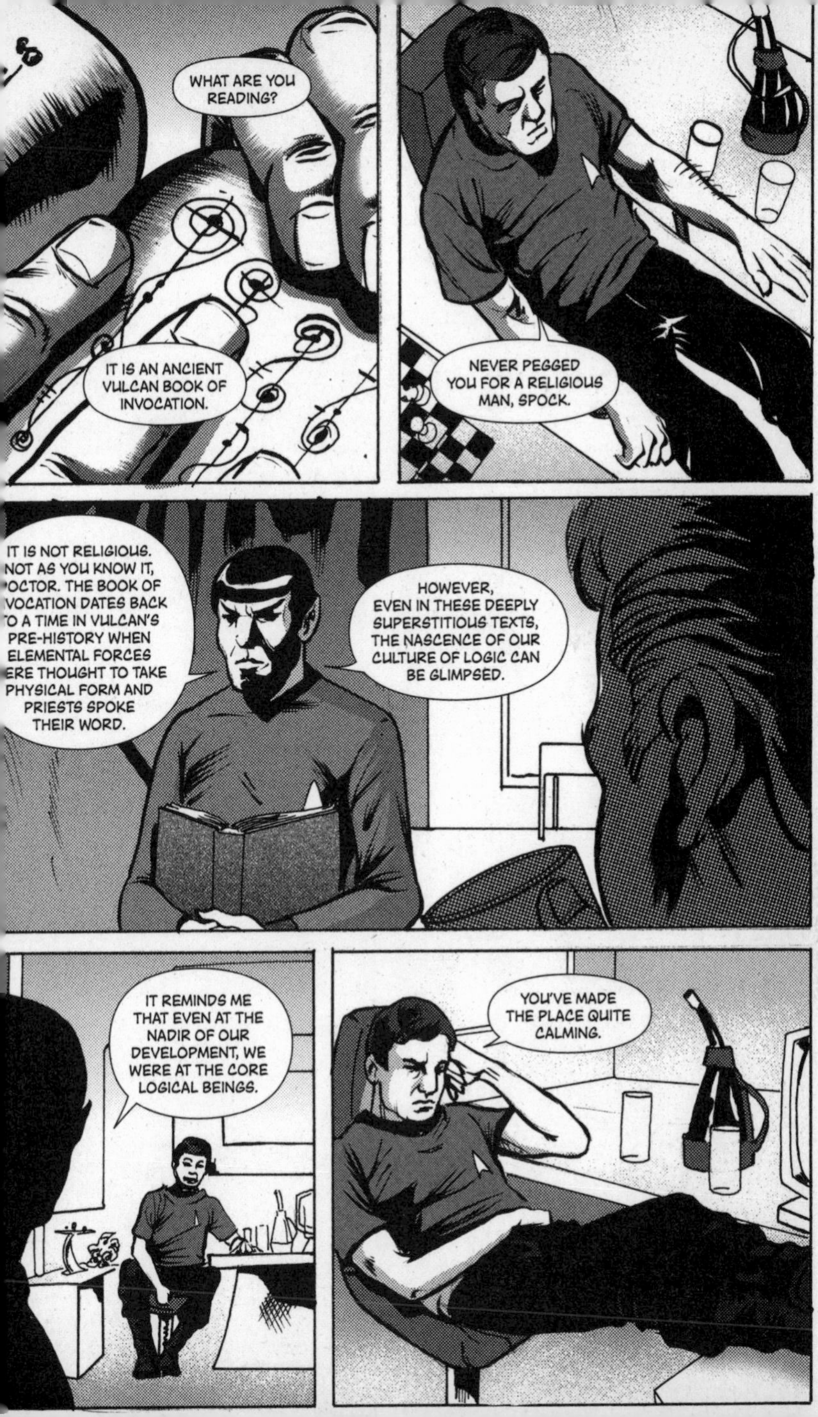
WHAT ARE YOU READING?
IT IS AN ANCIENT VULCAN BOOK OF INVOCATION.
NEVER PEGGED YOU FOR A RELIGIOUS MAN, SPOCK.
IT IS NOT RELIGIOUS. NOT AS YOU KNOW IT, OCTOR. THE BOOK OF VOCATION DATES BACK O A TIME IN VULCAN'S PRE-HISTORY WHEN ELEMENTAL FORCES ERE THOUGHT TO TAKE PHYSICAL FORM AND PRIESTS SPOKE THEIR WORD.
HOWEVER, EVEN IN THESE DEEPLY SUPERSTITIOUS TEXTS, THE NASCENCE OF OUR CULTURE OF LOGIC CAN BE GLIMPSED.
IT REMINDS ME THAT EVEN AT THE NADIR OF OUR DEVELOPMENT, WE WERE AT THE CORE LOGICAL BEINGS.
YOU'VE MADE THE PLACE QUITE CALMING.

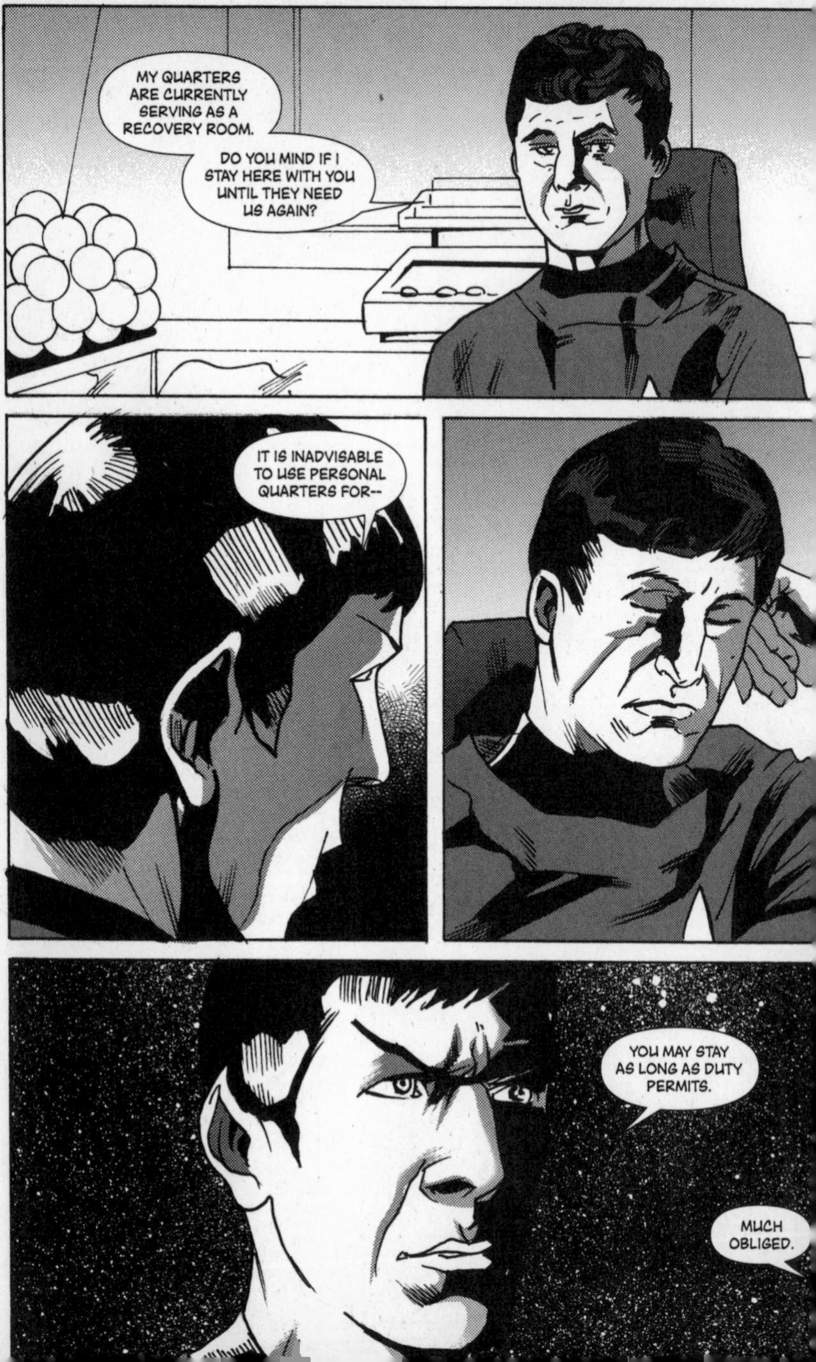
MY QUARTERS ARE CURRENTLY SERVING AS A RECOVERY ROOM.
DO YOU MIND IF I STAY HERE WITH YOU UNTIL THEY NEED US AGAIN?
IT IS INADVISABLE TO USE PERSONAL QUARTERS FOR--
YOU MAY STAY AS LONG AS DUTY PERMITS.
MUCH OBLIGED.

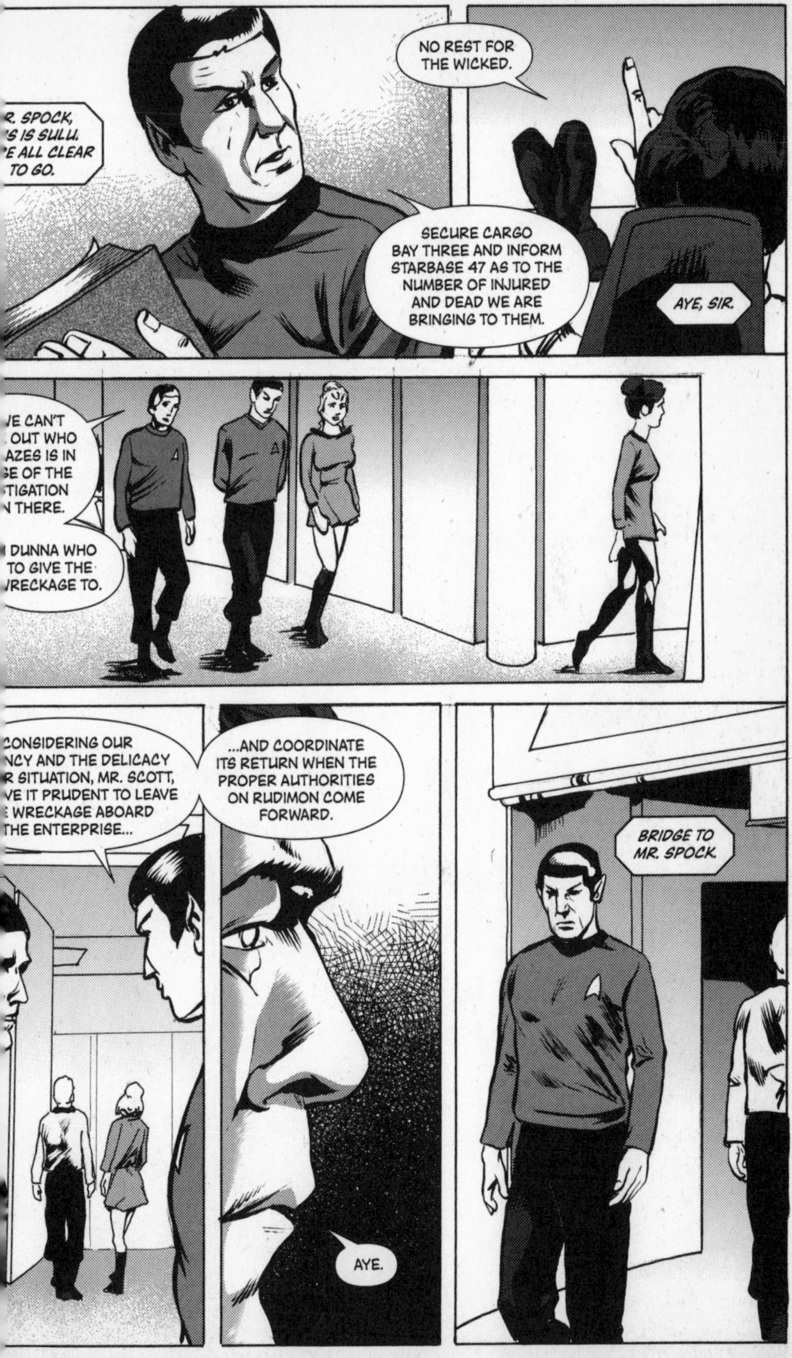
R. SPOCK, 'S IS SULU. 'E ALL CLEAR TO GO.
NO REST FOR THE WICKED.
SECURE CARGO BAY THREE AND INFORM STARBASE 47 AS TO THE NUMBER OF INJURED AND DEAD WE ARE BRINGING TO THEM.
AYE, SIR.
VE CAN'T OUT WHO AZES IS IN GE OF THE TIGATION N THERE.
DUNNA WHO TO GIVE THE VRECKAGE TO.
CONSIDERING OUR NCY AND THE DELICACY R SITUATION, MR. SCOTT, VE IT PRUDENT TO LEAVE WRECKAGE ABOARD THE ENTERPRISE...
...AND COORDINATE ITS RETURN WHEN THE PROPER AUTHORITIES ON RUDIMON COME FORWARD.
AYE.
BRIDGE TO MR. SPOCK.

SPOCK HERE.

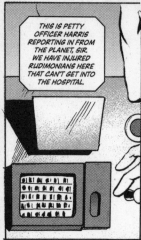

THIS IS PETTY OFFICER HARRIS REPORTING IN FROM THE PLANET, SIR. WE HAVE INJURED RUDIMONIANS HERE THAT CAN'T GET INTO THE HOSPITAL.

PRIORITIZE THE ENTERPRISE CRE PETTY OFFICER HARRIS.

WE WILL DEPART FOR STARBASE 47 AS SOON AS THE EVACUATION IS COMPLETE.

HOWEVER, COORDINATE WITH DR. MCCOY TO LEAVE ON RUDIMON ALL MEDICAL SUPPLIES THAT THE ENTERPRISE CAN AFFORD TO SPARE.

YES, SIR.

I'LL RETURN TO THE PLANET T ADDRESS THE GOVERNOR.

COMMANDER...

...GOVERNOR LAISU WAS KILLED IN THE BLAST.

ACKNOWLEDGED.

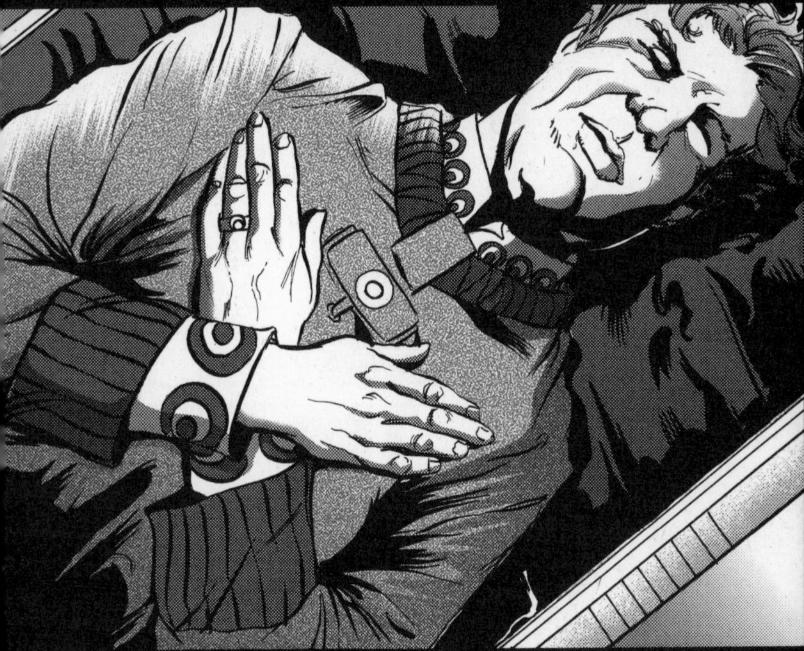

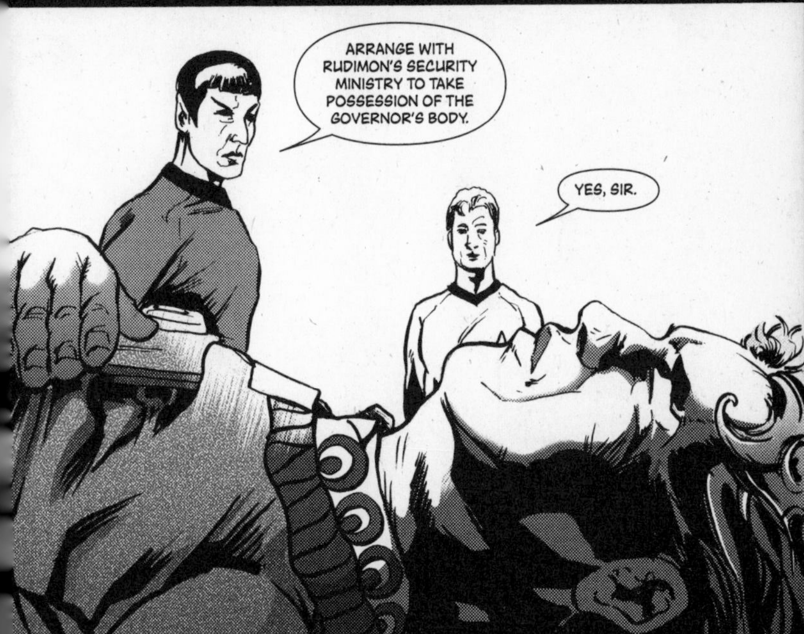
ARRANGE WITH RUDIMON'S SECURITY MINISTRY TO TAKE POSSESSION OF THE GOVERNOR'S BODY.
YES, SIR.

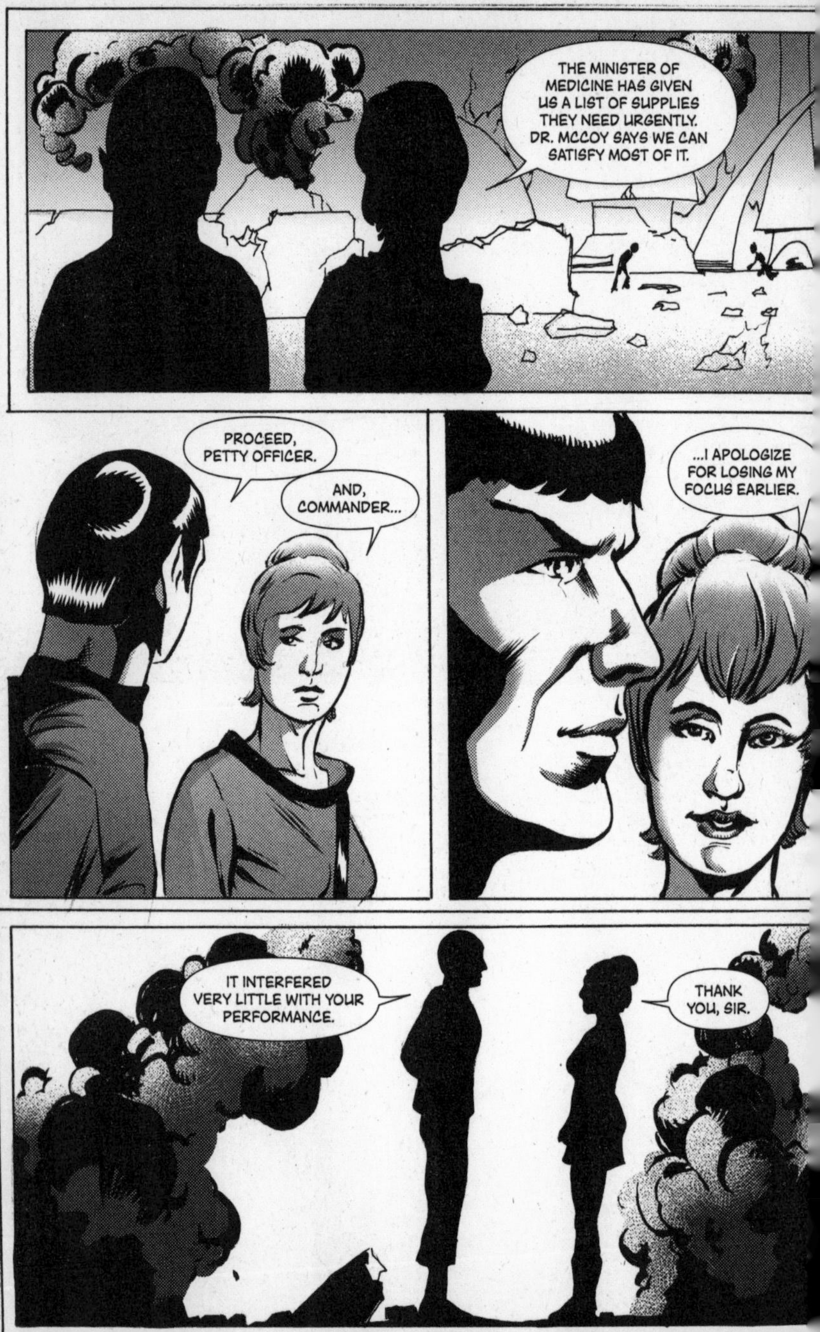
THE MINISTER OF MEDICINE HAS GIVEN US A LIST OF SUPPLIES THEY NEED URGENTLY. DR. MCCOY SAYS WE CAN SATISFY MOST OF IT.
PROCEED, PETTY OFFICER.
AND, COMMANDER...
...I APOLOGIZE FOR LOSING MY FOCUS EARLIER.
IT INTERFERED VERY LITTLE WITH YOUR PERFORMANCE.
THANK YOU, SIR.

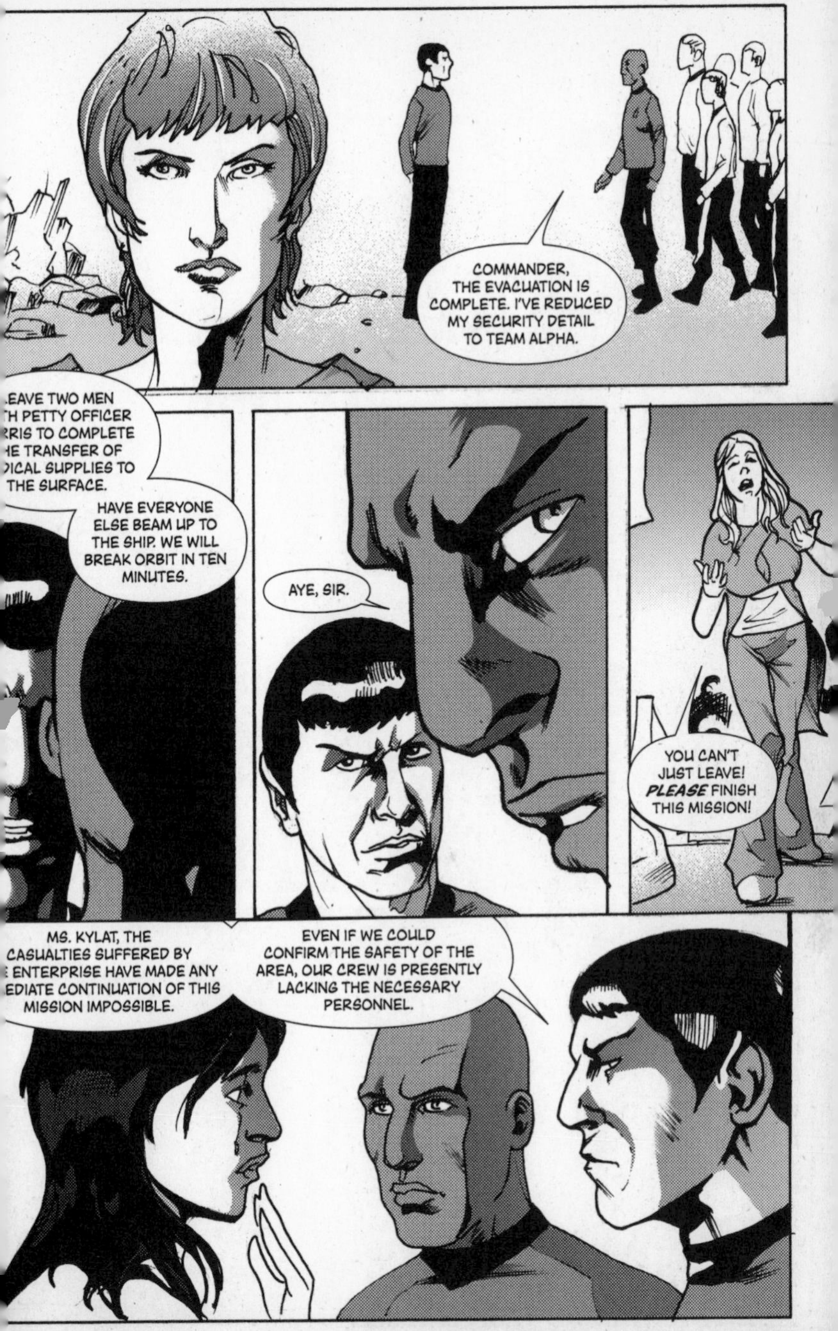
COMMANDER, THE EVACUATION IS COMPLETE. I'VE REDUCED MY SECURITY DETAIL TO TEAM ALPHA.
EAVE TWO MEN TH PETTY OFFICER RRIS TO COMPLETE HE TRANSFER OF DICAL SUPPLIES TO THE SURFACE.
HAVE EVERYONE ELSE BEAM UP TO THE SHIP. WE WILL BREAK ORBIT IN TEN MINUTES.
AYE, SIR.
YOU CAN'T JUST LEAVE! ***PLEASE*** FINISH THIS MISSION!
MS. KYLAT, THE CASUALTIES SUFFERED BY E ENTERPRISE HAVE MADE ANY EDIATE CONTINUATION OF THIS MISSION IMPOSSIBLE.
EVEN IF WE COULD CONFIRM THE SAFETY OF THE AREA, OUR CREW IS PRESENTLY LACKING THE NECESSARY PERSONNEL.

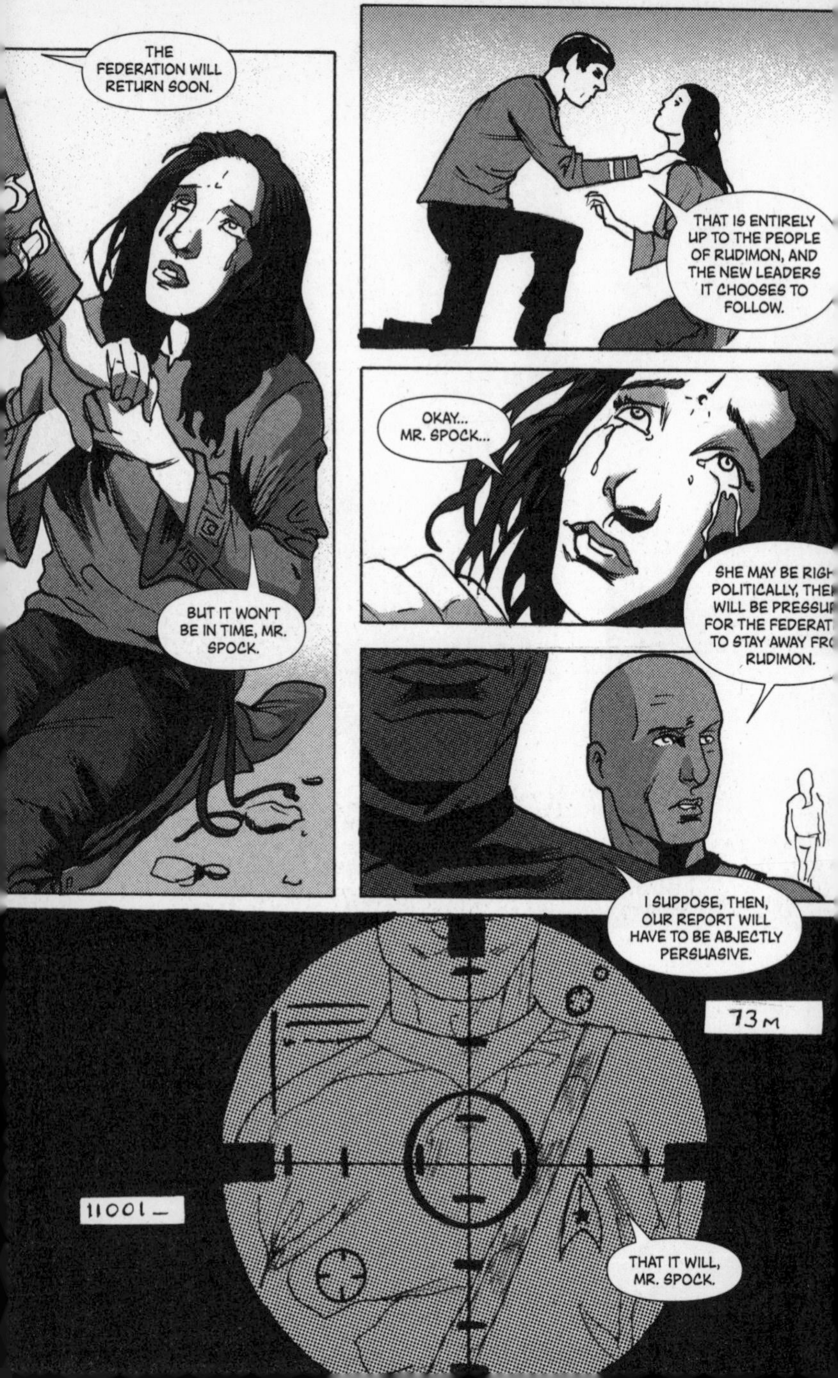
THE FEDERATION WILL RETURN SOON.
BUT IT WON'T BE IN TIME, MR. SPOCK.
THAT IS ENTIRELY UP TO THE PEOPLE OF RUDIMON, AND THE NEW LEADERS IT CHOOSES TO FOLLOW.
OKAY... MR. SPOCK...
SHE MAY BE RIGH POLITICALLY, THE WILL BE PRESSU FOR THE FEDERAT TO STAY AWAY FR RUDIMON.
I SUPPOSE, THEN, OUR REPORT WILL HAVE TO BE ABJECTLY PERSUASIVE.
73 M
11001_
THAT IT WILL, MR. SPOCK.

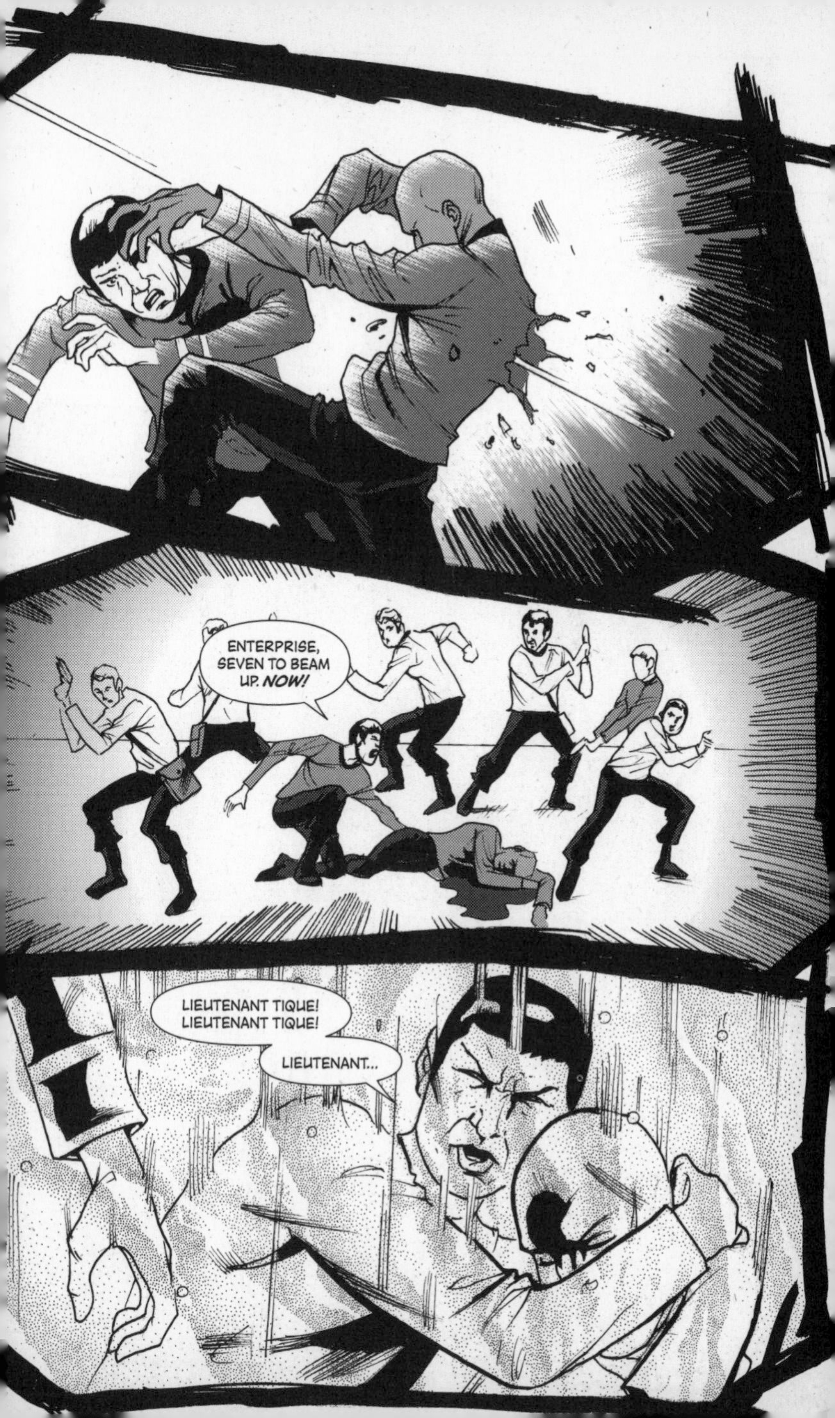

ENTERPRISE, SEVEN TO BEAM UP. *NOW!*
LIEUTENANT TIQUE! LIEUTENANT TIQUE!
LIEUTENANT...

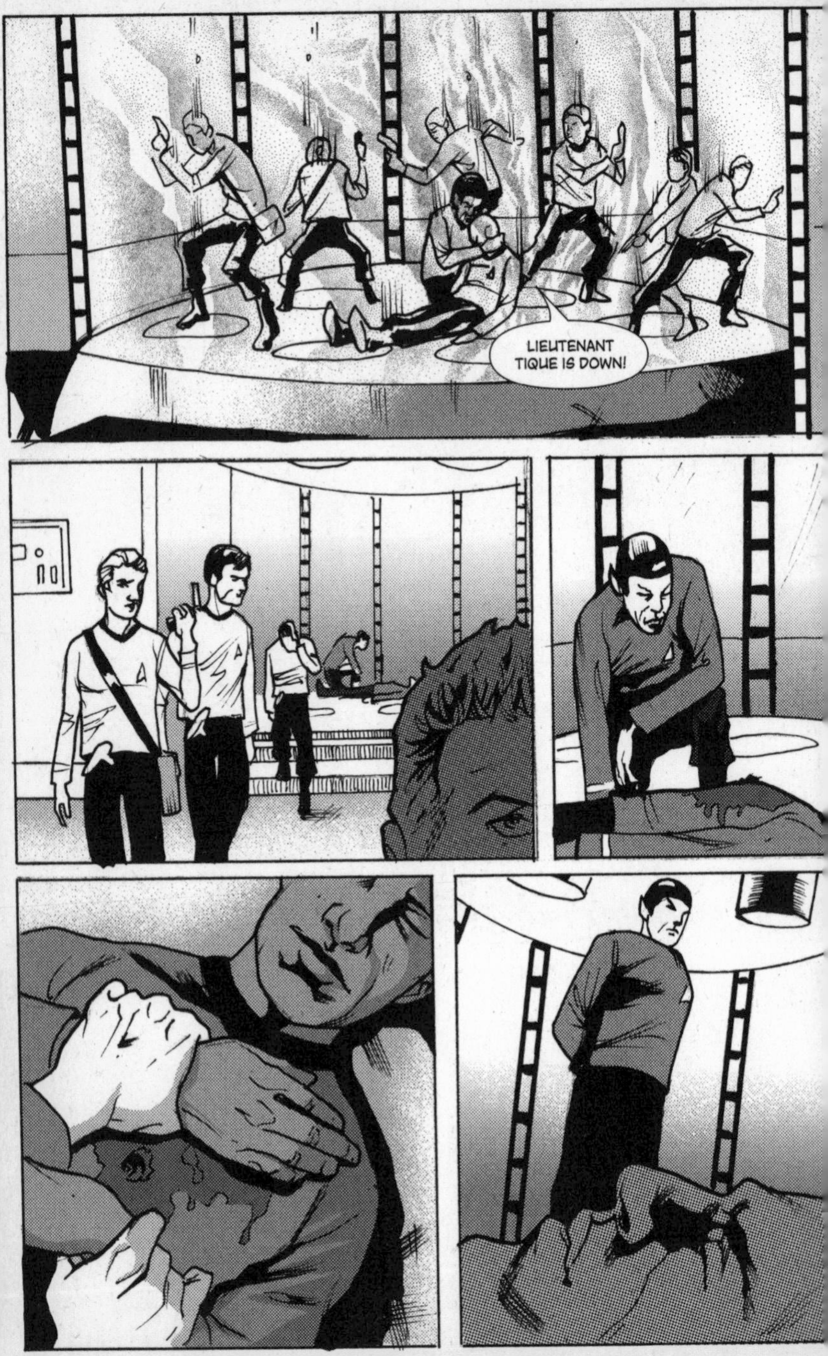
LIEUTENANT TIQUE IS DOWN!

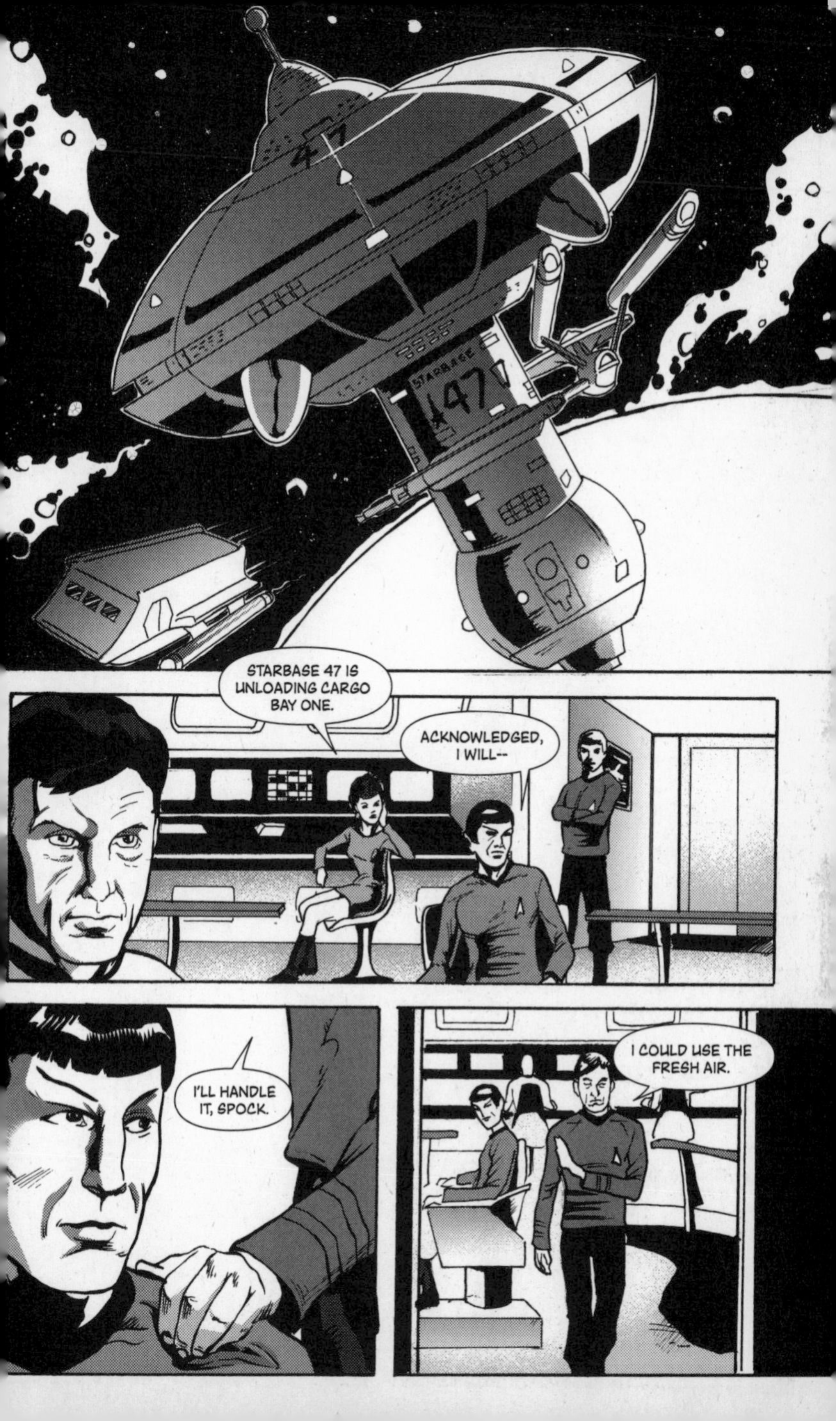
STARBASE 47
STARBASE 47 IS UNLOADING CARGO BAY ONE.
ACKNOWLEDGED, I WILL--
I'LL HANDLE IT, SPOCK.
I COULD USE THE FRESH AIR.

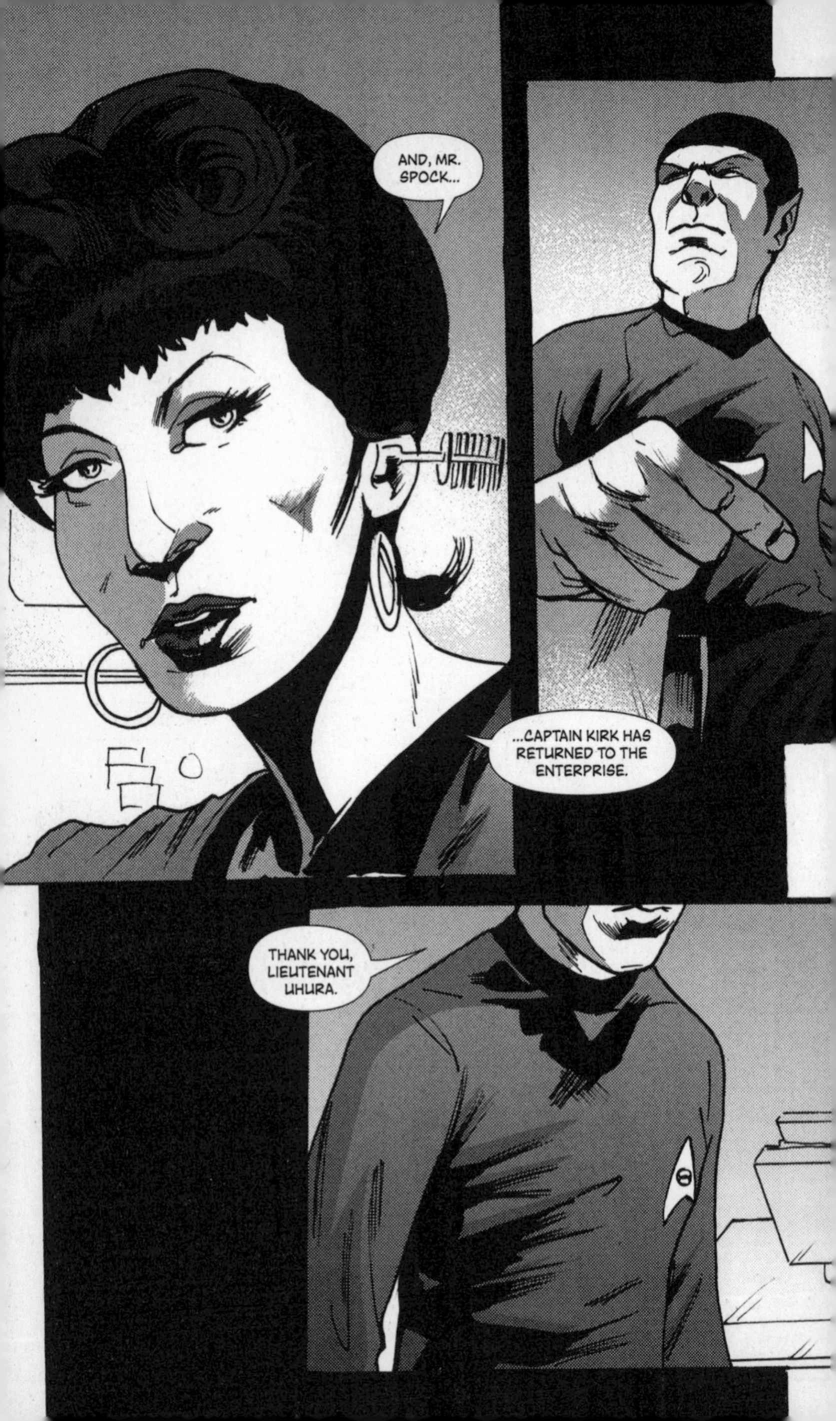
AND, MR. SPOCK...
...CAPTAIN KIRK HAS RETURNED TO THE ENTERPRISE.
THANK YOU, LIEUTENANT UHURA.

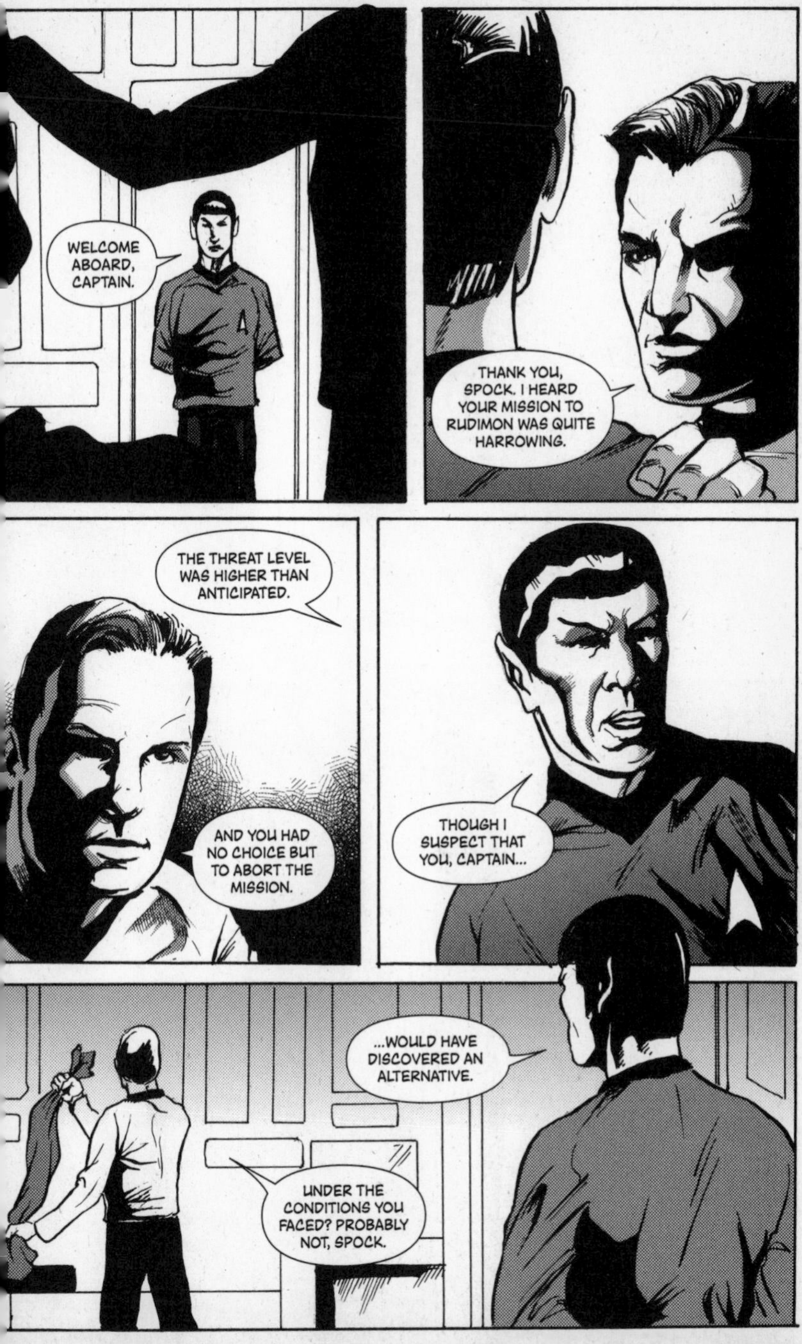
WELCOME ABOARD, CAPTAIN.
THANK YOU, SPOCK. I HEARD YOUR MISSION TO RUDIMON WAS QUITE HARROWING.
THE THREAT LEVEL WAS HIGHER THAN ANTICIPATED.
AND YOU HAD NO CHOICE BUT TO ABORT THE MISSION.
THOUGH I SUSPECT THAT YOU, CAPTAIN...
...WOULD HAVE DISCOVERED AN ALTERNATIVE.
UNDER THE CONDITIONS YOU FACED? PROBABLY NOT, SPOCK.

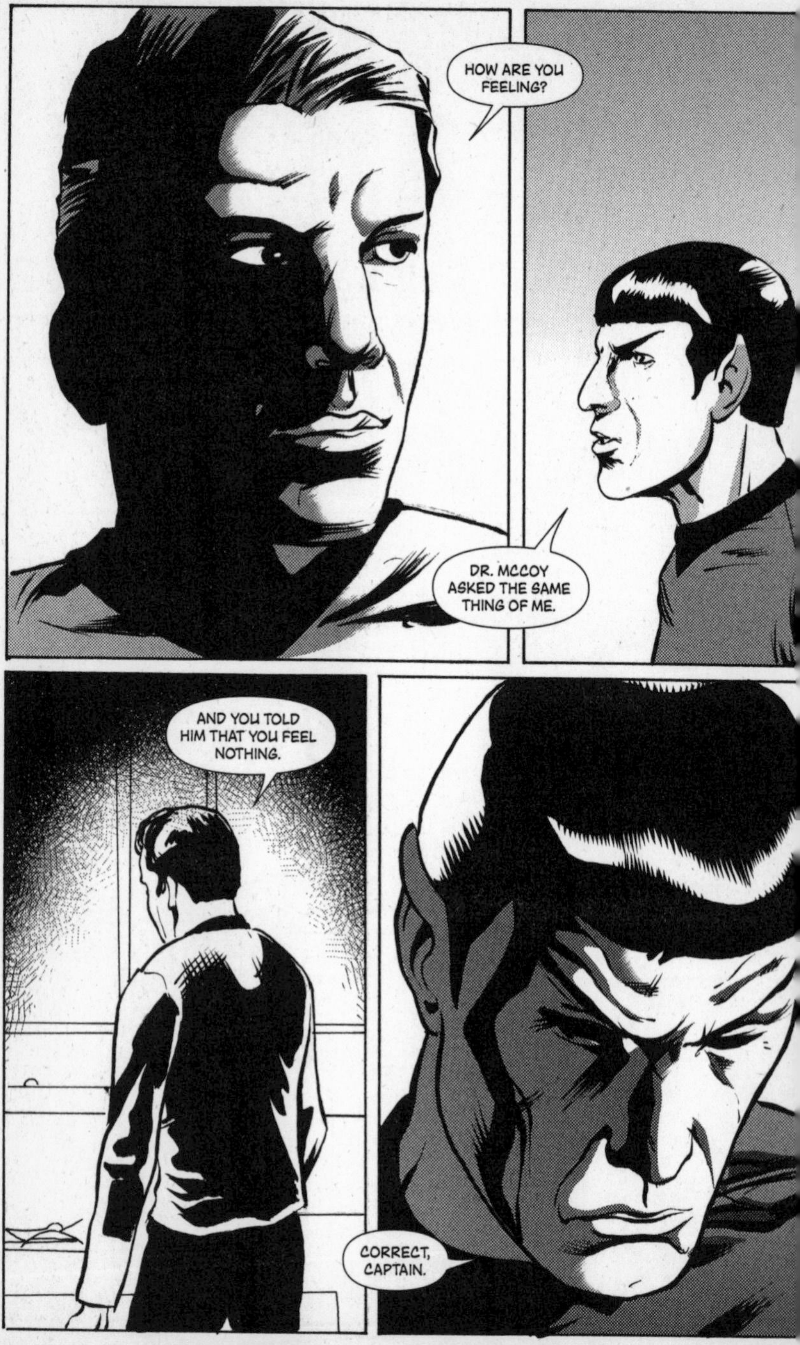
HOW ARE YOU FEELING?
DR. MCCOY ASKED THE SAME THING OF ME.
AND YOU TOLD HIM THAT YOU FEEL NOTHING.
CORRECT, CAPTAIN.

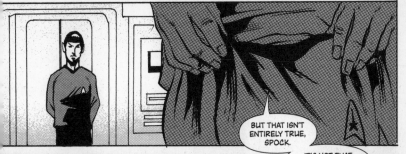

BUT THAT ISN'T ENTIRELY TRUE, SPOCK.

IT'S NOT THAT VULCANS HAVE NO EMOTIONS...

IT'S THAT YOUR EMOTIONS DON'T CONTROL YOU, AS THEY DO HUMANS MUCH OF THE TIME.

IS THAT CORRECT?

THAT IS CORRECT, CAPTAIN.

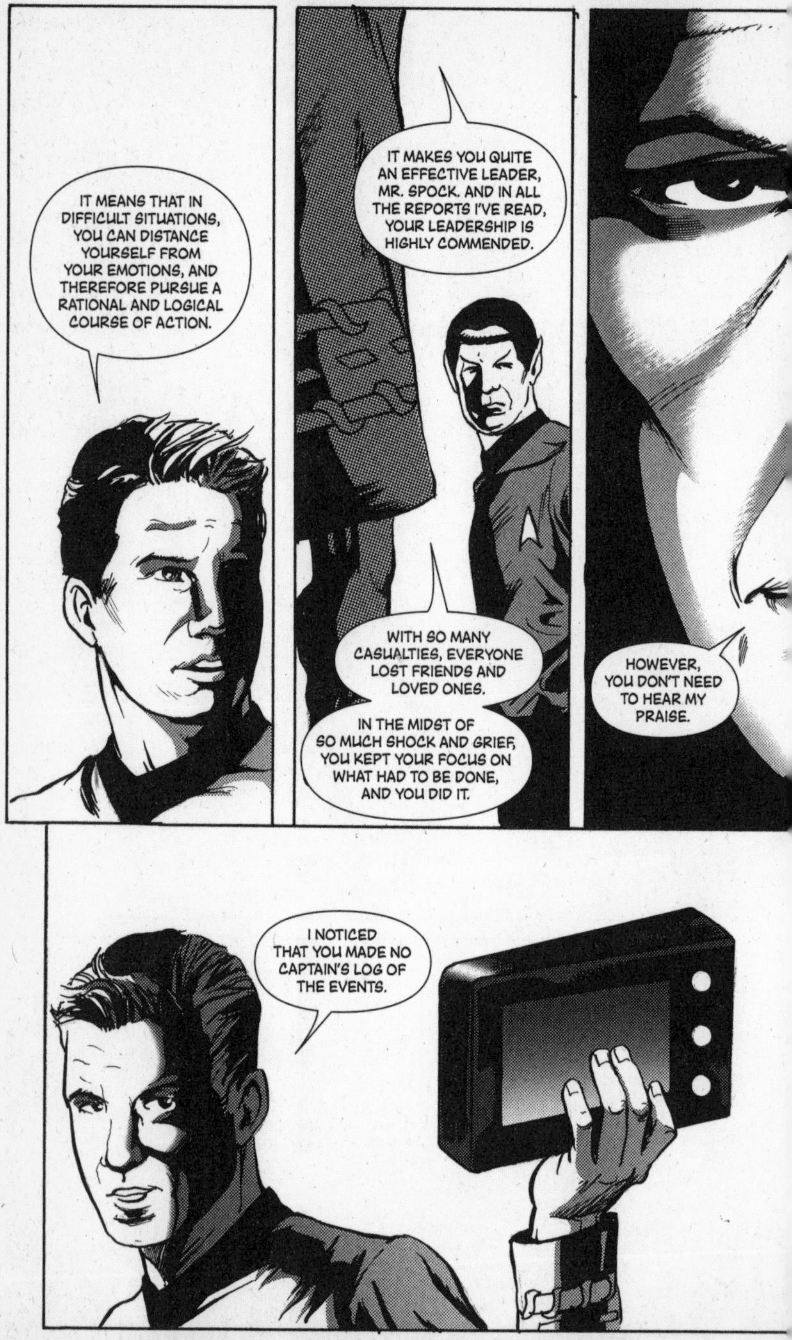
IT MEANS THAT IN DIFFICULT SITUATIONS, YOU CAN DISTANCE YOURSELF FROM YOUR EMOTIONS, AND THEREFORE PURSUE A RATIONAL AND LOGICAL COURSE OF ACTION.
IT MAKES YOU QUITE AN EFFECTIVE LEADER, MR. SPOCK. AND IN ALL THE REPORTS I'VE READ, YOUR LEADERSHIP IS HIGHLY COMMENDED.
WITH SO MANY CASUALTIES, EVERYONE LOST FRIENDS AND LOVED ONES.
IN THE MIDST OF SO MUCH SHOCK AND GRIEF, YOU KEPT YOUR FOCUS ON WHAT HAD TO BE DONE, AND YOU DID IT.
HOWEVER, YOU DON'T NEED TO HEAR MY PRAISE.
I NOTICED THAT YOU MADE NO CAPTAIN'S LOG OF THE EVENTS.

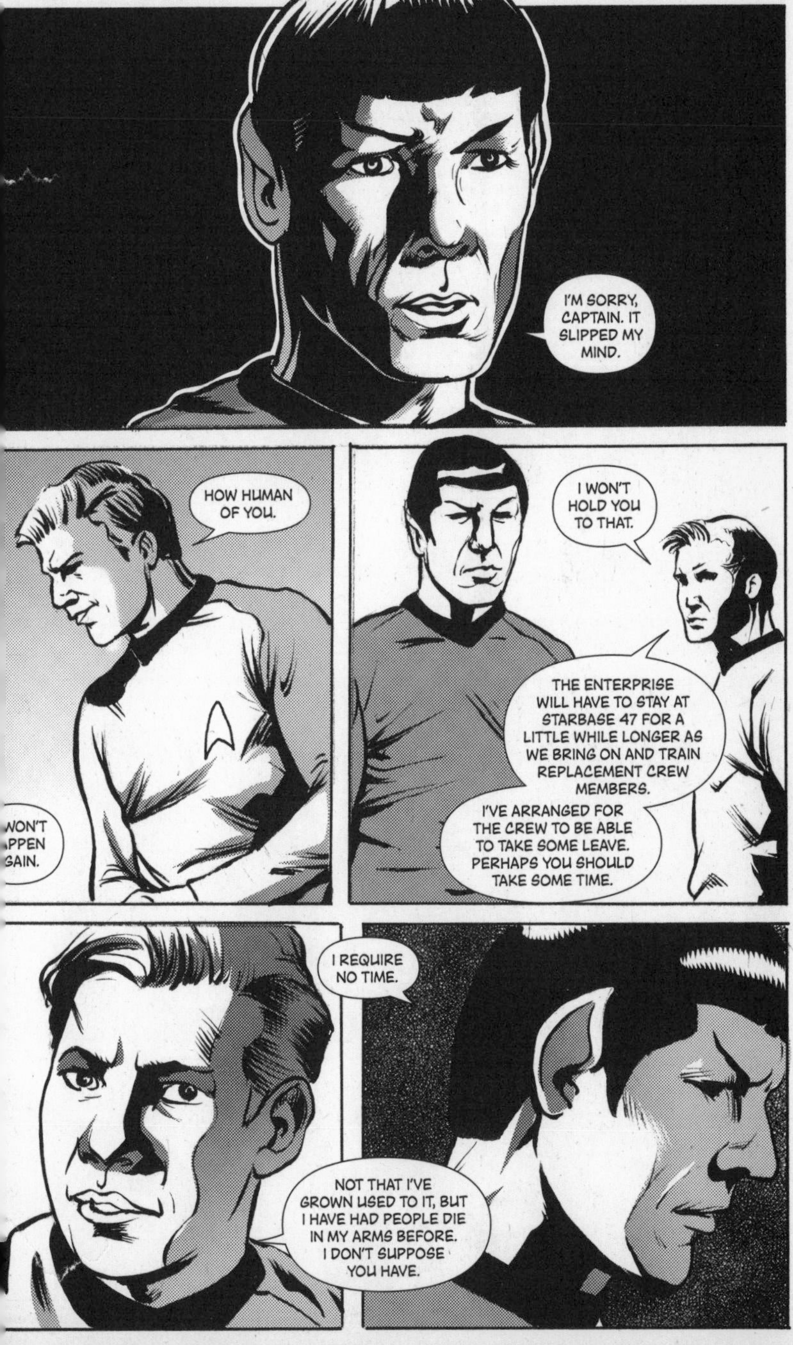

I'M SORRY, CAPTAIN. IT SLIPPED MY MIND.
HOW HUMAN OF YOU.
WON'T PPEN GAIN.
I WON'T HOLD YOU TO THAT.
THE ENTERPRISE WILL HAVE TO STAY AT STARBASE 47 FOR A LITTLE WHILE LONGER AS WE BRING ON AND TRAIN REPLACEMENT CREW MEMBERS.
I'VE ARRANGED FOR THE CREW TO BE ABLE TO TAKE SOME LEAVE. PERHAPS YOU SHOULD TAKE SOME TIME.
I REQUIRE NO TIME.
NOT THAT I'VE GROWN USED TO IT, BUT I HAVE HAD PEOPLE DIE IN MY ARMS BEFORE. I DON'T SUPPOSE YOU HAVE.

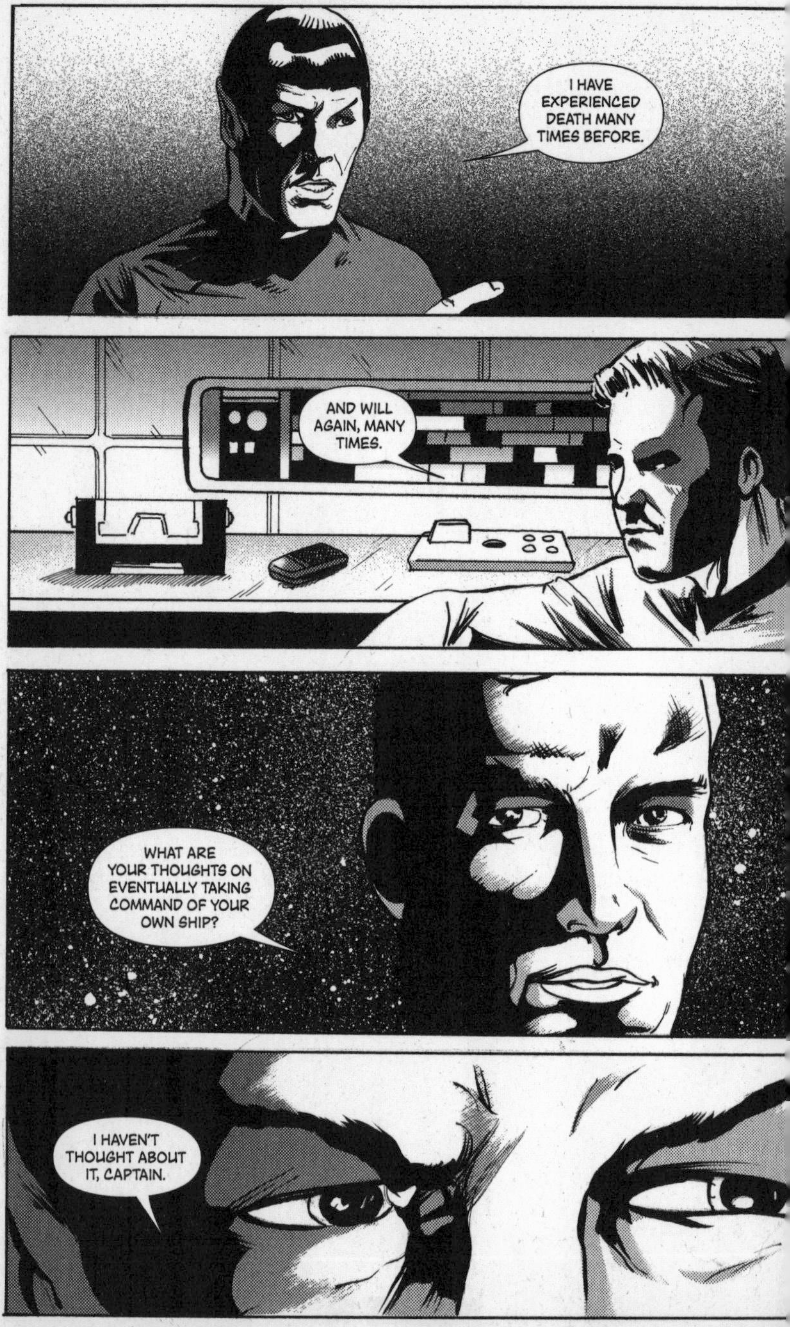
I HAVE EXPERIENCED DEATH MANY TIMES BEFORE.
AND WILL AGAIN, MANY TIMES.
WHAT ARE YOUR THOUGHTS ON EVENTUALLY TAKING COMMAND OF YOUR OWN SHIP?
I HAVEN'T THOUGHT ABOUT IT, CAPTAIN.

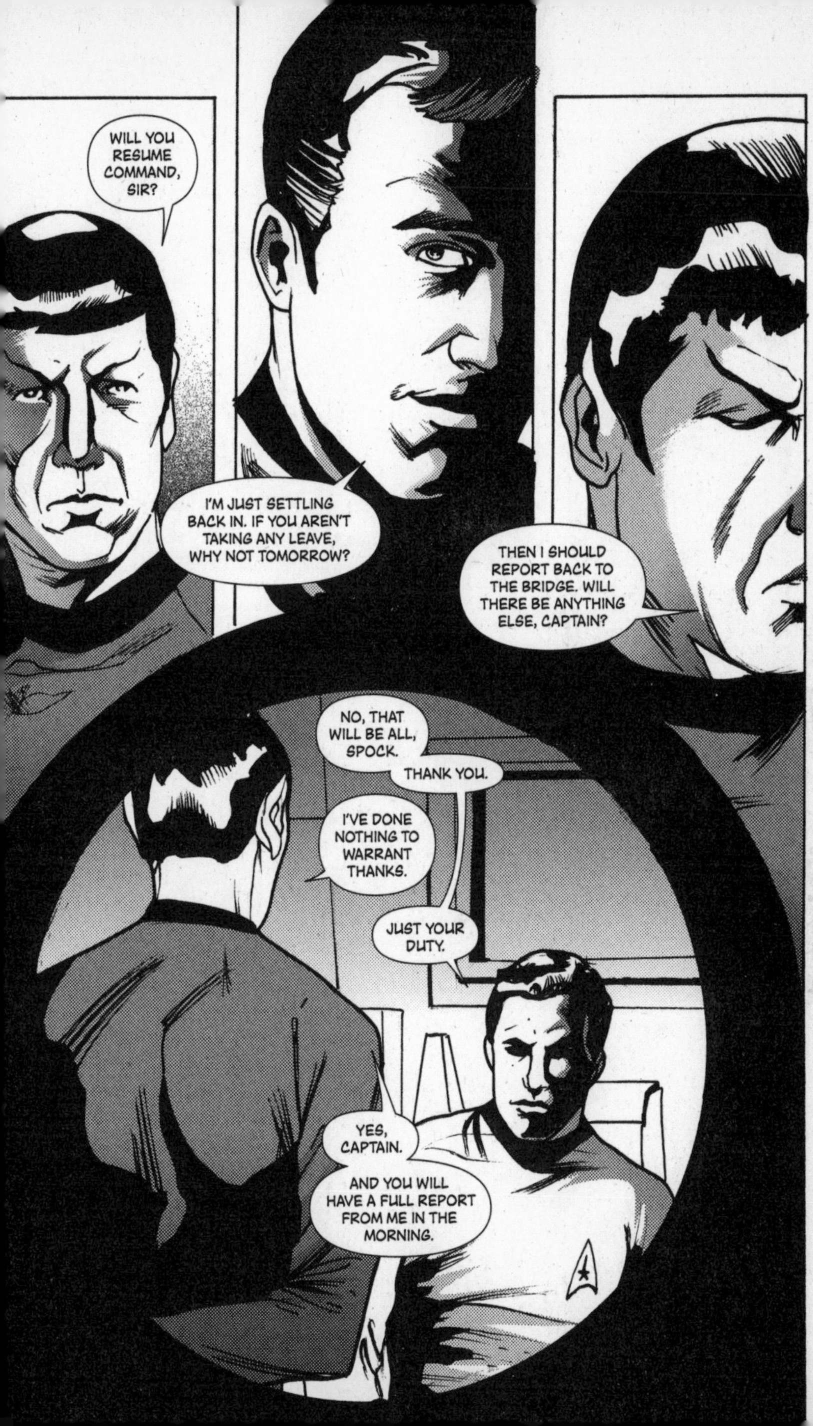
WILL YOU RESUME COMMAND, SIR?
I'M JUST SETTLING BACK IN. IF YOU AREN'T TAKING ANY LEAVE, WHY NOT TOMORROW?
THEN I SHOULD REPORT BACK TO THE BRIDGE. WILL THERE BE ANYTHING ELSE, CAPTAIN?
NO, THAT WILL BE ALL, SPOCK.
THANK YOU.
I'VE DONE NOTHING TO WARRANT THANKS.
JUST YOUR DUTY.
YES, CAPTAIN.
AND YOU WILL HAVE A FULL REPORT FROM ME IN THE MORNING.

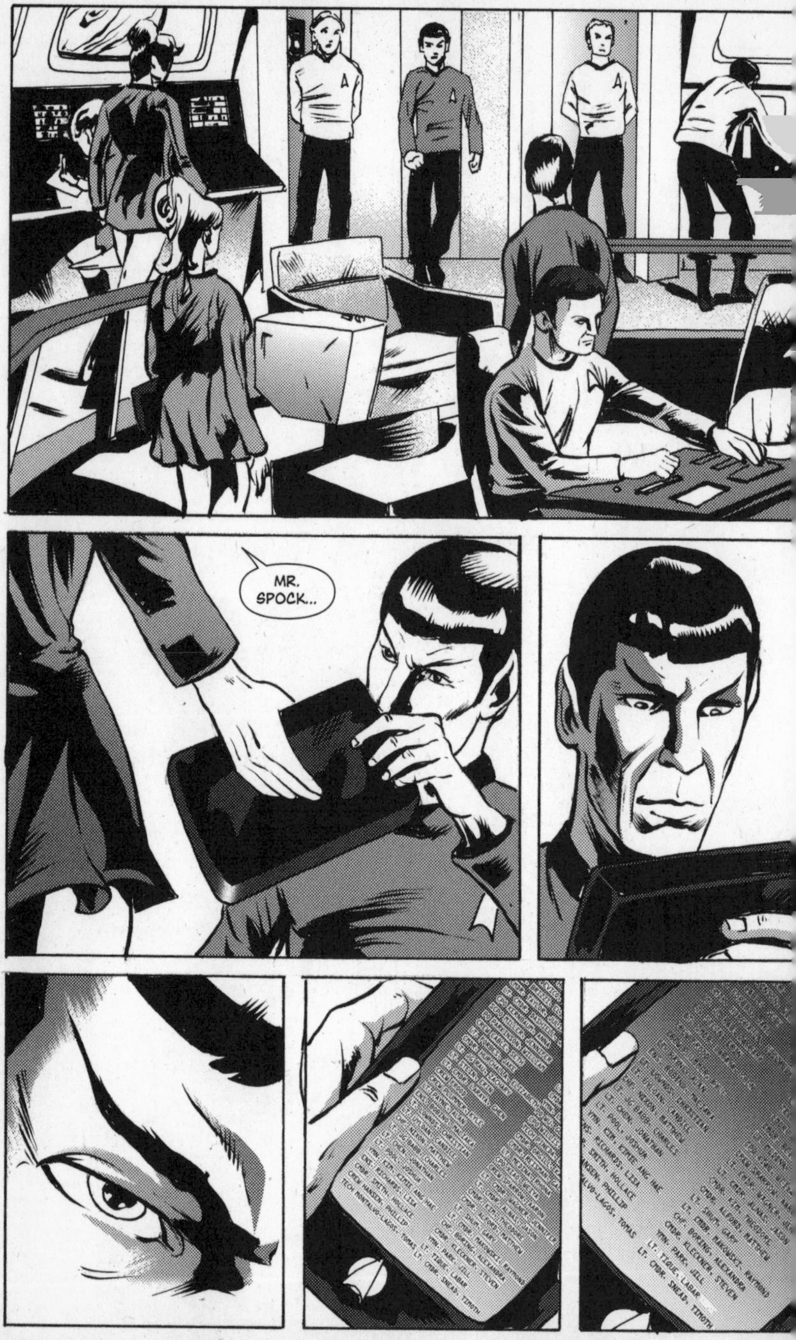
MR. SPOCK...

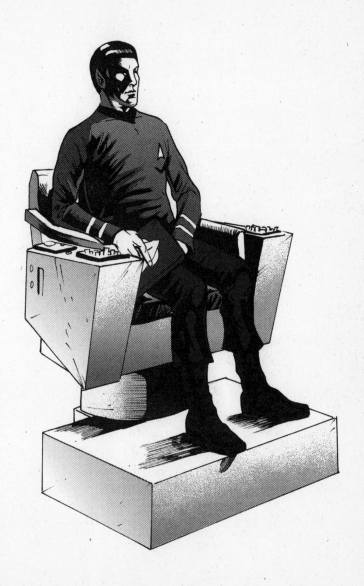

INALIENABLE RIGHTS

STORY BY NATHANIEL BOWDEN
PENCILS AND INKS BY HEIDI ARNHOLD
TONES BY DOMINIC PRESTERA

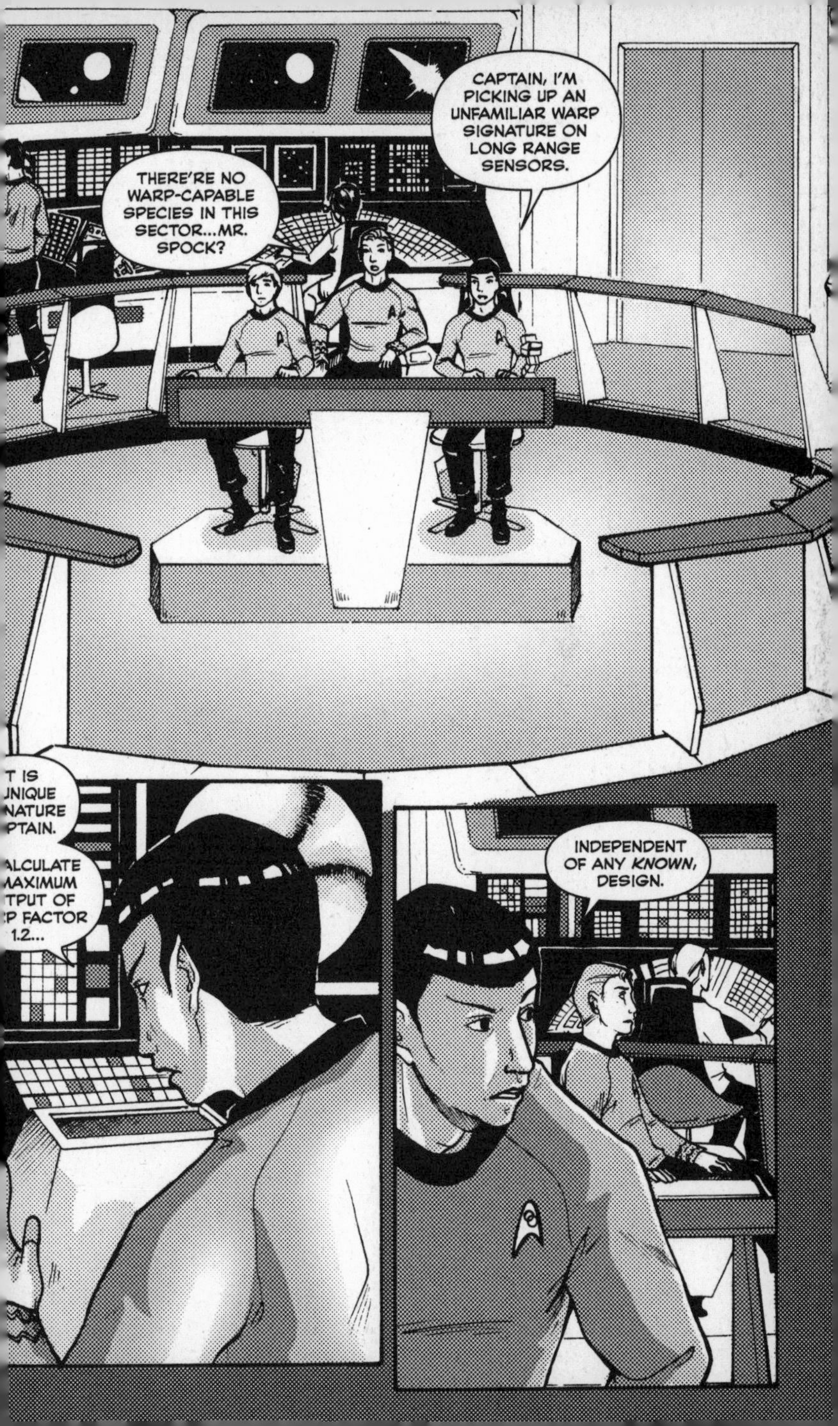
THERE'RE NO WARP-CAPABLE SPECIES IN THIS SECTOR...MR. SPOCK?
CAPTAIN, I'M PICKING UP AN UNFAMILIAR WARP SIGNATURE ON LONG RANGE SENSORS.
T IS UNIQUE NATURE PTAIN.
ALCULATE MAXIMUM TPUT OF P FACTOR 1.2...
INDEPENDENT OF ANY *KNOWN*, DESIGN.

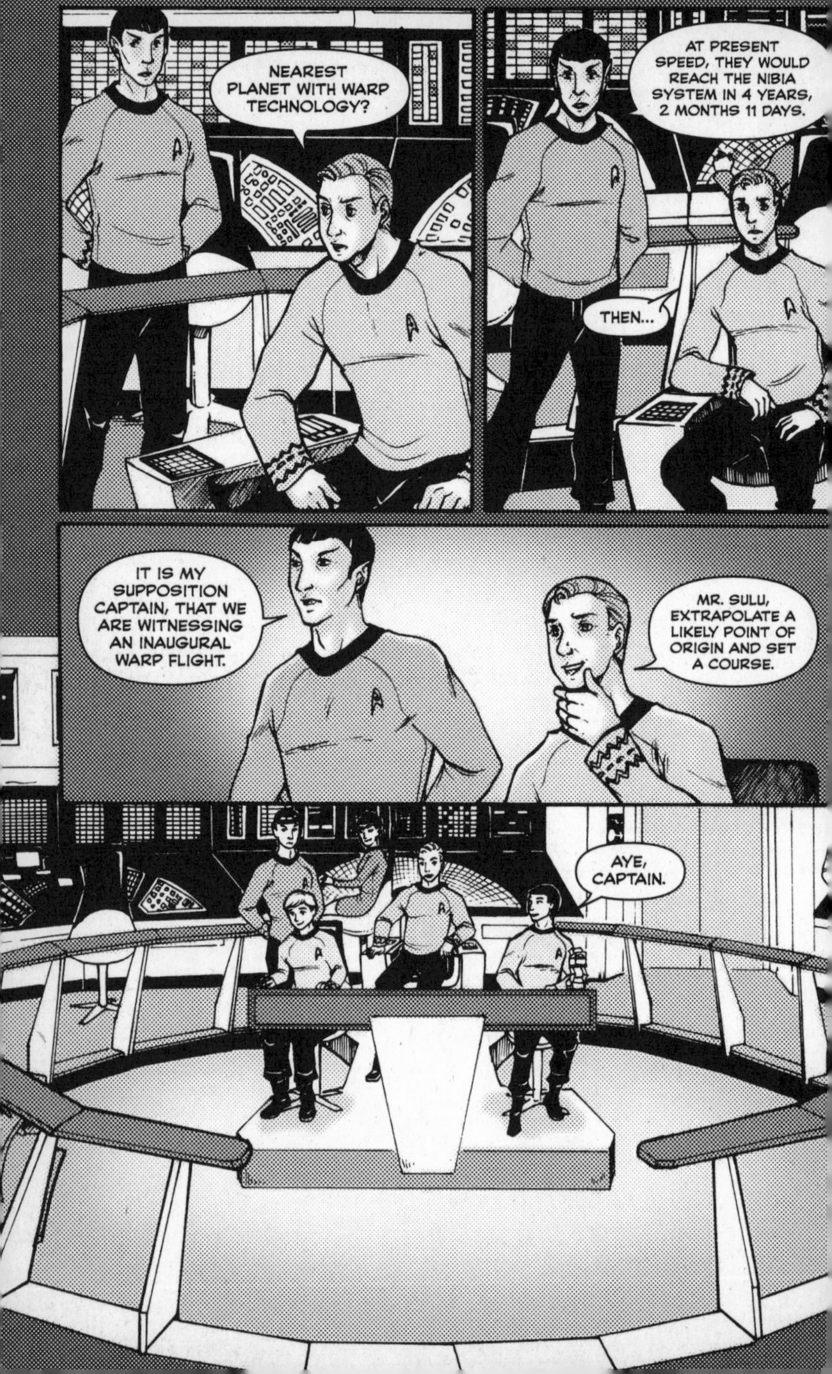
NEAREST PLANET WITH WARP TECHNOLOGY?
AT PRESENT SPEED, THEY WOULD REACH THE NIBIA SYSTEM IN 4 YEARS, 2 MONTHS 11 DAYS.
THEN...
IT IS MY SUPPOSITION CAPTAIN, THAT WE ARE WITNESSING AN INAUGURAL WARP FLIGHT.
MR. SULU, EXTRAPOLATE A LIKELY POINT OF ORIGIN AND SET A COURSE.
AYE, CAPTAIN.

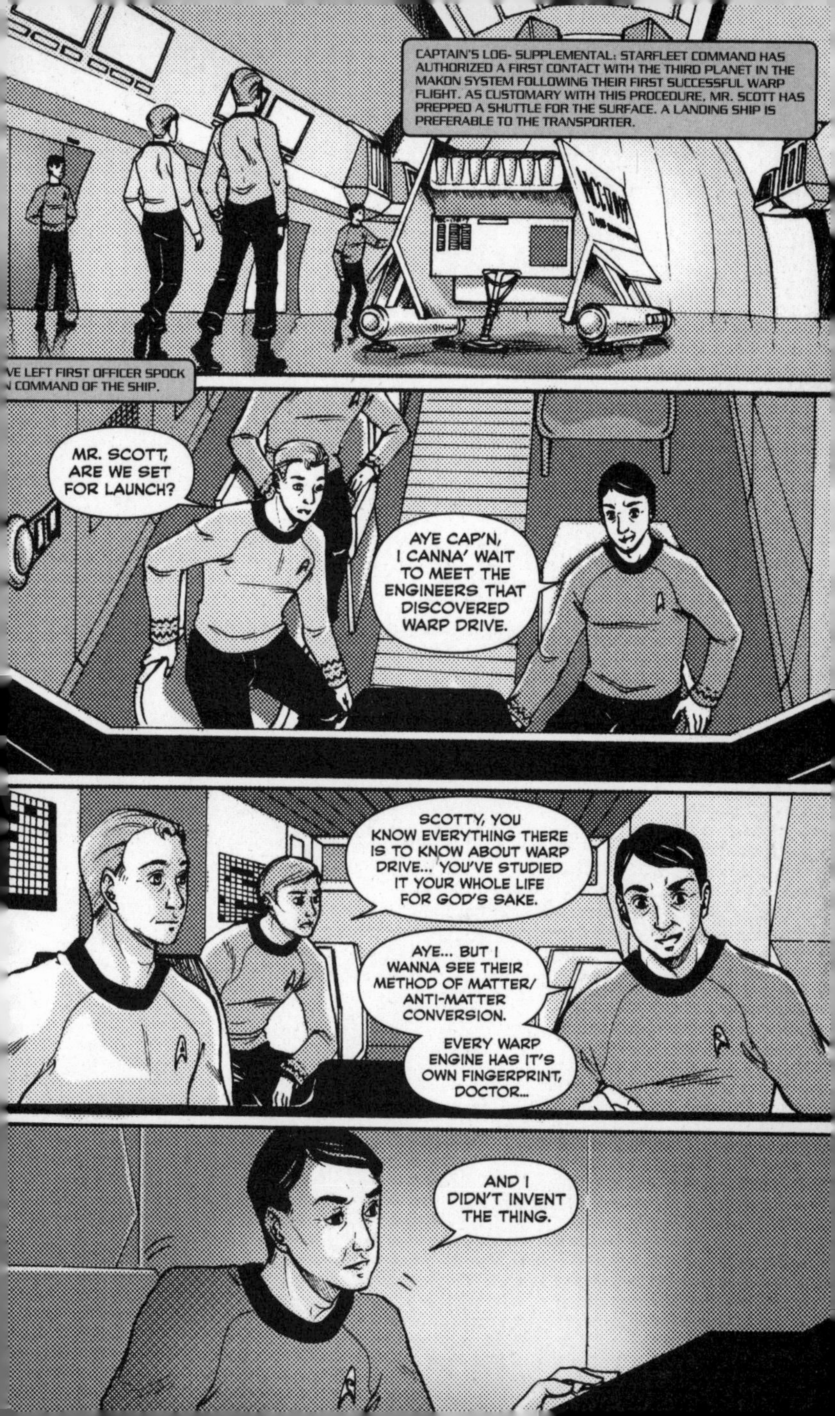
CAPTAIN'S LOG- SUPPLEMENTAL: STARFLEET COMMAND HAS AUTHORIZED A FIRST CONTACT WITH THE THIRD PLANET IN THE MAKON SYSTEM FOLLOWING THEIR FIRST SUCCESSFUL WARP FLIGHT. AS CUSTOMARY WITH THIS PROCEDURE, MR. SCOTT HAS PREPPED A SHUTTLE FOR THE SURFACE. A LANDING SHIP IS PREFERABLE TO THE TRANSPORTER.
VE LEFT FIRST OFFICER SPOCK
N COMMAND OF THE SHIP.
MR. SCOTT, ARE WE SET FOR LAUNCH?
AYE CAP'N, I CANNA' WAIT TO MEET THE ENGINEERS THAT DISCOVERED WARP DRIVE.
SCOTTY, YOU KNOW EVERYTHING THERE IS TO KNOW ABOUT WARP DRIVE... YOU'VE STUDIED IT YOUR WHOLE LIFE FOR GOD'S SAKE.
AYE... BUT I WANNA SEE THEIR METHOD OF MATTER/ ANTI-MATTER CONVERSION.
EVERY WARP ENGINE HAS IT'S OWN FINGERPRINT, DOCTOR...
AND I DIDN'T INVENT THE THING.

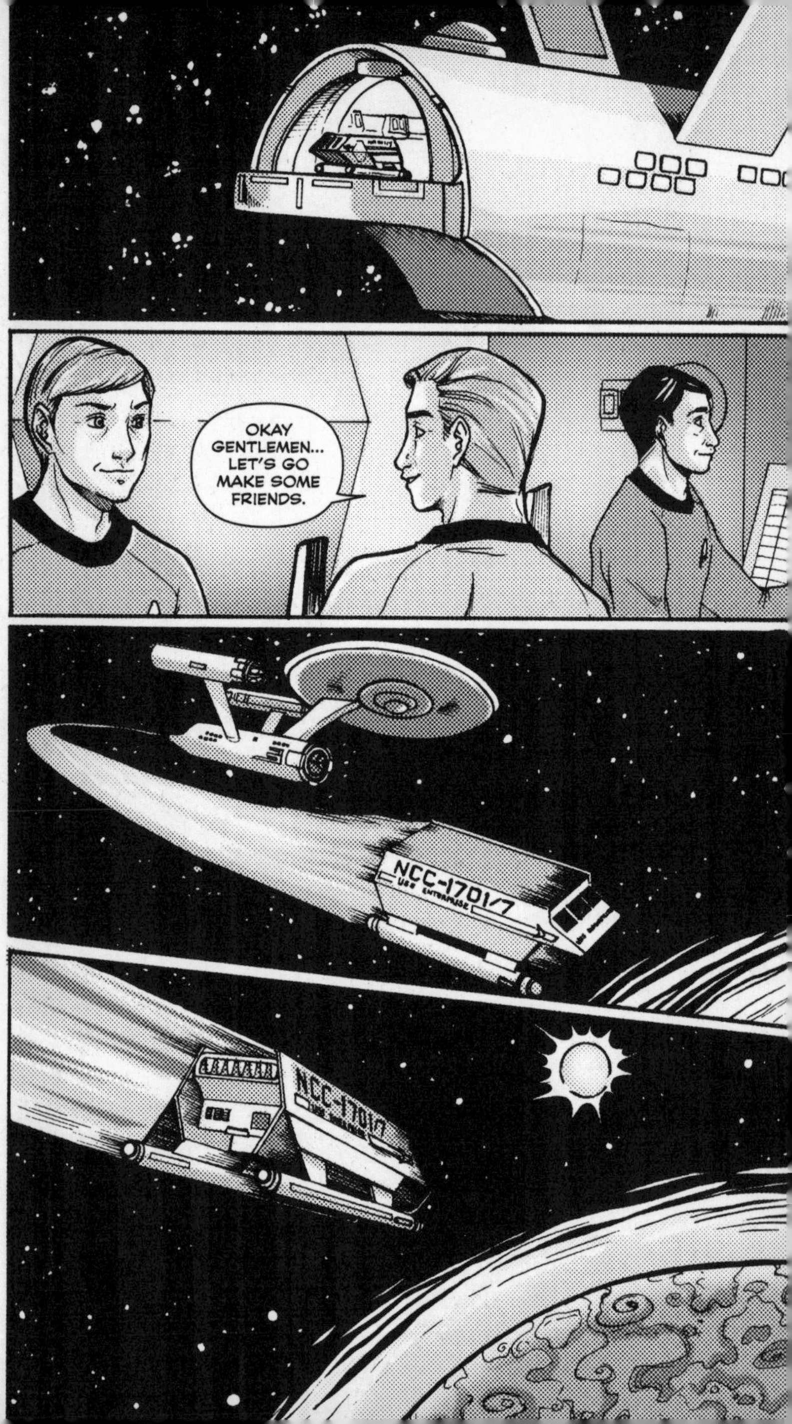
OKAY GENTLEMEN... LET'S GO MAKE SOME FRIENDS.
NCC-1701/7
USS ENTERPRISE
NCC-1701/7

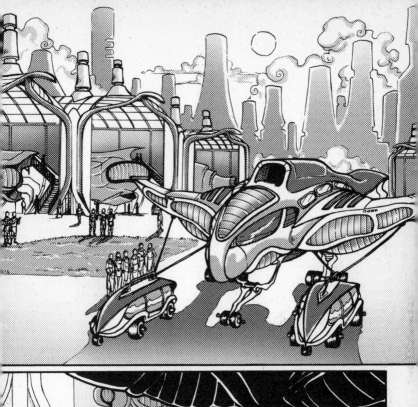

...RESULTS INDICATE IF THE COOLANT TANK HADN'T RUPTURED, IT MAY HAVE HIT WARP 2...

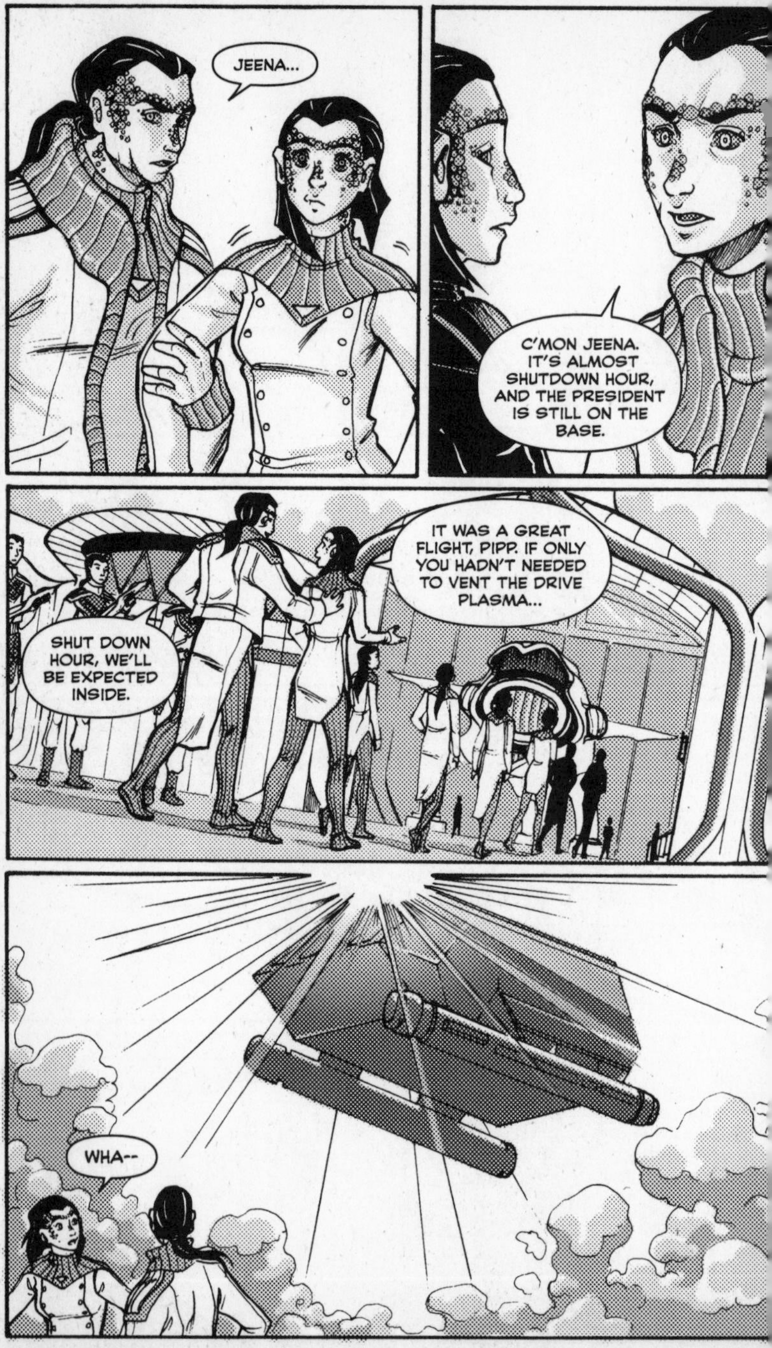
JEENA...
C'MON JEENA. IT'S ALMOST SHUTDOWN HOUR, AND THE PRESIDENT IS STILL ON THE BASE.
SHUT DOWN HOUR, WE'LL BE EXPECTED INSIDE.
IT WAS A GREAT FLIGHT, PIPP. IF ONLY YOU HADN'T NEEDED TO VENT THE DRIVE PLASMA...
WHA--

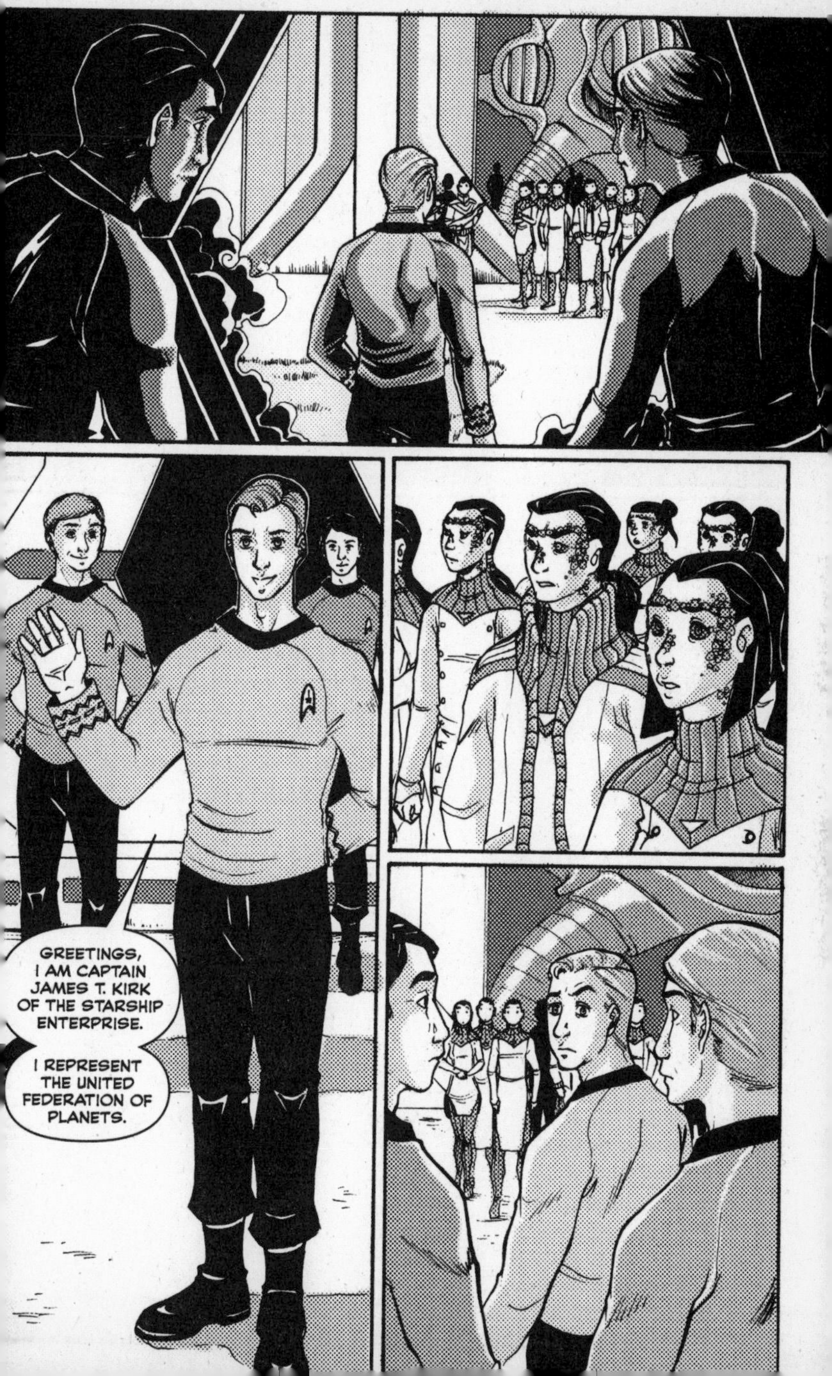
GREETINGS, I AM CAPTAIN JAMES T. KIRK OF THE STARSHIP ENTERPRISE.
I REPRESENT THE UNITED FEDERATION OF PLANETS.

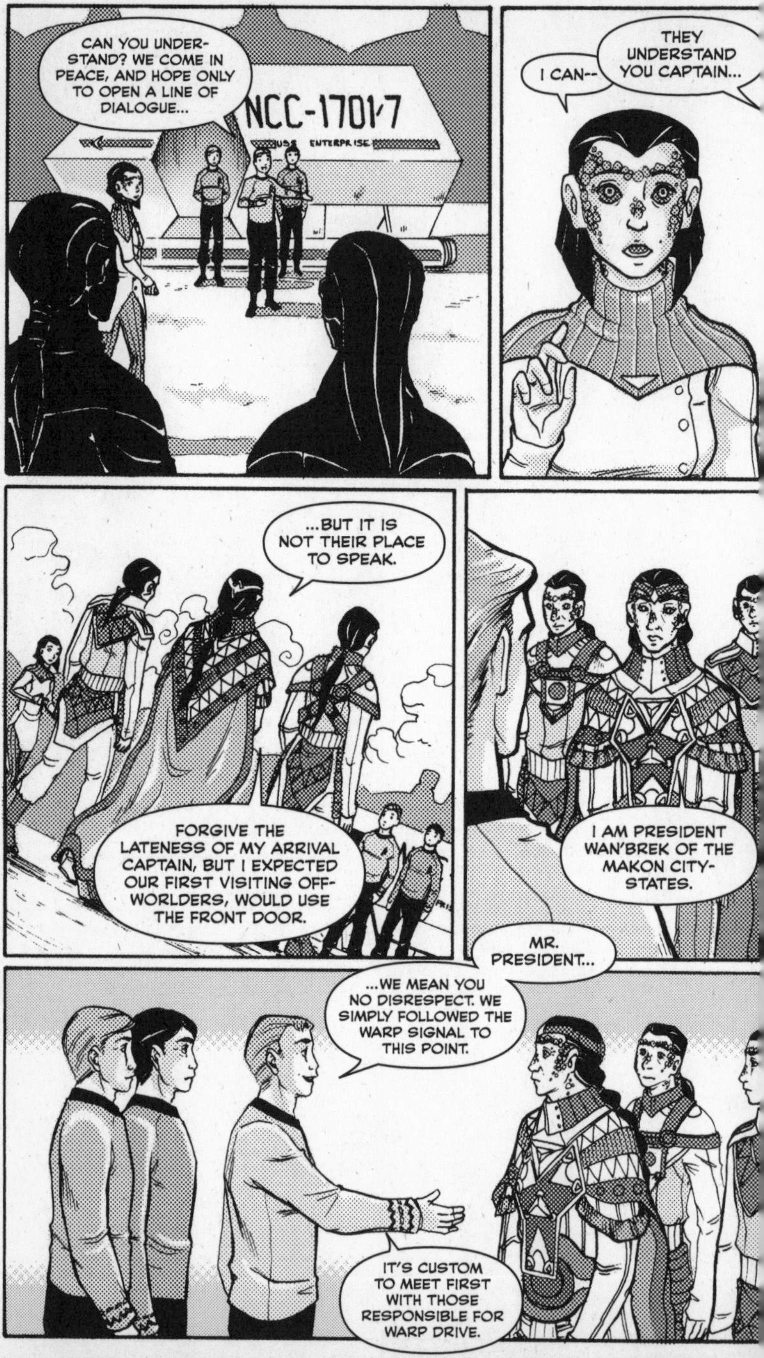
CAN YOU UNDERSTAND? WE COME IN PEACE, AND HOPE ONLY TO OPEN A LINE OF DIALOGUE...
NCC-1701-7
USS ENTERPRISE
I CAN--
THEY UNDERSTAND YOU CAPTAIN...
...BUT IT IS NOT THEIR PLACE TO SPEAK.
FORGIVE THE LATENESS OF MY ARRIVAL CAPTAIN, BUT I EXPECTED OUR FIRST VISITING OFF-WORLDERS, WOULD USE THE FRONT DOOR.
I AM PRESIDENT WAN'BREK OF THE MAKON CITY-STATES.
MR. PRESIDENT...
...WE MEAN YOU NO DISRESPECT. WE SIMPLY FOLLOWED THE WARP SIGNAL TO THIS POINT.
IT'S CUSTOM TO MEET FIRST WITH THOSE RESPONSIBLE FOR WARP DRIVE.

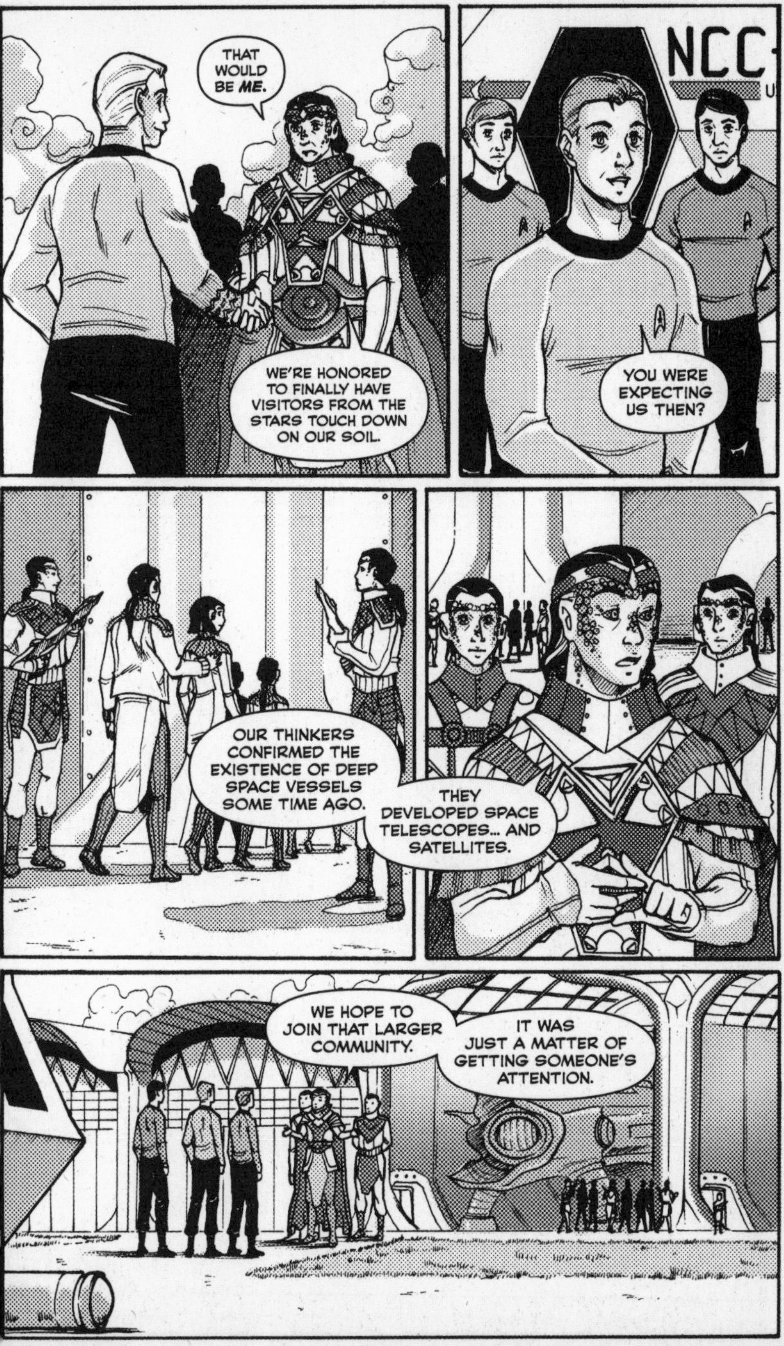
THAT WOULD BE *ME*.
WE'RE HONORED TO FINALLY HAVE VISITORS FROM THE STARS TOUCH DOWN ON OUR SOIL.
NCC-
YOU WERE EXPECTING US THEN?
OUR THINKERS CONFIRMED THE EXISTENCE OF DEEP SPACE VESSELS SOME TIME AGO.
THEY DEVELOPED SPACE TELESCOPES... AND SATELLITES.
WE HOPE TO JOIN THAT LARGER COMMUNITY.
IT WAS JUST A MATTER OF GETTING SOMEONE'S ATTENTION.

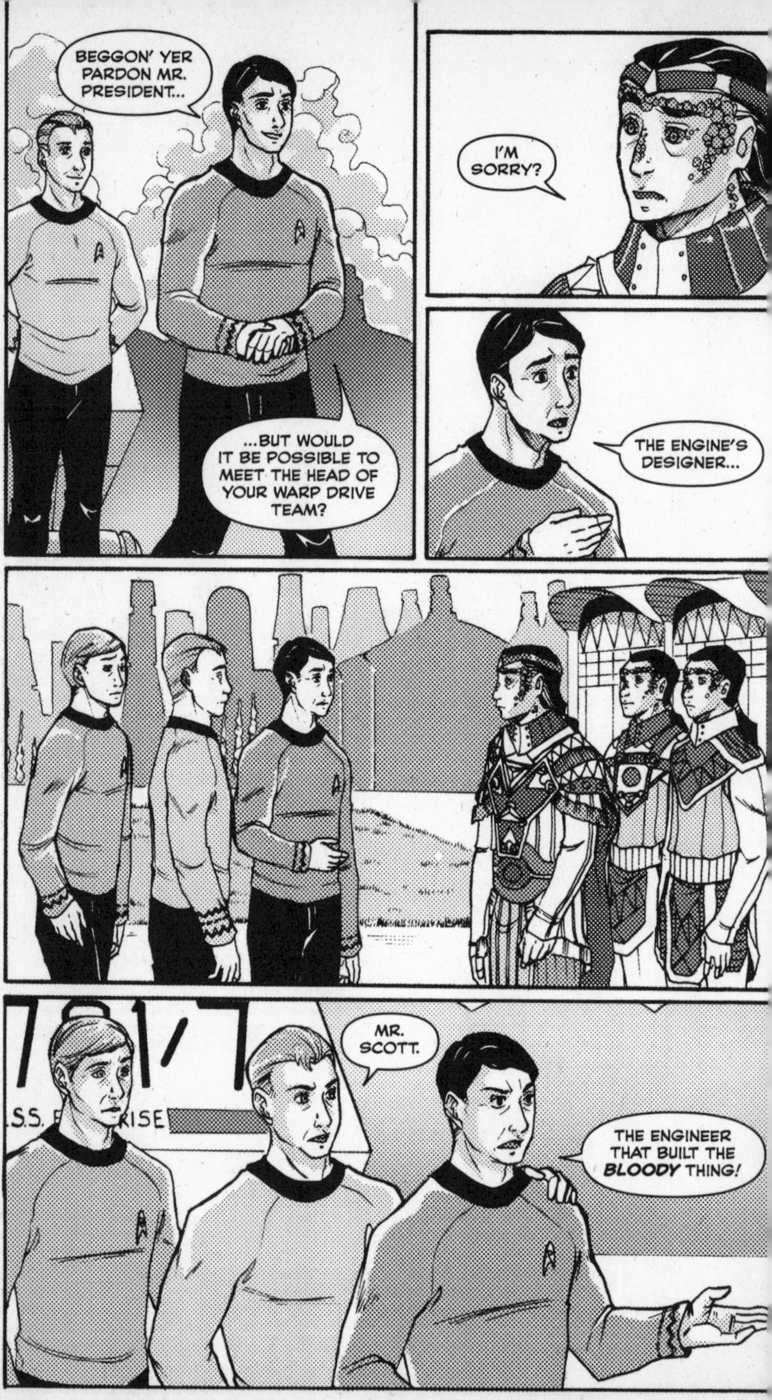
BEGGON' YER PARDON MR. PRESIDENT...
...BUT WOULD IT BE POSSIBLE TO MEET THE HEAD OF YOUR WARP DRIVE TEAM?
I'M SORRY?
THE ENGINE'S DESIGNER...
MR. SCOTT.
THE ENGINEER THAT BUILT THE *BLOODY* THING!

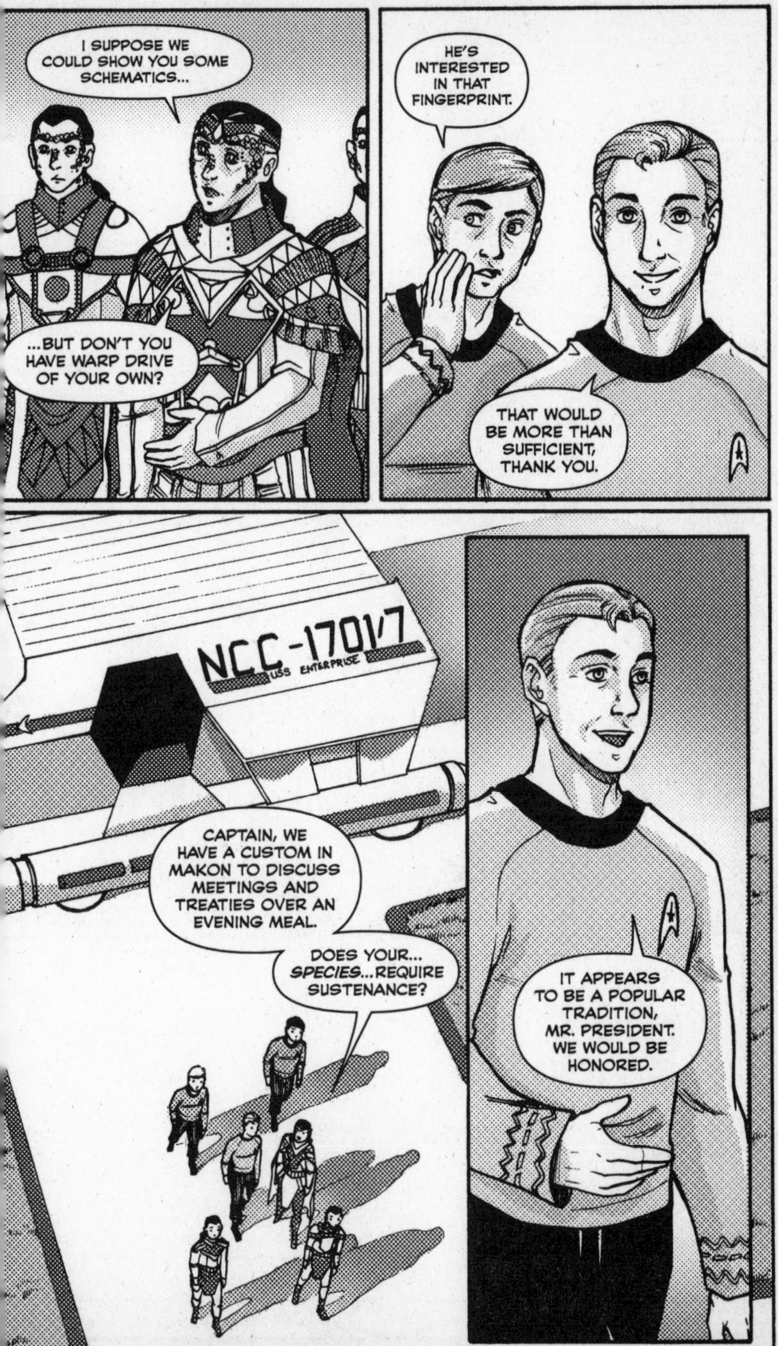
I SUPPOSE WE COULD SHOW YOU SOME SCHEMATICS...
...BUT DON'T YOU HAVE WARP DRIVE OF YOUR OWN?
HE'S INTERESTED IN THAT FINGERPRINT.
THAT WOULD BE MORE THAN SUFFICIENT, THANK YOU.
NCC-1701/7
USS ENTERPRISE
CAPTAIN, WE HAVE A CUSTOM IN MAKON TO DISCUSS MEETINGS AND TREATIES OVER AN EVENING MEAL.
DOES YOUR... *SPECIES*...REQUIRE SUSTENANCE?
IT APPEARS TO BE A POPULAR TRADITION, MR. PRESIDENT. WE WOULD BE HONORED.

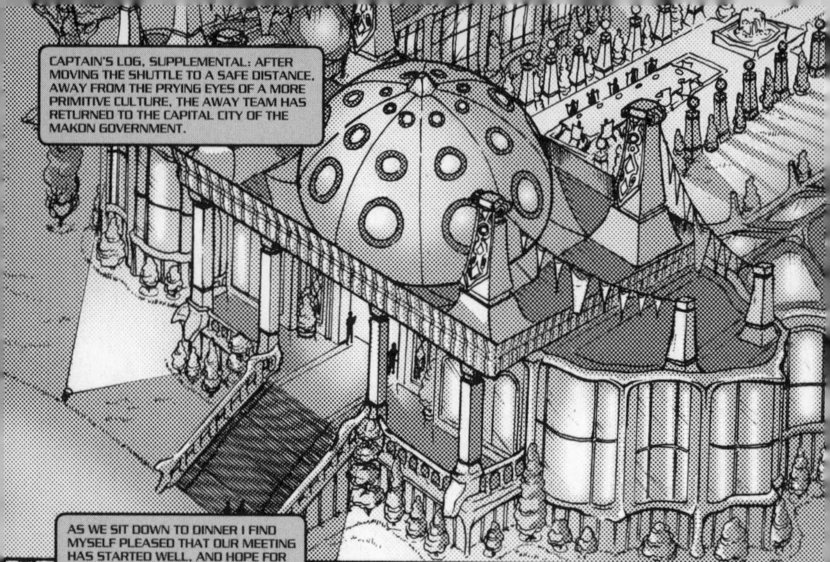
CAPTAIN'S LOG, SUPPLEMENTAL: AFTER MOVING THE SHUTTLE TO A SAFE DISTANCE, AWAY FROM THE PRYING EYES OF A MORE PRIMITIVE CULTURE, THE AWAY TEAM HAS RETURNED TO THE CAPITAL CITY OF THE MAKON GOVERNMENT.

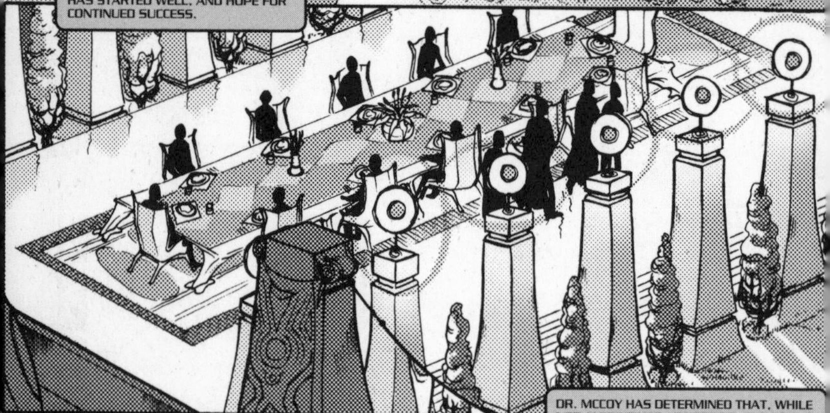
AS WE SIT DOWN TO DINNER I FIND MYSELF PLEASED THAT OUR MEETING HAS STARTED WELL, AND HOPE FOR CONTINUED SUCCESS.

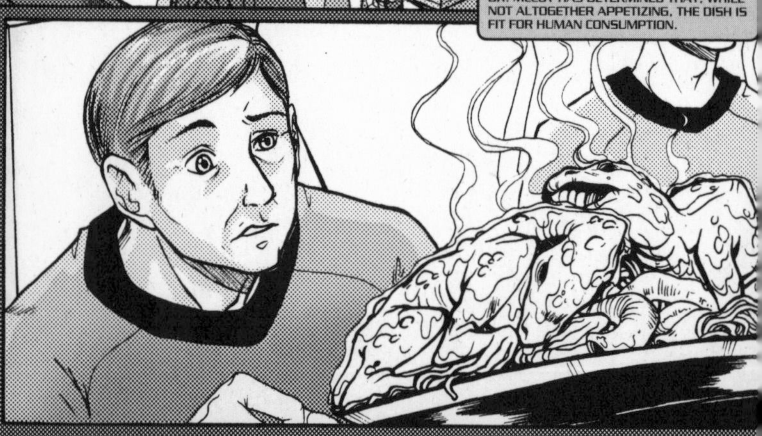
DR. MCCOY HAS DETERMINED THAT, WHILE NOT ALTOGETHER APPETIZING, THE DISH IS FIT FOR HUMAN CONSUMPTION.

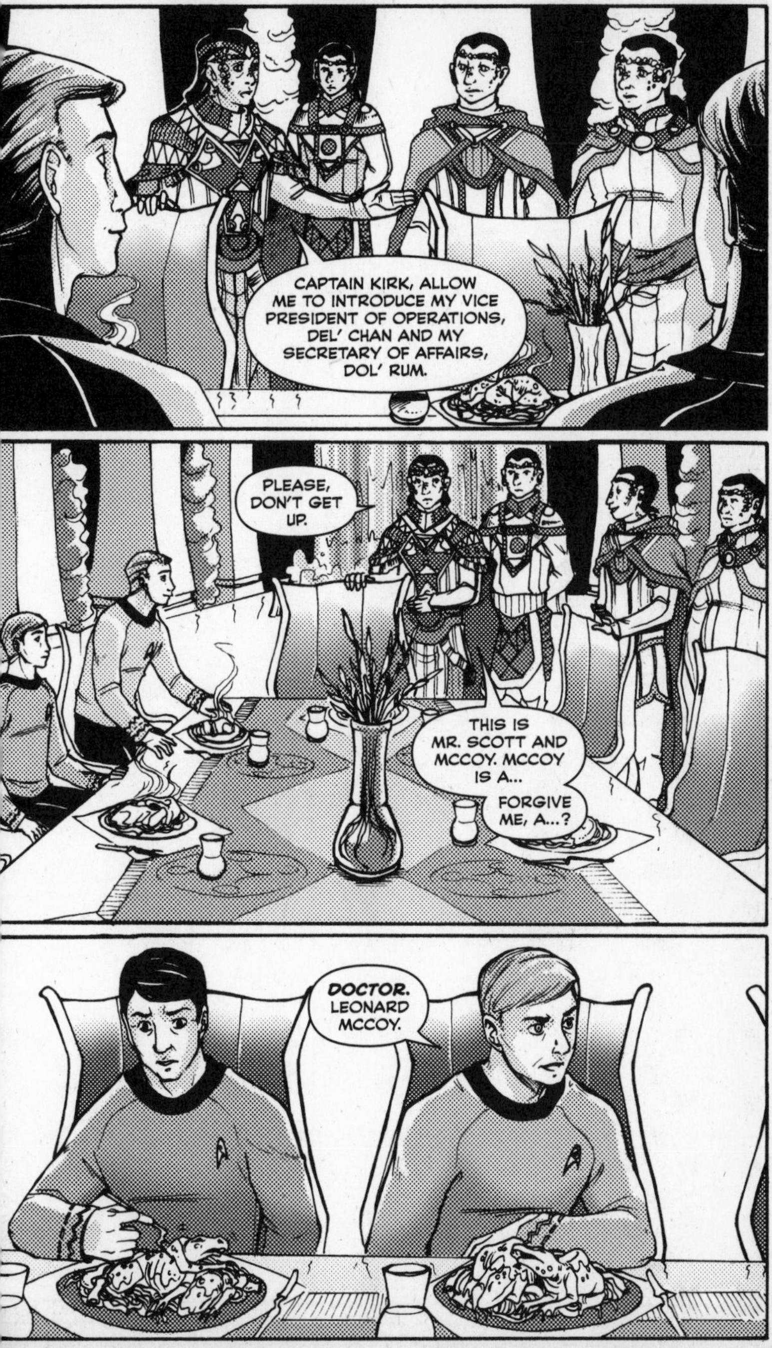
CAPTAIN KIRK, ALLOW ME TO INTRODUCE MY VICE PRESIDENT OF OPERATIONS, DEL' CHAN AND MY SECRETARY OF AFFAIRS, DOL' RUM.
PLEASE, DON'T GET UP.
THIS IS MR. SCOTT AND MCCOY. MCCOY IS A...
FORGIVE ME, A...?
DOCTOR. LEONARD MCCOY.

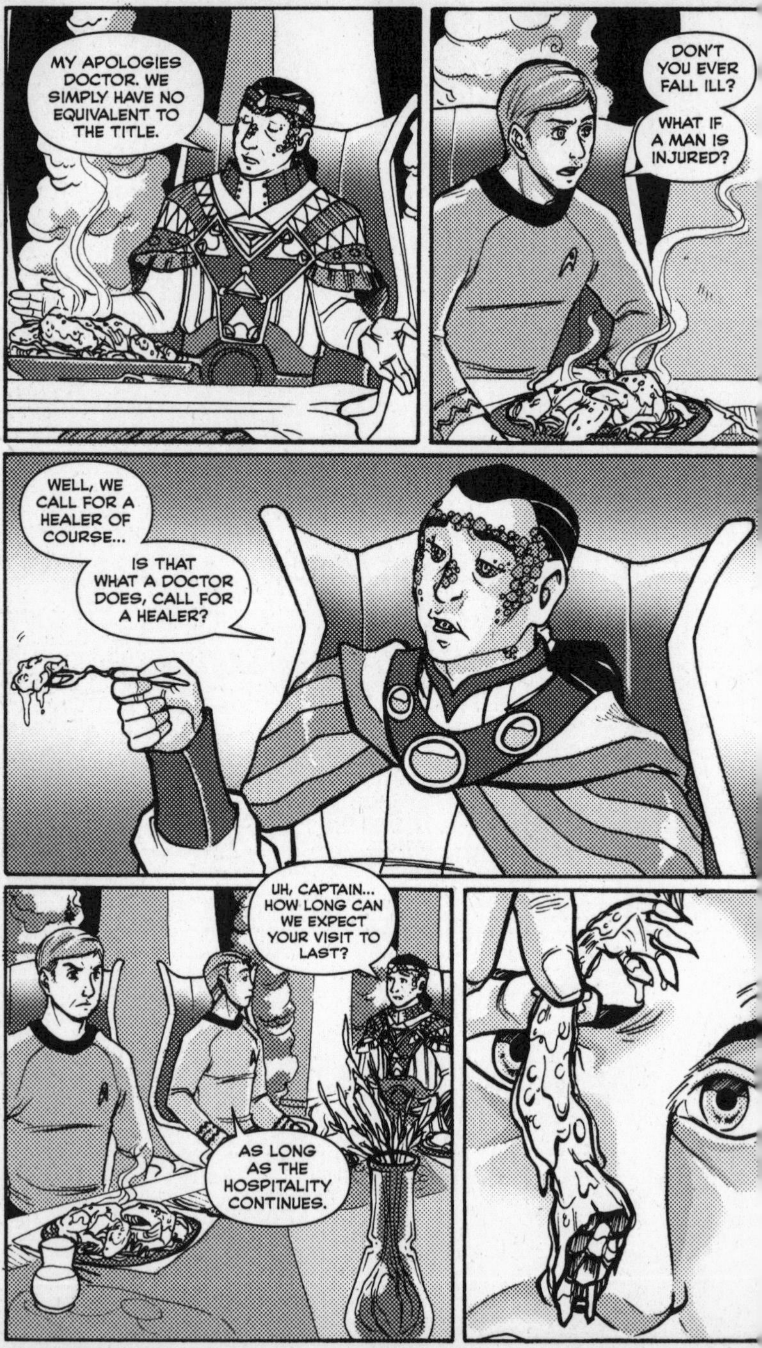
MY APOLOGIES DOCTOR. WE SIMPLY HAVE NO EQUIVALENT TO THE TITLE.
DON'T YOU EVER FALL ILL?
WHAT IF A MAN IS INJURED?
WELL, WE CALL FOR A HEALER OF COURSE...
IS THAT WHAT A DOCTOR DOES, CALL FOR A HEALER?
UH, CAPTAIN... HOW LONG CAN WE EXPECT YOUR VISIT TO LAST?
AS LONG AS THE HOSPITALITY CONTINUES.

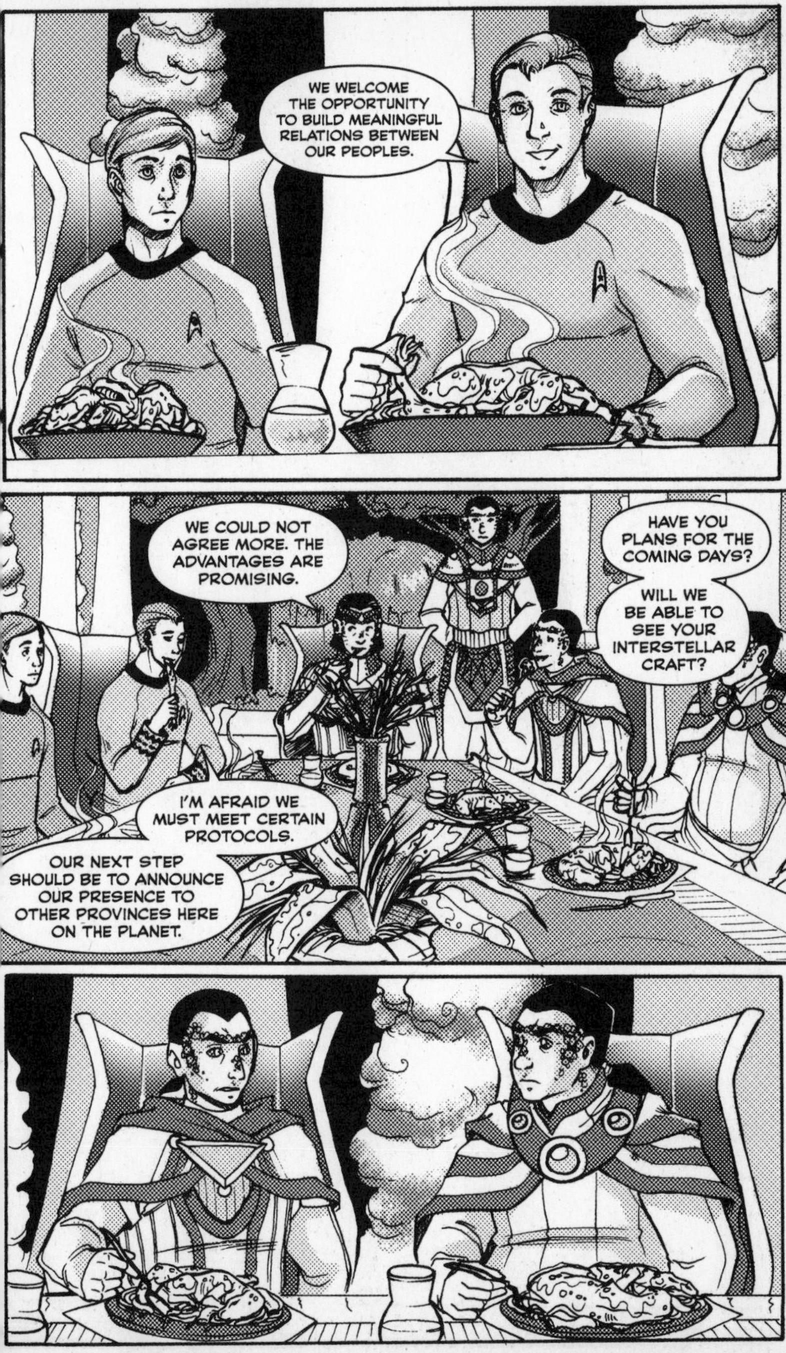
WE WELCOME THE OPPORTUNITY TO BUILD MEANINGFUL RELATIONS BETWEEN OUR PEOPLES.
WE COULD NOT AGREE MORE. THE ADVANTAGES ARE PROMISING.
HAVE YOU PLANS FOR THE COMING DAYS?
WILL WE BE ABLE TO SEE YOUR INTERSTELLAR CRAFT?
I'M AFRAID WE MUST MEET CERTAIN PROTOCOLS.
OUR NEXT STEP SHOULD BE TO ANNOUNCE OUR PRESENCE TO OTHER PROVINCES HERE ON THE PLANET.

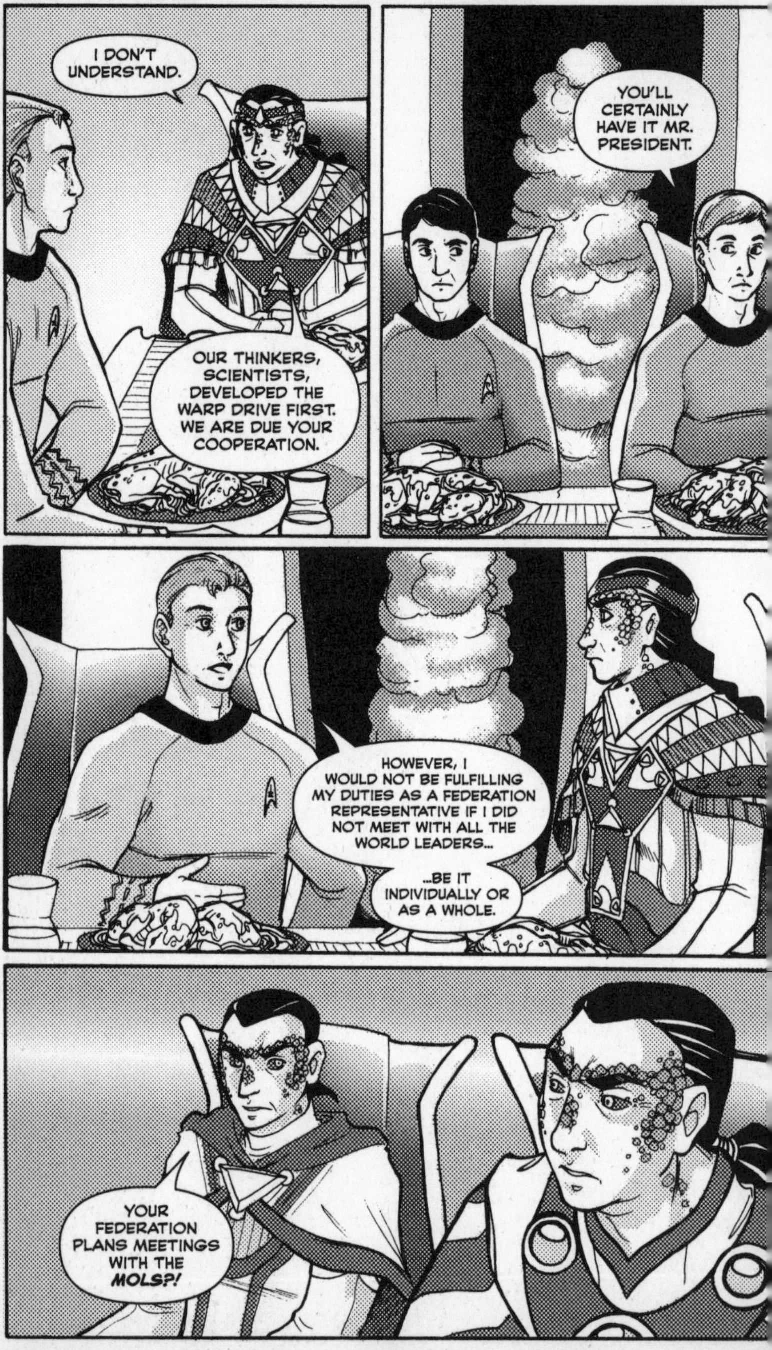
I DON'T UNDERSTAND.
OUR THINKERS, SCIENTISTS, DEVELOPED THE WARP DRIVE FIRST. WE ARE DUE YOUR COOPERATION.
YOU'LL CERTAINLY HAVE IT MR. PRESIDENT.
HOWEVER, I WOULD NOT BE FULFILLING MY DUTIES AS A FEDERATION REPRESENTATIVE IF I DID NOT MEET WITH ALL THE WORLD LEADERS...
...BE IT INDIVIDUALLY OR AS A WHOLE.
YOUR FEDERATION PLANS MEETINGS WITH THE *MOLS?!*

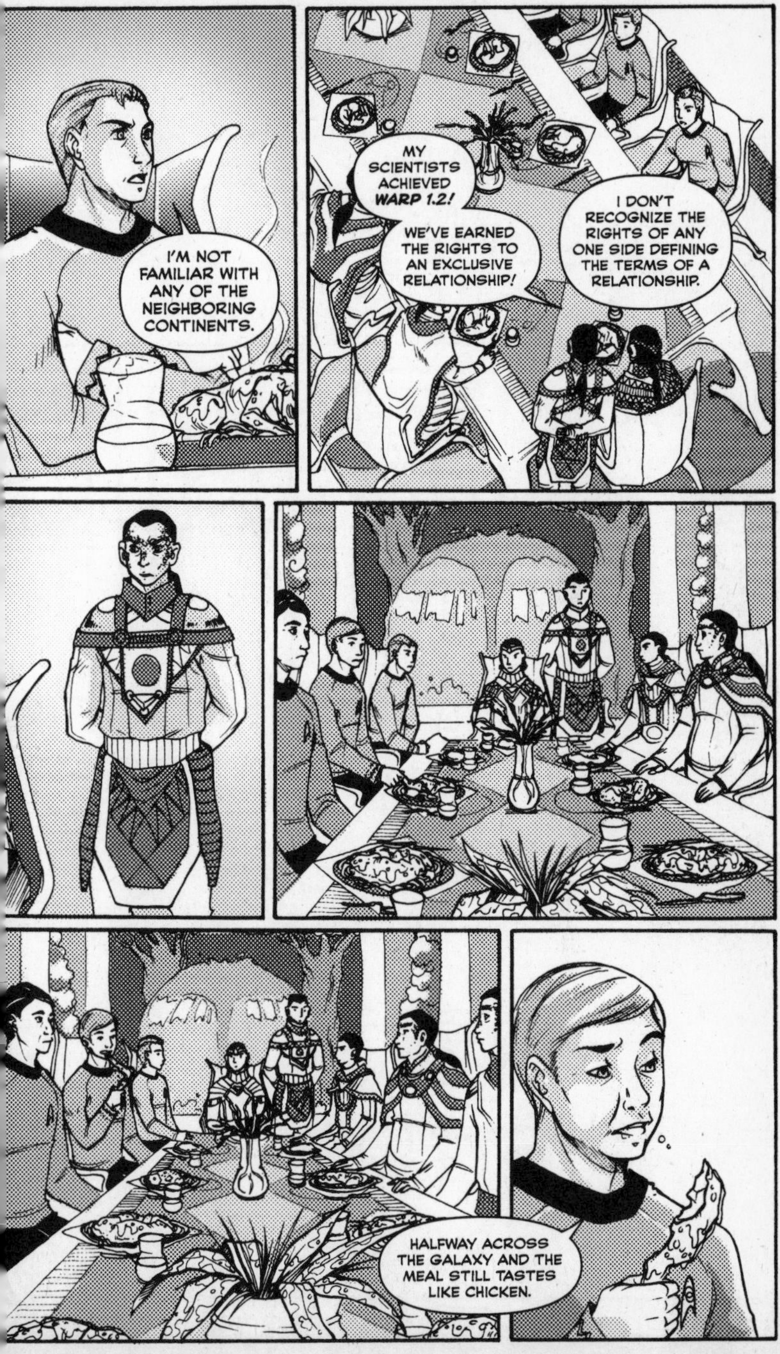
I'M NOT FAMILIAR WITH ANY OF THE NEIGHBORING CONTINENTS.
MY SCIENTISTS ACHIEVED *WARP 1.2!*
WE'VE EARNED THE RIGHTS TO AN EXCLUSIVE RELATIONSHIP!
I DON'T RECOGNIZE THE RIGHTS OF ANY ONE SIDE DEFINING THE TERMS OF A RELATIONSHIP.
HALFWAY ACROSS THE GALAXY AND THE MEAL STILL TASTES LIKE CHICKEN.

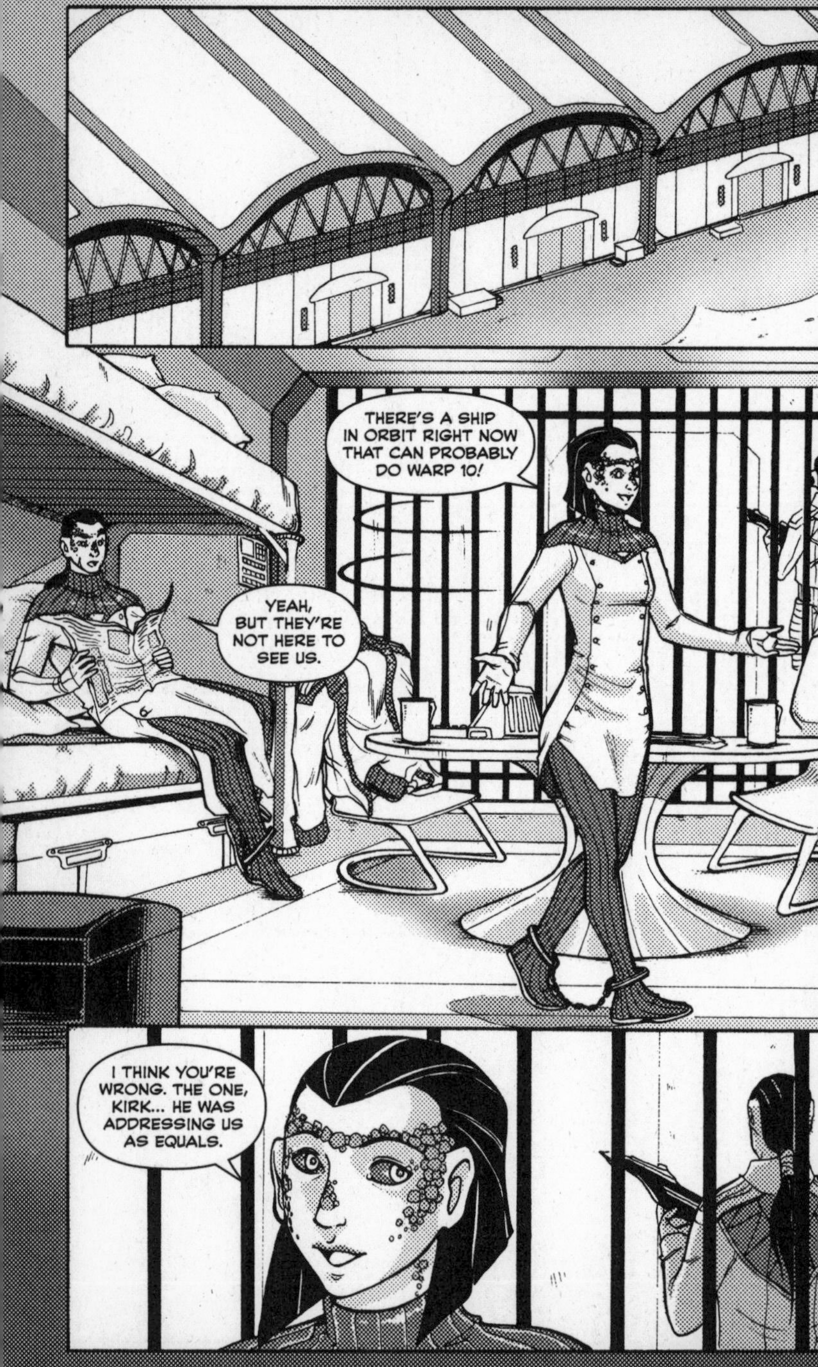
THERE'S A SHIP IN ORBIT RIGHT NOW THAT CAN PROBABLY DO WARP 10!
YEAH, BUT THEY'RE NOT HERE TO SEE US.
I THINK YOU'RE WRONG. THE ONE, KIRK... HE WAS ADDRESSING US AS EQUALS.

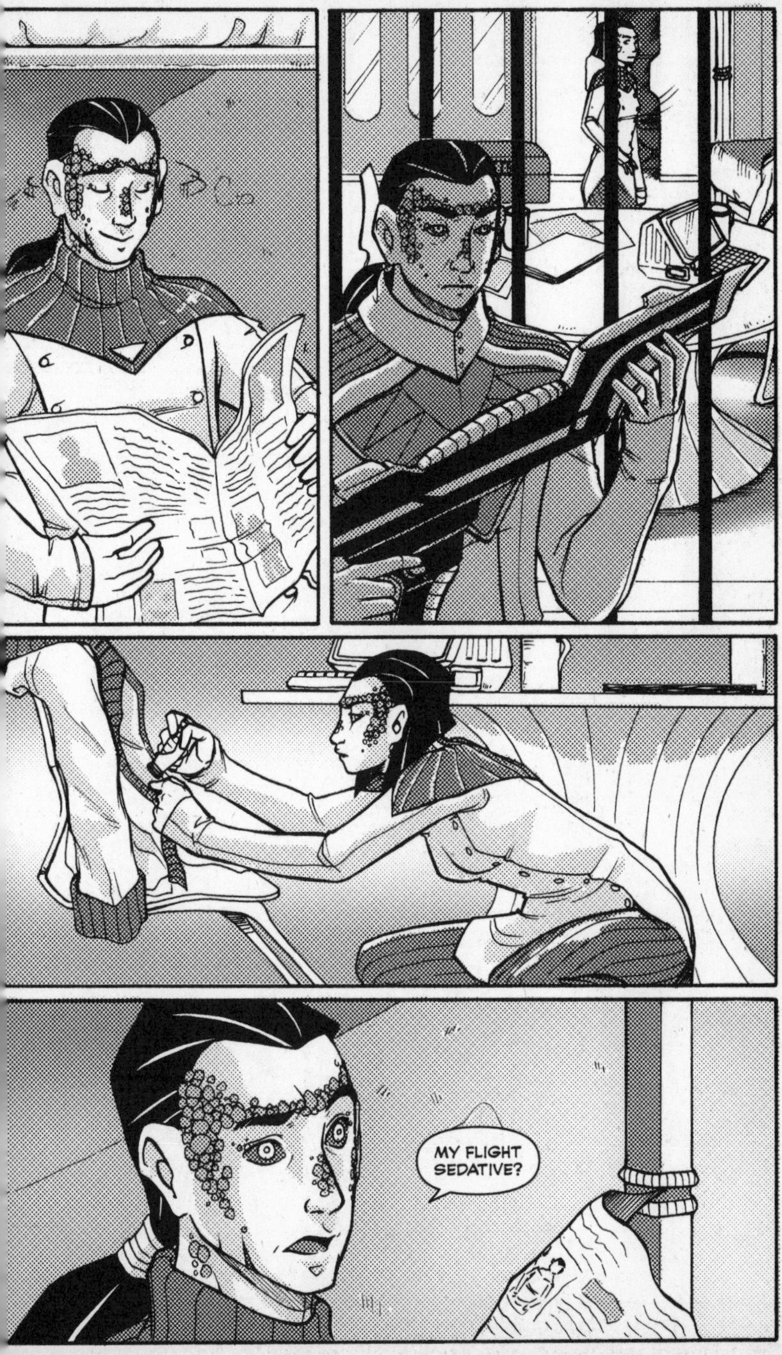
MY FLIGHT SEDATIVE?

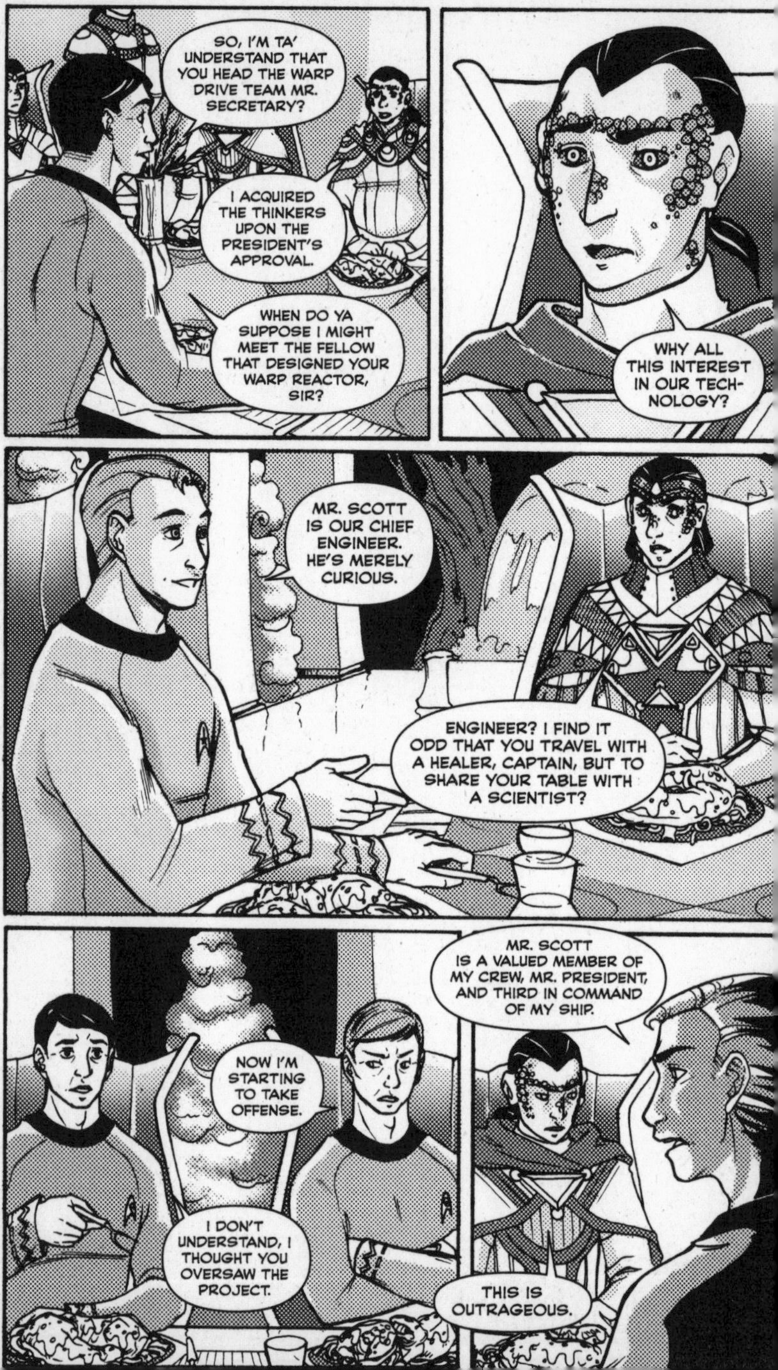
SO, I'M TA' UNDERSTAND THAT YOU HEAD THE WARP DRIVE TEAM MR. SECRETARY?
I ACQUIRED THE THINKERS UPON THE PRESIDENT'S APPROVAL.
WHEN DO YA SUPPOSE I MIGHT MEET THE FELLOW THAT DESIGNED YOUR WARP REACTOR, SIR?
WHY ALL THIS INTEREST IN OUR TECH-NOLOGY?
MR. SCOTT IS OUR CHIEF ENGINEER. HE'S MERELY CURIOUS.
ENGINEER? I FIND IT ODD THAT YOU TRAVEL WITH A HEALER, CAPTAIN, BUT TO SHARE YOUR TABLE WITH A SCIENTIST?
NOW I'M STARTING TO TAKE OFFENSE.
I DON'T UNDERSTAND, I THOUGHT YOU OVERSAW THE PROJECT.
MR. SCOTT IS A VALUED MEMBER OF MY CREW, MR. PRESIDENT, AND THIRD IN COMMAND OF MY SHIP.
THIS IS OUTRAGEOUS.

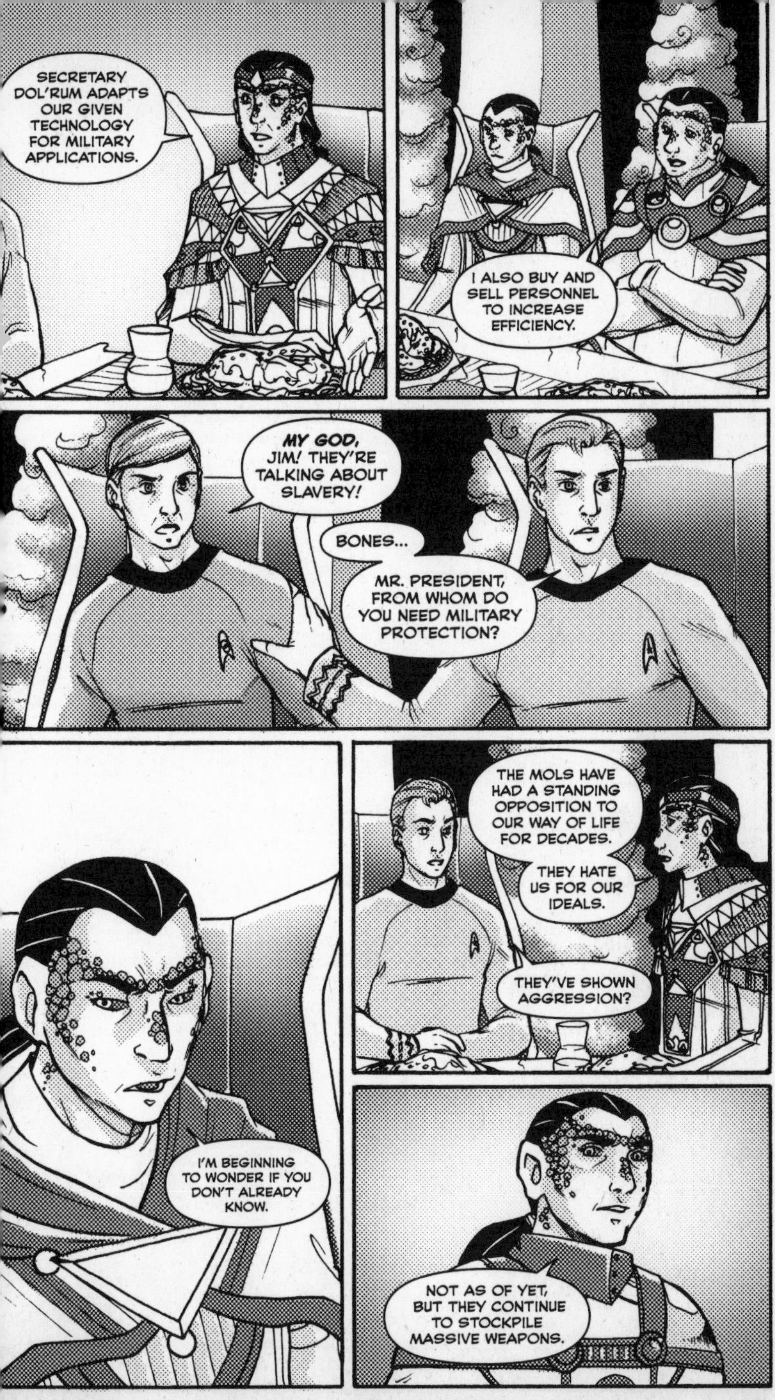
SECRETARY DOL'RUM ADAPTS OUR GIVEN TECHNOLOGY FOR MILITARY APPLICATIONS.
I ALSO BUY AND SELL PERSONNEL TO INCREASE EFFICIENCY.
MY GOD, JIM! THEY'RE TALKING ABOUT SLAVERY!
BONES...
MR. PRESIDENT, FROM WHOM DO YOU NEED MILITARY PROTECTION?
I'M BEGINNING TO WONDER IF YOU DON'T ALREADY KNOW.
THE MOLS HAVE HAD A STANDING OPPOSITION TO OUR WAY OF LIFE FOR DECADES.
THEY HATE US FOR OUR IDEALS.
THEY'VE SHOWN AGGRESSION?
NOT AS OF YET, BUT THEY CONTINUE TO STOCKPILE MASSIVE WEAPONS.

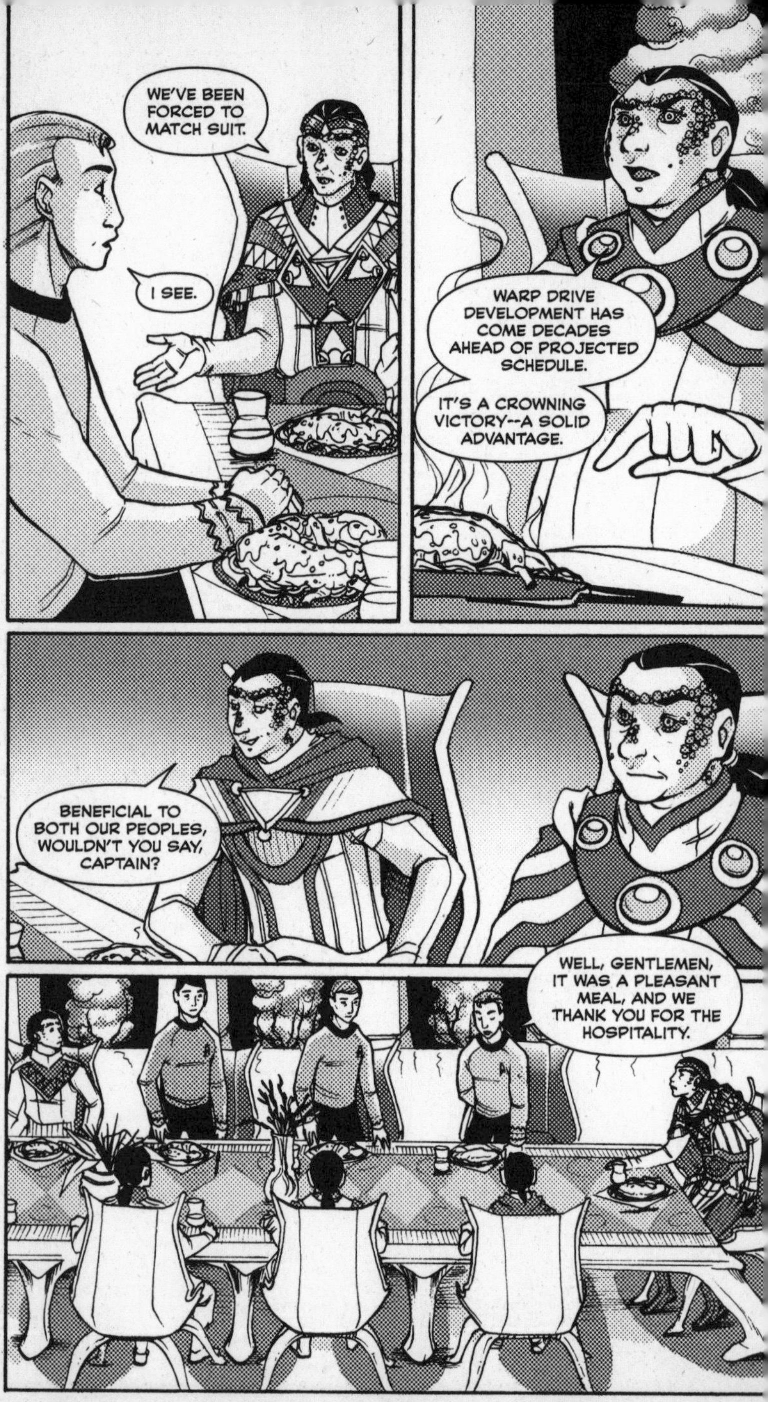
WE'VE BEEN FORCED TO MATCH SUIT.
I SEE.
WARP DRIVE DEVELOPMENT HAS COME DECADES AHEAD OF PROJECTED SCHEDULE.
IT'S A CROWNING VICTORY--A SOLID ADVANTAGE.
BENEFICIAL TO BOTH OUR PEOPLES, WOULDN'T YOU SAY, CAPTAIN?
WELL, GENTLEMEN, IT WAS A PLEASANT MEAL, AND WE THANK YOU FOR THE HOSPITALITY.

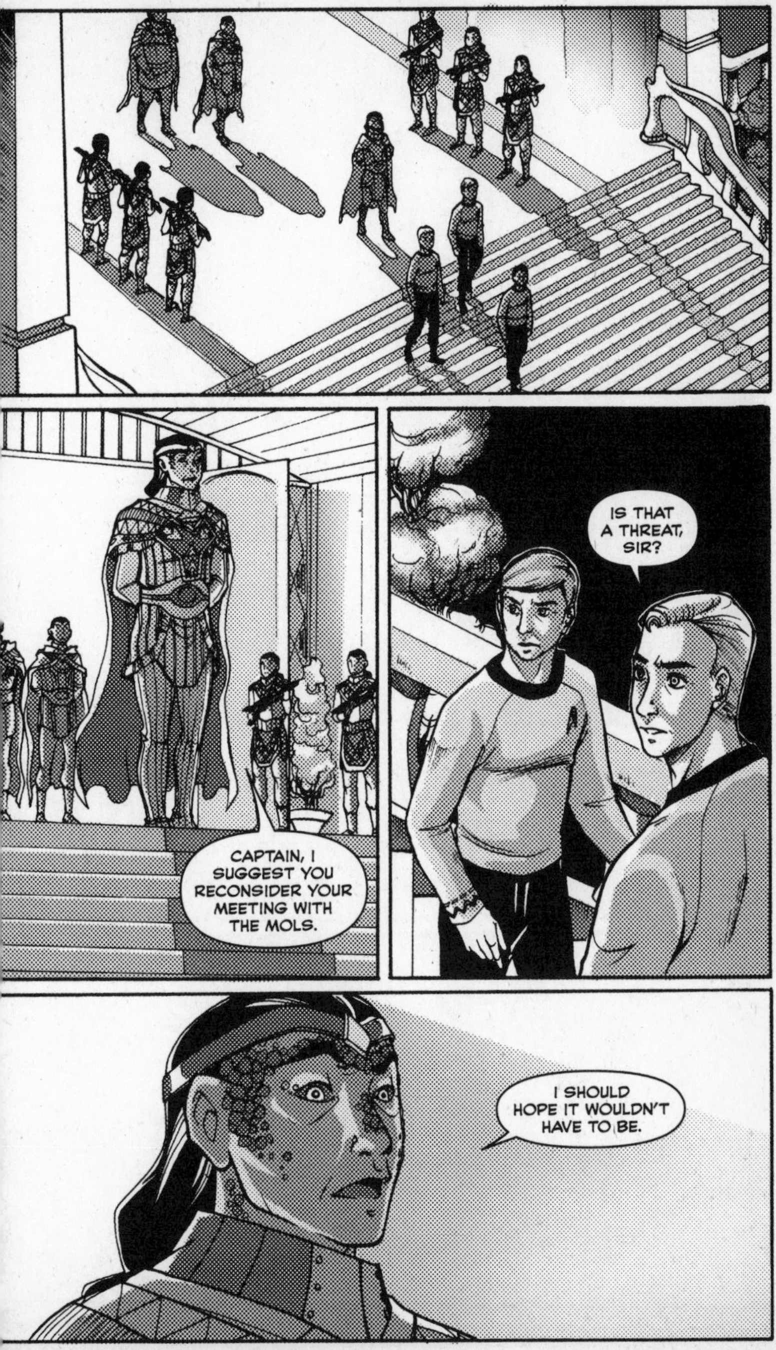
CAPTAIN, I SUGGEST YOU RECONSIDER YOUR MEETING WITH THE MOLS.
IS THAT A THREAT, SIR?
I SHOULD HOPE IT WOULDN'T HAVE TO BE.

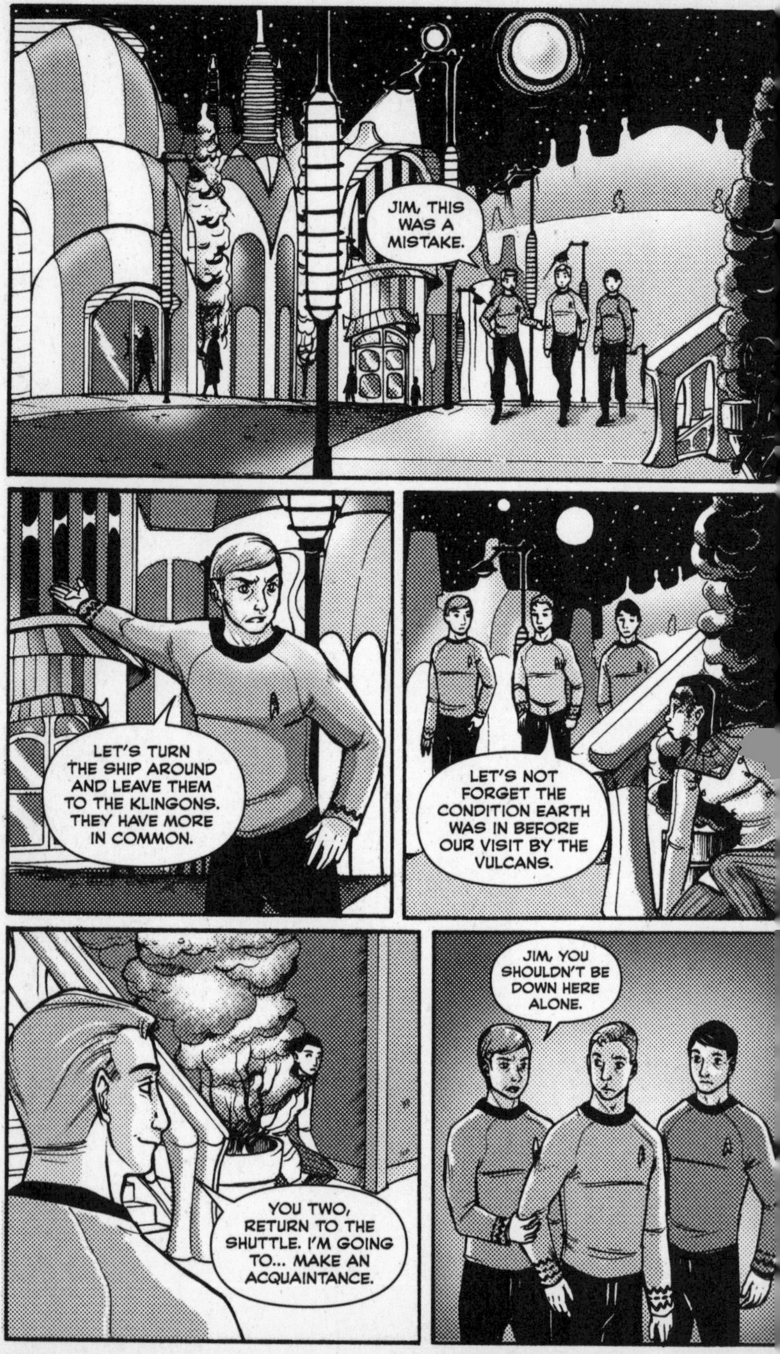
JIM, THIS WAS A MISTAKE.
LET'S TURN THE SHIP AROUND AND LEAVE THEM TO THE KLINGONS. THEY HAVE MORE IN COMMON.
LET'S NOT FORGET THE CONDITION EARTH WAS IN BEFORE OUR VISIT BY THE VULCANS.
YOU TWO, RETURN TO THE SHUTTLE. I'M GOING TO... MAKE AN ACQUAINTANCE.
JIM, YOU SHOULDN'T BE DOWN HERE ALONE.

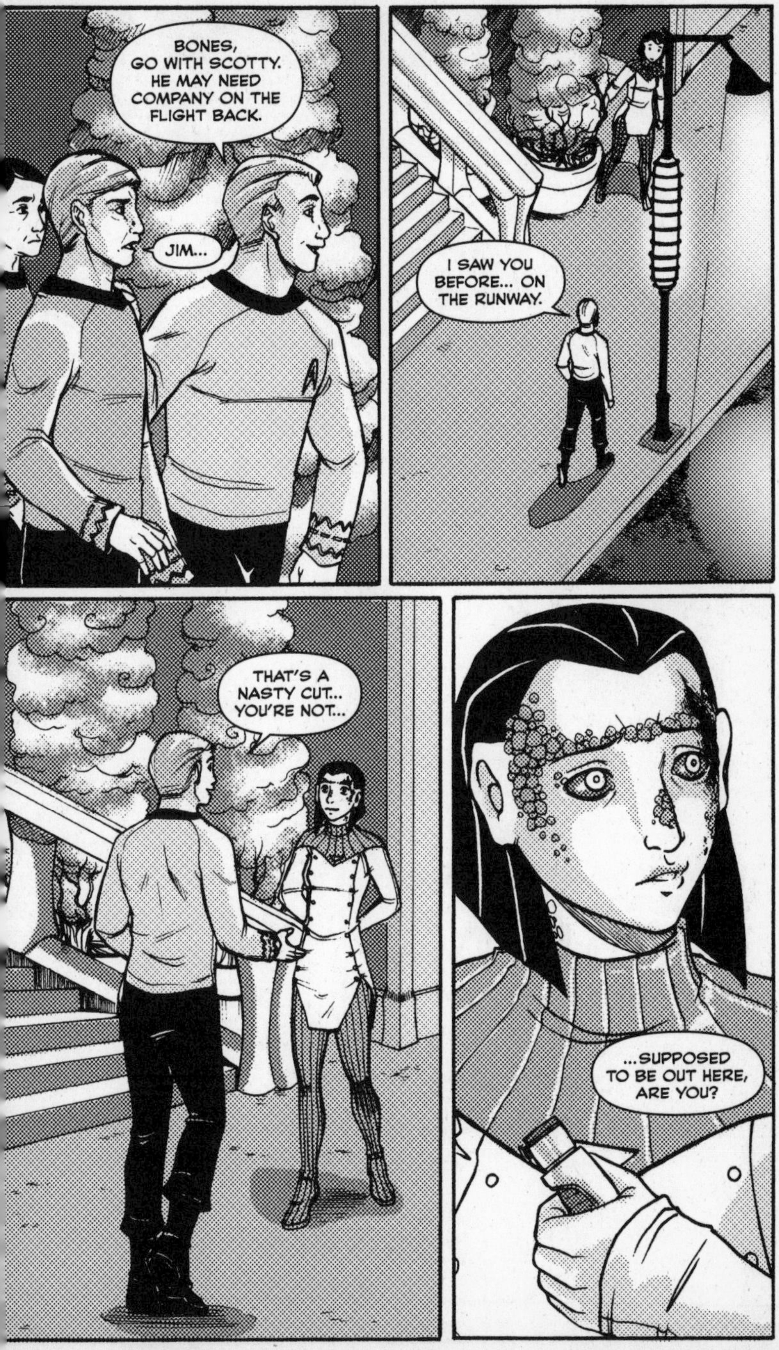
BONES, GO WITH SCOTTY. HE MAY NEED COMPANY ON THE FLIGHT BACK.
JIM...
I SAW YOU BEFORE... ON THE RUNWAY.
THAT'S A NASTY CUT... YOU'RE NOT...
...SUPPOSED TO BE OUT HERE, ARE YOU?

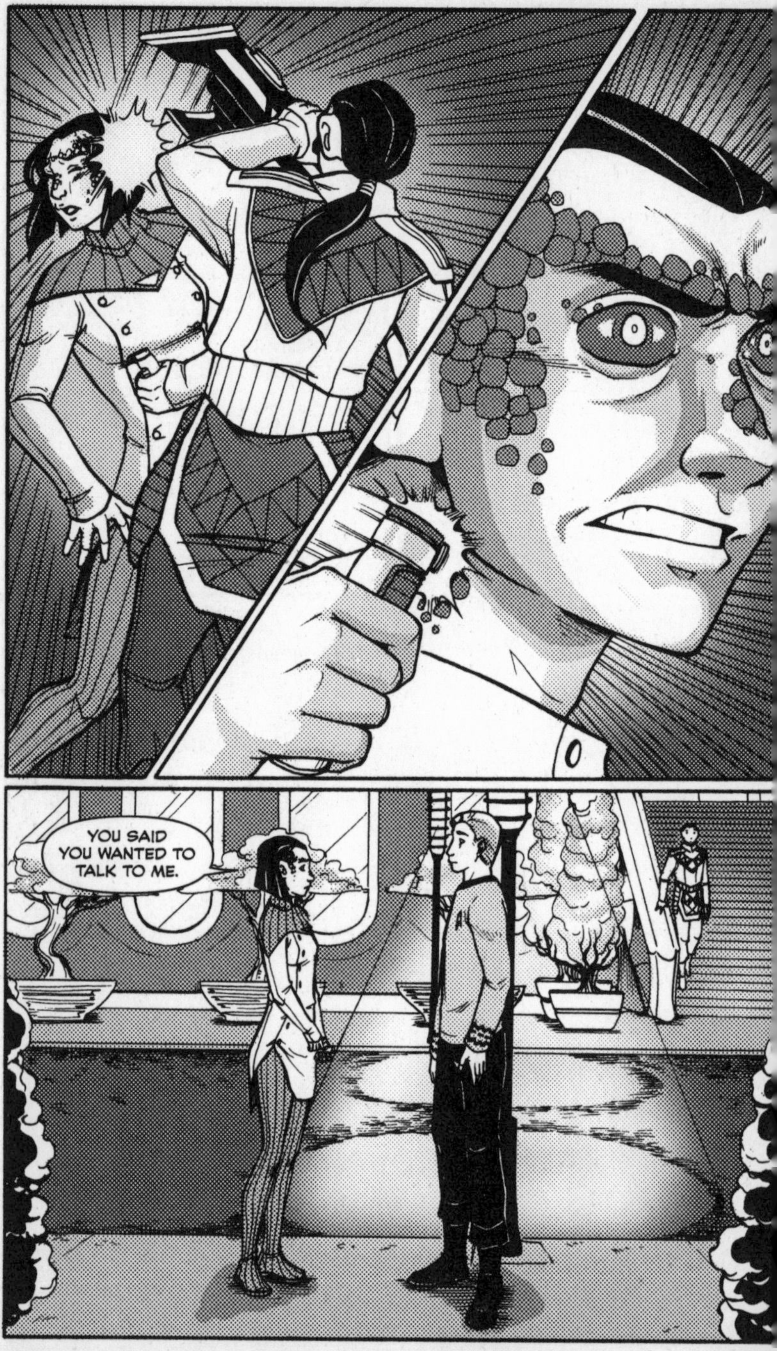
YOU SAID YOU WANTED TO TALK TO ME.

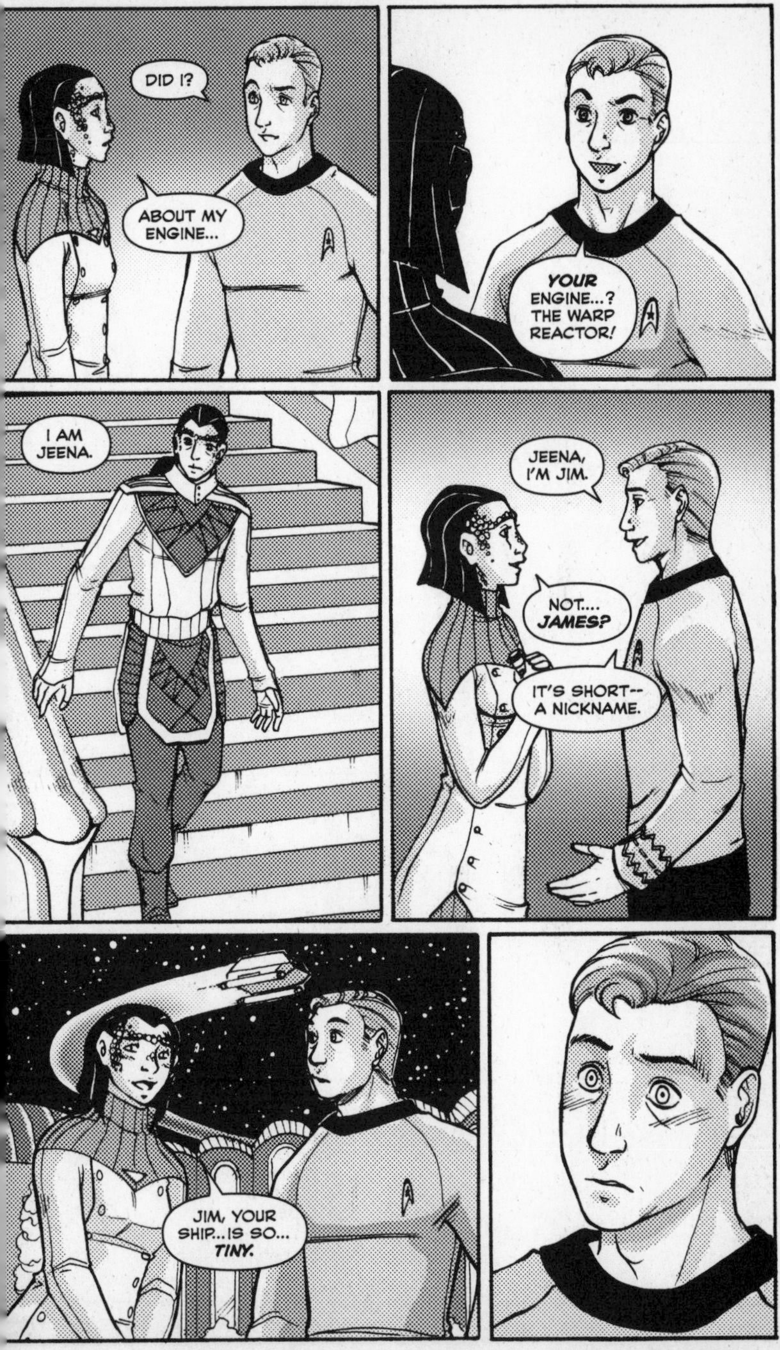
DID I?
ABOUT MY ENGINE...
YOUR ENGINE...? THE WARP REACTOR!
I AM JEENA.
JEENA, I'M JIM.
NOT.... JAMES?
IT'S SHORT-- A NICKNAME.
JIM, YOUR SHIP...IS SO... TINY.

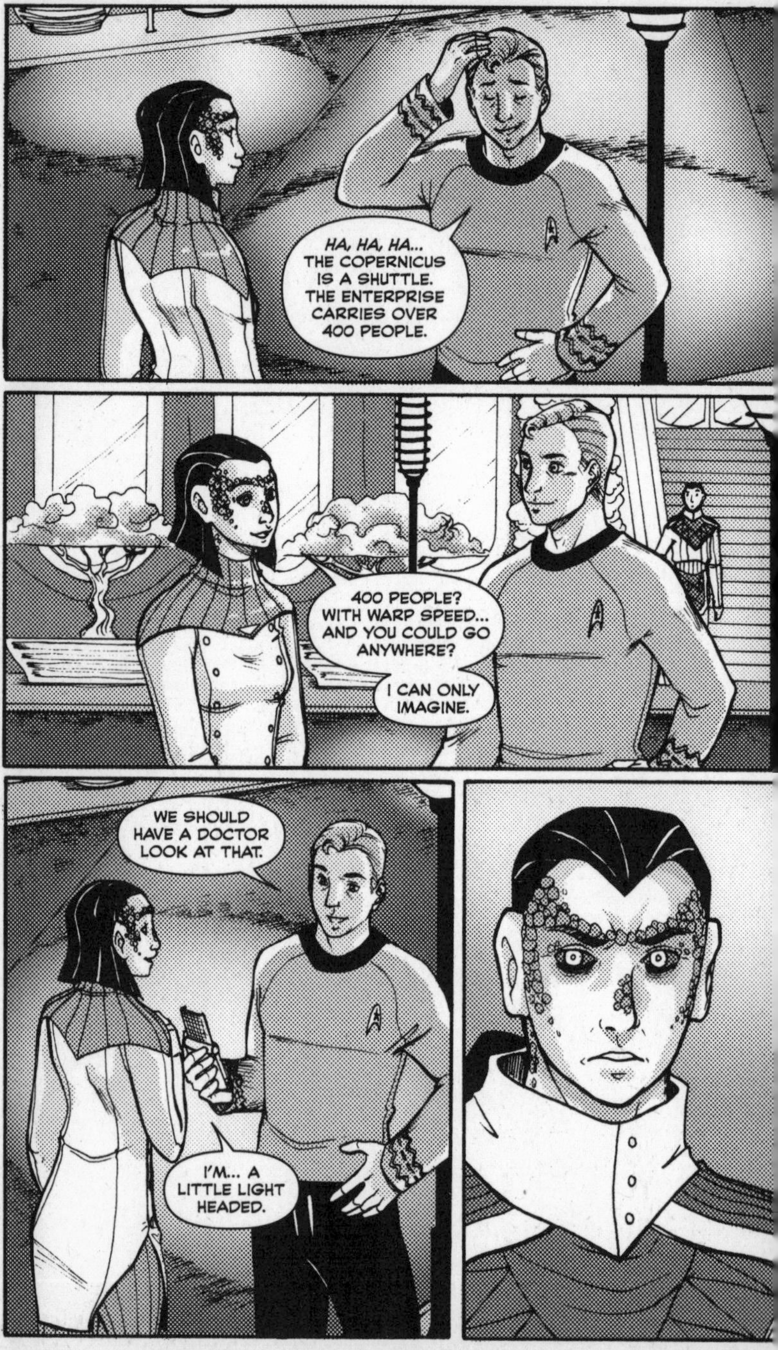
HA, HA, HA... THE COPERNICUS IS A SHUTTLE. THE ENTERPRISE CARRIES OVER 400 PEOPLE.
400 PEOPLE? WITH WARP SPEED... AND YOU COULD GO ANYWHERE?
I CAN ONLY IMAGINE.
WE SHOULD HAVE A DOCTOR LOOK AT THAT.
I'M... A LITTLE LIGHT HEADED.

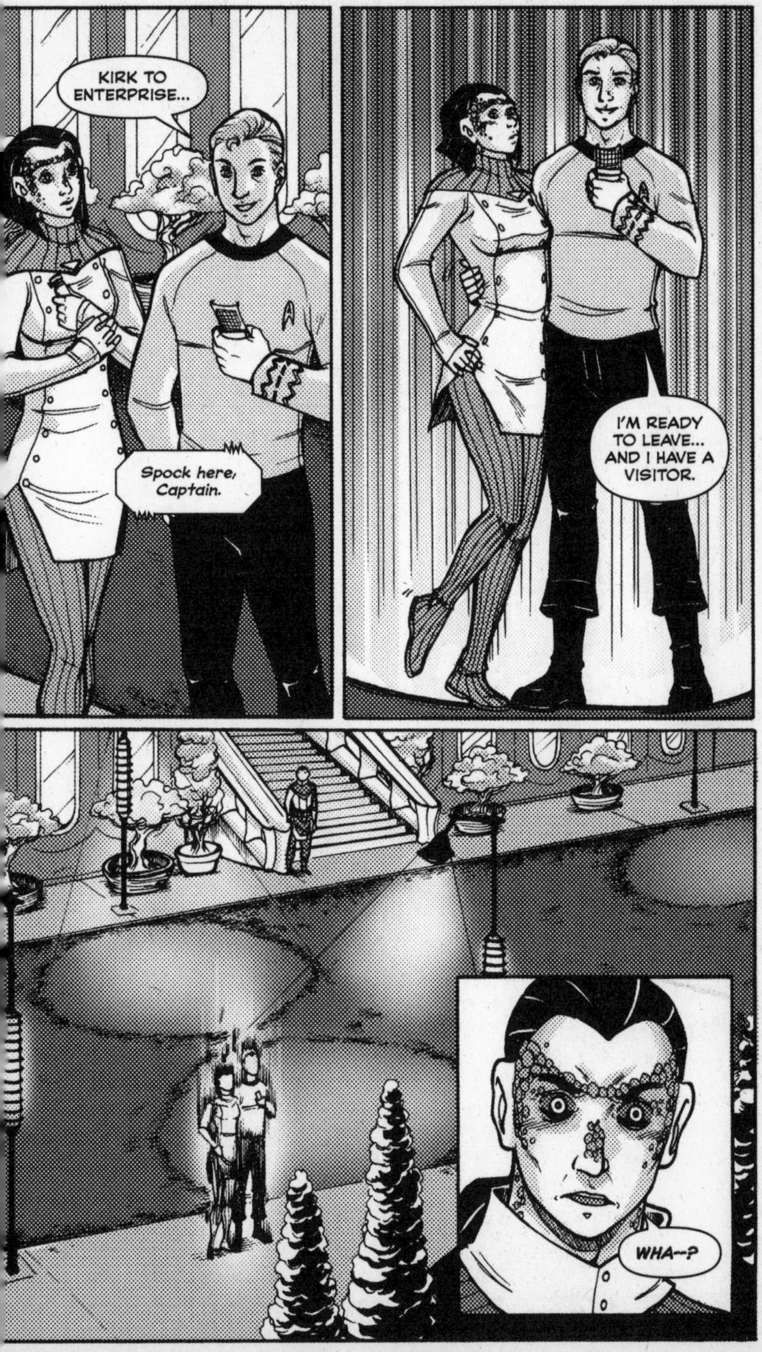
KIRK TO ENTERPRISE...
Spock here, Captain.
I'M READY TO LEAVE... AND I HAVE A VISITOR.
WHA--?

THERE'S A FEW MINOR DIFFERENCES AT THE MICRO-CELLULAR LEVEL, BUT THE DERMAL REGENERATOR SHOULD HAVE NO PROBLEM COMPENSATING.

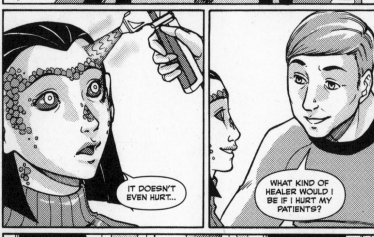

IT DOESN'T EVEN HURT...

WHAT KIND OF HEALER WOULD I BE IF I HURT MY PATIENTS?

JEENA... THERE'S SOMEONE I THINK YOU SHOULD MEET.

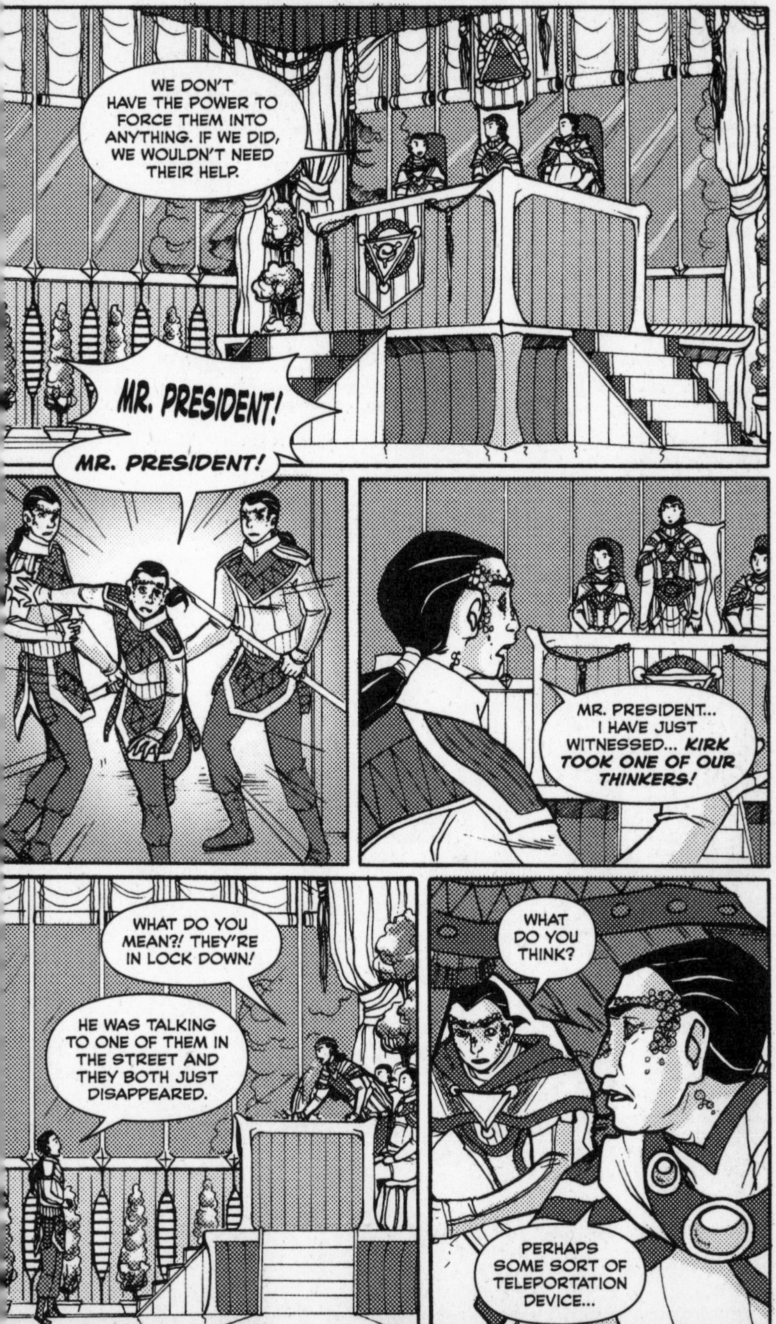
WE DON'T HAVE THE POWER TO FORCE THEM INTO ANYTHING. IF WE DID, WE WOULDN'T NEED THEIR HELP.
MR. PRESIDENT!
MR. PRESIDENT!
MR. PRESIDENT... I HAVE JUST WITNESSED... KIRK TOOK ONE OF OUR THINKERS!
WHAT DO YOU MEAN?! THEY'RE IN LOCK DOWN!
HE WAS TALKING TO ONE OF THEM IN THE STREET AND THEY BOTH JUST DISAPPEARED.
WHAT DO YOU THINK?
PERHAPS SOME SORT OF TELEPORTATION DEVICE...

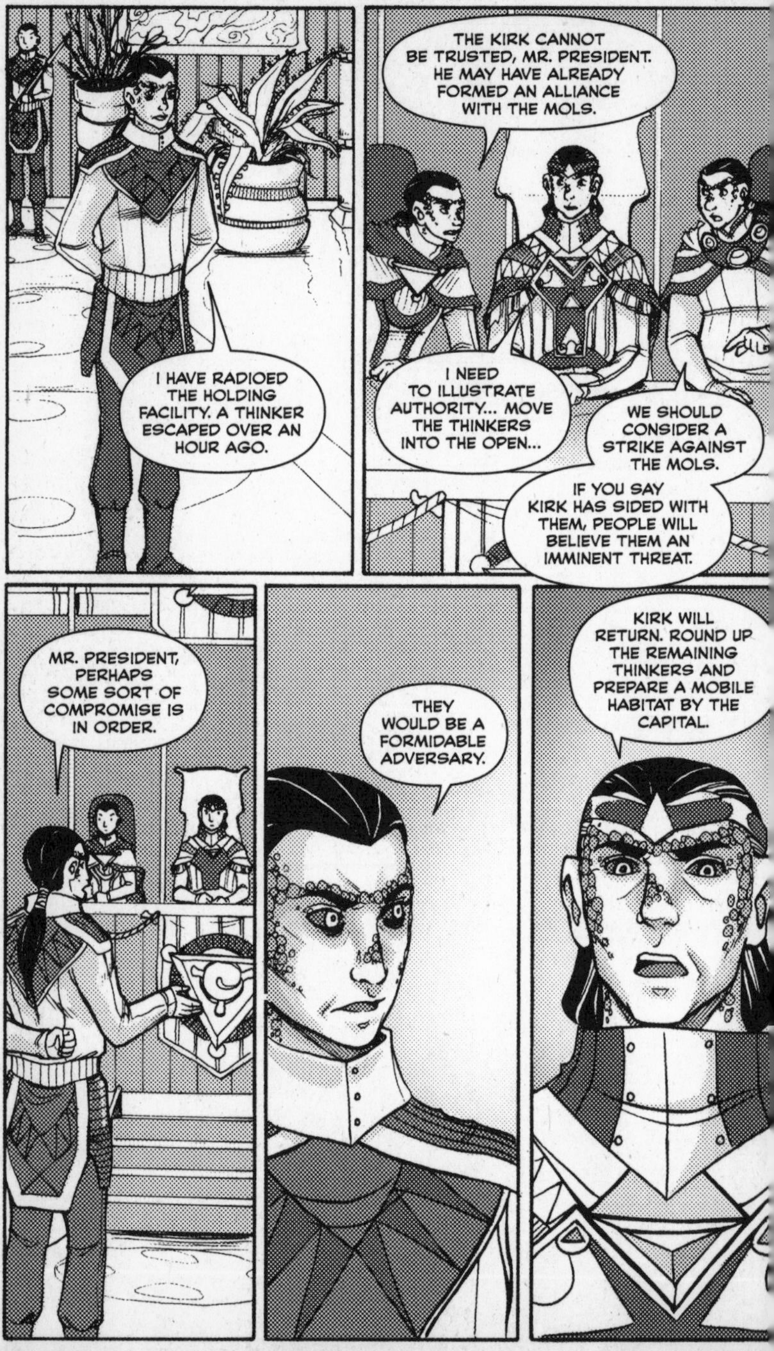
I HAVE RADIOED THE HOLDING FACILITY. A THINKER ESCAPED OVER AN HOUR AGO.
THE KIRK CANNOT BE TRUSTED, MR. PRESIDENT. HE MAY HAVE ALREADY FORMED AN ALLIANCE WITH THE MOLS.
I NEED TO ILLUSTRATE AUTHORITY... MOVE THE THINKERS INTO THE OPEN...
WE SHOULD CONSIDER A STRIKE AGAINST THE MOLS.
IF YOU SAY KIRK HAS SIDED WITH THEM, PEOPLE WILL BELIEVE THEM AN IMMINENT THREAT.
MR. PRESIDENT, PERHAPS SOME SORT OF COMPROMISE IS IN ORDER.
THEY WOULD BE A FORMIDABLE ADVERSARY.
KIRK WILL RETURN. ROUND UP THE REMAINING THINKERS AND PREPARE A MOBILE HABITAT BY THE CAPITAL.

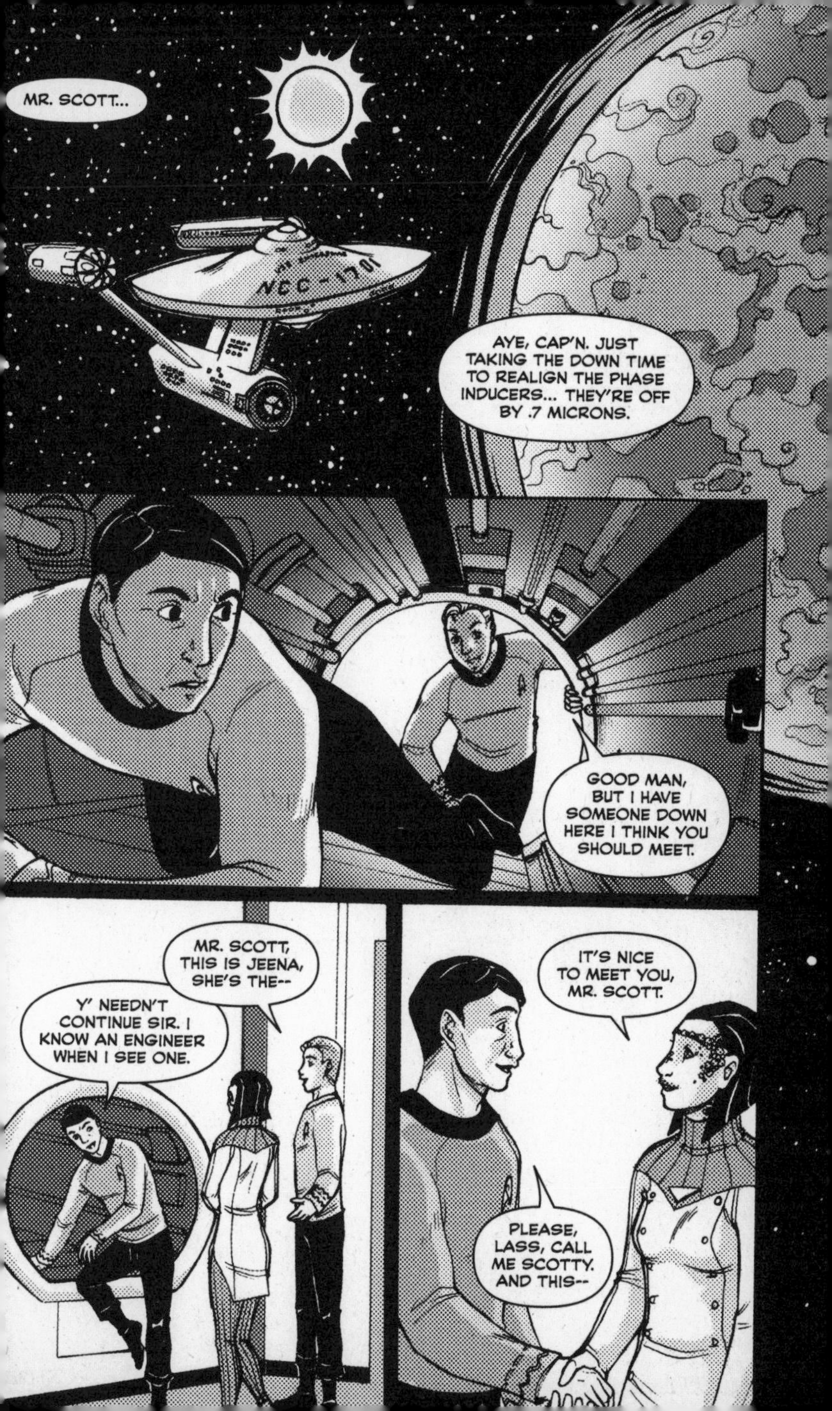
MR. SCOTT...
NCC-1701
AYE, CAP'N. JUST TAKING THE DOWN TIME TO REALIGN THE PHASE INDUCERS... THEY'RE OFF BY .7 MICRONS.
GOOD MAN, BUT I HAVE SOMEONE DOWN HERE I THINK YOU SHOULD MEET.
MR. SCOTT, THIS IS JEENA, SHE'S THE--
Y' NEEDN'T CONTINUE SIR. I KNOW AN ENGINEER WHEN I SEE ONE.
IT'S NICE TO MEET YOU, MR. SCOTT.
PLEASE, LASS, CALL ME SCOTTY. AND THIS--

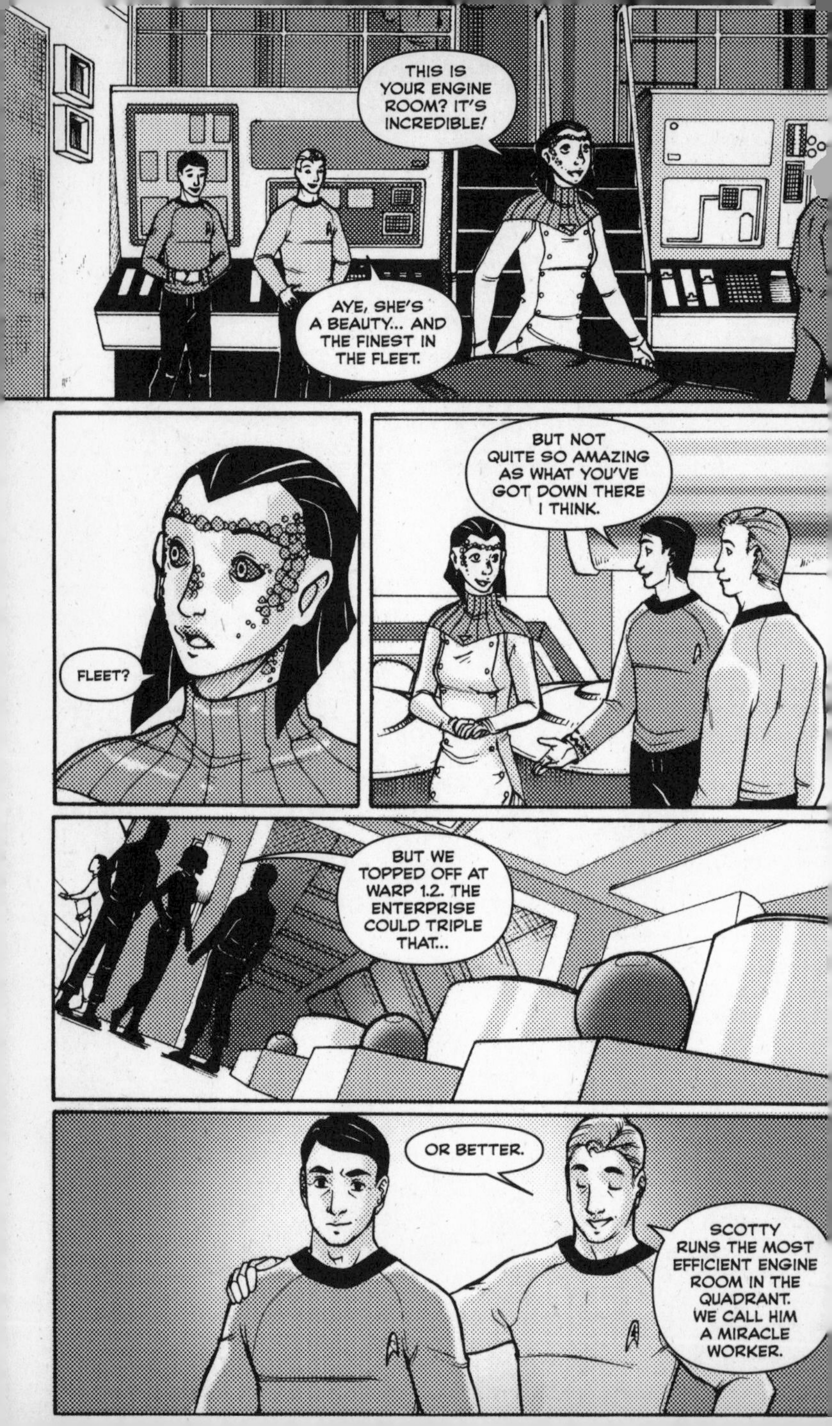
THIS IS YOUR ENGINE ROOM? IT'S INCREDIBLE!
AYE, SHE'S A BEAUTY... AND THE FINEST IN THE FLEET.
FLEET?
BUT NOT QUITE SO AMAZING AS WHAT YOU'VE GOT DOWN THERE I THINK.
BUT WE TOPPED OFF AT WARP 1.2. THE ENTERPRISE COULD TRIPLE THAT...
OR BETTER.
SCOTTY RUNS THE MOST EFFICIENT ENGINE ROOM IN THE QUADRANT. WE CALL HIM A MIRACLE WORKER.

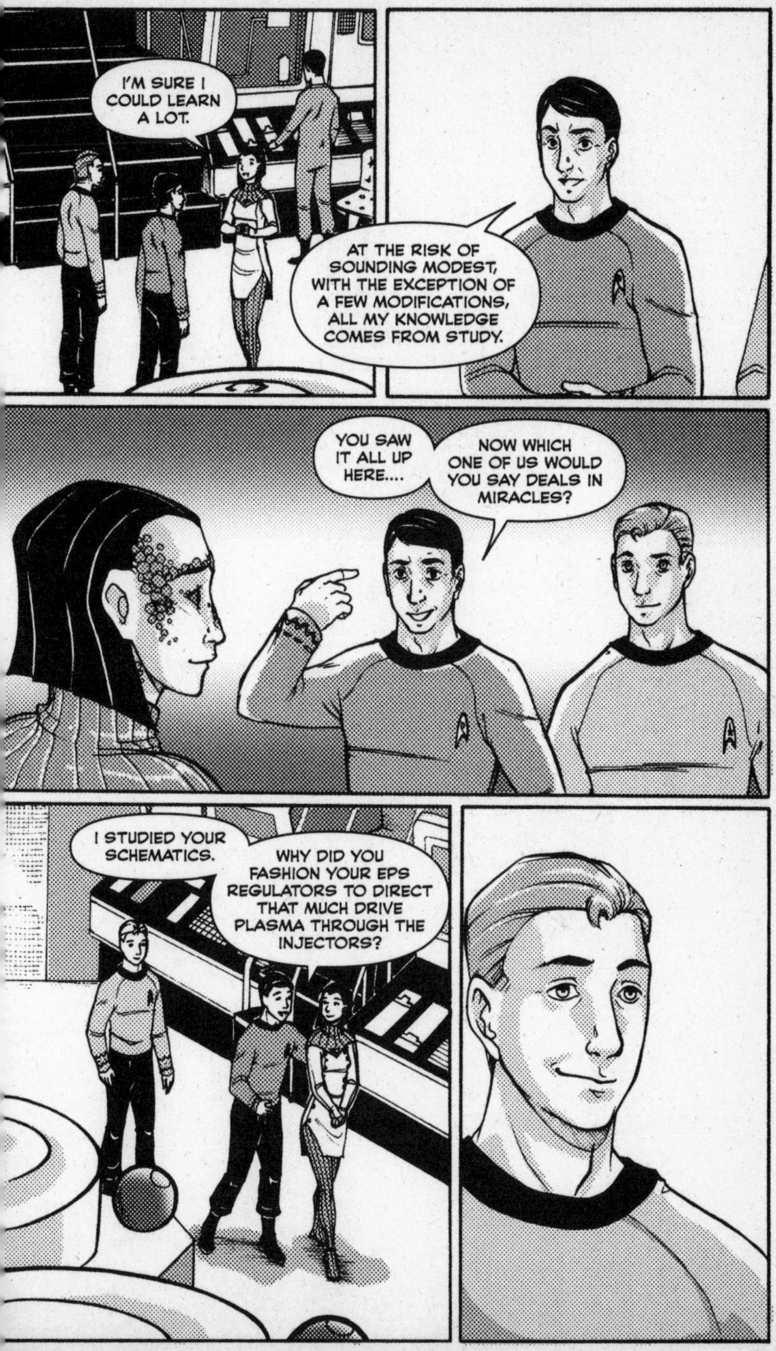
I'M SURE I COULD LEARN A LOT.
AT THE RISK OF SOUNDING MODEST, WITH THE EXCEPTION OF A FEW MODIFICATIONS, ALL MY KNOWLEDGE COMES FROM STUDY.
YOU SAW IT ALL UP HERE....
NOW WHICH ONE OF US WOULD YOU SAY DEALS IN MIRACLES?
I STUDIED YOUR SCHEMATICS.
WHY DID YOU FASHION YOUR EPS REGULATORS TO DIRECT THAT MUCH DRIVE PLASMA THROUGH THE INJECTORS?

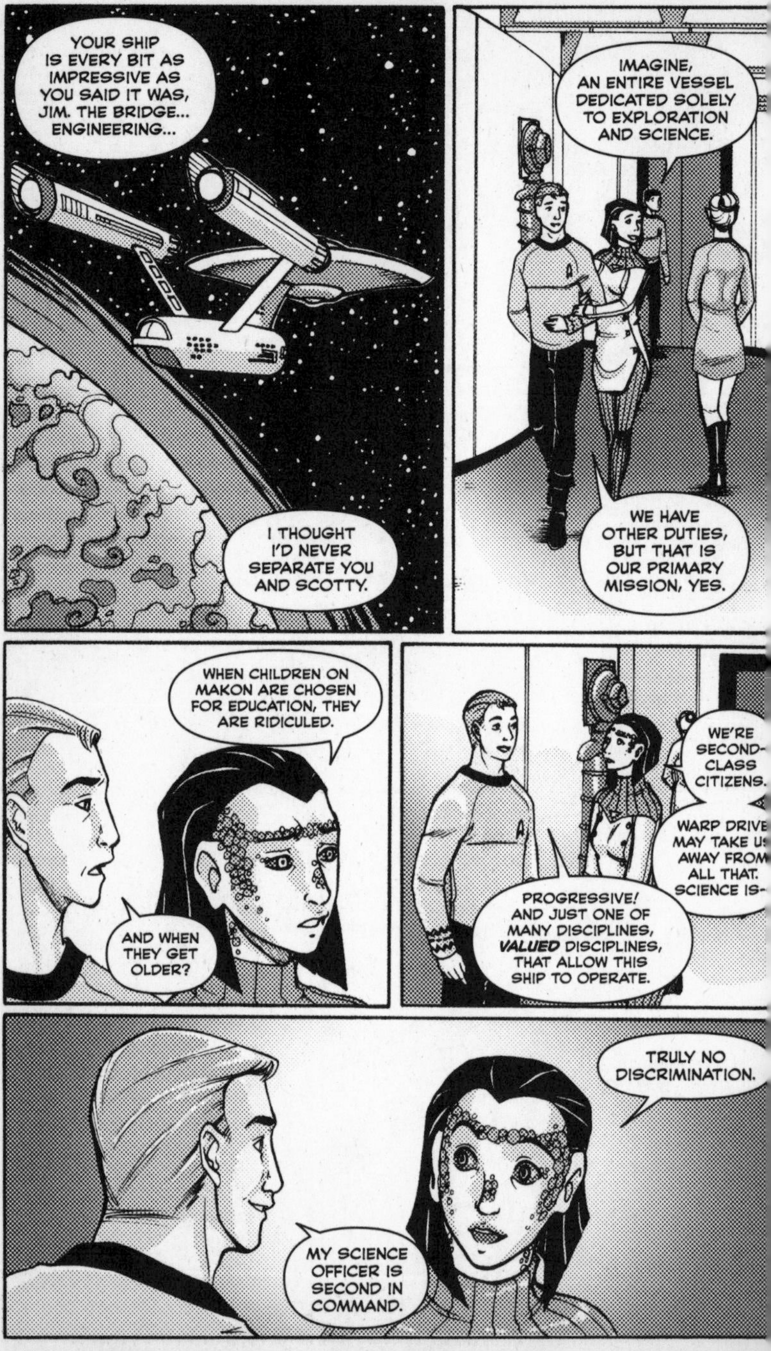
YOUR SHIP IS EVERY BIT AS IMPRESSIVE AS YOU SAID IT WAS, JIM. THE BRIDGE... ENGINEERING...
I THOUGHT I'D NEVER SEPARATE YOU AND SCOTTY.
IMAGINE, AN ENTIRE VESSEL DEDICATED SOLELY TO EXPLORATION AND SCIENCE.
WE HAVE OTHER DUTIES, BUT THAT IS OUR PRIMARY MISSION, YES.
WHEN CHILDREN ON MAKON ARE CHOSEN FOR EDUCATION, THEY ARE RIDICULED.
AND WHEN THEY GET OLDER?
WE'RE SECOND-CLASS CITIZENS.
WARP DRIVE MAY TAKE U AWAY FROM ALL THAT. SCIENCE IS-
PROGRESSIVE! AND JUST ONE OF MANY DISCIPLINES, *VALUED* DISCIPLINES, THAT ALLOW THIS SHIP TO OPERATE.
TRULY NO DISCRIMINATION.
MY SCIENCE OFFICER IS SECOND IN COMMAND.

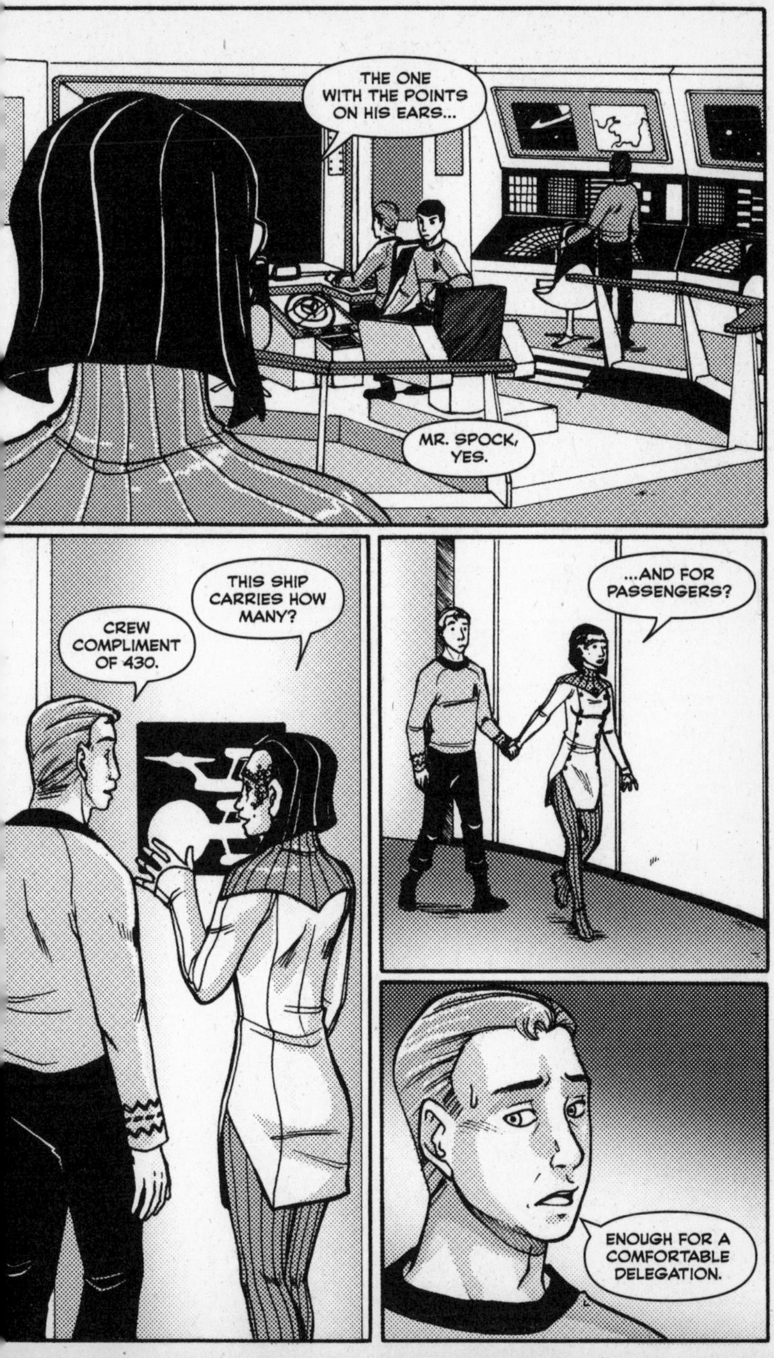
THE ONE WITH THE POINTS ON HIS EARS...
MR. SPOCK, YES.
THIS SHIP CARRIES HOW MANY?
CREW COMPLIMENT OF 430.
...AND FOR PASSENGERS?
ENOUGH FOR A COMFORTABLE DELEGATION.

BUT THE CREW... THEY ALL HAVE THEIR OWN ROOMS?

MOST HAVE BUNKMATES.

BUT HIGHER-RANKING OFFICERS ARE AFFORDED A FEW EXTRA AMENITIES... PRIVACY...

3F 121

DECK 5... WE'VE HAPPENED BY MY QUARTERS.

HM... ONE PLACE ON THE SHIP I HAVEN'T SEEN...

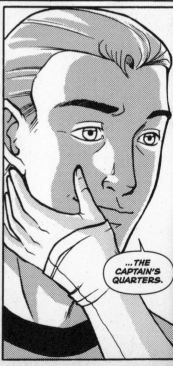

...THE CAPTAIN'S QUARTERS.

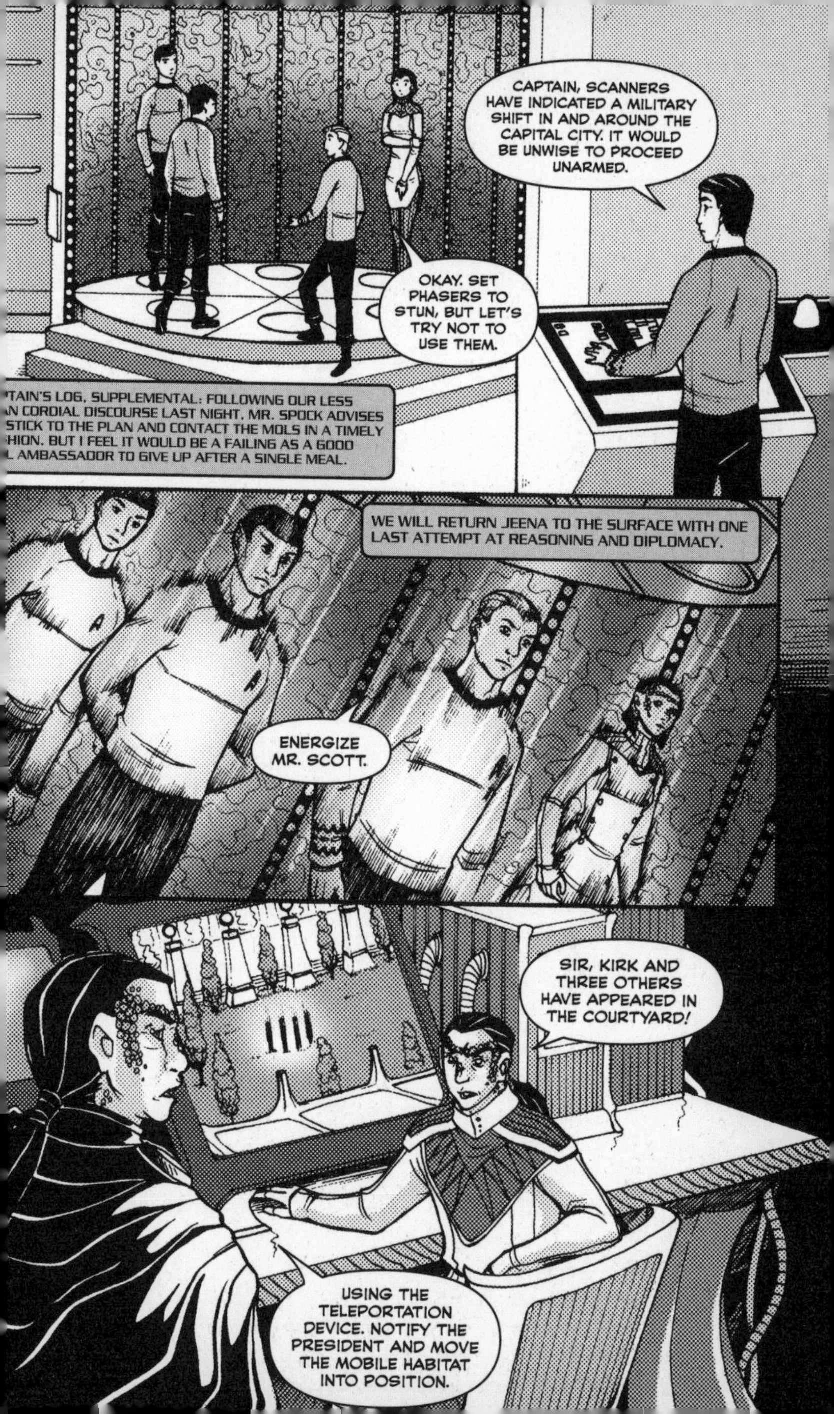

CAPTAIN, SCANNERS HAVE INDICATED A MILITARY SHIFT IN AND AROUND THE CAPITAL CITY. IT WOULD BE UNWISE TO PROCEED UNARMED.
OKAY. SET PHASERS TO STUN, BUT LET'S TRY NOT TO USE THEM.
PTAIN'S LOG, SUPPLEMENTAL: FOLLOWING OUR LESS N CORDIAL DISCOURSE LAST NIGHT, MR. SPOCK ADVISES STICK TO THE PLAN AND CONTACT THE MOLS IN A TIMELY HION. BUT I FEEL IT WOULD BE A FAILING AS A GOOD L AMBASSADOR TO GIVE UP AFTER A SINGLE MEAL.
WE WILL RETURN JEENA TO THE SURFACE WITH ONE LAST ATTEMPT AT REASONING AND DIPLOMACY.
ENERGIZE MR. SCOTT.
SIR, KIRK AND THREE OTHERS HAVE APPEARED IN THE COURTYARD!
USING THE TELEPORTATION DEVICE. NOTIFY THE PRESIDENT AND MOVE THE MOBILE HABITAT INTO POSITION.

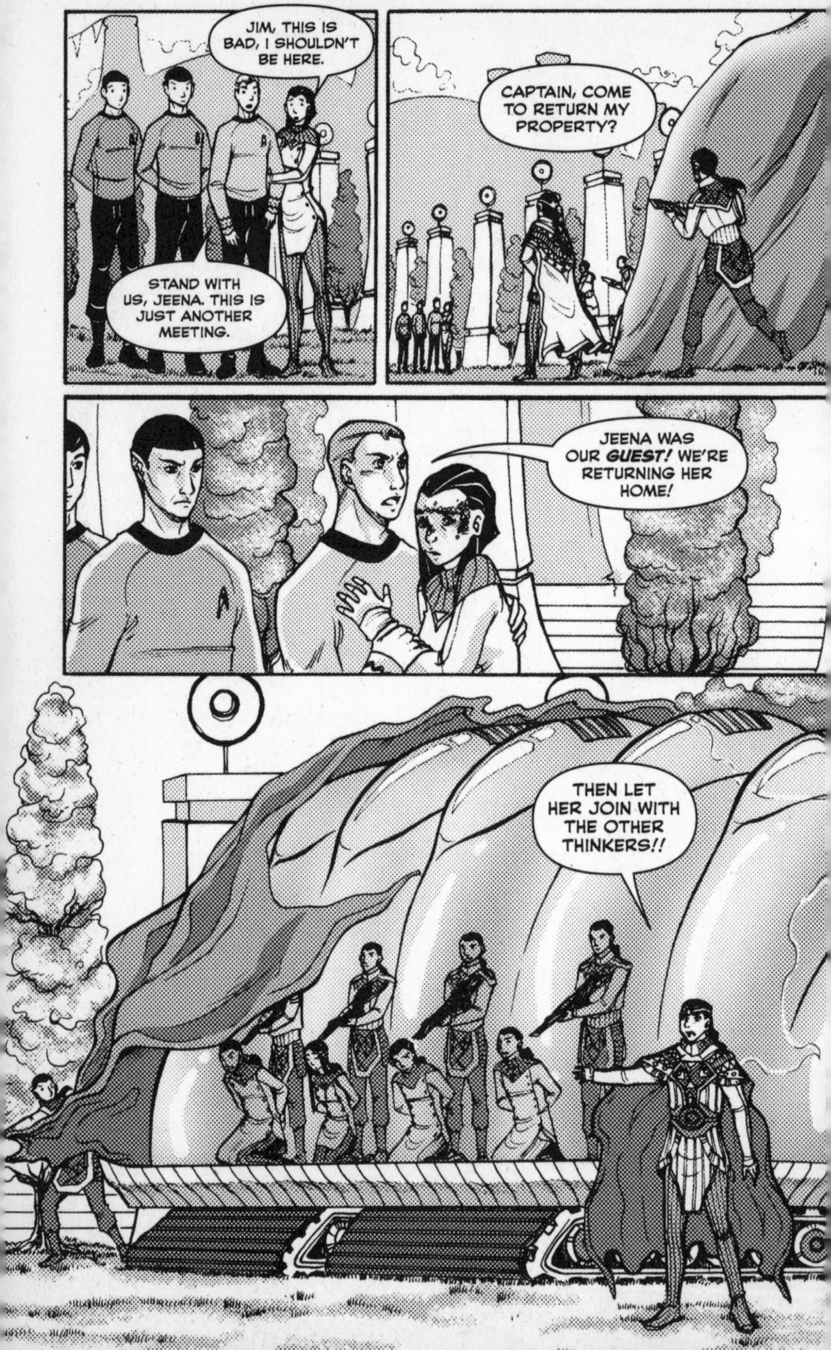
JIM, THIS IS BAD, I SHOULDN'T BE HERE.
STAND WITH US, JEENA. THIS IS JUST ANOTHER MEETING.
CAPTAIN, COME TO RETURN MY PROPERTY?
JEENA WAS OUR *GUEST!* WE'RE RETURNING HER HOME!
THEN LET HER JOIN WITH THE OTHER THINKERS!!

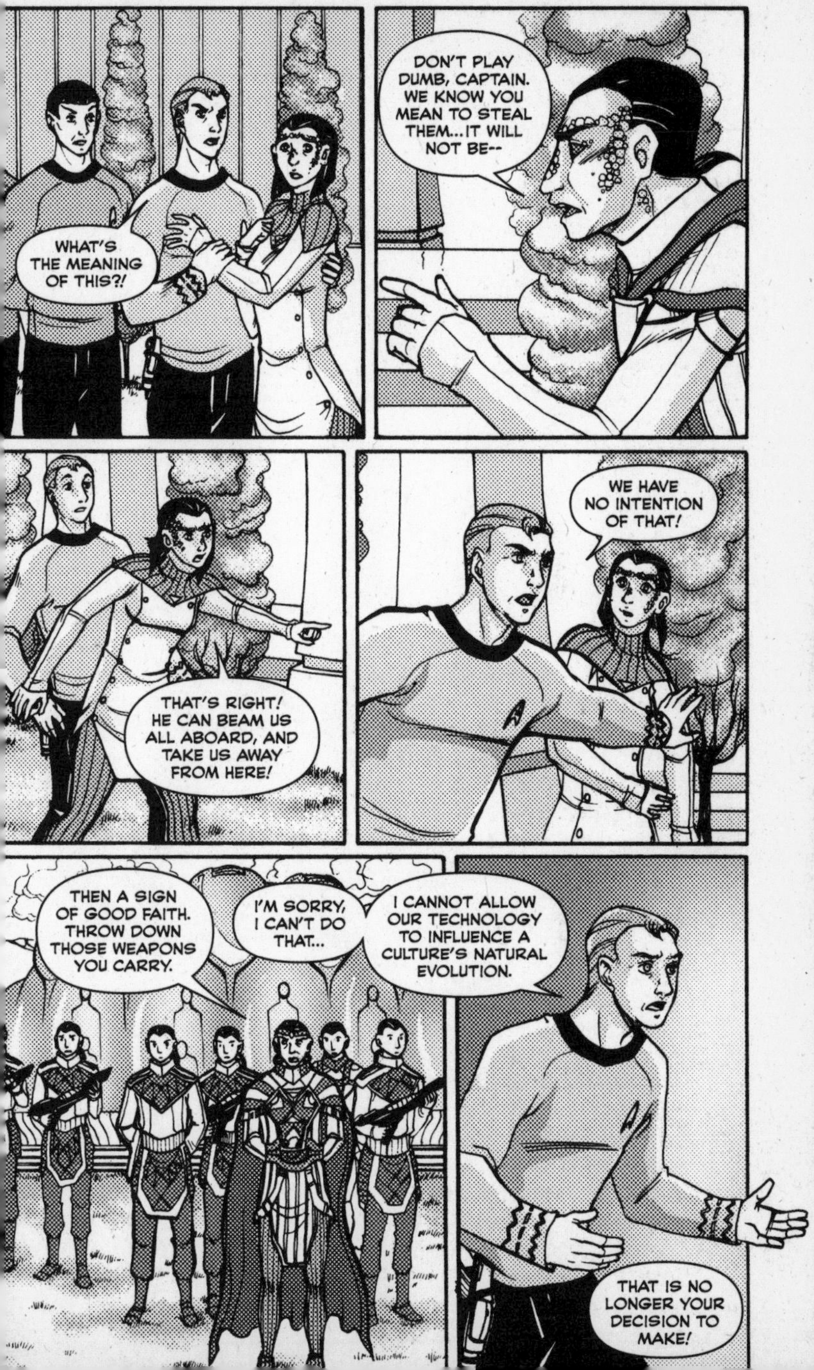
WHAT'S THE MEANING OF THIS?!
DON'T PLAY DUMB, CAPTAIN. WE KNOW YOU MEAN TO STEAL THEM...IT WILL NOT BE--
THAT'S RIGHT! HE CAN BEAM US ALL ABOARD, AND TAKE US AWAY FROM HERE!
WE HAVE NO INTENTION OF THAT!
THEN A SIGN OF GOOD FAITH. THROW DOWN THOSE WEAPONS YOU CARRY.
I'M SORRY, I CAN'T DO THAT...
I CANNOT ALLOW OUR TECHNOLOGY TO INFLUENCE A CULTURE'S NATURAL EVOLUTION.
THAT IS NO LONGER YOUR DECISION TO MAKE!

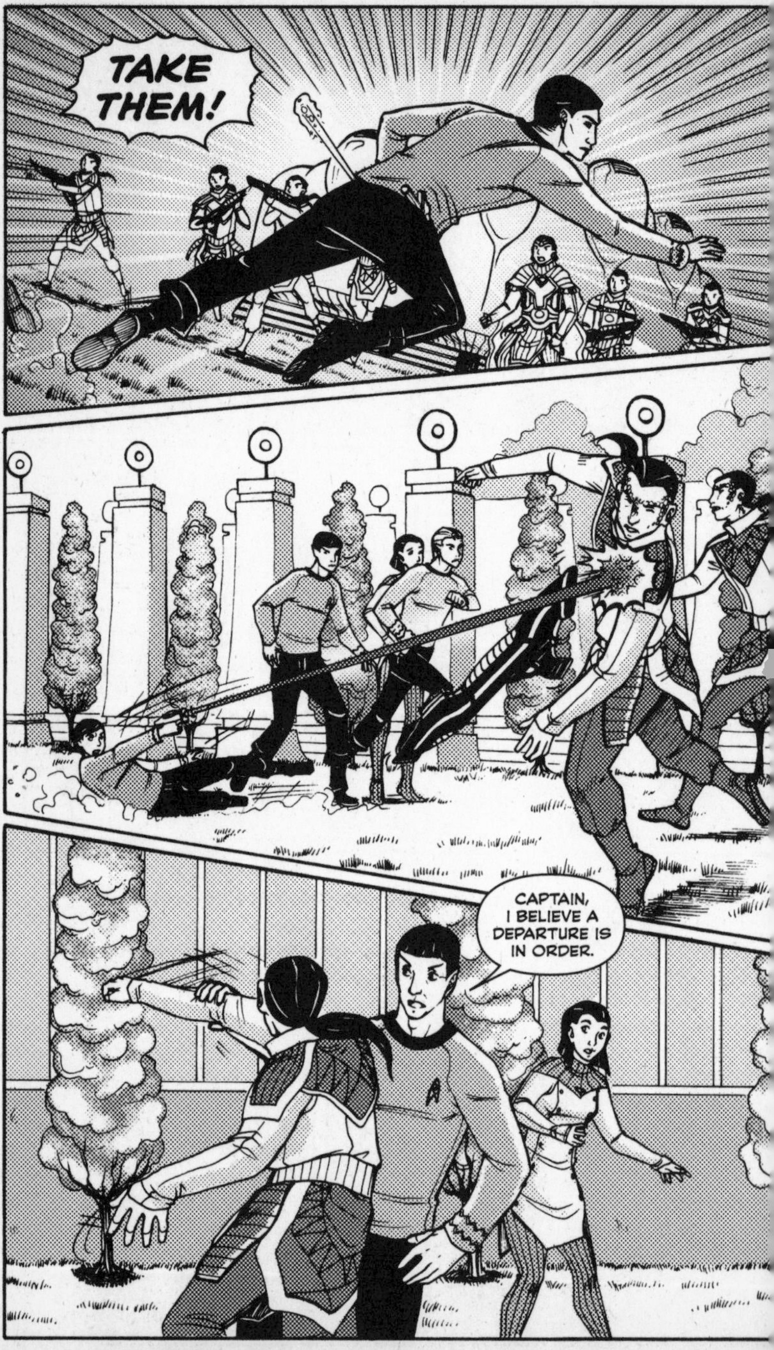
TAKE THEM!
CAPTAIN, I BELIEVE A DEPARTURE IS IN ORDER.

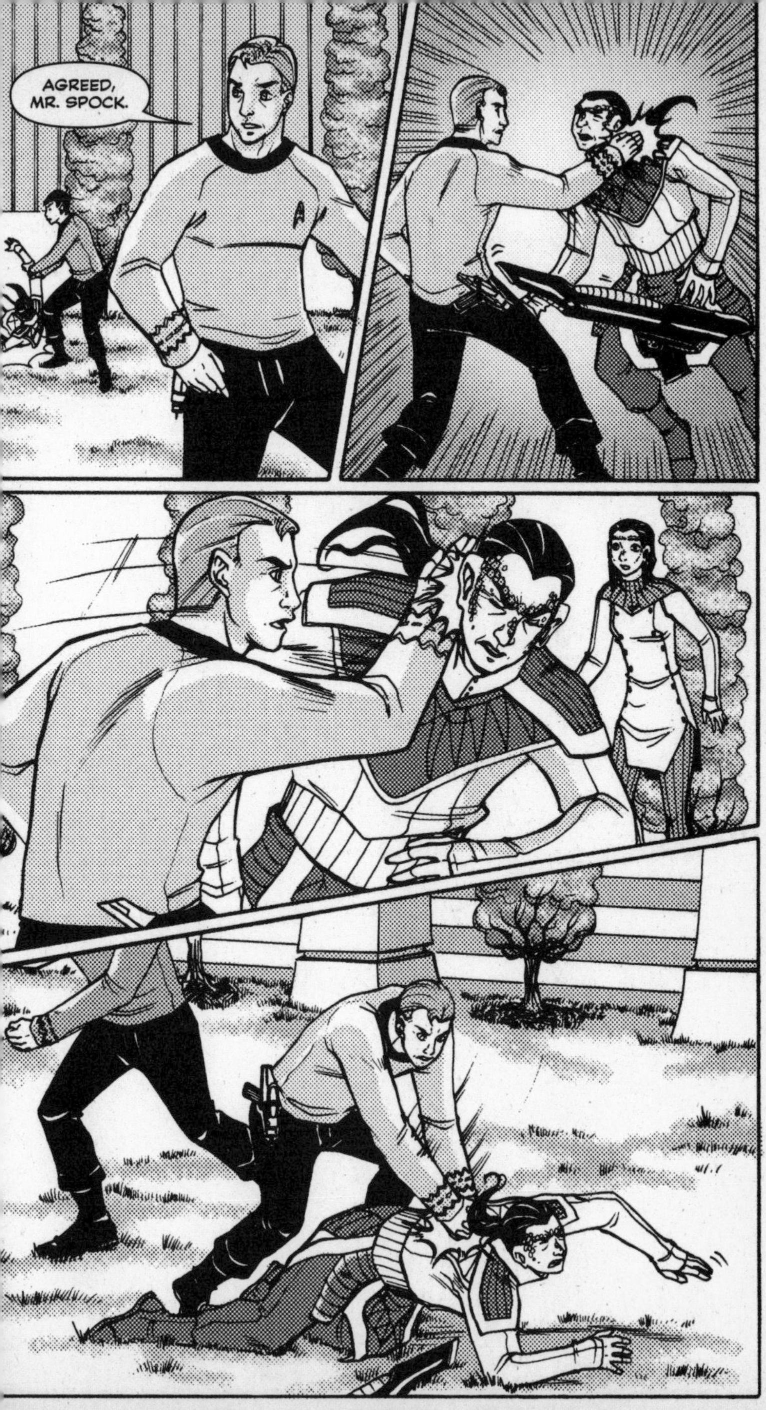
AGREED, MR. SPOCK.

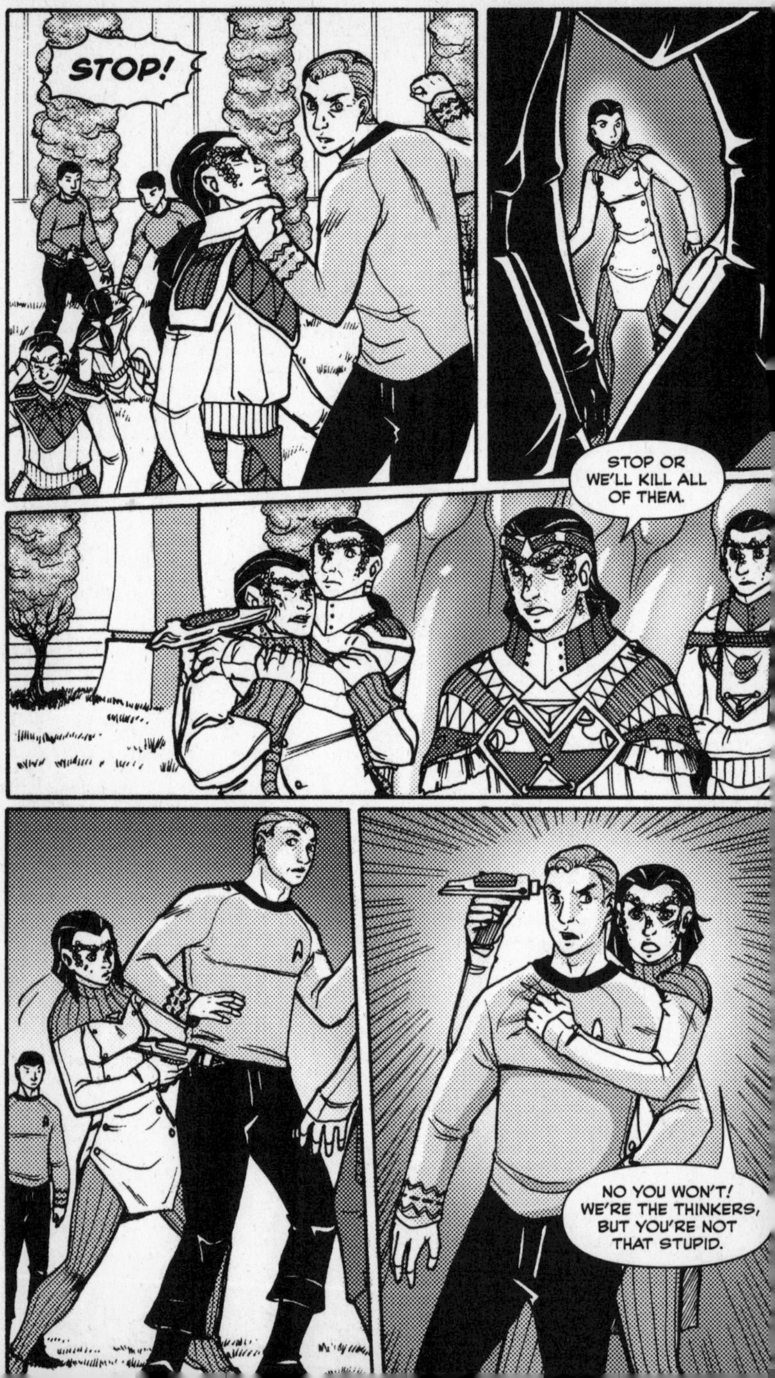
STOP!
STOP OR WE'LL KILL ALL OF THEM.
NO YOU WON'T! WE'RE THE THINKERS, BUT YOU'RE NOT THAT STUPID.

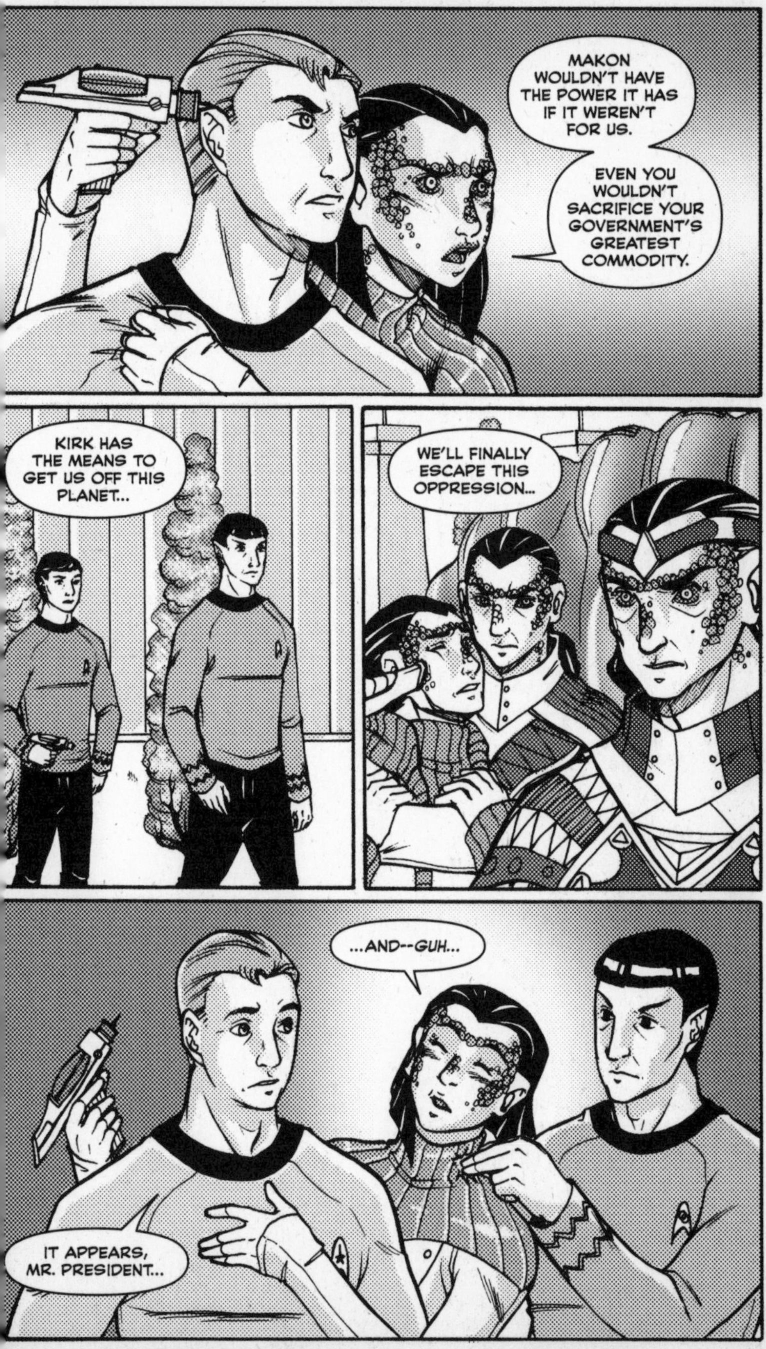
MAKON WOULDN'T HAVE THE POWER IT HAS IF IT WEREN'T FOR US.
EVEN YOU WOULDN'T SACRIFICE YOUR GOVERNMENT'S GREATEST COMMODITY.
KIRK HAS THE MEANS TO GET US OFF THIS PLANET...
WE'LL FINALLY ESCAPE THIS OPPRESSION...
...AND--GUH...
IT APPEARS, MR. PRESIDENT...

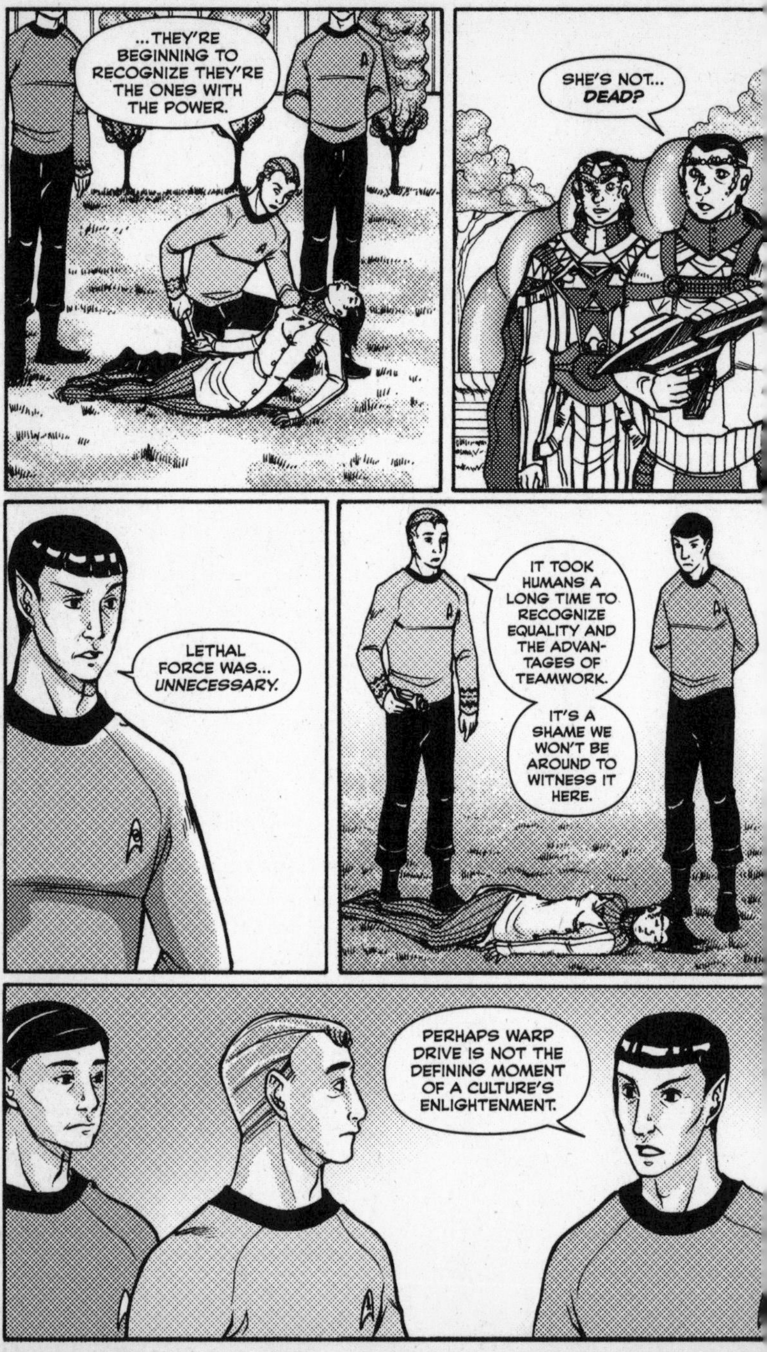
...THEY'RE BEGINNING TO RECOGNIZE THEY'RE THE ONES WITH THE POWER.
SHE'S NOT... *DEAD?*
LETHAL FORCE WAS... *UNNECESSARY.*
IT TOOK HUMANS A LONG TIME TO RECOGNIZE EQUALITY AND THE ADVANTAGES OF TEAMWORK.
IT'S A SHAME WE WON'T BE AROUND TO WITNESS IT HERE.
PERHAPS WARP DRIVE IS NOT THE DEFINING MOMENT OF A CULTURE'S ENLIGHTENMENT.

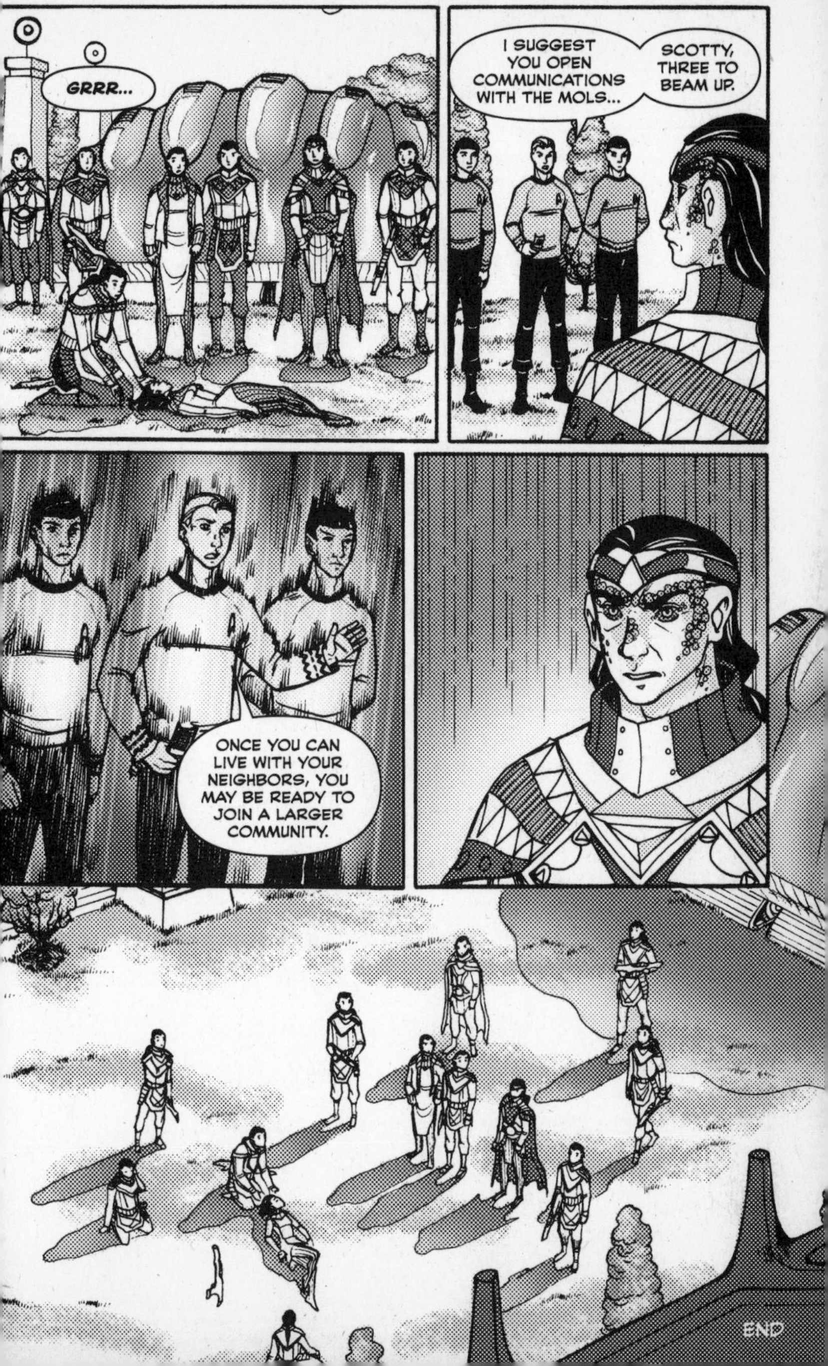
GRRR...
I SUGGEST YOU OPEN COMMUNICATIONS WITH THE MOLS...
SCOTTY, THREE TO BEAM UP.
ONCE YOU CAN LIVE WITH YOUR NEIGHBORS, YOU MAY BE READY TO JOIN A LARGER COMMUNITY.
END

NEW FROM POCKET BOOKS

STAR TREK®
MYRIAD UNIVERSES
INFINITY'S PRISM

Three all-new novels
exploring three different alternate realities by

William Leisner
Christopher L. Bennett
James Swallow

Available wherever books are sold

And don't miss the second volume
ECHOES AND REFRACTIONS
coming in August!

Turn the page for a preview of
A Less Perfect Union
by William Leisner

Myriad Universes: Infinity's Prism

More than a hundred years after the Terra Prime movement achieved its dream of an isolationist Earth, humanity is once again at a fork in the river of history . . . and the path it follows may ultimately be determined by the voice of a single individual: the sole surviving crewmember of the first *Starship Enterprise*™ . . .

A Less Perfect Union

S unrise over Death Valley.

    At the first hint of light, the nocturnal creatures that gave the lie to this place's name started scurrying for the cool shade of their burrows. The temperature, which had dipped down to almost 20 degrees Celsius overnight, had already started to climb again, heading for an expected 50 degrees.

And T'Pol, who had spent the last half hour staring at the ceiling of her bedroom, lifted the thin sheet off her body and pushed herself slowly up out of bed. She slid her bare feet into an old pair of slippers and shuffled into the kitchen, where she turned on the tap and waited patiently for the ancient pump to draw enough water up from the underground spring to fill her teakettle.

The pump, like the house it was in, was over two hundred years old. The small adobe structure had been built just after World War III by a small group of religious cultists who wished to separate themselves from the rest of their violent race. This locale, one of the most forbidding on the planet, proved ideal to this purpose: no one had discovered any evidence of the group's ritual mass suicide until two years after the fact.

Once she'd coaxed enough water out of the spigot, T'Pol placed the kettle on a small heating unit and then reached for her tin of chamomile tea. She was not quite as cut off from the world as the original inhabitants had been—that would be close to impossible on twenty-third-century Earth. But her nearest neighbors, in the town of Furnace Creek several kilometers away, were very protective of their privacy, and hers by extension. One of them, though, a Mister Timbisha, made regular sojourns into Beatty for supplies and provisions, and occasionally gifted her with small comforts, such as tea or fresh fruits. One time, he had brought a small jar of *plomeek* seeds, obviously smuggled to Earth by black marketers. Each time she went out to gather new leaves from her small shaded garden, she wondered how he had known what they were, and how much they must have cost him to obtain. The one time she had offered to compensate him, he refused, saying, "Some of us still remember how much Earth owes you."

Now that T'Pol thought about it, though, Mister Timbisha had been an elderly man when she first moved to the Southern California desert. Most likely . . . yes, she remembered now: Timbisha had died, like so many humans she'd known over the years. He'd been dead for . . . decades? Could that be right? Hadn't she seen him just . . . No. But if he was dead, who was it who had been bringing her her tea?

And with her thoughts returned to tea, the whistle of the kettle finally penetrated her consciousness, though she had the sense that the water had been boiling for some time.

She squeezed her eyes shut, willing her disorganized

thoughts and memories to reorder themselves. The scent of chamomile as it was released and carried by the steaming water helped in that regard. Sighing, she lowered herself into a chair at the kitchen table, both gnarled hands drawing warmth from the ceramic cup.

It had been growing increasingly difficult for her to maintain her mental disciplines as the years went by. She'd struggled with her failing abilities for a long time, particularly since her time in the Expanse, and the damage she'd inflicted on herself through the abuse of trellium-D. But matters had gotten to the point recently that she'd begun to worry that she was developing Bendii Syndrome or some other infirmity. She'd lived on Earth for so long, without the benefit of a Vulcan physician; she could be suffering from any number of undiagnosed conditions . . .

But that was just paranoia. T'Pol still retained enough of her logical faculties to understand her current difficulties had begun just over a month ago, shortly after hearing the news about Elizabeth Cutler: at the age of 147 years, the last surviving human member of Jonathan Archer's *Enterprise* crew had died of natural causes at her home in Tycho City, attended by five generations of her progeny.

And with her passing, T'Pol was alone, in yet one more sense.

T'Pol was startled out of her thoughts by a quiet alarm bleeping throughout the house, indicating that the property's proximity sensors had been tripped. Bighorn sheep occasionally came down from the surrounding mountains in search of greenery to graze, but not as the sun was on its way up. Setting her cup down, T'Pol stood and reached for one of the kitchen drawers, from which she withdrew an outdated but still functional phase pistol.

She then activated a small countertop viewscreen, each of its three panels showing different views from the rooftop visual sensors. A man in denim pants and a plain blue cotton shirt was approaching from the direction of the old National Park Visitors Center, following the faint footpath that led to her front steps. T'Pol moved quickly through the house to the foyer and peered outside through a small optical lens set in the door. The man walked with both hands held away from his body, palms forward and empty. He was purposely presenting himself as harmless as he approached, but that did not mean he in fact was. Once he got within fifty meters of the house, T'Pol pushed the door open and aimed her pistol at his chest. "Do not come any closer," she called to him.

The man did as he was told, at the same time lifting his hands a bit higher. "I mean you no harm, Lady T'Pol," he shouted back.

"Nor do I intend to harm you," T'Pol replied. "However, my intentions are subject to change if you do not leave this property right now."

"Ma'am, my name is Christopher Pike, and I'm—"

"I do not care who you are, or what your reasons are for tracking me to my home. I do not welcome visitors, and I will defend my home and my privacy to the fullest."

The man now closed his hands into fists, and dropped

them to his sides as he pulled himself up straight to his full height. "Lower your weapon, Commander," he called out in a voice that came from the inner depths of his being and rang with the characteristic authority of a starship captain. The muzzle of T'Pol's phase pistol actually dipped slightly as her long-dormant yet deeply etched military instincts responded to the man's tone and bearing.

Her lapse was only momentary. "Starfleet stripped me of my commission a long time ago," T'Pol informed him.

The man—Pike—started walking again, now ignoring the weapon aimed at him. "Once a Starfleet officer, always a Starfleet officer, they say."

"If you're here on official Starfleet business, shouldn't you be in uniform?"

He cracked a small grin. "I grew up in the Mojave; I know better," he told her. "If I had come to Death Valley in that heavy velour turtleneck, before long I would be begging you to use that phaser on me."

T'Pol lowered her pistol arm to her side, realizing there was no deterrent factor if Pike was making jokes about it. No doubt he'd faced more frightening foes in his life than a 176-year-old hermit lady. "What is this about, Mister Pike? What could Starfleet possibly want with me more than a century after my discharge?"

"Well, it's not Starfleet, per se. It would perhaps be more comfortable for us both if we were to discuss this inside."

T'Pol tried—and failed—to suppress a sigh of resignation. She took a step back, holding the door open for

Pike, and then indicated the small parlor that made up the front of the house. It was sparsely furnished and undecorated, as befitting one who did not entertain. Pike took a seat on a hard wooden mission chair as T'Pol settled onto a threadbare but comfortable sofa. "Lady T'Pol, I was asked by Prime Minister Winston to come speak with you. He intends to petition the Interstellar Coalition to admit Earth as a member. And he wants your support in that goal."

T'Pol raised one eyebrow. "Indeed? And what makes him believe I'd give it?"

"Because you know from firsthand experience that a partnership between humans and nonhumans can work." Every muscle in T'Pol's body tensed at that, from the base of her neck to the fingers still wrapped around the phase pistol in her lap. Somehow, she managed to control her emotional retort as Pike obliviously continued, "You were right there at Captain Archer's side, from the launch of the NX-01 to his court-martial."

"I fail to see the relevance of these statements," T'Pol told Pike calmly, changing her hold on the pistol to minimize the chance of accidentally discharging it. "Carter Winston is not Jonathan Archer."

"No, but like Archer, the prime minister wants to extend the hand of friendship and cooperation to the other powers of the galaxy."

"Carter Winston is a businessman. He spent a lifetime manipulating commodities markets on dozens of colonies and other Earth-subjugated worlds, amassed several financial fortunes, and then used his wealth and reputa-

tion to launch a political career, leading him prematurely
to United Earth's most powerful governmental office.
Forgive me if I find the comparison inapt."

"Listen, I'm as cynical about politicians as the next person," Pike said, lowering his voice to affect the sense that
he was sharing a confidence. "But like you said, the guy is
a businessman first, and a damned smart one, too. But if
the business of politics is getting votes and keeping yourself in power, then petitioning for Earth's admittance into
the Interstellar Coalition is a losing deal for him."

T'Pol cocked her head and narrowed her eyes at the
human. "You're going to tell me now that Winston is ad-
vocating this union selflessly, for a higher, more noble
purpose."

"What if I did?"

"I would tell you that you were correct: it would be
a losing deal for him," she said, a small touch of regret
coloring her tone. "Are you familiar with the reasons
Vulcans renounced emotion, Mister Pike?"

"Because of war," the Starfleet captain answered. "You
nearly wiped yourselves out, right?"

"Correct. The emotions of fear and hatred are too
powerful and too destructive. Your people have turned
those emotions against extraterrestrials, which is perhaps
the only reason you have avoided the fate my ancestors
suffered. And no matter the best intentions of Prime
Minister Winston or yourself, a proposal like this will
only serve to rekindle that fear and hatred. I have seen it
happen too many times over the past one hundred and
nine years, as recently as just this past week."

"So, when I report back to the prime minister, I should tell him, don't even bother?"

"I would advise phrasing the message a bit less bluntly."

Pike slid forward to the edge of his chair and leaned toward her. "Would that be the same advice—less bluntly phrased—you gave Captain Archer when he decided to act as mediator at Weytahn?"

T'Pol narrowed her eyes at Pike. That was, in fact, the essence of what she'd told Jonathan when he'd first proposed negotiating a peaceful settlement between Vulcan and Andoria over the long-disputed planet, which Vulcan called Paan Mokar. But that was irrelevant. "As I have already said, Carter Winston is not Jonathan Archer."

"I understand," Pike said. "But let me ask you: at that point in history, was Jonathan Archer yet 'Jonathan Archer'?"

"He's gotcha there, T'Pol."

When she was first introduced to Jonathan Archer, he was suspicious and headstrong, and highly mistrustful of the Vulcans, whom he blamed for holding his father's warp engine research back for decades. Even after the successful negotiations at Weytahn, it would be years before T'Pol developed the kind of unquestioning regard for Jonathan they were now talking about.

"I understand you have misgivings," Pike continued. "More than anyone else on Earth, I'd bet. But I'd also bet that you have more reasons to want to see things change than most humans. Our best chance of effecting those changes is with your support, even if it's just tacit."

A Less Perfect Union

T'Pol said nothing for a long time. The last thing she wanted to do, so soon after the disaster of her visit to Berkeley, was to put herself out there again, trusting in supposedly well-intentioned humans. But if there was even the slightest chance that she could help advance Jonathan's last unfinished mission . . . "I will have to meditate on the matter before reaching any decision," she finally told Pike.

"Of course." Pike stood up and started to put his right hand out to her, before he remembered the Vulcan aversion to casual physical contact. "Thank you again for your time and your indulgence, ma'am."

"Captain Pike . . ." He stopped at the door and turned back. "Why did the prime minister send *you* here to make his case?" she asked.

"Because it's my ship that will be undertaking the diplomatic mission to the Coalition," he told her. "And because he thought you might be more favorably inclined if you were asked by the captain of the current *Starship Enterprise.*"

Her heart seemed to skip a few beats at the mention of that piece of information. Still, she kept herself steady and said in a dismissive tone, "Sentimentality is an emotion."

"That's what I thought," Pike said, a corner of his mouth twitching upward. "Good day, ma'am."

"Good day, Captain," she said, and stood staring at the door for several seconds after he'd left, deep in thought.